Gallipoli Diaries

Nothing can alter what happened now: Anzac stood and still stands for reckless valour in a good cause, for enterprise, resourcefulness, fidelity, comradeship and endurance that will never admit defeat.

CHARLES BEAN
OFFICIAL HISTORIAN, WORLD WAR I

'At the landing, and here ever since'

AFTER EIGHT MONTHS ON THE BEACH SOME OF THE DIGGERS HAD BECOME REAL
CHARACTERS, WITH THE MOST CELEBRATED BEING THOSE WHO HAD BEEN THERE
FROM DAY ONE. (INITIALLY DRAWN AT GALLIPOLI FOR *THE ANZAC BOOK*, 1916.)

Gallipoli Diaries

The Anzacs' Own Story Day by Day

Jonathan King

Kangaroo Press

GALLIPOLI DIARIES: THE ANZACS' OWN STORY DAY BY DAY
First published in Australia in 2003 by Kangaroo Press
An imprint of Simon & Schuster (Australia) Pty Limited
20 Barcoo Street, East Roseville NSW 2069

A Viacom Company
Sydney New York London Toronto

Visit our website at www.simonsaysaustralia.com

Cataloguing-in-Publication data:

Gallipoli Diaries:
the Anzacs' own story day by day.

  Bibliography.
  Includes index.
  ISBN 0 7318 1205 0.
  1. World War, 1914–1918 – Campaigns – Turkey – Gallipoli
  Peninsula – Personal narratives, Australian. 2. Soldiers –
  Australia – Diaries. I. King, Jonathan, 1942– .

940.426

Endpapers: *The Landing at Gallipoli, 1915* by Charles Dixon (1872–1934)
reproduced courtesy of Parliament House Gift Collection, Joint House Department, Canberra, ACT

Cover design by Avril Makula GRAVITY ADD
Internal design by Anna Soo
Typeset in 11 on 15 Sabon
Printed in China through Phoenix Offset

10 9 8 7 6 5 4 3 2 1

CONTENTS

To the Anzacs:

Those 8,709 brave Australian 'diggers' who died
fighting at Gallipoli

and
their 2,701 Kiwi 'cobbers',

not to mention
the Brits and their Allies
who were killed in that bold but hopeless campaign.

And
not to forgot the poor old Turks
who lost more than anybody else defending their homeland.

PREFACE
LISTENING TO THE ANZACS

As the Preface for *Gallipoli Diaries* should really have been written by those soldiers who fought at Gallipoli, the author is passing on the words of wisdom of the last ten veterans of that terrible campaign. I had the privilege to spend time from the mid-1990s to 2002 with these last ten, sadly watching them pass away one by one until there was just Alec Campbell, the last survivor who died in 2002. The Preface belongs to these last ten men as what they had to say was so important and after all they were the ones who inspired me to collect the stories of other Anzacs for this book.

I was fascinated by these old warriors as vital last witnesses to one of the nation's most important stories. That was why I filmed my interviews with them for the documentary *The Last Anzacs*. They might have all been over 100 years of age but to a man they all still wanted to pass on one message — Gallipoli had been a great mistake and they would never have volunteered to fight there if they had their time over. Of course they had hindsight but each had an especially memorable message that is worth repeating as a foundation for this book.

Les Leach, a New Zealander who carried water at Gallipoli and moved to Sydney when he returned, died in November 1997. He said 'Nobody really knew what was going on at Gallipoli and the British authorities seemed to be just as confused as us privates in the trenches'. Ted Matthews, from Sydney, who was a corporal in signals, was the last man to die who had landed on that first Anzac Day 25 April 1915. He died in 1997 aged 101. Before leaving this planet, he said 'Stop glorifying Gallipoli — from the mistaken landing onwards, the British mucked the whole thing up and we should never had followed them. But if they had had an Australian in charge we could have won the battle at Gallipoli'.

Before he died, Doug Dibley, from New Zealand, who served as stretcher bearer at Gallipoli alongside 'Simpson and his donkey' said, 'the slaughter was so bad there we had to shoot men to stop some of

LES LEACH

TED MATTHEWS

DOUG DIBLEY

JACK BUNTINE (SEATED RIGHT)

FRED KELLY

the more terrified from deserting'. Jack Buntine, from Melbourne, a great fighter and 'crack shot' who was a sniper at Gallipoli and won a military medal in the war said before he died in December 1998, 'Australians were the only all volunteer Army so we were keen to fight. But even though there were no better fighters than Australians we could never have won at Gallipoli because the odds were too great — but even so Australia learnt nothing at all from Gallipoli — nothing at all'.

Fred Kelly, from Sydney, who had been an infantryman also died in December 1998. To him, Gallipoli was 'a terrible experience' and he detested the place. 'It was ridiculous to even attempt to land on the beach because it was so narrow let alone to climb the ridges as they were never ending and exposed to enemy fire'. Len Hall, from Perth who died in February 1999, threatened to swap sides. His military career was the stuff of a colourful feature film. He landed at Gallipoli, fought with the Light Horse at the bloody battle of the Nek, rode in the charge of the Light Horse at Beersheba under General Harry Chauvel and rode to liberate Damascus with Lawrence of Arabia. But at the end of his life he said, 'Next time I would fight for the Turks against the invading Australians as they are such good people and it was their land not ours'.

Frank Isaacs of Perth who fought as a infantryman and died in April 1999, said, 'Australians paid the highest price of all per capita with more deaths in proportion to population than any other nation because all the other nations let Australians down when it came to fighting as the French kept deserting and the British had no stomach for tough battles. We were suckers'.

All of the last three, who had survived into the new millennium and were celebrated on commemorative postage stamps, warned Australians against idealising Gallipoli. Walter Parker, a water carrier at Gallipoli who died in January 2000 at 104, became a pacifist who opposed all wars. He begged his son not to fight in World War II, only to see him killed. He said, 'Gallipoli achieved nothing and just showed war is not a means of settling disputes — all those deaths of young Australians to no purpose'. Roy Longmore, of Melbourne who had been a tunneller at Gallipoli and died in in June 2001 at 106, emphasised all the mistakes. 'We landed on the wrong beach, tried to attack impossible positions, were badly equipped and not even prepared for winter — shocking leadership'.

The last man standing was Alec Campbell of Hobart who died at 103 just after Anzac Day 2002. He was the nation's last living link with Gallipoli, and so had the last word about the battle. Having enlisted at 16 and served as a water carrier at Gallipoli and seen so many of his comrades killed as he moved around the trenches at Anzac Cove, he warned 'I was a foolish young man to have gone off to that war and I would never do it again. Never go to war with a foreign power again to fight in far-off shores if it has nothing to do with Australia'. Campbell who was also opposed to Australians fighting in modern wars alongside the USA, said 'We had no time for the British whatsoever and it was a mistake for Australians to blindly follow another foreign power into war so we should not repeat that mistake. We should only go to war to defend our shores from attack'.

As these last living voices had so much to say about what really went on at Gallipoli, I decided to find many more voices to tell the big story from the ordinary soldier's point of view. After casting the net around Australia, I was able to unearth a wide enough sample to tell the story more fully. Now, instead of the words of ten Anzacs, *Gallipoli Diaries* gives voice to over two hundred soldiers who were there through extracts from their diaries and letters. Their words reinforce the urgent message of those last ten Gallipoli Anzacs. Even though these writers of 1915 did not have the advantage of hindsight, they knew something was wrong.

LEN HALL

SOURCES

There were 50,000 Australians fighting in Gallipoli and so these extracts present only a small part of what is available. There were many different types of soldiers doing very different jobs including sniping, defending trenches, shooting or capturing enemy soldiers, carrying water etc. There were also many different categories of soldiers, such as ambulancemen, doctors, machine gunners, Light Horsemen, generals and privates.

Consequently, the soldiers have different points of view and interests. Some get things right and others get things wrong. They did not have much information since there was strict censorship. Also, many soldiers got misleading information and listened to rumours on the 'bush telegraph', and some did not know what battles were taking place, while others did not know where they were or which army units, leaders or soldiers were fighting what battles. It would have been hard to find out the true facts in that military settlement at Gallipoli. Having visited Gallipoli a few times, I can confirm what a confusing collection of hills, dry creek beds, gullies and plateaus the landscape presents. I also sympathise with the soldiers who, like the author, could not spell.

FRANK ISAACS

WALTER PARKER

ROY LONGMORE

ALEC CAMPBELL

They abbreviated many items, got senior officers' titles wrong as well as ranks and army units and generally used their own personal shorthand in writing. Their extracts are reprinted here more or less as they were written warts and all.

But all of their thoughts and feelings were accurate as they came from the heart and so give the reader an understanding of the daily routine of the campaign. It was a miracle these men bothered to write as much as they did. Our thanks to the ordinary Australians who preserved these diaries and letters and the Australian War Memorial that cares for most of them. The nation now has an important record of this event. I hope the soldiers who wrote the extracts would be pleased to see them published.

The source for each soldier's extract is recorded in the References at the end of the book chapter by chapter. The References are listed in the order in which the extracts appear in the text. The reference for each extract is only mentioned once in each chapter.

Having been inspired by those last ten Gallipoli veterans to tell the story from the words of the men in the trenches, let us hear from these voices which have been silent for too long.

ACKNOWLEDGEMENTS

The author wishes to thank the following kind people:

THE ANZACS
The last ten surviving Anzacs from Gallipoli whom the author interviewed and who inspired this book: Ted Matthews, Les Leach, Jack Buntine, Fred Kelly, Frank Isaacs, Doug Dibley, Len Hall, Walter Parker, Roy Longmore, Alec Campbell. The hundreds of soldiers who wrote the diaries and letters in this book. The custodians who cared for those diaries and letters including their families who have kindly shared them with the nation; and Charles Bean the visionary Gallipoli correspondent and his Australian War Memorial: the custodians of today.

SIMON AND SCHUSTER
Jon Attenborough who shared the vision, Julia Collingwood who worked so hard to make it happen, and the helpful Helen Golic along with the book's editor Howard Gelman.

RESEARCHERS
Glenda Lynch, Researching Australia who selected and transcribed most of the extracts in this book; Military Historian Peter Bastick; military adviser Barry Billing, writer and researcher Will Baillieu.

SUPPORTERS
The visionary Tony Webster whose Webster Publishing backed the project from the start, Radio 2GB and Channel 9's Kerri-Anne Kennerley who promote history, the Sydney Writers' Festival and Curtin University.

AUSTRALIAN WAR MEMORIAL
Those who helped locate and transcribe the diaries, letters and honour roll including Margaret Lewis, Kerrie Leech, Carmel McInerny, Peter Stanley, and Ian Kelly.

SUPPLIERS: WORDS & PICTURES
Mrs Diana Baillieu, Mrs Anthony Caillard, Andy Webster, Jonathan Webster, Michael Digby, Bob Hyman, Patti Finn, Wilbur Wright, John Cox, the Paul family of Raymond Terrace, the Scobie family of Maitland NSW, and John Nicholson of Dalebrook, Carcoar NSW.

And last but not least my wife and resident editor Jane King

SPONSORS
Singapore Airlines who flew the author to Gallipoli to research this book, and QANTAS who flew the author around Australia to interview the last ten Anzacs.

WRITERS

The author also wishes to thank the writers, artists, photographers from Gallipoli who produced *The Anzac Book* from their dugouts and trenches in 1916; Les Carlyon whose monumentally brilliant bible *Gallipoli* has been a turning point in scholarship and which he consulted extensively because of its detail, accuracy, critical approach and sheer substance.

Other references included; Kevin Fewster's *Gallipoli Correspondent: the frontline diary of C.E.W. Bean*; Robert Reid's book *Gallipoli*; Michael McKernan, *Padre, Australian Chaplains in Gallipoli and France*; Peter Burness, *The Nek*; Robert Rhodes James, *Gallipoli*; Helen Mitchell, *Suvla to the Somme*; Phil Taylor and Pam Cupper, *Gallipoli. A Battlefield Guide*; Anthony Hill, *Soldier Boy. The True Story of Jim Martin the youngest Anzac*; Albert Facey, *A Fortunate Life* and a never-ending library of books about Gallipoli that have been consulted.

APOLOGY

If the author has forgotten anybody or any book he apologises and if contacted will make amends in any future edition.

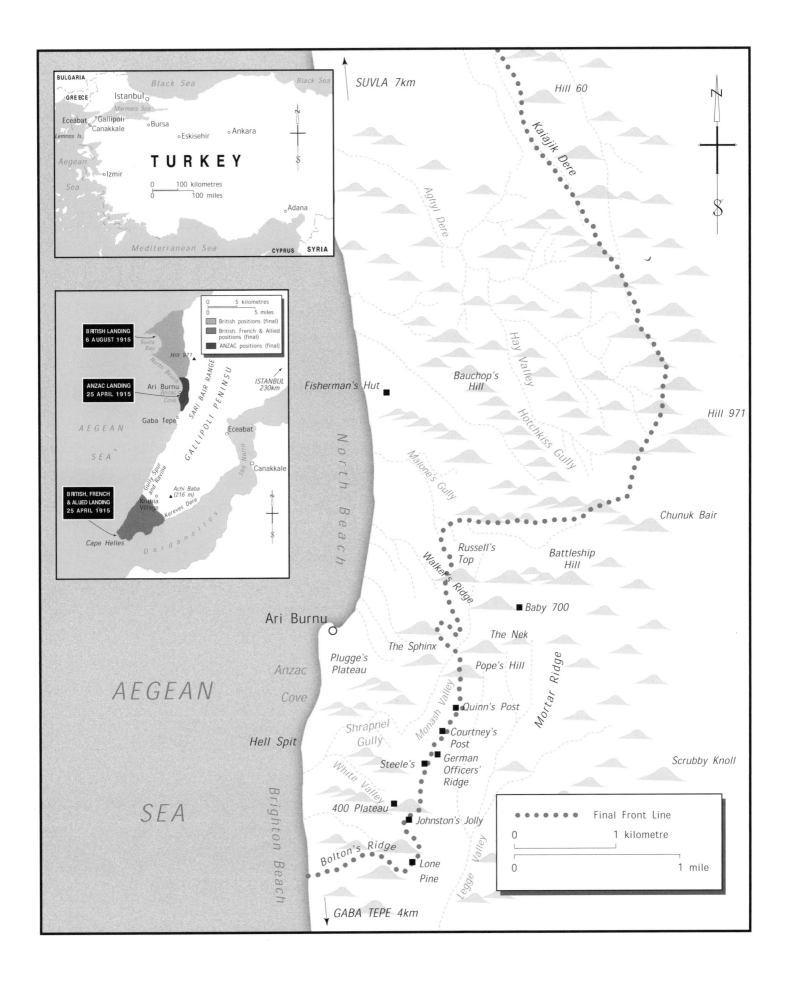

SUVLA 7km

Hill 60

Karajik Dere

Aghyl Dere

Hay Valley

Bauchop's
Hill

Hotchkiss Gully

Hill 971

Malone's Gully

Chunuk Bair

Fisherman's Hut

Russell's
Top

Battleship
Hill

Walker's Ridge

■ Baby 700

The Nek

The Sphinx

Pope's Hill

Ari Burnu

Plugge's
Plateau

Anzac
Cove

Mortar Ridge

Monash Valley

■ Quinn's Post

Hell Spit

Shrapnel
Gully

■ Courtney's
Post

Scrubby Knoll

Steele's ■

German
Officers'
Ridge

White Valley

AEGEAN

400 Plateau ■

■ Johnston's Jolly

Bolton's Ridge

SEA

Brighton Beach

North Beach

■ Lone
Pine

Legge Valley

••••••• Final Front Line

0   1 kilometre

0   1 mile

GABA TEPE 4km

Turkey inset map:

BULGARIA

GREECE

Black Sea

Black Sea

Istanbul

○ Gallipoli

Eceabat ○
Canakkale

○ Bursa

Marmara Sea

○ Eskisehir

○ Ankara

Lemnos Is.

TURKEY

Aegean
Sea

○ Izmir

0   100 kilometres
0   100 miles

○ Adana

Mediterranean Sea

CYPRUS   SYRIA

Gallipoli landings inset map:

0   5 kilometres
0   5 miles

British positions (final)

British, French & Allied
positions (final)

ANZAC positions (final)

BRITISH LANDING
6 AUGUST 1915

Suvla
Bay

Hill 971 ▲

North Beach

ANZAC LANDING
25 APRIL 1915

Ari Burnu
Anzac
Cove

SARI BAIR RANGE

ISTANBUL
230km

Gaba Tepe

GALLIPOLI PENINSU

Eceabat

AEGEAN

SEA

The Narro

Canakkale

BRITISH, FRENCH
& ALLIED LANDING
25 APRIL 1915

Gully Spur and Ravine

Achi Baba
▲ (216 m)

Krithia
Village

Kereves Dere

Cape Helles

Dardanelles

INTO THE FIRING LINE — AT LAST

So through Churchill's excess of imagination, a layman's ignorance of artillery and the fatal power of a young enthusiast like Churchill to convince older and more cautious brains, the tragedy of Gallipoli was born.

CHARLES BEAN, WAR CORRESPONDENT AT GALLIPOLI

Gallipoli Diaries was compiled to give a voice to the soldiers who fought this historic battle. Excerpts from their letters and diaries provide the reader with a picture of the daily life of an Anzac soldier. The words are from officers and privates and even war correspondents who tell their story of the campaign from start to finish. These selected writings may not be the whole story of the battle but they give a soldier's perspective of the nine-month campaign. Through these writings, a reader will come to understand how the Anzacs were transformed during the Gallipoli campaign. They went to Gallipoli as soldiers of the British Empire but came out of the battle as Australians.

This book also honours a special request. Once they knew they might die, the soldiers often wrote in their diaries and letters (sometimes just before they were killed) that they wanted to be remembered by the people back home in Australia. Their writings reveal them as men of exceptional calibre. They wrote these letters and diaries for many different reasons — some used their diaries as therapy, perhaps to share their fear, or to keep sane. Others simply wanted to tell folks back home the truth about the horrors of battle (though sometimes they made light of the reality of war in order to deal with it). What the mothers and wives thought of these letters describing killings, woundings and deaths, we don't know but they must have found it difficult.

Gallipoli Diaries is the first chronicle of every one of the 240 days of the campaign and the first time the actual days of the week have been identified using many diaries and letters. Gallipoli was a day-by-day experience with the soldiers living each day to the full, as it could be

AS HEAD OF THE BRITISH ADMIRALTY, WINSTON CHURCHILL EXERTED A LOT OF INFLUENCE IN THE 1915 DECISION TO LAND BRITISH AND ALLIED TROOPS AT GALLIPOLI. AWM H12243

their last. Down in the trenches, a weekday was very different from a Saturday or a Sunday, when church services often took place as well as letter writing, bathing, washing or changing clothes (if they had any spare clothing), delousing old clothes, killing fleas, visiting a hospital and even resting. Not that weekends, Saturdays or Sundays were always available for such pastimes. The landing at Anzac Cove was on a Sunday as was the August offensive against Lone Pine and the main evacuation in December was over a Saturday and Sunday — a day that was only sacred when war didn't intrude.

The book is meant to be accessible to the lay reader who may not have a background in military history or the battle at Gallipoli. Hopefully, readers will find out what the daily routine was like for the soldiers themselves. They wrote about everyday events in plain easy-to-read English. To give a comprehensive picture of the whole campaign is difficult, because it encompassed a large geographic area and

FROM THEIR LANDING ONWARDS, THOUSANDS OF SOLDIERS KEPT PERSONAL DIARIES MOSTLY WRITTEN IN PENCIL.

approximately 50,000 Australian soldiers took part in the battle. Many of them had different experiences in their different locations. I walked over the terrain from north to south and I can confirm that it is many kilometres distance from Suvla Bay to North Beach and further down past Ari Burnu and Anzac Cove, moving on to Brighton Beach right down to Gaba Tepe.

Anzac Cove is also many kilometres from the southern theatre of Cape Helles, a large area where thousands of British, French and other troops fought.

The 50,000 soldiers in the Australian Imperial Force who served in the nine-month campaign on the Gallipoli peninsula in 1915 were members of the legendary Australian and New Zealand Army Corps. The AIF was the only all-volunteer army in World War I. While the book focuses on the Australian contingent, the New Zealanders also played a significant role in the Gallipoli campaign. The Anzacs were part of a multi-national British led expedition trying to capture the Dardanelles peninsula from the Turks. The plan, devised by the then First Lord of the Admiralty, Winston Churchill, directed the Anzac forces to land on the western side of the peninsula, capture all the Turkish gun emplacements, march to the eastern side of the peninsula capturing gun emplacements along the coast right up to Constantinople (Istanbul) which the Allies also hoped to capture. At the same time, Anglo-French forces would land on the southern tip of the peninsula at Cape Helles, fighting their way up the peninsula and joining the Anzacs before marching on to Constantinople to conquer Turkey. Although the Anglo-French campaign at Cape Helles on the southern tip of the Gallipoli peninsula was equally important, this book focuses on the Australians who landed on the western shore at what became known as Anzac Cove — the generic name used in this book.

Once the British controlled Turkey, the Allies planned to free Russian ships trapped in the Black Sea allowing them to sail through the Bosporus and Dardanelles into the Mediterranean to help Britain and her Allies win the war. In theory it was a brilliant plan but in reality the rugged terrain of the Gallipoli peninsula made the entire adventure impossible.

It certainly was a hopeless task as the rugged Turkish coastline was too well defended by well-armed soldiers. The attack on the Dardanelles peninsula cost the Australians 8,709 dead, and Britain lost 21,255 soldiers during the campaign with France losing 10,000, New Zealand 2,701, India 1,558 and Newfoundland 49. Turkish casualties included 86,692 killed.

Of the 12,000 Australians who landed on that first day, approximately 2,000 were killed in the first 24 hours. That momentous event was

APART FROM SINGING THE PRAISES OF THE ANZACS, *SYDNEY MORNING HERALD* CORRESPONDENT CHARLES BEAN, WHO COVERED GALLIPOLI FROM START TO FINISH, BECAME ONE OF THE GREAT CHAMPIONS OF THE AIF. HE COVERED THE FIGHTING TILL THE END OF THE WAR, THEN HELPED ESTABLISH THE AUSTRALIAN WAR MEMORIAL IN CANBERRA. AWM G01561

THE ECCENTRIC BRITISH
JOURNALIST ELLIS ASHMEAD-
BARTLETT COVERED GALLIPOLI
FOR A RANGE OF FLEET
STREET NEWSPAPERS, AND
HELPED START THE LEGEND OF
THE FEARLESS ANZACS WITH
HIS COLOURFUL STORIES.

commemorated the following year as Anzac Day with street processions all over Australia. Later the event was promoted as a day of national memorial.

Newspaper correspondents painted a picture of heroic feats in describing the Anzacs. Their reports laid the foundation of the Anzac national legend. They wrote about bronzed gladiators who refused to say die when they landed at the wrong beach on an impossible suicide mission. Despite the precarious landing, reports described how the Anzacs repeatedly charged at Turkish guns pointing straight at them from the hills above and captured Turkish positions against murderous enemy fire.

London's *Daily Telegraph* reporter who sent stories to many Fleet Street newspapers, Ellis Ashmead-Bartlett, set the tone: 'In the face of murderous enemy fire this bold race of athletes continued to scale the highest cliffs'. Britain's poet laureate, John Masefield, added that 'the ANZACS were the finest body of young men ever brought together in modern times. For physical beauty and nobility of bearing they surpassed any man I have ever seen; they walked and looked like the kings in old poems, and reminded me of the Shakespearean line "Baited like eagles having lately bathed".'

Even the normally restrained Lt Gen. Sir William Birdwood, the commanding officer at Anzac Cove, sang their praises. 'No words of mine could ever convey to readers at their firesides in Australia, New Zealand and the Old Country, one half of what all their boys have been through, nor is my poor pen capable of telling them of the never-failing courage, determination and cheerfulness of those who have so willingly fought and given their lives for King and country's sake.' *Sydney Morning Herald* correspondent, Charles Bean, who became Australia's official World War I historian and subsequently founded the Australian War Memorial, also summed up the campaign in words that perpetuated the legend: 'ANZAC stood, and still stands for reckless valour in a good cause, for enterprise, resourcefulness, fidelity, comradeship and endurance that will never admit defeat.'

The Anzacs would be involved in bigger and more decisive battles as the war progressed, especially in Flanders and France where 48,617 Australians died. Gallipoli, however, was the first international combat involving Australia, which became a nation only fourteen years earlier. Since then, the Anzac legend formed at Gallipoli has captured the nation's imagination and has never been dislodged from the popular psyche where it seems to grow in stature year by year.

It's easy to be wise after the event. Gallipoli, however, was a monumental failure. As Australia's last veteran of the 25 April landing

OPPOSITE: BRISBANE'S BERT
WHITE, WHO COULD NOT SEE
ANY REASON TO REMOVE HIS
'FAG' FOR AN OFFICIAL PRE-WAR
PORTRAIT WITH A MATE, WAS
TYPICAL OF THE IRREVERENT
LARRIKIN WHO VOLUNTEERED
TO FIGHT AT GALLIPOLI.

Ted Matthews said in 1997, 'From the mistaken landing onwards, the British mucked the whole thing up'. British politicians did make a mistake deciding to invade Turkey on the Gallipoli peninsula. They appointed military commanders because of their social status but with little military experience who were not only incompetent but also unapproachable. British reconnaissance failed to detect the difficulty of the terrain. While Turkish intelligence learned of Allied plans, the British failed to discover Turkey expected the attack. Officers organised the trench system so poorly that these defences did not properly protect soldiers during the fighting. Officers were also derelict in organising proper burials, the dead lying unattended for weeks and sometimes not buried at all, allowing decomposing corpses to spread disease. The British administrators also failed to deliver adequate food and water for the troops. The British tacticians mounted a hopeless series of attacks at Helles across open ground in broad daylight against impenetrable Turkish defences sending thousands to certain death. Impossible offensives were also mounted at Anzac Cove in August against Hill 971, Chunuk Bair and the Nek at the cost of thousands of lives. Finally, the British commanders took so long to decide to evacuate the peninsula that thousands more soldiers died from shelling and sickness. In short,

THESE QUEENSLANDERS, MANY OF WHOM SAID THEY WERE JUST LOOKING FOR 'A BIT OF FUN' WERE TYPICAL OF THE RAW RECRUITS WHO ENLISTED IN THE AIF IN 1914 AND WERE TRAINED IN TIME FOR GALLIPOLI.

it was in Shakespearean terms a tragic comedy of errors mismanaged by larger than life, cane-carrying caricatures of Col. Blimp complete with their mandatory handle-bar moustache.

Sometimes, the perspective of history can turn bloody disasters into triumphs and Gallipoli was a victory of sorts for the Anzacs, who succeeded in hanging on to that beach for nine months despite hopeless British military leadership. The British do not celebrate Gallipoli, as do the descendants of Australians who landed on that first Anzac Day. In the first year of the 21st century, so many Australian 'pilgrims' visited Gallipoli for the dawn service that the event was transferred from Anzac Cove to North Beach, where a commemorative memorial was built. The Australian government contributed $1.2 million to build the memorial and the New Zealand government $0.3 million while the Turkish government gave an undisclosed amount. This memorial, dedicated by Prime Minister John Howard on 25 April 2001, became the showpiece of a new Gallipoli Peninsula Peace Park. A commemorative stone wall with a series of panels now tells different parts of the Gallipoli story from the landing to the evacuation. Above, fly the flags from the Allied nations who helped restore peace along with the Turkish flag. The memorial park can accommodate up to 15,000 people and the organisers hope it will be adequate for the 2015 centenary.

When the last Gallipoli veteran died in 2002, Australia lost a living link with one of the most important events of its first century as a nation. Through the diaries and letters in this book, we can regain the immediacy of that time. Those soldiers were witnesses not only of a celebrated battle but also of a nation's defining moment — which began when they leapt from the boats and scrambled up that beach at Anzac Cove. That was another Australia, defined by its colonial ties and now lost forever. Those young men believed in the British Empire so strongly that they volunteered to fight for 'king and country', and were glad to risk their lives for that cause.

Some, like Maj. E. Brind, from the 23rd Battalion, wrote regularly, typically starting his letters with, 'Dear Mum Here's the weekly start for the home letter. It's astounding how the days go past and you are at the end of the week really before you know it has properly started. There has been a crowded week this week. First I'm awfully sorry to tell you our little Diggley Doc. Has gone to swell the number of Australians who have given their lives for the cause'. They wrote letters to keep sane or to break the routine, as Capt. Stanton explained. 'This place is worse than even Broadmeadows for Furpheys' and 'I used to think fellows were exaggerating when they talked of the monotony of this life but there is no doubt about it, we take not the least bit of notice of the

LYING IN WAIT FOR THE
ANZACS TO LAND AT GALLIPOLI
WAS ONE OF THE GREAT
SOLDIERS OF WORLD WAR I,
MUSTAFA KEMAL (AKA
ATATURK), FOURTH FROM LEFT,
WHO DEFENDED THE
PENINSULA WITH THESE
OFFICERS OF THE ANAFARTA
FORCE WHICH HE COMMANDED.
AWM P01141.001

everlasting bang bang and I can tell you John Turk's index finger hangs on the trigger very lightly at night time, he wastes thousands of rounds of ammunition.'

The writings reveal recurrent themes among the soldiers. Firstly, they all wanted to prove themselves and were anxious to do some good, to show they were pulling their weight. Invariably, they volunteered for the most dangerous missions. Many wrote home excitedly that, 'At last I am in the firing line'. They were always unselfish towards their mates. Charles Bean noted that when the wounded refused to take more than one or two sips of a water bottle needed by others on the battlefield, he felt 'they were so unselfish one could have cried'.

Some soldiers describe the campaign at Gallipoli as if it was a sporting contest and the landing itself like running onto the field in a football match against enemy bullets from the other team. For Lt L. Richards, who played International Rugby for both Australia and England, the battle was like a world football event. 'I don't feel the coming danger any more than I have felt anxious the night before an international football match', he wrote before landing.

Many Aussies were known as cheerful jokers who made light of hardship, as Maj. Brind of the 23rd Battalion noted on a cold December day. 'We have had a touch of winter in the trench. The chaps have stuck it out well in spite of the intense cold, though I don't think that any of them will volunteer for Arctic exploration when we get home.' Shivering, as winter approached, Capt. Bill Knox told his wife that his many layers of clothes would have equipped him to sail south on any Antarctic expedition mounted by Sir Ernest Shackleton. Some Anzacs even appeared to laugh in the face of certain death. They seemed at the same time brave, fearless, cavalier, foolhardy and reckless, and preferred to die showing their worth rather than stay alive as cowards. As Col. Monash wrote on 14 May to his wife, 'the men have been living for weeks in squalor, dirt and rain, with most of them in rags yet they are laughing and singing and joking and indulging in chaff and horse-play until it is their turn tomorrow to face the awful ordeal of the trenches'.

WHEN THEY WROTE THEIR LETTERS HOME, MOST SOLDIERS ON THE BEACH, LIKE GALLIPOLI'S YOUNGEST ANZAC JAMES MARTIN, 14, BEGGED FOR LETTERS FROM HOME – WHICH IN HIS CASE NEVER ARRIVED.

On 31 August, Trooper I.L. Idriess, 5th Australian Light Horse Regiment, wrote that 'I did not know Gus Gaunt was such a sprinter before. To see him running naked from the beach with a bucket of water in his hand and a Turk bullet whistling merrily just overhead was very amusing. I was looking on'. On 30 October, Capt. Ivor Williams of 21st. Battalion, described the enemy with an affectionate nickname as he played down threats. 'Turko threw some more shells at us today, but again did no damage'. And on 19 May, Charles Bean wrote that in midst of battle 'they seemed such simple, frank chaps, light-hearted with all the fascinating freshness of Australians playing their game there just like children and all the time the enemy was firing away over their heads'.

Not that the slaughter of their comrades left them unmoved. On 15 August, Sgt. C.C. St. Pinnock, of the 8th Light Horse Regiment, wrote, after they charged the Turks, that 'they were waiting ready for us' so 'we did not get ten yards'. Then, 'the second line came on and got the same reception, and so on until the whole of the 8th and 10th were practically wiped out. Really too awful to write about. All your pals that had been with you for months and months blown and shot out of all recognition. There was no chance whatever of us gaining our point, but the roll call after was the saddest, just fancy only 47 answered their names out of close to 550 men. I simply cried like a child. It is really too awful'. Pte. J. Pasini also wrote to his mother on 6 June revealing that 'a man's life is valued at nothing in this war!'.

Australians looking for comfort to compensate for the tragedy of Gallipoli and the passing of these brave men need go no further than the most poignant memorial of all, which ironically was written by their enemy. In 1935, to commemorate the twentieth anniversary of the battle, Turkish president and poet Kemal Ataturk (aka Mustafa Kemal), who defended Gallipoli against the Anzacs, had a large memorial placed at Anzac Cove with one of his own poems inscribed.

> You heroes that shed your blood and lost your lives, you are now lying in the soil of a friendly country, therefore rest in peace. There is no difference between the Johnnies and the Mehmets to us, where they lie side by side, here in this country of ours. You their mothers who sent your sons from far away countries wipe away your tears; your sons are now lying in our bosom and are in peace. After having lost their lives on this land they have become our sons as well.

Against this epic background, the story of Gallipoli can now be told in the words of the soldiers who lived through it.

THE GERMAN OFFICER IN CHARGE OF THE TURKISH FORCES RESISTING THE ANZACS' LANDING AT GALLIPOLI WAS THE FORMER CAVALRY LEADER, GENERAL OTTO LIMAN VON SANDERS.

THE YOUNGEST PERSON TO BE
CAUGHT UP IN THE
ENTHUSIASM TO VOLUNTEER
FOR WAR WAS 14-YEAR-OLD
JAMES MARTIN FROM
MELBOURNE, POSING HERE
WITH HIS SISTER MILLIE
BEFORE SAILING OFF FOR
GALLIPOLI WHERE HE DIED
BEFORE HIS 15TH BIRTHDAY.

PROLOGUE
ANZAC EVE
24 April 1915

As this may be the last opportunity I have of talking to you, I want to say briefly that, in the event of my going out, you are to believe that I do so with only one regret, which is, the grief that this will bring to you and Bert and Mat. For myself, I am prepared to take my chance. While, on the one hand, to win through safely would mean honour and achievement, on the other hand to fall would mean an honourable end.

COL. JOHN MONASH, LETTER TO WIFE, 24 APRIL 1915

EN ROUTE TO GALLIPOLI, THE AIF TRAINED AT MENA CAMP, EGYPT, BELOW THE PYRAMIDS. AWM PO1436.007

After dark on 24 April, the bulk of the troops in the Australian Imperial Force's special Australian New Zealand Army Corps (the Anzacs) were transported along with their New Zealand comrades across the Mediterranean Sea by a fleet of 200 ships. The troops were heading for the Gallipoli peninsula ready, willing and able to land on those fatal shores. The months of training at places like Mena Camp at Giza, Egypt, were over. Now ready for combat, the Anzacs were moving inexorably towards their historic rendezvous. Thousands of soldiers from the Australian Imperial Force's special Australian New Zealand Army Corps were on the eve of their first action on a beach on the coast of Turkey. The British commanders believed the landing would take place on a wide beach just north of Gaba Tepe, which was meant to be an entrance to fairly flat fields over which the Anzacs could march. Nobody knew that logistical error would mean the troops landed much further north at a narrow beach perched under steep cliffs which became known as Anzac Cove. The medical corps estimated they would have to evacuate 3,000 of the Anzacs who would be too badly wounded to fight. No arrangements were made for burials. For some this mistaken landing would be a baptism of fire that would change their lives forever, and for others, it meant death.

At the same time, British and French troops were getting ready to land at the southern tip of the Gallipoli peninsula at Cape Helles as part of a combined campaign to capture the Dardanelles. The British 29th Division planned to land at five different beaches in the south. Although the Anglo-French action was equally important, this book is concerned with the Australians who landed on the beaches at Anzac Cove (with New Zealand comrades beside them). Months later, the British would also land to the north of Anzac Cove at Suvla Bay. Over time the three major assaults on the peninsula would come to be known under one generic heading — 'Gallipoli'.

It was a tense moment made even more tense because of the extra waiting. The landing had been put back from Thursday 23 April for 48 hours because of severe weather. Now the men hoped they would be second time lucky. Only the senior officers knew what was happening and the atmosphere aboard ship was one of acute apprehension that night before the landing. As the ships approached their destination, the tension among the troops mounted to a fever pitch. Some of them knew they were approaching the Turkish coast, some also realised this was the western coast of the Gallipoli peninsula and a handful knew it was the beach near Gaba Tepe.

Officers in charge of the landing had read the special order from Lt Gen. Sir William Birdwood, Commander of the Anzacs, which made it

AS WATER WAS SUCH A PRECIOUS RESOURCE, A GROUP OF SOLDIERS WOULD OFTEN WASH AND SHAVE IN THE SAME TUB.

clear that 'In conjunction with the Navy we are about to undertake one of the most difficult tasks any soldier can be called on to perform' but 'that we shall succeed I have no doubt, simply because I know your full determination to do so. Lord Kitchener has told us that he lays special stress on the role the army has to play in this particular operation, the success of which will be a very severe blow to the enemy — indeed as severe as any he could receive in France. It will go down in history to the glory of the soldiers of Australia and New Zealand'.

After asking all soldiers to 'listen attentively', Birdwood admitted that 'we are going to have a real hard and rough time of it, until at all events, we have turned the enemy out of our first objective'.

Claiming that 'Hard, rough times none of us mind' Birdwood warned that 'the country wither we are bound is very difficult' so 'we may not be able to get our wagons anywhere near us for days so men must not think their wants have been neglected if they do not get all they want. On landing it will be necessary for every individual to carry with him all his requirements in food and clothing for three days'. Finally Birdwood warned them 'to take the very greatest care not only of food but ammunition the replenishment of which will be very difficult'. He urged them to 'make an effort to try and refrain from starting on your water bottle until quite late in the day. Once you start drinking you cannot stop, and a water bottle is very soon emptied'. Also, he warned, 'You must not waste ammunition by firing away indiscriminately at no target' but wait until we 'find the enemy in well entrenched positions when all our ammunition will be required to turn them out'.

That night, the 4,000 soldiers of the 3rd Brigade of the First Australian Division were 'lying in wait' thinking and feeling different thoughts about the coming battle. They would be the first to lead the charge. Waiting also were three men who wrote down their thoughts on that night — a Lieutenant, a Lieutenant General and a war correspondent.

24 April 1915

Lt Richards from the 1st Battalion Australian Imperial Force summed up the feelings of soldiers when he wrote, 'To-morrow is the all-eventful day. We have our bully beef and biscuits with a full water bottle for two days or more. There is no water on the Gallipoli landing place at all, so we have to take great care of our water and fill ourselves up to the neck before landing.

'At 3.30 a.m. the first landing parties comprising the 1st Brigade will face the music which will probably be poured out to them from the

IT WAS WHILE TRAINING IN EGYPT THAT THE BONDS OF FRIENDSHIP STARTED FORMING. THEY WOULD LATER TRANSLATE INTO THE LEGENDARY 'MATESHIP' AMONG GALLIPOLI SOLDIERS WHO TEAMED UP IN PAIRS TO LOOK AFTER EACH OTHER.

trenches only a few hundred yards from the open beach, but it is just possible that the fleet will have cleared the Turks back from their advanced positions.

'At 8 a.m. the Engineers and 1st Field Ambulance go ashore in small barges [and] rowing boats. Of course, our landing will be free from rifle fire but there are two forts 800 ft. and 600 ft. high back 2 miles with a clear range on to the landing place. The fleet which includes the *Queen Elizabeth*, *London* and *Prince of Wales* may hold these forts up and keep them busy. Let's hope!

'I listened to Maj. Croxton speaking from the bridge deck this afternoon. He gave particulars of the numbers and the battalions landing and what was expected of them. His speech was full of fine humour, dealing chiefly with our funky condition and likely fear. It was hardly the kind of speech one would expect on the eve of big doings, as there was plenty of ridicule, nonsense, but no hard facts or detailed information. It seemed more as though we were preparing for a pantomime instead of grim warfare. I don't mean for one moment that he would have made us melancholy and miserable but he would have given us something like an idea of what to expect.

'*Later* — Now, however, that I have gone over the sketch plan of the whole country over which our action is to take place, I am more satisfied and prepared for the scene of our work to-morrow. These two fortified points are our objective right enough and it's going to be a regular inferno, that is, of course, if the fleet does not blow the forts to hell … If we can get possession of these two points the towns and forts on both sides of the Narrows will get the "axe" right enough. Anyhow, there is some satisfaction in knowing that we Australians have got a chance of distinguishing ourselves at last. It will be hard and thrilling work right enough, in fact a gigantic task for the first time in action, but I think they will make good right enough. My money, anyhow, is on our boys tomorrow.

'At night as soon as lights go out the fellows get asking questions about one another, and it's astounding the home truths that are told. A fellow soon finds out if he is unpopular. The jokes they get off are startling sometimes. They also had a go at the number of lance corporals appointed, but they treated me very mildly indeed. I find that I must take the stripe and wear it. This does not bother me now as there is a likelihood of promotion if the fighting is going to be as bad as it looks at present.

'Our A.M.C. arrangements or rather equipment have been badly catered for. There is a serious insufficiency of bandages and drugs through the whole business. Even haversacks had to be improvised to-day owing to the stretcher squads being broken down from 6 men to 4 men each, thereby making 9 extra squads and no equipment for them. I have got the remains of a cold clinging to me yet, but as I am taking all precautions it will soon wear off. I took care to have some cough lollies with me but I am nursing them very carefully. Into my overcoat I have sewn a piece of waterproof sheeting as the coats do not keep the water out very well, and added extra pockets to my coats for possible convenience and emergency sake. I also have a waterproof bag to carry my notebook and camera in. I have 7 rolls of films (8 exposures in each) which will have to do me for a time, until we reach civilisation I suppose.

'Gallipoli has mythology interests as the great warrior of the Siege of Troy — Achilles — is buried here, or at any rate there is a place described as the "Tomb of Achilles". Lemnos Island is known also to mythology as it was here that Vulcan landed when he was thrown out of Mount Olympus by Juno.

'There was a glorious sunset tonight. It was just like a stage setting with the lovely deep red-coloured orb disappearing between the purple hills and the dainty rose pink sky. I was drawn away from it to get more bully beef and biscuits in my mess tin.

'To-night, although the fellows are naturally a little excited, they are in good spirits. They have shown up splendidly (comparatively speaking) since we left the loafing and waiting ground in the sands of Egypt. There has been a stronger tendency for sacred music also of late, with mouth organ and concertina. Only a few minutes ago they were playing and singing "Nearer my God to Thee" and "Lead Kindly Light". It's wonderful how religion gets them down when there is danger about. This ordeal should also test and bring my lack of faith home to me and give me a new light in that direction, as I walk blindly and aimlessly now.'

Lt Richards, who played International Rugby for both Australia and England said, 'I don't feel the coming danger any more than I have felt anxious the night before international football match. For my own part there is nothing to fear but at last (since Brother Charlie's death) I realise there are other folk and that I must take care of myself and live for them'. He also noted that 'Rather a good concert took place on the well deck to-night. This is a clear sign of the fellows' coolness, though the main songs were of the sad sob kind.' Finally Richards got rid of surplus weight. 'I have a few letters that must be acknowledged. I will look them over and tear them up now. Just why I could not explain at all but nevertheless I must!! That's the lot'.

One of the senior officers, Col. John Monash, later the Commander in Chief of Australia's army in France, reflected on the apprehension of the soldiers when writing to his wife. 'We have received our sailing orders, and inside of a few hours shall be in the thick of the greatest combined naval and military operation in history, with Australia in the pride of place. — That we shall succeed I do not entertain any doubt, but that I shall come through unscathed and alive is not so certain. — As this may be the last opportunity I have of talking to you, I want to say briefly that, in the event of my going out, you are to believe that I do so with only one regret, which is, the grief that this will bring to you and Bert and Mat. — For myself, I am prepared to take my chance. — While, on the one hand, to win through safely would mean honour and achievement, on the other hand to fall would mean an honorable end. — At best I have only a few years of vigour left, and then would come decay and the chill of old age, and perhaps lingering illness. — So, with the full and active life I have had, I need not regard the prospect of a sudden end with dismay. — I am greatly comforted to know that you will be well provided for, and will be surrounded by many friends, who, for my sake, will help you to win through all difficulties that may beset you in the future. — I am sure you know how deeply I have always loved you, and how in all things I have tried to act in your best

AWARE OF THE REGION'S
MYTHICAL ASSOCIATIONS WITH
EPIC SAGAS, THE MORE
CLASSICAL SCHOLARS AMONG
THE ANZACS COMPARED THEIR
LANDING WITH THE VOYAGES
OF PIONEER NAVIGATORS AS
SHOWN HERE IN THIS DRAWING
FOR *THE ANZAC BOOK*, WHICH
WAS PRODUCED BY THE
SOLDIERS WHILE THEY WERE
AT ANZAC COVE.

interests. — I know also that you have loved me dearly, and will honor my memory.'

Sydney Morning Herald correspondent, Charles Bean, summed up the anticipation of Anzac Eve when he wrote in his diary, 'This morning I was waked by the motion of the ship ... Staff officers have been advised to take off their brassards whilst in close touch with the enemy ... so the bright colours have for the moment disappeared ... one sometimes is inclined to think of the utter hopeless wastefulness of this whole war ... we know what a tremendous job it is this assault on a strong fortress ... It's a great gamble the whole thing really ... and a lot of Australians — boys who began their life on the Murray or in a backyard in Wagga or Bourke or Surry Hills will be left lying in Turkey

WANDERING spirits, seeking lands unknown,
Such were our fathers, stout hearts unafraid.
Have we been faithless, leaving homes they made,
With their life's blood cementing every stone?
Nay, when the beast-like War God did intone
His horrid chant, was our first reckoning paid
For years of ease. Their restless spirits bade
Us fight with those whose Homeland was their own.

Rest easy in your graves, the spirit lives
That brought you forth to claim of earth the best.
Ours it is now, and ours it shall remain;
Mere jealous greed no honest birthright gives.
Shades of our fathers, hear our faith confessed,
We shall defend your Empire or be slain.

Capt. JAMES SPRENT,
A.M.C. (3rd Field Amb.).

... some of the positions tomorrow I believe are "to be taken at all costs". The lights of the ship will go out presently ... I will fill my brandy flask and then to bed'.

They were approaching Gallipoli, where the very bay itself seemed to be holding its breath in the blackness of the night in anticipation of the terrible events of the morrow. No matter how apprehensive the men were, there was no turning back. As Charles Bean reported at '12 midnight: the ships have sailed from Lemnos!'.

When that clock struck midnight on the 25 April 1915, the Anzacs sailed toward their rendezvous with history.

THERE WERE MORE THAN ENOUGH TALENTED POETS AMONG THE ANZACS TO PUT FINE WORDS TO THE CLASSICAL IMAGES DRAWN FOR *THE ANZAC BOOK*.

This photograph was taken in secret on the morning of the landing by a soldier sheltering among the men who had made it to the safety of the cliffs at Anzac Cove. It shows how those still arriving in open boats were 'sitting ducks'.

CHAPTER 1
25 APRIL
The Landing

All men are now lined up on deck and the orders issued, 'no rifles are to be loaded … equipment to be left unbuckled … silence to be strictly maintained in the boats. Bayonets to be fixed the moment of landing & the first line of trenches to be taken at the point of "cold steel". At precisely 3.10 a.m. countless numbers of small craft … push off together for the unknown.'

ANONYMOUS SOLDIER OF THE 3RD BRIGADE

Sunday 25 April
DAY 1

MAJ. E.G. SINCLAIR-MACLAGAN, THE COMMANDER OF THE BRAVE MEN OF THE 3RD BRIGADE WHO LANDED FIRST AT GALLIPOLI ON 25 APRIL 1915. AWM H12187

At last the time had come. The anxious waiting was over. As journalist Charles Bean, notebook and pencil in hand, noted, 'It is still too dark to see what I am writing but the dawn is slowly growing … it is well past four just when the men of the 3rd Brigade should be rushing out of their boats … then at 4.38 for the first time listening eagerly … I heard the distant echo of rifle firing the men had landed and the battle had begun.'

The first Australian soldiers to land were the 3rd Brigade (known as the all Australian brigade) led by Maj. E.G. Sinclair-MacLagan. He had four battalions (the 9th, 10th, 11th and 12th battalions) made up of about 1,000 men each to a total of 4,000 soldiers.

The second wave of soldiers were the 1st and 2nd Brigades also of about 4,000 men each comprising a supporting force of 8,000. The 2nd Brigade would land ahead of the 1st Brigade. In all about 12,000 Australians landed on the first day. The ordinary soldiers who rushed ashore that day had no idea of the historic nature of their mission. Some did not even know what country they were attacking due to official secrecy, nor who they would be shooting at.

The soldiers who landed from the 25th of April onwards discovered that their task was a difficult one. The cliffs of the rugged Turkish coastline were too steep and the terrain was defended by well-armed enemy soldiers who were continually reinforced and supported by highly skilled German officers. These Turkish soldiers were also perched on cliff tops overlooking the beaches chosen by the Allied landing forces. After all this was the wrong beach, a mile north at Ari Burnu where the cliffs were much steeper than the flat terrain of the intended landing site, Gaba Tepe. According to Charles Bean, had the troops landed where they were meant to at Gaba Tepe the results could have

BY THE TIME THE SUN ROSE OVER THE GALLIPOLI PENINSULA ON 25 APRIL, THE ANZACS WERE ALREADY BEING FERRIED IN OPEN BOATS TO ANZAC COVE FROM THE SHIPS AT ANCHOR AS THIS PHOTOGRAPH BY CHARLES BEAN REVEALS.

actually been worse as 'the Turks who must have heard we intended landing there, had made that place exceedingly strong — so I doubt if we could have landed there'.

Yet the men rose to the challenge. Despite heavy enemy fire, they stormed the beach and charged up steep cliffs, driving fleeing Turks before them. Although 2,000 Australians were killed in the first 24 hours, some soldiers achieved miraculous feats of strength before the Turks brought in reinforcements and mounted massive counterattacks. Athletic climbers like Capt. Arthur Seaforth Blackburn, Capt. Eric Tulloch, Capt. Joe Lalor, Lt Ivor Margetts, Capt. Alfred Shout and Lt Hedley 'Snowy' Howe not only got to the top of the cliffs overlooking the landing beach but some to the top of hills far inland. From this vantage point, they could see below them the sparkling waters of their coveted Dardanelles shipping channel. On this first day, these heroic fighters reached strategic positions on the Gallipoli Peninsula that Anzacs would never reach again — Scrubby Knoll, Chunuk Bair, Battleship Hill, Baby 700 and the notorious Nek (which the Anzacs tried to capture in August but failed losing hundreds in the attempt).

These advance soldiers could almost have run down the hill on the eastern side of the peninsula towards the Dardanelles, but this was not the battle plan. The soldiers were so far in front of the line that no supporting reinforcements could join them. Had they not turned back, they would have been cut off from their base on the beach. Once these brave soldiers retreated, no Allied soldier ever got so far inland again in the nine-month campaign. Although it had been a valiant effort, by the end of the first day, the Anzacs occupied only a square kilometre of land, their front line less than 900 metres from the sea. Some of the leaders, including Lt Gen. Birdwood, considered evacuating the troops.

Further south along the Peninsula at Cape Helles, the British-led Allied forces, which included soldiers from France and other nations also met with fierce resistance. The Anglo-French forces were able to entrench on some beaches but on others, aggressive counterattacks (at beaches like Y Beach) forced them to evacuate by 26 April. With the Australian and New Zealand action on Anzac Cove, the Anglo-French assault was essential to the campaign to take the peninsula and the Dardanelles.

There were other heroic deeds on that first day. Many well-known accounts of familiar personalities were written, including the records of Charles Bean, and the exploits of Pte. John Simpson Kirkpatrick known as 'the man with the donkey'. Pte. Albert Facey published his life story, *A Fortunate Life*, in 1981. Corp. Ted Matthews, who was the last survivor of the 25 April landing at Gallipoli, landed on that first day and gave many interviews before he died at 101. Ted Matthews was given a state funeral in 1997. The New Zealanders also have their share of heroic stories. They fought bravely alongside the Australians as part of the Anzac force.

The 3rd Brigade landed first followed by the 2nd Brigade which came right behind, then the 1st Brigade. The diary entry of an anonymous soldier from the 3rd Brigade begins the story, 'Arrived with the rest of the Fleet, consisting of Battleships, Cruisers, torpedo-destroyers, transports etc at a quarter to three. It is now black dark, the moon having gone down, sky clear & sea calm. Everyone is in a state of eager excitement, men move around the deck noiselessly and speak in whispers. We can now see the high black peaks of the shores of the Peninsula about 5 miles distant ... transport boats are lowered and steam pinnaces and destroyers also come alongside to take the boats in tow.

'All men are now lined up on deck and the orders issued, "no rifles are to be loaded ... equipment to be left unbuckled ... silence to be strictly maintained in the boats. Bayonets to be fixed the moment of landing & the first line of trenches to be taken at the point of cold steel" ... at precisely 3.10 a.m. countless numbers of small craft ... push off together for the unknown ... the scream of a shell and the water is thrown fifty feet skywards ... three shrapnel shells burst high over our heads and the contents come down like hail in the water near by ... our battleships commence & immediately there is the roar of a hundred guns & the whole place is illuminated ... the concussion is awful, one would fancy the whole mountain-side had fallen ... we are now within a mile of the shore & the row and din has increased ... the whole side of the mountains seem to be sending forth tongues of flame and the bullets fairly rain upon us — the water is churned up from rifle-fire, machine-guns, maxims, shrapnel and common shells ... seven of the boys in our boat are killed & God knows how many in the others ... the boats bottom scratch on the rocky shore ... 50 yards from land and to wade ashore with the feeling on you that you are at least one of the first to put foot on Turkish soil ... silent forms lay scattered on the beach everywhere: some gone to their last resting place ... some writhing in their last agonies, others with their life-blood fastly oozing out.

'Now we have commenced up those steep cliffs, parts of which one has to almost pull himself branch by branch ... in many places to fall back again ... We are near them now, only 50 yards away ... then a roar and a yell ... as we are charging at them ... they are out of their trenches ... On and on, up those awful cliffs and through the dense scrub, where every few yards a Turk jumps out with his bayonet ready ... Then the second line of trenches and again the third, just as the dawn of a new but bloody day is breaking. The top of the mountain is now strongly outlined against the grey morning sky (our goal) but yet fully two miles away. We now ... form up in some sort of a line, that has been hopelessly confused ... at this moment there is a "burr" overhead and on looking up we see two of our own flying-machines hovering over the enemy and dropping smoke-bombs to direct the fire of our warships ... Now for the first time our rifles ... fire (10 rounds rapid is the order) charge magazines again and up and at them ... until at last ... we gain the mountain peaks. The goal is reached but at what a cost.

'We now take advantage of all cover and pour in volley after volley, till the rifles are red hot and the wood-work smoking ... An hour of this and then the order comes down the line, to advance at right form, so we push on and by 3 o'clock we have them driven 3 or 4 miles inland. Then the order to get down and dig in — dig in for your lives — entrenching tools out and as one man digs the next is pouring in volley after volley ... As soon as it grows dark the order is passed down to the officers to select so many men to go back to the landing place at the beach for ammunition … after nearly two hours we get there … But oh God the sight of the dead and wounded absolutely covering the little sandy beach … there is an enormous staff of medical men etc. there but it is absolutely impossible to attend to all, so that many a life … expires on the beach for want of looking after … Each man now seizes a box of ammunition & off in feverish haste for the firing-line … at midnight we regain the firing-line, worn-out, weary and hungry … No chance of sleep as the enemy are ever at us, and so the night advances to the dawn of a new day and thus was the work of our first day's bloody battle.'

An unnamed Pte. No. 94, from A Company, 9th Battalion, 3rd Brigade, who was on the first boat to land, described the danger enemy machine guns posed to the landing force. 'The first man ashore on the peninsula was Lieutenant Chapman of the 9th, followed closely by Colonel Lee, Major Robertson, Major Salisbury, Captain Ryder, Dr. Butler and the men of our landing boat. In the darkness before the dawn, men gathered on the beach beneath the cliff. Packs were thrown off and bayonets fixed. All this time a machine gun on the cliff above us had been pouring a hail of bullets into the landing parties.

'Dr. Butler had lost some of his stretcher-bearers in that deadly fire and this made him very angry. "Come on, Queenslanders, we must take that gun" he cried and started climbing the cliff revolver in his hand. We stormed up the cliff behind him. Sergeant Fowles and Patrick Courtney were on either side of me as we climbed the cliff and both were shot dead. But we rushed the gun, bayoneted the Turks who formed the gun crew and silenced it, smashing the gun so it could never be used again.'

Pte. A.R. Perry who was in the 3rd Brigade also landed with this first wave. He was in the 10th Battalion and was wounded along with some of his mates not long after coming ashore. 'Thousands of bullets began to fly around and over us, sometimes barely missing. Now and then one heard a low gurgling moan, and turning, one saw near at hand some chum, who only a few seconds before had been laughing and joking, now lying gasping, with his life blood soaking down into the red clay and sand. "Five rounds rapid at the scrub in front" comes the command of our subaltern. Then an order down the line "Fix bayonets!" Fatal order was it not, perhaps some officers of the enemy who shouted it? (For they say such things were done). Out flash a thousand bayonets, scintillating in the sunlight like a thousand mirrors, signaling our position to the batteries away on our left and front … One wonders how anyone could live amidst such a hail of death-dealing lead and shell. "Ah, got me!" says one lad on my left, and he shakes his arms. A bullet had passed through the biceps of his left arm, missed his chest by an inch, passed though the right forearm and finally struck the lad between

SGT. HERBERT FOWLES, A QUEENSLAND TEACHER, WAS ONE OF THE VERY FIRST TO LAND WITH THE 9TH BATTALION IN THE 3RD BRIGADE. HE WAS KILLED WHILE TRYING TO CAPTURE A MACHINE GUN ON ONE OF THE FIRST RIDGES HE SCALED.

THESE ANZACS JUST HAD TO
HOPE AND PRAY THEY WERE
NOT SHOT IN THE OPEN BOATS
AS THEY WERE TOWED BY
STEAM-POWERED VESSELS ON
25 APRIL. ONCE CLOSER IN,
THE ROWERS LOWERED THEIR
OARS AND ROWED THE
SOLDIERS AS CLOSE TO THE
BEACH AS POSSIBLE.
AWM P02194.003

him and me … a man from the 9th Battalion started to bind up his wounds as he was bleeding freely. All the time shrapnel was hailing down on us. "Oh-h" comes from directly behind me and looking around, I see a poor little Lieutenant of C Company has been badly wounded. From both hips to his ankles blood is oozing through pants and puttees, and he painfully drags himself to the rear. With every pull he moans cruelly. I raise him to his feet and at a very slow pace start to help him to shelter past a file of bleeding men some shot through the leg "using their rifles as crutches" … Alas! I have only got him about 50 yards from the firing line when bang-swish! And we were both peppered by shrapnel and shell. My rifle butt was broken off to the trigger guard, and I received a smashing blow that laid my cheek on my shoulder. The last I remember was the poor little Lieutenant groaning again as we both sank to the ground'. When he came around, Pte. Perry found himself on a troopship heading for hospital with other wounded. But he wrote that 'I would not have missed it for all the money in the world'.

Pte. R.G. Hamilton was also in the 3rd Brigade landing with the first wave as a member of the 9th Battalion. Although also wounded, he was lucky to be evacuated at the end of that first day, which he described in a letter to his family. 'Just a line to let you know that I am still numbered amongst the living … I will try to give you an idea of our landing though I do not suppose it will interest you much but you see I have nothing else to write about … on the twenty fourth of April we sailed away for the Dardanelles we were told that night that we were to land next morning about two o'clock, that night we transferred on to a torpedo boat destroyer which was capable of holding about 300, just before daylight we came in sight of our destination and disembarked on to small rowing boats capable of holding about 30.

'I was picked for a rower and was in the first boat, we got about 50 yards in the boats (the shore was about 300 yards away) when the

Turks opened a terrific fire on us, both rifle and machine guns, however we kept on going and eventually landed with only three casualties out of our boat, about the same time as we were landing there was hundreds of small boats, from cruisers, gunboats and transports also landing. When we got ashore we fixed bayonets and charged their first line of trenches, but they would not stay but cleared back to their main body which was about two miles away and we only got a few, after a short respite of about half an hour they opened fire again also their artillery and land batteries and our gunboats, talk about an inferno, well I'm deaf yet from it, then shrapnel fell around us like hailstones, however we kept at it all day fighting against fearful odds but being continually reinforced, thereby holding the ground that we had gained during the early part of the day, but at an awful cost which you will see when the casualty list come out.

'I am glad to say … I was in the firing line all day with the exception of half an hour while I helped one of our wounded officers back to the dressing station. It was terrible to see your comrades shot down around you, shattered to pieces with shells and shrapnel others shot or wounded with bullets. I had some very narrow escapes, once whilst digging a small embankment in front of me with my entrenching tool a machine gun turned onto me, I had the tool right in front of my head and four or five bullets hit it in less than a second, but one missed and

THE SOLDIERS WHO FOLLOWED THE FIRST WAVE OF LANDINGS AT ANZAC COVE ON 25 APRIL WERE NOT SO HEAVILY OPPOSED, ENABLING THESE STAFF MEMBERS FROM THE DIVISIONAL HEADQUARTERS TO WADE ASHORE SAFELY. AWM G00903

hit my puttee leaving a hole three or four inches in length and only grazed the skin, the machine gun then shifted to the next man and shot him instantly. I finished what I was doing and started shooting.

'It was very late that evening when I did get hit, though our right flank had retired about half a mile, I was one of them, we lined the top of a ridge and was told to hold it at all cost, the hail of bullets that were fired at us was terrific, another machine gun found me but I was behind a small bush, it stripped all the leaves off the bush and one caught me in the foot smashing the bone and going right through the bottom of the boot, I had to go back then and was eventually sent on to the boat about eleven o'clock that night. Well, I wont tire you with any more news now, you will be bored before you get half through this, and there is no other news to tell you.'

Pte. James Suggett-Hagan was in the 2nd Brigade, in the 3rd Battalion and so was in the second wave that landed. 'We arrived in Gulf of Saroo at 4.45 a.m. Can now see enemies fort guns and field batteries engaging our warships. We are warned to prepare to disembark onto torpedo boats. A and B Companies of 3rd Battalion disembark onto T.B.D. *Rattlesnake* at 5.10 a.m. Shells dropping all around our boat and bursting overhead. The roar of guns and the rattle of musketry is terrible.

'About 50 yards from shore we transfer from T.B.D. into rowing boats amid a continual shower of shrapnel. We now begin to lose our men. Whole boatloads vanish as a result of murderous artillery fire from the Turks' machine guns. About 15 yards from shore we get beached. Water too shallow for boats. We are ordered to wade ashore.

'Those who got ashore were ordered to take all possible cover. Beach was littered with dead and wounded men. Our battalion was ordered into action immediately. We got into a sort of formation, discarded our packs and charged for our lives.

'At 6.30 a.m. we were side by side with 3rd Brigade men and fighting fiercely ... Our first mountain gun spoke up at 7.30 a.m. and we cheered like one man ... The warships were giving the enemy a frightful doing. The Queen Lizzie, in particular, was bursting 5 inch lyddite right amongst them whilst they were advancing in Indian file from WALKER'S RIDGE towards QUINN'S POST. Our chaps were holding on admirably.

'At 10 a.m. the most terrible battle of the day commenced. The enemy now had his artillery in good going order and he gave us particular HADES backed up by several massed attacks. The butchery on both sides was gruesome and in places we were very hard pressed ... by noon we were well dug in. It was decided that a further advance at that time was impossible and we were told to dig in and fortify ... After

ONE OF BRAVEST SOLDIERS ON THE FIRST DAY WAS MILITARY CROSS WINNER CAPTAIN ALFRED SHOUT OF 1ST BATTALION. HE SCALED THE CLIFFS ABOVE ANZAC COVE AND BEFORE BEING ORDERED TO RETREAT, REACHED THE TOP FROM WHERE HE COULD SEE THE SPARKLING WATERS OF THE DARDANELLES — WHICH THEY EVENTUALLY HOPED TO CONTROL. AWM G01028

LT COL. ROBERT SCOBIE LED
HIS MEN ASHORE ON THE FIRST
DAY AT GALLIPOLI, AND
STRUGGLED BACK TO THE
BEACH WHEN WOUNDED IN THE
FACE. HE WAS LATER KILLED
WHEN HE BRAVELY LED HIS
MEN INTO BATTLE DURING THE
AUGUST OFFENSIVE.

noon the fire died down considerably and things were VERY SLOW until about 5.30 p.m. when the enemy made another massed assault which was the worst one of the day. It was no use and was repulsed with great loss. … Desultory fire throughout the night … THUS ENDED ONE OF THE WORST DAYS I HAVE EVER WITNESSED.'

One of the others landing with the 2nd brigade in this second wave was Lt Col. Robert Scobie of the 2nd Battalion, a veteran of the Boer war, who was also wounded. He wrote to his wife, Flora. 'We started to disembark at 6.30 a.m and when we got to the beach there were dead and wounded lying everywhere. Our men marched up to the place of formation under the cliffs, and soon we were away. It was very rough country, with a low scrub on it, very steep and rugged, going up abruptly to about 400 feet from the beach'. Despite the challenge, Scobie confirms members of 'The Third Brigade got in about two miles on to a ridge facing the Dardanelles' and he 'took two companies up to support their left passing tents and dug-outs, dead and wounded men' but then 'We got it from shrapnel' which 'just came down in showers'.

Although Scobie sheltered 'in a little drain cut out by water', he was 'fool enough to sit up to tell the men to root in and got it on the nose, and of course it bled some, just spouted out, and each time a shell came along I ducked and it spouted more. I began to feel weak, and decided to go to the rear, and left Richardson in charge. Somehow I got out between our fellows and the Turks on the way in and was mighty lucky to escape and only for the whisky flask I am sure I wouldn't be here'. Having drunk whisky to dull the pain Scobie had 'a recollection of staggering down a creek with my revolver in my hand, and having another whisky, then listening for our big guns, to see which direction to take, went straight towards them, and came upon Third Battalion men who put on another bandage, and applied more whisky, and here I am'.

Scobie concluded that 'I am of the opinion that if the position of the Turks had been reversed, the Australians would have tipped the landing Turks back into the sea. We got a terrible knocking about, but it was naturally so, for we had a tough job. It was a very bad landing place'. Having served with distinction in the Boer War from 1899–1902, Scobie would have known what combat was like. Most soldiers who landed on that day had never been in battle. Unlike many of the battlefields in which he had fought in South Africa, Scobie said Anzac Cove 'had big tough hills all around, very difficult to climb with all our kit and the enemy was well entrenched above'. They had little hope, he said as 'there were guns and machine guns everywhere, and the Turks who also knew the country had already marked off the ranges. But I'll bet if the positions had been reversed, we would have wiped them off the land into the sea on that night ... We had a terrible list of casualties'.

Lt Col. Scobie recovered from losing the bridge of his nose and was nursed back to health coincidentally by his sister Louisa Stobo, who worked in the same Cairo Army hospital. However, he was killed leading the 2nd Battalion in its charge against Lone Pine on 6 August. Lt Col. Scobie ordered his men to retreat in the face of a murderous enemy counterattack and bravely covered their retreat himself by throwing bombs at the enemy.

Driver J.H. Turnbull was also in this 2nd Brigade in the 8th Battalion, and so landed in the second wave after which he too was wounded. 'Reveille at 4 a.m. Most of us spent a restless night. Breakfast was at 4.30 a.m. and Warships opened up a bombardment and Turks replying from batteries ashore. We can see shrapnel shell

FROM THIS PHOTOGRAPHER'S POSITION HALFWAY UP THE FIRST CLIFF ABOVE ANZAC COVE ON 25 APRIL, IT IS POSSIBLE TO SEE BOTH THE SHELTER PROVIDED BY THE CLIFFS AND THE EXTENT OF THE ANZACS' CLIMB AFTER LANDING ON THE BEACH.

THE FIRST ANZACS ASHORE
WERE FROM THE 9TH BATTALION
OF THE 3RD BRIGADE. THEY MET
THE WORST OPPOSITION FROM
ENEMY FIRE AS SHOWN IN THIS
ILLUSTRATION BY JOHN L.
CURTIS.

THE FIRST ANZACS ASHORE
WERE FROM THE 9TH BATTALION
OF THE 3RD BRIGADE. THEY MET
THE WORST OPPOSITION FROM
ENEMY FIRE AS SHOWN IN THIS
ILLUSTRATION BY JOHN L.
CURTIS.

bursting high in air over our ships. We were half way through our hot stew when the order "Fall in on deck" was passed down to us. We formed up on deck and waited till about 5.30 a.m. Watching shells bursting over our ships and on the Turks ashore. It was all strange to us. Everyone very quiet then a Destroyer came along side us after landing the 3rd Bde. We boarded her and she steamed for the shore. We could see the broken scrub covered hills in front of us. Shrapnel overhead accounted for a few of us.

'The Destroyer stopped and we transhipped into boats manned by Bluejackets in charge of boys. Middies. Steam pinnaces towed half a dozen boats to the shore. We passed a pinnace towing a string of boats back to the Destroyer. The Quartermaster of the pinnace was a big bearded Bluejacket. The Officer in charge was a 15 yr Middy. The Middy was sitting with his legs hanging over the gunwale of the boat. He was holding his hand to his side. He called out to us. "Go on Australians you have them on the run and you have just captured a Krupp Gun". With that blood rushed from his mouth. He was shot through the lungs. A moment or so later a trawler passed us sandbagged up to the bridge the Captain of whom yelled out to us. "You have just captured a Krupp Gun and Turks are on the run".

'The water all round our boats was whipped up by shrapnel fire. Some boats were half full of wounded. Our boat grounded some distance from the beach. We waited a few seconds until the boat was hit by shrapnel. Then Col. Gartside told us to hop out. We needed no second order. I was in the stern. I hopped over the side into 4ft. of water and made for the beach. We crossed a narrow strip of sand to the prickly holly covered hills in front of us and we began our climb. You could hear the commands D. Coy. here. 14th Platoon here or No. 1 Sec. 14th Platoon here and so on. By the time the Coy. was on top of the first ridge we were in our places. That ridge was swept with shell fire and in a few minutes dead and dying were all round us. We scrambled down the other side of the Ridge into a Gully also swept by Shellfire we stormed up over another ridge passing dead and wounded until we came under machine gun fire. I saw men in front of me wearing the blue and white colour patches for the first time. Men of the 3rd Bde 12th Batt. He saw my red and white colours and wanted to know who I was. The 8th Bn 2nd Bde.

'Just then they made a dash forward I with them. I was lying behind a bush when a machine gun spoke and was cutting the twigs of the bush over my head and next I got a graize through the right arm. Another bullet smashed the woodwork of my rifle ... There were several wounded men in the vacinity we got as many as we could into the shelter of the trench. They were crying out for water and we had very little. We crawled out of the trench again and got the bottles from the Turks ... We hung on to our trench until late in the afternoon when some New Zealanders reached us. As my arm was troubling me I then made my way back to a dressing station on the beach ... I passed men going up to reinforce the line. When I arrived at the Beach the sight was awful. Dead and wounded were in long rows on the strip of sand. Doctors, First Aid men and Stretcher bearers working at top speed. Bearers would bring a wounded man in and find out he died on the way. He was put to one side. The doctors would look at others and shake their heads (a hopeless case) and pass on to another whom they have a chance of saving ... The sea at the water's edge was red with blood. Bearers after bringing their patients in would dip their stretches in the water to wash the blood from them ... I got my arm dressed and had my first meal for the day with a New Zealander. It then began to rain. I camped on the beach that night. At day break I was making my way up a Gully looking for my Battalion when I met E. Alsop and W. Butterworth. Geelong lads 8th Bn. having a meal. I joined in with them and found out I also had a bullet through my haversack ... We rejoined our Batt. on the extreme right. They were digging charging and shooting in turns all night. By dawn they had a good trench.

ONCE ASHORE THE ANZACS HAD TO RUSH TO THE SAFETY OF THE OVERHANGING CLIFFS TO GET OUT OF THE LINE OF FIRE FROM THE TURKISH DEFENDERS SHOOTING AT THEM FROM ABOVE. THIS PHOTO IS A RE-ENACTMENT STAGED AT GALLIPOLI A FEW DAYS BEFORE THE EVACUATION.

'The 3rd Bde. were the first to land about 4.30 when we were having breakfast. That was when the bombardment first sped up. The 9th Bn leading. Their Col. was killed in the boats. Two boats had all their men killed and were drifting about … The 2nd Bde then landed about 5.30 a.m. under shrapnel fire with small loss and took up a position on the 3rd Bdes right. The 5th, 6th and 7th Battalions must have landed just before us. These Battalions made a rapid advance and almost got across the peninsula before the Turks could re-organise … At dusk the 8th Bn got orders to dig in. They dug in for their lives. Alternatively using the shovel and rifle. The 5th 6th and 7th eventually fell back into our trenches and held the Turks. The Turks charged again and again but were met with heavy rapid rifle fire. Not able to make any further advance.'

A medical orderly responsible for rescuing some of these wounded men was Pte. R.G. Richards, of the 1st Field Ambulance, who noted 'No bugle call to wake up this morning, having left Lemnos about 1 a.m. but most of us were active before the sun rose, a brilliant and pleasing red glow. It was just the same as the sunset last night. A stage setting with the flashes and booming of the cannon to enliven matters. From just before daylight as we approached "Gallipoli"; there was a wholesale roaring and spitting of big guns. Our warships being particularly aggressive. The roar of guns did not bother me much but as we were landing onto the torpedo boat "Scourge" at 8.30 a.m. a shell came just over No. 13 transport and stirred up the water to a height of perhaps 60 feet, within 150 yards of us. This brought home to me the grim reality of war, but to my surprise I was not much troubled and took 7 photos before landing up over our knees in water from the rowing boats into which we were transferred from the "Scourge".

'As we were landing a schrapnel shell burst 150 yards away and threw a shower of bullets into the water; rather a pretty display. 20 minutes later we with stretchers climbing the steep rough hills looking for wounded, but it was about 1 o'clock when I got my first case and from then until 6 p.m. I got fully 21 dressings to do. The wounded were in splendid spirit and told me that in landing at 3 a.m. this day the Turks were right down on the beach but were soon driven back over the terrible ridges for a distance of 2 miles. But alas! Our fellows got knocked about badly before this.

'Seeing that the Turks had been pushed back and three guns taken it was surprising to me to find only a few dead and wounded Turks. While our officers and men were knocked about. In a fairly well sheltered valley I waited for an hour within a short distance of the attacking party. The word was continually being sent back that help was badly needed on the left flank. A whole Battalion of men were sent in but it was too late, the Turks had brought about a successful counterattack and driven our men back chiefly by the use of machine guns and shells. Showers of these shell bullets were falling all around our positions, and it fairly made us shake. Machine guns were being pushed forward by the New Zealanders, they only just passed our little party when a Captain got a bullet through his calf and Lt with a shattered forearm both came under my treatment.

ONE OF THE FIRST POSITIONS GAINED BY THE ANZACS ON 25 APRIL WAS PLUGGE'S PLATEAU JUST ABOVE ANZAC COVE, WHERE WAR CORRESPONDENT CHARLES BEAN PHOTOGRAPHED THESE SOLDIERS HEADING FURTHER INLAND COMPLETE WITH PACK, RIFLE AND SPADE. AWM G00907

'A fellow came along and asked me to go up and fix up his pal whose foot was shot. With a stretcher Watts and I went but 100 yards along the valley the bush was thick and the water worn track so rough that we discarded the stretcher and proceeded on all fours up to the firing trenches upon which our fellows had been driven back to. Here was a poor devil with his heel and sole of his foot blown away and although in great pain he was what might be considered cheerful. I cut his boot off and dressed it, bleeding was then not heavy. Now the trouble was to get him away with rifle fire pinging overhead and through the bushes within a foot of us, this safely done the way out was awful but my patient skidded down the steep side on his hand and seat while I went forward holding the limb. In the bottom of the gorge I got him onto my back and made good progress, but as the foot started to bleed heavily I had to put a tie onto the artery at the thigh. Fully two hours had past before we got back to the boats taking wounded aboard the transports, and he bore up wonderfully well right throughout. In his belt was a large sum of money which he said contained over 100 pound. When we got back I was pretty well finished, it was a hard job for me but truly terrible for the patient. While he was waiting he got out a sovereign and made me take it.

'It was a remarkable day right enough and a day in which it was easy to pick out the wasters also the brave men. I am delighted with our Australian troops, the way they take the gruel is splendid. At times there was a shortage of ammunition and reinforcements were badly wanted. But seeing they had landed everything under shell fire I should say they did very well ... It was heart wrenching to hear the plaintiff and only too ominous call of "More ammunition wanted on the left" What a doleful story these words really unfold. Also the call for reinforcements that ran back from mouth to mouth told of dire troubles that was being experienced on the other side of the hill. "Reinforcements hurry up on the right" what a significant sentence especially when uttered by the parched lips of a wounded man.'

Summing up the first day in his official dispatches, as optimistically as he could, Gen. Sir Ian Hamilton, Commander in Chief of the Mediterranean Expeditionary Force, concluded the landing had been more of a success than a failure. He had watched the action from his ship, *Queen Elizabeth*. The General's report contrasted strongly with the reality already reported by the soldiers. Gen. Hamilton praised the soldiers of the 3rd Brigade for disembarking from the ships claiming 'all these arrangements worked without a hitch and were carried out in complete orderliness and silence'. At first, he said he had aimed for a safe landing spot explaining that 'A rugged and difficult part of the

coast had been selected for the landing, so difficult and rugged that I considered the Turks were not at all likely to anticipate such a descent'. Although he admitted his plan went wrong, he claimed that the mistake turned out for the better saying 'the actual point of disembarkation was rather more than a mile north of that which I had selected' but 'it proved itself to be a blessing in disguise, inasmuch as the actual base of the force of occupation has been much better defiladed from shell fire'. He conceded, however that 'it increased the initial difficulty of driving the enemy off the heights inland'. He also claimed the 'boats were close to the shore before the enemy stirred … the moment the boats touched land the Australians leapt ashore like lightening and each man as he did so went straight at his bayonet to the enemy. So vigorous was the onslaught that the Turks made no attempt to withstand it and fled from ridge to ridge pursued by the Australian infantry'.

He then emphasised the achievements of the landing force, claiming that 'despite determined counter-attacks' by Turks early in the day 'the 3rd Brigade had held their ground with equivalent stubbornness'. They had 'put out of action three of the enemy's Krupp guns' and later in the day the Anzacs also 'handsomely repulsed' subsequent Turkish 'counter-attacks' and 'the line held firm' with 'the

AS SOON AS THEY GOT ASHORE COMMANDING OFFICERS ESTABLISHED DUGOUTS LIKE THIS ONE CONSTRUCTED FOR MAJ. GEN. BRIDGES, WHO NOT ONLY HAD A PICNIC TABLE BUT ALSO AMPLE REFRESHMENTS.

help of the guns of H.M. ships' he claimed even when 'the Turks were reinforced to a strength of 20,000 men'. At the end of the day it was 'a consolation to know that the Turks suffered even more seriously' and 'the whole surrounding country is still strewn with their dead of this date'. Although he did not mention the actual death toll of the Anzacs, at least Gen. Sir Ian Hamilton did admit that 'casualties had been deplorably heavy'.

Australian soldiers had fought bravely that first day and managed to secure a toehold on the beach. But even before official counting it was clear about 2,000 soldiers had been killed. It had been a lost cause from the moment they landed on the wrong beach according to one senior officer, Lt Col. Rosenskjar of the 26th Battalion. He noted in his official report that 'The larger tows had not even reached the beach grounding in 3 ft. of water. The men on leaving were in water up to their waists on leaving the boat ... Turks had concealment whereas Australians were faced by precipitous ridges and tortuous ravines which formed their first battlefield, also including confusing scrub covered gullies. They faced an impossible task even for the best trained troops in the world.'

Lt Col. Rosenskjar went on to report that the ground was also unknown to the invading army. They had expected to find a low sandy beach with cover on landing. Instead, they found themselves in the wrong spot with the Turks using machine gun fire killing or wounding several

THE COMMANDER-IN-CHIEF OF THE MEDITERRANEAN EXPEDITIONARY FORCE WHO CONTROLLED THE ANZACS WAS BRITAIN'S GEN. SIR IAN HAMILTON, SECOND FROM RIGHT, PICTURED WITH (LEFT TO RIGHT) COMMODORE KEYS, VICE ADMIRAL DE ROEBECK AND GENERAL BRAITHWAITE. AWM H10350

officers, including the two Company Commanders. Although some positions were captured, the troops were too scattered to make progress.

Taking stock at the end of the day, the Commander in Chief of the Anzacs, Lt Gen. Sir William 'Birdy' Birdwood, fortunately weighed both good and bad reports. He then wrote an urgent memo to his superior officers telling them just how hopeless the situation was and suggesting Gen. Sir Ian Hamilton consider evacuating. Crossing his fingers, Birdwood gave his report to a messenger who took it to the *Queen Elizabeth,* where Gen. Sir Ian Hamilton was in command.

That night, as Charles Bean reported, a dismal rain set in slowly drenching the soldiers whether they were lying wounded on the cliff slopes or the beach, or carrying wounded down to the hospital barges or just huddling in an open trench or dugout somewhere in that black night. But the rain didn't worry these exhausted soldiers. What they wanted most of all was to know what they were meant to do next.

BY THE TIME ALL THE ANZACS FROM THE FIRST WAVE HAD COME ASHORE AND UNLOADED THEIR SUPPLIES AT ANZAC COVE, SOME OF THE DIARISTS CLAIMED ANZAC COVE WAS JUST AS BUSY AS ANY MAIN STREET IN AN AUSTRALIAN CAPITAL CITY.

41

WITH 2,000 ANZACS KILLED AND THOUSANDS WOUNDED IN THE FIRST 24 HOURS, EVERY AVAILABLE VESSEL WAS NEEDED TO TRANSPORT CASUALTIES FROM THE BEACH, INITIALLY TO HOSPITAL SHIPS MOORED OFF ANZAC COVE, THEN TO HOSPITALS AT LEMNOS AND OTHER BASES.

CHAPTER 2
26–30 APRIL
The Morning After

Units hopelessly intermixed but everywhere the desire to get at the enemy — plenty of dash in fact — dash perhaps in excess. No one can say that for troops who had never been under fire — who did not know what they were coming to — that their attitude could have been better. Forward — forward must have been the cry.

LT WILLIAM HENRY DAWKINS, DIARY,
TUESDAY 27 APRIL

They may have felt lucky to be alive but when surviving soldiers woke up the morning after the landing, they realised their predicament. Some soldiers couldn't sleep because of sporadic enemy fire and the difficulty of finding a safe ditch or trench to lie in. The invasion had been a bloodbath. At least 2,000 of the 12,000 Australians who had landed on the beach were killed in the first 24 hours. By 3 a.m. on 26 April — under the necessary cover of darkness — at least 1,700 wounded were taken off the beach and additional rows of wounded men lay under the shelter of the cliff, on that little strip of sand at Anzac Cove.

The difficult circumstances of his troops certainly worried Anzac Commander, Lt Gen. Birdwood, a practical officer who had sent a message to his commander suggesting evacuation. If the Allies had evacuated over the next few nights (before the Turks had mustered all their reinforcements) they might have lost some men in the retreat but probably would have saved thousands of lives. Their position on the beach was untenable. They were at the bottom of steep cliffs with the enemy above shooting at them. In the next eight months another 6,500 men would be killed.

Lt Gen. Birdwood explained that 'the men are thoroughly demoralized by the shrapnel fire to which they have been subjected all day after exhaustion and gallant work in the morning. Numbers have dribbled back from the firing line and cannot be collected in this difficult country ... if troops are subjected to shell fire again tomorrow morning there is likely to be a fiasco as I have no fresh troops with which to replace those in the firing line. I know my representation is most serious, but if we are to re-embark, it must be at once.'

Gen. Sir Ian Hamilton's decision, however, condemned the Allied soldiers to another eight months of hopeless hell. Hamilton discussed the situation with Adm. C.F. Thursby who was in charge of the fleet. Thursby said it would take three days to evacuate. He was short of ships and boats for an evacuation, and his remaining vessels could not get close enough to the beach to collect the men because of enemy shelling. Gen. Hamilton wrote his fatal reply to Birdwood. 'Your news is indeed serious. But there is nothing for it but to dig yourselves right in and stick it out. It would take at least two days to re-embark ... make a personal appeal to your men and Godley's to make a supreme effort to hold their ground.' He added a PS. 'You have got through the difficult business, now you only have to dig, dig, dig, until you are safe.'

Ill-advised though it might have been, one of the war's toughest military decisions had now been taken. At 2.30 a.m. on 26 April, a messenger rowed ashore at Anzac Cove to deliver Hamilton's reply to Birdwood's headquarters where it was read out to 'a small crowd in the know', according to Charles Bean. It seems that by then Birdwood had accepted the situation and had decided the Anzacs were sufficiently entrenched to hang on to their precarious toehold on the beach. Charles Bean commented on Hamilton's order to Birdwood to remain. 'That clearly settled it'. The leaders had now refused to allow the Anzacs to leave the beach — so Bean said they 'would either stay there or cease to exist'. Not that the soldiers themselves would mind according to Bean as 'there was no question of demoralisation among the troops in the firing line'.

Fortunately, not much fighting took place on 26 April around Anzac Cove. During a failed advance around 400 Plateau some soldiers were killed including the 4th Battalion commander Lt Col. A.J. Onslow-Thompson (who had managed Colonial wool pioneer John Macarthur's historic Camden Park Estate before the war).

Quiet also prevailed down at Helles where 20,000 British troops had now landed, although it would turn out to be the quiet before a storm. Only an estimated 6,000 Turks defended the Helles area by 26 April. The British didn't realise the Turks were undermanned. While they waited to advance, Turkish reinforcements poured into the hills making the British offensive impossible. No evacuation would take place at

IT WAS ONLY WHEN THE DIFFERENT UNITS MANAGED TO HAVE A ROLL CALL, AFTER THE LANDING, THAT THEY REALISED HOW MANY OF THEIR NUMBER HAD BEEN KILLED.

Helles either because the commanding officer Maj. Gen. Aylmer Hunter-Weston had ordered the soldiers to 'dig in and make all preparations for a Turkish attack' adding 'there will be no retiring. Every man will die at his post rather than retire'.

The troops on the ground knew nothing about the high-level decisions to stay or retreat, nor did they seem to doubt their mission as their letters and diary notes confirm.

Monday
26 April
DAY 2

More soldiers landed on the second day to take their place alongside those sheltering under the ridges, in trenches or dugouts. More supplies also landed and piled up high on Anzac Cove.

The Anzacs hoped the Turks had been subdued. 'The first surprise', Bean noted with great relief 'was that the expected bombardment did not come'. There was some fighting admittedly and plenty of firing (both machine gun and rifle) along with shrapnel at the front line. This firing also claimed lives later in the day. If Lt Tiegs was any example, the soldiers themselves at Anzac Cove were certainly prepared to stick it out. As this second day dawned revealing dead and wounded all around him the optimistic Lt Tiegs wrote, 'Am feeling well in health, but my leg is cold and very sore if I move ... The enemy artillery appears to be quieted for they were not answering. It is reported our boys are doing

WITHIN DAYS OF ARRIVING, THE ANZACS HAD CONSTRUCTED LANDING PIERS FOR LOADING SUPPLIES WHICH THEY STACKED UP ON THE BEACH AT ANZAC COVE. IT MAY HAVE BEEN SHELTERED BY CLIFFS BUT IT SOON BECAME VERY CRAMPED. AWM P01130.001

well. Stores and water is being taken ashore from a ship … Her name is "Clan MacGilivray". Our casualties yesterday were about 2,000. British troops landed on end of peninsula about 8 miles lower than us and meet with no opposition till about 6 miles in land. They captured a Turkish regiment and are supposed to be two miles from our boys and expect to join hands tonight. The French also landed on Asiatic side, have not heard how they got on. Battleships kept up a steady bombardment, up till late at night but the Turkish fire appeared to slacken. Casualties today reported about 250'.

Down at Cape Helles, the British, who had landed at Y Beach, had to clear out. The reinforced Turkish defenders suddenly appeared in increasing numbers forcing them back into the sea. The British had no option but evacuate. This may have been an unauthorised evacuation and against Maj. Gen. Hunter-Western's orders but it certainly saved lives. Helles was a tough place and Maj. David French of the Dublins on V Beach was just glad to have made it through that first night. He had lost most of his men when the Turks 'practically wiped out those in the three boats ahead' when 'only two reached the shore un-hit'. He had 'run about 150 yards through the water the bullets striking the sea all around us' until 'they put one through my left arm'. With his good arm, he then dug into a low cliff where he lay bleeding overnight. 'I shall never forget that night. Heavy rifle fire incessantly. Drizzling with rain. Wounded groaning on all sides and surrounded by dead. I admit I thought it was all up.'

By the third day Bean reported that 'most of the dugouts were finished' and it was just as well because the Turks fired off shells, machine guns and rifles from the cliff tops. Some soldiers and officers near the front line were killed including Maj. F.D. Irvine, of the 1st Brigade, and Col. H.N. MacLaurin, commander of the 1st Brigade. They were shot trying to look over the top of their trench. Maj. Brudenell White was hit by shrapnel in his dugout though not seriously wounded.

The Anzacs were fighting to secure a viable foothold up from the beach. The soldiers thought only of digging in and advancing when possible. As Henry Dawkins wrote, 'Still digging for water hard. Position being consolidated. At 4 p.m. the right centre tries to make an advance but unsupported by infantry or artillery. They are under the fire of shrapnel — have to retire. Quite a stream of men come down the valley and I think things look serious but they calm down later. Lt Plant comes in with 30 worn out men of 9th Btn. Distribute tea etc to many

Tuesday 27 April
DAY 3

men and officers in a worn out state. The casualties are large especially among the officers — 3rd and 2nd Bdes apparently suffering most. Units hopelessly intermixed but everywhere the desire to get at the enemy — plenty of dash in fact — dash perhaps in excess. No one can say that for troops who had never been under fire — who did not know what they were coming to — that their attitude could have been better. Forward — forward must have been the cry. One platoon I hear even got into Kyadere [an area approximately two and a half miles inland]. Saw Col. MacLagan and staff very much cut up at the loss he had sustained. Could only muster 1,000 men.'

At Helles an anonymous midshipman recorded his first impressions of continuous shrapnel fire in his diary. 'One hears a bang, a long drawn out scream, then a sharp "Pah!" and a lot of little thuds as the bullets come down'.

Wednesday 28 April
DAY 4

By the fourth day the troops had succeeded in digging themselves in and had survived Turkish counterattacks that were less ferocious than expected. Allied warships were now regularly shelling Turkish positions on the hill tops and marines from the Royal Naval Division (RND) arrived as reinforcements, supporting the Anzacs who had been fighting for five days. The latest threat at Anzac Cove was from snipers in hidden positions who were now picking off vulnerable soldiers, including Maj. Brown of the 3rd Battalion who was hit three times. Bean said the call went out to track down the snipers. 'They have found the cubby hole of a sniper — not I am told the sniper himself —with 100 expended rounds of ammunition, 300 unexpended, 3 weeks rations and a little well of water in it.'

According to Warrant Officer John Treloar, a daily routine had already been established. 'Since we have landed here the fashion has been early rising; beginning with 1 a.m. last Sunday, but 5.30 has been the latest I have risen so far. We have now got a fair number of Turkish prisoners and some of them have I think given some useful information. Some say they like the soldiering, some the reverse, but they are putting up a very good and stubborn fight. Germans seem to be serving in the artillery, but infantry do not seem to include any. I have had the opportunity of speaking to a few men of their experiences. Most talk very little and some say it was just Hell. I think many, ever so many gallant acts have been performed that the world will never hear of. In one case in a small retirement a man brought a wounded comrade back and under heavy fire crossed the skyline — which deed assumes a higher

AFTER ESTABLISHING THEIR SETTLEMENT ASHORE, THE ANZACS ASSEMBLED THEIR WEAPONS AND AMMUNITION IN PLACES LIKE REST GULLY FROM WHICH THEY PLANNED TO ATTACK THE TURKS ON THE RIDGES ABOVE.
AWM P00591.004

degree of pluck when one realises how quick the enemy's men are to take advantage of opportunities ... Australia should be proud when it hears of the feat of the 1st Aust. Divn., though some of the men say they would never have done it unless they had gone mad temporarily ... We are now beginning to realise the total number of casualties ... Perhaps when the casualty lists reach Australia the people there will begin to realise the terrors of war. We are also beginning now to receive identity discs and personal effects of the killed. It is very pathetic in some cases to receive letters written to meet the eventuality, which has now taken place.'

Meanwhile, at the south end of the Gallipoli peninsula, where the British and French had landed and dug in, the first battle of Krithia began on 28 April. The Allies advanced towards the village of Krithia (now Alcitepe) trying to reach Achi Baba ridge where the Turkish reinforcements had arrived. The Allies failed to win this first battle of Krithia and the fighting dragged on for days claiming many British and French.

Thursday
29 April
DAY 5

By the fifth day, army engineers had constructed four jetties made of pontoons. They were floating bridges on which stores could be landed from barges sent from the ships out at sea beyond the range of Turkish fire. Sections of the beach were organised for stores and equipment hospital tents had been erected, as well as wireless stations, Red Cross stations, and canteens. Bean noted the supplies included 'everything needed for the support of an army, supplies, transport, water and ambulances'.

THE MOST POPULAR LEADER AT ANZAC COVE WAS THE COMPETENT, PRACTICAL AND PLAIN SPEAKING COMMANDER OF THE AUSTRALIAN AND NEW ZEALAND ARMY CORPS (ANZAC) LT GEN. SIR WILLIAM BIRDWOOD, ALSO KNOWN AS 'BIRDY', WHO WAS DESCRIBED BY SUPERIOR OFFICERS AS 'THE SOUL OF ANZAC'.

Signaler R. Stanley revealed that some of the men at least got the traditional issue of fortifying rum. 'Re-organising our Bdge, and having a good feed of bully beef and biscuits. Three men hit with spent bullets, while organising. Shrapnel bursts around us and wounds a few more. War boats still fire at intervals. Issue of rum in evening. During night Turks try several ruses, and break out into storms of fire. Engineers, at great risk, put barbed wire in front of our trenches. We now have the mastery of their fire and know that we have a strong position. The 3rd Bdge however stands by.'

STRETCHER BEARERS HAD THEIR WORK CUT OUT FOR THEM DURING THE LANDING AND OVER THE NEXT FEW DAYS. WOUNDED SOLDIERS WERE CARRIED DOWN TO THE BEACH — ITSELF OFTEN UNDER FIRE — AND THEN EVACUATED TO HOSPITAL SHIPS. AWM A05784

In *Genesis* God created the world in six days before resting on the seventh. The Anzacs also seem to have established their fortified settlement by the end of the sixth day — though they couldn't rest on the seventh day many soldiers attended their first church services at Anzac Cove the following day, Sunday. The 1st Australian Division and some of the infantry battalions were reduced to less than half their original strength. Another setback came when, after a two-hour battle with a Turkish torpedo vessel, the Australian submarine *AE 2* was

**Friday
30 April**
DAY 6

sunk. It torpedoed an enemy gunboat earlier and so great things were expected of the submarine, but now it was lost in the Sea of Marmara with all crew captured.

Just before *AE 2* sank, crewmember Albert Knaggs noted, 'The enemy torpedo vessel lowered a boat to take us off, in which there was a German officer, but she could only take five hands so we had to swim for it. When we got aboard we saw that her torpedo tubes were empty and a German sailor who could speak English told us they had both been fired at us but missed. Aboard the torpedo boat the officers were deep in the dark cabin in the forward mess deck. While our clothes were being dried the torpedo boat proceeded to Gallipoli and made fast alongside a hospital ship, where we were interviewed by General Liman von Sanders who was in command of the Peninsula. At 8 p.m. the torpedo boat proceeded to Constantinople where we arrived the next morning.'

Aware of heavy losses, Col. John Monash, reviewed his options. He was meant to be preparing for a forward move against the Baby 700 hilltop, from where Turkish gunners were shooting down at Anzacs. Col. Monash now complained to his superior officer, Maj. Gen. Alexander John Godley, that he did not want to advance because his

BY 26 APRIL, SOME OF THE WOUNDED SOLDIERS WERE BROUGHT DOWN FROM THE FRONTLINE TO THIS 3RD BATTALION DRESSING STATION WHERE THEY WERE PATCHED UP AND EITHER SENT BACK INTO BATTLE OR EVACUATED TO HOSPITAL SHIPS. AWM G00920

troops were still scattered all over the place 'in expectation of a further advance I should like you to know that, at the moment of writing, my Brigade is by no means an organised command, capable of coordinated action. The Battalion Commander (except 14th) has yet more than, one half of his personnel in his own hands. The units of the Brigade on landing were scattered all over the whole line, in fragments in many cases as small as 8 or 10 men. These are gradually being located, and pieced together, but the process is painfully slow. One half Battalion (16th) has been in a very difficult position since Monday and continuously under attack, and badly requires relief, which I shall soon be able to give. At the moment I suppose I could not count on more than 2,000 rifles actually in proper touch with me. By tomorrow I hope to have this position vastly improved'.

During the last days of April, the situation improved and there were hopeful signs that the landing force had regrouped. As Charles Bean wrote, 'Many of the wounded have now been shipped out to hospitals across the sea, and Turkish prisoners are brought into camp each day in increasing numbers giving themselves up and the Turk is said to be afraid of us'. But when the campaign moved into the following month, Bean and his fellow diary and letter writers would see the worst side of warfare.

SO MANY SOLDIERS DIED DURING THE BIG COUNTERATTACKS BY THE TURKS ON 19 MAY THAT BOTH SIDES AGREED ON A TRUCE ON 24 MAY TO BURY THE DECOMPOSING BODIES LYING BETWEEN THE OPPOSING TRENCHES TO MINIMISE THE SPREAD OF DISEASE. AWM HO3920

CHAPTER 3
MAY
Burying the Dead

THE PRICE

DEAD figures writhe and beckon in my dream;
  Wild eyes look into mine;
While I, bewildered, watch the bloody stream
  With misty eyes ashine.

It rends my heart, and I am nothing loath
  To have the murder cease.
Horror it is and carnage, yet are both
  Part of the price of peace.

Corpl. COMUS, 2nd Bat., A.I.F.

The ground was simply covered with dead between the trenches at various points and after the day's work of burying, estimates of 12,000 Turks killed have been made ... Amongst this awful mass of dead Turks were some of our boys who had been killed on the 1st and 2nd days' fight and had lain there since ... The bodies were horrible to look at being black and swelled up stretching out the clothing and in many cases when they were touched falling to pieces.

WILLIAM DEXTER, ANGLICAN CHAPLAIN,
DIARY, 24 MAY 1915

PRIVATE ALBERT JACKA WON
AUSTRALIA'S FIRST VICTORIA
CROSS WHEN HE LEAPT INTO A
TURKISH TRENCH ON 19 MAY,
SHOT FIVE TURKS, BAYONETED
ANOTHER TWO, TOOK THE REST
PRISONERS AND CAPTURED THE
TRENCH ALL ON HIS OWN.

During the 'merry month of May' as some soldiers referred to the spring campaign, camp life settled down to a routine. At Anzac Cove the Turks launched counterattacks against hard won Allied positions which were fiercely defended by the Anzacs. For their part, the Anzacs tried to advance up the steep cliffs and ridges, especially in the early part of the month but mostly in vain. Pte. Albert Jacka became the first soldier to be recommended for a Victoria Cross when he captured a Turkish trench against great odds.

The Turks threw shells, shrapnel and bullets at the Australians and New Zealanders and this took a heavy toll. Casualties included Gen. William Bridges and Pte. John Simpson Kirkpatrick, 'the man and his donkey', and many more wounded who were treated at Gallipoli or shipped to hospitals at Lemnos or other medical centres. Despite the fighting, precious little ground changed hands. It was a stalemate. In fact, the front line changed little all month and the strategic positions already carried names or nicknames by which they would be known for the rest of the campaign. Allied advances were also limited by the withdrawal during May of warships from the British fleet, which had been shelling the Turkish positions. The commanders feared their ships would be torpedoed and some were sunk.

As the Anzacs could not break out of their 'prison', they spent a lot of time fortifying their dug outs, trenches and tunnels. The Australians and New Zealanders were eventually joined by Indians, Gurkhas and Maoris. As the month dragged on, one urgent task became most important — to bury the dead. Spring temperatures meant the bodies which had been mounting up for some time would rot creating an unbearable stench.

At Helles at the bottom of the Gallipoli peninsula, British forces engaged the enemy in fierce battles with horrendous death tolls and thousands of casualties. The high command decided that, as Anzac Cove on the western shore was a stalemate, Allied forces should advance up the peninsula from the southern tip held by the British and French. To increase their chances of success, Gen. Hamilton asked Lt Gen. Birdwood for his two strongest brigades, the 2nd Australian and the New Zealand Brigade. During the first week the battle dragged on making Helles the worst place to be that month. Keen to cover the main events, war correspondent and diligent diarist Charles Bean sailed from Anzac to Helles where he reported on the fighting.

End of Week 1

At Anzac Cove the month started with the Anzacs gearing up for an impending attack (planned for 2 May) against the Turks. Down south at Helles, the Turks had reinforced their numbers and also planned a determined counterattack against the British and French clinging to the tip of the peninsula. The Turks got in first as they started their counterattack as night fell on 1 May. An early casualty, Maj. White noted in his diary, 'Got hit in the left side with a shrapnel bullet-skin not penetrated but a big bruise … our HQ frequently shelled by enemy … great sight to see all the naval guns firing'.

The bigger picture became clearer for Lt McHenry when rowing his boat ashore. 'The usual early morning artillery duel was commenced this morning by the Turks who at 4.30 a.m. poured shrapnel onto our position until the warships stopped it. The fighting continued unabated during the day and it was rumoured that the "Goeben" was sunk in the Dardanelles. During the evening I was told to take charge of a rowing boat to go ashore with messages for the officers and had my first glimpse of the shore and my first experience of really being under fire.

Saturday 1 May
DAY 7

CHAPLAIN WILLIAM DEXTER, WHO HELPED BURY THE DEAD ON 24 MAY, SAID 'THE GROUND WAS SIMPLY COVERED WITH DEAD BETWEEN THE TRENCHES' AND 'THE BODIES WERE HORRIBLE TO LOOK AT BEING BLACK AND SWELLED UP STRETCHING OUT THE CLOTHING'. AWM HO3955

The cliffs present a strange sight with everyone dug in and sheltered against the enemy's shrapnel, which is poured on the position during the day. Bdr. Bill was hit severely in the thigh … Read, Turner and Benson were hit although not seriously enough to put them out of action. Sgt. Smith L.O. was hit in the arm pit just before he got to shore. During the day A sub. Gun was put out of action by a direct hit. Indians, Australians, English soldiers and sailors are all mixed up ashore and each little group has its fire and cooks its mess in the shelter of its dugout. Saw Mr C.E.W. Bean who perhaps has changed his opinion of the Australians by now.'

Sunday 2 May

DAY 8

THE CARTOONIST FOR *THE ANZAC BOOK*, DAVID BARKER, COULD NEVER RESIST HAVING A GO AT ANY OF THE ANZACS IF THEY ASKED STUPID QUESTIONS.

The Ass: 'Are you wounded, mate?'
The Victim: 'D'yer think I'm doing this fer fun?'

Although some of the Anzacs led by Col. John Monash tried to seize the strategic hill top of Baby 700 above Monash Valley with the help of the New Zealanders, they failed due to heavy opposition and also 'friendly fire'. As Bean reported, 'Just when Colonel Monash was discussing another move the whole of our artillery opened up on the ridge held by our men … along the top of the ridge can be seen our dead lying like ants shriveled up or curled up some still hugging their rifles'.

Fortunately, the Turks also failed with a fierce attack aimed at dislodging Anzacs from their positions further down the hills towards Anzac Cove. At Helles, the Anglo-French forces stopped the Turks counterattack for the second time. The Turks killed many British and French troops but did not dislodge them. A stalemate ensued at both Anzac Cove and Helles.

Not that these battles worried Capt. King, who was more concerned with digging a deep trench. 'Had a darn good sleep and got up at about 6 a.m. and issued rations to the chaps. Then the shrapnel began to come and it hailed around about us and hit everything around me but myself. We deepened our sleeping place about three feet, it was not deep enough. We captured a wireless party this morning, an Officer and about seven men — they had an Observation Station. Very hot to-day — a bit of a breeze. Got a paper to-day Feb. 11th, English one. Carried a few rounds of ammunition to a gun in the Valley, fifty more of our Drivers came ashore last night, one of them got hit while coming over S. Hayes. The War boats had a good go in last night and the Infantry had a bit of a go in, otherwise things were just about the same'.

Major White was not too preoccupied by battles to record in his diary that he 'Saw a blackbird yesterday, heard him singing gaily! Some pretty wildflowers here too'.

Although Britain's Royal Naval Division were meant to have bolstered the strength of the Anzacs since their recent arrival, Bean claimed these are 'decidedly jumpy … Australians have to be put in amongst them to steady them down' as they were firing at their own officers and trying to bayonet anybody who moved about in the dark. 'What I have seen of them has been rather feeble — in fact hopeless' Bean concluded.

The offensive led by Monash was still the talk of the optimists among the troops. The soldiers liked to think it succeeded especially as the price paid was so high. Lt Small confirmed that 'Our troops made a successful advance and according to the number of injured coming in they paid dearly for it. Same story. In the morning we made bombs … When we had made 25 we were told to get into full marching order and go up to the ridge our fellows took last night. When we got there we had to cut a communications path to the top and then sap towards the trench to enable the wounded to be brought up and down.

'What a pitiful sight they presented. They had been 20 hours lying all over the place with great gaping wounds. Some had both legs broken and the pain they endured coming down the steep sides was almost unendurable. We soon had water food and ammunition up to them and shortly afterwards I was astounded to hear they were about to retire at dark. The wounded were all out but further up the gully they were still coming down in a steady stream. Norm Durack, J. Sinclair and Self were left to cut steps to facilitate matters while the others retired quietly. By this time all the ammunition was down and the Infantry had retired; we were still coping with the wounded and I am sorry to say some of our fellows would not do so preferring to seek safety and leave the helpless to move for themselves.'

Monday
3 May
DAY 9

Lt Small spoke for many when he complained of having had 'a restless night' before he 'started work at 11. The snipers were giving a deal of trouble on the ridge owing to the "dead ground" sheltering them. To get rid of the nuisance it was decided to sap forward and then make a new firing line. Our boys could then command the valley. Our shift started at 11 a.m. and finished at 3 p.m. The snipers took particular objection to us because we would persist in throwing muck over the parapet. On our way home we saw a horrible sight. Away up on the

Tuesday
4 May
DAY 10

face of one of the cliffs were the bodies (15) of some poor fellows who had charged on Sunday night at 7 p.m. They were hanging in all sorts of positions. They could not be buried as the enemy controlled that position. At night the right centre appeared to be heavily engaged. Our shift went on guard at 8 p.m. each man doing one hour.'

Wednesday 5 May
DAY 11

Charles Bean travelled down to Cape Helles by boat on 5 May to cover the next offensive. Gen. Hamilton redeployed some of the Anzacs to help the Anglo-French forces in their difficult stalemate against the Turks. Bean was sad to leave his mates at Anzac Cove noting, 'We know the Turks have lost heavily. But our missing are probably lying out there beyond our lines — one knows indeed that many of them are'.

Some soldiers, like Lt McHenry, were 'marooned' on a stationary ship offshore. 'Monotony — monotony. The life aboard ship is rotten when our pals are on shore chancing their lives, we are doing miserable guards and piquets over horses. I mounted guard tonight again, cold and windy too. Evidently I'm still livery eh?'.

Thursday 6 May
DAY 12

The second battle of Krithia started with an Allied attack on 6 May and dragged on until 8 May, costing thousands of lives on both sides. With Anzac reinforcements, the Allied force mounted an extensive offensive, further inland towards a hill called Achi Baba, in an attempt to enlarge the beachhead gained earlier. They failed. Charles Bean was covering this battle, 'watching British shells exploding over the hill and looking for any signs of the British reaching the hill itself'. They had still only gained 'just a foothold — no more'.

In amongst this bloodbath, a horse saddler, James Parker, reported seeing his first Turkish prisoners. 'Left Bty … walked into Base to draw horse feed and mens' rations. While there, met Jack Biggsley and found out all 2nd Inf. Bde. and New Zea. had just landed. Glad to find out both he and Bert were A1. Stopped with cart half way back under cover to have rations brought up by hand. While there, big Artillery duel started. Saw Turk prisoners in enclosure … Got rations to Bty. by 12 a.m. had dinner in installments as guns going off and on from 11 a.m. to 7 p.m. All Btys. and ships firing, our and French Inf. Advanced 1,500 yds. More heavy firing during night. Improved our pits and dugouts during afternoon … During day several shells fell close to Bty. on left rear bursting 100 yds. in rear of us. The 6th shelled Turks out of trench during afternoon. Saw the F. Art. and Inf. on our right advancing and capturing trenches. Lancashire Fusiliers from Egypt landed and passed us on our right. Sikhs, and Gurkhas and British troops coming and going to trenches alongside us. Pack horses and mules taking ammunition up day and night. Fired 390 shells.'

Friday
7 May
DAY 13

The British and the Australian support troops could not reach the Achi Baba hill. Bean said they were told to dig in like the Anzacs had at Anzac Cove. 'The order came that the Turks could see us on the open field from Achi Baba and to dig in as fast as we could or they'll have their shrapnel on to you in a few minutes.'

Whether they were dug in or not, the second battle for Krithia raged on with successive waves of Anglo-French troops throwing themselves at relentless Turkish fire. According to Sgt. Parker, 'Big guns started again 7 a.m. We started about 8 a.m. Aeroplanes up every day. 6th knocked a machine out at 9.30 a.m. Big attack in full swing again. Fired 489 shells. Cleared out some trenches. Our troops advanced a fair bit. Lot of wounded coming back. Turks heavily shelled best part of day and through night. Also saw our ships shelling Asiatic side of Dardanelles. Shells dropping on our flank batteries both to front and rear. Krithia road heavily shelled by Turks about 500 yards from us. Amm. Wagon + gen. service wgn. Blown up at Base camp. Australians nick-named "White Gurkhas". Amm. brought up to us during night, also rations. 97th Bty moved up on our left. Bty. came up on our right. Many interesting chats with British and Indians, New Zea. and Australian troops coming back past our position, many of them wounded, also French Artillery men.'

End of Week 2

Saturday
8 May
DAY 14

A fortnight into the campaign and far from the hell breaking loose at Helles, Corp. McKern was tempted to celebrate his Saturday at Anzac Cove with a dip in the ocean.' Easy day went to beach with Alan, had swim we had to leave in a hurry owing to shrapnel. Gave sortie at night.' The water was much less inviting at Helles. The second battle of Krithia finally ground to a halt. Bean had been appalled at the number of his fellow Australians being killed and left to die in no-man's-land. He was criticised by officers for what they called, 'Dam fool actions' as

THE ANZAC SETTLEMENT LOST ONE OF ITS FAVOURITE SONS DURING THE 19 MAY TURKISH COUNTERATTACK WHEN JOHN SIMPSON KIRKPATRICK (RIGHT), 'THE MAN AND HIS DONKEY', WAS MACHINE GUNNED WHILE TRANSPORTING THE WOUNDED BACK FROM THE FRONTLINE ON HIS TRUSTY STEED, 'MURPHY'. AWM J06392

he ducked out of a trench and pulled a wounded man back to safety. The carnage was so bad that day, he could not help himself. 'Men were crying out in No Man's Land "Stretcher-bearer! Stretcher-bearer!!" but a messenger running past replied "You wont see them tonight my boy — they're rarer than gold. You wont get them along here" which was an idiotic thing to say prompting one of the wounded to reply "You might let us think we will" … I saw one poor devil out of the hundreds lying there crawling along who had been hit in both legs — trying to get back to cover so I dragged him by both legs into a ditch got hold of two packs put them around him and left'. Bean said that 'He had torn open his trousers as they generally do to see the wounds and was bleeding pretty freely. I don't fancy he can have lived — poor chap'. The battle had been such a costly disaster, even Gen. Hamilton had to admit failure, justifying this as best he could in his report. 'The operation has been a failure but the troops have done all that flesh and blood could do.' To succeed in future 'more and more munitions will be needed'.

Gen. Hamilton's report was a gross understatement, according to Corp. C. Roberts of the 8th Battalion. 'It was perhaps the most important day in the history of the 2nd Brigade, or if not the most important, then surely the most disastrous. The losses on the day of the landing at Anzac, were not to be compared with the casualties of today. An hour before the advance reinforcements from Egypt brought the battalions up to full strength. From the camping ground our troops advanced leisurely, to the foot of a ridge … The enemy had noticed the movement, and commenced shelling a small dwelling, where some dispatch riders had sheltered.

'Hardly had the reinforcements been allotted to their several companies, when the word came to advance. It appeared that all the officers were not fully acquainted with the direction of attack, and in some instances it was a case of follow the leader. The enemy … commanded a clear view of any troops advancing. Immediately the attack commenced the Turks brought artillery fire to bear upon us, their shooting was very accurate … It was not a pleasant thing to contemplate, working our way through that curtain of fire, seeing the men falling at every shell … The alternative … was to cross the creek, and work in the open … There was little to choose between; death followed every man … the men were literally mown down, but still the remainder pushed on, until within 300 yards of the enemy's line. Here they halted waiting for reinforcements which did not, and could not come. The larger part of the brigade were either killed or wounded … The field behind us was strewn with the bodies of our dead and wounded. No aid could be given the wounded, on account of the coverless country. And many perished that night.'

Sunday
9 May
DAY 15

The second battle for Krithia may have been over — apart from a follow up night attack on the 9 May by the Turks — but the day at Cape Helles was spent digging deeper in preparation for the next conflict. They also tried to pull out the wounded and bury bodies where possible. Although as Bean admitted, 'Wounded were crying "I'm in agony. Oh, I'm in agony"' but 'one knew that there was no earthly chance of many of the men near the front line being taken in … it made you mad to think of the dull, stupid, cruel, bungling that was mismanaging the medical arrangements run by the British. Everything is late with the British staff — nothing up to time — no evidence of brains that I have seen'.

Back at Anzac Cove, Corp. McKern heard for the first time of the unjustified sinking by Germany of the Cunard passenger liner, *Lusitania,* with the loss of 1,198 innocent lives. 'Sleeping nearly all day. Plenty of shrap. at night. 14th advanced, gave Turks hell with grenades. Mountain batteries also knocked them about badly. Corp. Kirby and self dropped about a doz. Reinforcements in front of us. Dum dum wound in side paining me. Went down to Post Office 4th Batt. this morning, wonderful changes everywhere. Regular Batt. stores, cook houses, dressing stations etc. Tremendous waste through bayonets, equipment etc. lying about everywhere. R. M. L. I. sent thanks and appreciation to D and A. Coy for relieving them in isolated trench under heavy fire. The platoon relieving them came back only five strong. News of Lusitania.'

Monday
10 May
DAY 16

By 10 May, the British medical authorities at Cape Helles recorded that 10,000 casualties had been evacuated from the 29th Division since 26 April. Back at Anzac Cove, the Turks continued their strong defence. Salvation Army Chaplain, William McKenzie, recorded how he survived a close shave. 'After landing the Beach became a "hot shop" with shrapnel shells and all sought shelter — over a dozen were fired. I had a very narrow squeak. I got covered with earth when I threw myself on the road for safety. A number of shells fell near us. However I got safely up the Hill tho' both shrapnel and bullets were flying overhead. The men's welcome to me was very warm and hearty. They were most grateful to greet me once more. I camped with the "Div." at the dressing station to be near to the wounded etc. I slept none the first night, as a fusillade of bullets flew over our heads the whole night and kept us a great row. I improved my "dugout" next day tho' it was very damp and uncomfortable, however, the sun got over it next day and so the third night I slept soundly. It was pleasing to be able to get the Col.'s body the first night I was in the firing line and we buried him at 9 p.m. in an exposed position and for safety I had to kneel in a crouching position to conduct the burial. He had been dead a fortnight. I had to perform a number of burials that day as indeed every day.'

Tuesday 11 May
DAY 17

At Cape Helles, Gen. Hamilton visited surviving troops noting they were 'caked with mud, hagged with lack of sleep, pale as the dead, many of them slightly wounded and bandaged, hand or head, their clothes blood stained their eyes blood shot'.

Down on the ground, Sgt. James Parker recorded the activities. 'Very quiet till 3 p.m. A few shells dropped near HQ's. and Aviation ground about 7 p.m. No damage … Biplanes up all morning and shelled by enemy. Rained during morning, cold wind blowing. Tommies searching paddocks for snipers, getting another on our right near 8th French Bty. Put up water trough at well, rear of Bty's. right flank. Good water in C Sub's trench, so dug a small well there. About 3 p.m. was over at horselines about clothing requis. when shells started coming over again, some dropping in front and one right of Bty. and then a lot in right rear of us among Ind. and British transport camps, mules and horses. Heard Japan and China were at war, also Lusitania torpedoed and sank off Queenstown. Rained heavy during night.'

Wednesday 12 May
DAY 18

As the transporting of the wounded continued down at Cape Helles, the French medical authorities reported 12,610 casualties had been evacuated since 25 April, out of their total strength of 22,450. For the moment, the Anglo-French military command was postponing future attacks against Achi Baba and Krithia.

Others were also being buried at Anzac Cove where the firing continued as Lt Ward noted. 'Reveille at 6 a.m., feed up horses. Went ashore without horses on a Torpedo. Landed amid rifle shots. Marching up valley to the trenches. Saw one poor chap taken out to sea for burial, plenty of music. 7.30 p.m. just finished digging a dugout for my pal and self. He has now gone to get some hot water to make a cup of cocoa. Snipers are starting so we are lying low. Bullets flying all around, nobody takes any notice we'll wake up when a few of us get picked off. Laid our blankets out and now comfortable as can be.'

Thursday
13 May
DAY 19

Having listened to the firing for days at Anzac, Col. Monash as a musician with a highly developed ear, noted that 'the bullet which passes close by (say within ten or twenty feet) has a gently purring hum' while 'the bullet which passes well overhead, especially if fired from a long range, has a sharp sudden crack like a whip' and 'our own rifle fire sounds like a low rumble of the drums or growl'. But, 'the enemy's rifle fire is a medley of sharp cracks like crackers exploding overhead' and 'the enemy's shrapnel sounds like a gust of wind in a wintry gale ... our own artillery is an ear-splitting reverberating echo'. He reasoned that when we are back home 'we shall not be able to sleep amid perfect quiet unless someone rattles an empty tin outside the bedroom door'.

Meanwhile out at sea, seaman Spalding heard the news that one of the Allied ships was sunk. 'This morning early H.M.S. "GOLIATH" was sunk by Torpedo. Only 150 saved. We have seen her for the last two or three days at her station near Suddul Bahr about a mile up the Straights from us. Submarine having been reported in Aegean yesterday, it was at first thought that she had been sunk by her, but it appears that a Turkish Torpedo Boat crept down the straits unobserved and torpedoed the 'GOLIATH' and got away again. Being at such an hour of the night there was a terrible loss of life. We on board knew nothing of it till this morning. An explosion would attract no notice on account of the continual noise of gunfire. Our troops on shore are said to be advancing slowly. This afternoon the camp on Helles beach was shelled severely from Asiatic coast. Several horses and some men killed. I saw six or seven large shells burst within half an hour. One burst close to the ship and a hot piece of shell fell on deck.'

Friday
14 May
DAY 20

Although sweet dreams must have been few and far between, Lt Leslie Ward managed to have one, as he confided in his diary. 'Having been up through the night I over slept, and was dragged out of a beautiful sleep; and the company in my dreams was not kaki soldiers or Turks! Three others and myself left camp straightway to go aboard the ship for a few utensils, we are now sitting on a little pinnace waiting to go out to the "Devanaha". Its a most glorious morning and the sea looks lovely and calm. We will have a swim going back. No sooner had we got out to sea than our pinnace was ordered to at once return ... So we were landed back on the shore. In five minutes all Troop Ships had lined up. I believe it was a submarine scare. However, we had a swim with shrapnel flying all around us.'

MOST OF THE ANZACS TEAMED UP WITH A MATE TO DOUBLE THEIR CHANCES OF SURVIVAL AND WHEN ONE OF THEM WAS SHOT, THE OTHER VOWED TO CARRY THE WOUNDED MATE TO SAFETY, AS SHOWN HERE IN THIS COMPOSITE PHOTOGRAPH. THIS BOND BETWEEN SOLDIERS LAID THE FOUNDATIONS OF AUSTRALIAN MATESHIP.

Maj. White's dreams of gallant soldiering had also been dispelled. He wrote to his wife that 'I am obviously not a soldier because I do not like modern war. One needs the courage of a lion, cunning of a serpent and instincts of a rabbit — as a hole in the ground is the only place of moderate safety and I am writing in one now'.

Yet these dangers did not get the men down. Col. Monash wrote to his wife that 'the men have been living for weeks in squalor, dirt and rain, with most of them in rags yet they are laughing and singing and joking and indulging in chaff and horse-play until it is their turn tomorrow to face the awful ordeal of the trenches'.

End of Week 3

Saturday
15 May
DAY 21

Up to 15 May, many of the soldiers killed were lower ranking officers. Then disaster struck when Maj. Gen. Sir William Bridges, Commander of 1st Australian Division and one of the highest-ranking officers at Gallipoli, was mortally wounded while inspecting forward positions in Monash Gully. He was commander of the 1st Australian Division and a former Inspector General of the permanent Australian army. This tragedy was nevertheless just part of the day's events for W.O. John Treloar. 'When I looked out on Anzac Cove this morning I found that most of the transports had gone — to Alexandria and then, I think, to England. All our horses will be disembarked at Alex., I expect, here we will have mule carts owing to the difficult country in which we are operating. So far, of course, there has been little need of transport, for we are practically stationary. Really the only transport work at present going on is the supply of food, ammn. and water, and this is all done at night.

'This afternoon we were rather shocked to hear our General [Maj. Gen. Bridges] had been wounded. I can't say the event was unexpected, for he has shown what I thought a rather rash contempt of fire. His wound is, I believe, very serious and we hardly expect him back. He has been replaced temporarily by Brig.-Gen. H.B. Walker, DSO, an Imperial Officer who has been employed as OC, 1st Inf. Bde. since the death of Colonel MacLaurin [killed in action 27/4/1915]. We heard today also of the heavy losses sustained by the 2nd Inf. Bde. at Cape Helles. Apparently the fighting there has been very severe and the Victorian Bde. has sustained many casualties. In our new Headquarters we are not exempt from shell fire; but those that do come generally burst where they can do no harm. I went to bed in the evening feeling very tired. It will be glorious when the time comes for us to cease our strenuous labours and return to our beloved Australia.'

Maj. White added that Bridges was 'severely wounded in the right thigh by a rifle bullet ... it was not only the femoral artery but another artery and vein and when the stretcher bearers started carrying him down to the beach, Bridges said "Don't have me carried down, I don't want to endanger any of your stretcher bearers" but they insisted'.

MAJ. GEN. WILLIAM THROSBY BRIDGES, WHO WAS SHOT IN MAY WHILE WALKING AROUND THE TRENCHES, WAS THE HIGHEST RANKING AUSTRALIAN OFFICER KILLED AT GALLIPOLI.

A sombre mood hung over the Anzac Cove area as Maj. Gen. Bridges' condition deteriorated. Maj. White confided to his diary. 'Very depressed. General Bridges condition serious. I sent a cable to Mrs Bridges yesterday'.

Rather than dwelling on this looming tragedy, Col. Monash consoled himself with the confirmation that Australians were better soldiers than the rest. 'Apart from many things which cannot be written about yet, the thing above all others which stands out uppermost in the terrible fighting which has been incessant since our landing on 25 April is the magnificence of our Australian troops. I have had plenty of opportunity of comparing them with the troops of British regular units and Territorials, and the British officers are the first to admit that for physique, dash, enterprise and sublime courage, the Australians are head and shoulders above any others. Throughout the whole of the fighting there has never been a murmur of complaint, in spite of the hardships and privations and continuous hours and hours of toil and deafening clamour. The men are as docile and patient and obedient and manageable as children, yet they are full of the finest spirit of self-devotion. For the most perilous enterprises, whenever volunteers are called for, every man in sight offers instantly, although often it means certain death to many of them. They are always cheerful, always cracking jokes, always laughing and joking and singing … The 16th Battalion on 1 May, at dusk, charged the "Razor Ridge" singing "Tipperary" and "Australia will be there" … I am convinced that there are no troops in the world to equal the Australians in cool daring, courage, and endurance.'

Charles Bean arrived back at Anzac Cove by boat from Cape Helles on 17 May. He noted that all the British warships had by then deserted the waters off Anzac Cove (for fear of being torpedoed). 'Shells were still dropping into the water very fiercely' although 'the men on the beach were going about working careless of any fire, in the good old Anzac way … The doctors say there is no hope for General Bridges.' Maj. White revealed in the secrecy of his diary that Bridges was not the only officer to die. 'Villiers Stuart was killed today and we all went to his funeral'.

Ambulance man Corp. A. Coulter got away for a brief spell saying, 'Sailed for Imbros daybreak. Very pretty island entrance like Nth. Head valleys and trees plenty warships and transports also Submarines'.

On that same day in another part of Gallipoli, soldiers were watching planes rather than submarines as Corp. McKern reported 'Holmes wounded. Enemy being reinforced German aeroplane visits us. 2nd Brigade return from Cape Helles, did fine work but lost heavily'.

Tuesday
18 May
DAY 24

On hearing that the Maj. General had died, Maj. White praised Maj. Gen. Bridges for his 'capability of leading troops in the field', saying his 'calm judgment and imperturbability in times of stress were most inspiring'. According to Charles Bean, a Morse code message received at headquarters that day from the enemy warned that 'We will put you into the seas tomorrow, you Australian bastards. Big guns we will give you; we will give you mines you Australian bastards'.

Nothing actually happened that day, apart from a little morning shelling on the beach, and men like Chaplain Dexter had other more domestic concerns. 'The bed was hard, the pillow (my waterbottle) was worse, my overcoat was not long enough to cover me altogether and the guns wakened us at about 4.30 a.m … Our dugout was on the side of the hills of a narrow valley looking out on the sea; the dugout itself was just part of the hillside cut away. The angle of the hill was very steep and a floor about 6' broad was levelled off. Crouching against the back was quite good enough to escape the shrapnel … But as they went over us they struck the bottom of the little side valley in which we were and by 8.00 a.m. had caused several casualties amongst the 7th Battalion not 30 yards away … Round the valley on our right the ground rises steeply to the crest of the plateau about 600' high and a windy road at the bottom of the valley leads right up. This road has been made up by our men, that is improved, but at some parts it is a death trap where stray bullets come over a depression in the hill at the end of the valley and drop right in the road … I went back with Col Wanliss to the 5th Battalion … further up the main valley … The 5th Battalion was originally 1,000 strong. They have received 400 reinforcements = 1,400 and now their strength is 460 after 3 weeks' fighting. Practically the whole regiment wiped out'.

Wednesday
19 May
DAY 25

The day after the Morse code warning, the Turks did launch a major counterattack — their biggest yet — as they had warned. They attacked along the entire Anzac frontline. Screaming out 'Allah' and assorted Arabic war cries, they charged the Australian trenches suicide style. The Anzacs were so well fortified since the landing that the Turks could only break through in a few places. It was a frightening moment but the Anzacs prevailed, shooting thousands of Turkish soldiers before they reached the Anzac trenches. The Turks suffered at least 10,000 casualties compared to 160 Australians killed and 468 wounded. During the fighting, the 22 year old Pte. Albert Jacka of the 14th Battalion from Melbourne set an heroic example at Courtney's Post by running across no-man's-land and jumping into a Turkish trench killing five Turks, bayoneting two and taking two prisoners. Pte. Jacka called out 'I managed to get the beggars, sir', when Lt K.G.W. Crabbe arrived with reinforcements. Pte. Jacka noted in his diary that 'Lieut Crabbe informed me that I would be recommended'. Crabbe had indeed recommended Jacka for a Victoria Cross, which he was awarded later in the year while still serving at Gallipoli. Jacka, who went on to the Somme where he fought even more heroically, became one of the highest decorated Australian soldiers of World War I.

Sadly, one of those killed was the highly popular John Simpson Kirkpatrick, 'the man and his donkey'. Simpson rescued hundreds of wounded men, carrying them from the front line on his donkey. He was shot dead by machine gun fire even as he led his donkey up towards the front to collect another soldier wounded in battle. Something of a maverick larrikin, Simpson had operated alone and without orders. Having found a Turkish donkey and seen how many soldiers needed rescuing he just saved as many as he could.

Lance Corp. Smith recorded some of the day's action in his diary. 'Came on duty in trenches last night at 9 p.m. was on watch till 12 p.m. Then had to stand by our rifles till dawn. About 3.30 a.m. word came along that the enemy were advancing — presently we heard heavy firing on our left and received orders to fire low — the Turks came on in twos and threes up the gully and over the ridge but did not succeed in reaching our parapets. There were hundreds of them in the scrub just below us and we poured in a heavy rifle fire supported later by artillery — the fight lasted till about 8 a.m. — the Turks left about 200 killed in front of our trenches — the three chaps in the same recess as me were shot dead and I had three bullets through my cap. The enemy then began to shell our parapets from point blank range but did not do much damage. we were relieved at 12 a.m. In the afternoon the Light Horse captured a trench that had been giving them trouble — all night heavy fusillades — Turks fearing attack.'

Having lost so many men in their suicidal attacks, Turkish officers appeared above their trenches with white flags and started burying their own dead. Turkish doctors also emerged and started treating and recovering Turkish wounded. Taking a chance an Australian General went out to meet them on no-man's-land, gave them cigarettes and suggested an official truce be negotiated a day or so later to bury all the dead. He then ordered them back into their trenches before firing resumed.

**Thursday
20 May**
DAY 26

Unaware of the impending truce, Pte. Lennie was still bringing his diary up to date. 'The Turks charged our trenches Wednesday night and got a warm reception there are dead Turks everywhere 2,000 killed and 5,000 wounded. But I think there are more Turks. They flew the white flag with the Red crescent which is equal to our red cross yesterday so our Officers got out of the trenches also the Turkish General and had a conversation between the trenches the Turks wanted to bury there dead so our heads gave them permission But instead of Burying the unfortunate dead they were picking up rifles and ammunition so our boys would not stand that.'

Friday
21 May
DAY 27

Negotiations got under way between the Australians and Turks for the burial of the dead. The Turks selected an emissary to finalise the arrangement. Looking at the beach and the limited water supplies, Bean prophetically noted 'we only have two old water pontoons for all the men but one single storm would finish them both off and there is no reserve at all on the beach'. He blamed British mismanagement. 'Surely it can't be beyond the resources of the Mediterranean Expeditionary Force to safeguard over and over again our water supply.'

For his part, Capt. King was more worried about supplies of ammunition. 'Was awakened this morning about 3 a.m. and carried ammunition to 4th Battery; the firing was pretty hot all night, a lot of firing by the guns and rifles, every now and then. Had breakfast late and then went up to firing line and had a shot at the Turks and they were not two hundred yards off; they were digging in their trenches. Had sleep this afternoon and it was very hot. Carried ammunition to guns tonight.'

End of Week 4

Saturday
22 May
DAY 28

Finally the Turks sent an envoy from Gaba Tepe to Anzac Cove where Maj. Thomas Blamey met him on the beach. The Anzacs blindfolded the Turk for the last part, not because many Australians were swimming naked but so he would not see their operational headquarters. Having agreed on a truce with Anzac officers, the envoy then returned to organise the burial of the dead from the Turkish side.

Lt Col. Reynell explained how important these burials were to the troops. 'We got orders to go at once and relieve the New Zealand

Auckland Regt. in the trenches. The trenches are like a rabbit warren and it took me till 6 p.m. to get everybody settled down and get every man prepared to meet the various quips and cranks and merry jests that brother Turk is primed up with by his German confreres. There are scores of dead men mainly Turks lying within twenty yards of some of these trenches and although most of them have been dead nearly 3 weeks the stench is still very ripe. They can't be buried as there are Turk snipers all round in the thick bush who pick off anybody who shows over the parapet. When I was looking round one trench that we were to relieve I suddenly came on a dead New Zealander in an advanced stage of decomposition that had been dragged into the trench by the N.Z. men with a crooked stick. It was a very unpleasant object and I was glad they had buried him by the time our men came to occupy the trench. By using the periscope one can see all round … Our fellows have shot 5 Turks since occupying the trenches.'

WHEN THE TURKISH EMISSARY VISITED THE ANZAC HEADQUARTERS TO NEGOTIATE THE BURIAL TRUCE, A COUPLE OF NAKED ANZAC SWIMMERS CARRIED HIM ON A STRETCHER AROUND THE BARBED WIRE FENCE PROTECTING ANZAC COVE FROM ATTACK.
AWM G00989

73

Sunday 23 May
DAY 29

The Anzac leaders sent a message around the beach and outlying trenches that the truce was scheduled for the following day. Soldiers used the 23 May opportunity to take a few final potshots at the enemy with 'considerable gun fire' right up to the deadline, Bean noted.

Meanwhile at Cape Helles, Capt. Norm Hollis of the Australian Field Ambulance, was more worried about protecting his unusual pet than burying a few dead soldiers. 'No doubt by this time you have received one of my cards which, however, do not convey much information. Even now I can't tell you very much ... I suppose the papers will inform you pretty accurately as to our movements. This country and climate suits our fellows down to the ground and except for a cold here and there we are all enjoying the best of health.

'The "tucker" leaves nothing to be desired except that shrapnel figures a little too prominently on the menu. Our casualties in the battery have been very slight. We have been detached from the Australians who landed further north, and are operating with British at Cape Helles. Needless to say we have been entirely successful and are confident of a glorious victory. We have all housed ourselves very comfortably in dugouts ... It would amuse you mightily to see some of

ALTHOUGH ESTIMATES VARIED, AUSTRALIAN BURIAL PARTIES BURIED AT LEAST 160 ANZACS WHILE TURKISH BURIAL PARTIES BURIED APPROXIMATELY 3,000. BURYING THE DEAD WAS DIFFICULT BECAUSE, AS CHAPLAIN WILLIAM DEXTER EXPLAINED, WHEN THEY WERE TOUCHED THE BODIES OFTEN FELL TO PIECES. AWM H03954

the graceful dives that are executed when shrapnel bursts over us. I saw one of the French native troops dive or fall backwards into a trench … all that could be seen of him was a pair of rolling eyeballs and a smile a mile wide. Our mascot, a monkey had a remarkable experience the other day during a particularly heavy shelling … I looked round and saw our monkey in mid-air in the centre of a mass of flying shell, earth and smoke. However, he came down with only a bit of skin off his nose and not a bit the worse for his experience.'

At last the day of the truce came enabling both sides to bury the dead. Bean noted it would 'improve life in the trenches as some of our men were actually sick because of the stench'. The Australians buried their dead on their half of the no-man's-land, while the Turks did the same on their half with men from both sides exchanging cigarettes. The Australian Medical Corps Burial parties who found 'the dead very thick indeed' spent the day identifying Australian or New Zealand bodies and burying them where they lay. Others, like Lt Gen. Birdwood, Maj. Gen. Godley and Col. Monash, walked about reconnoitering for future battles — as did Turkish officers. At least 'Our men got a good day's rest', Bean said.

Monday 24 May
DAY 30

Chaplain Dexter was certainly relieved that the dead — grotesque as they were — could be buried at last. 'Things very quiet this morning. Raining and things generally miserable. At 7.30 a.m. armistice began for the purpose of burying the dead. The smell is something awful. Some of the bodies have been lying in the heat of the sun for 4 weeks and of course all are unrecognisable. It is only by identification discs that the corpses are known. The actual cessation of hostilities did not take place until 8.00 a.m., for one sniper kept going somewhere in the Turkish lines. It was arranged that a central line between the trenches be fixed. Each on their own half of the ground could take their dead away and also rifle and ammunitions … The ground was simply covered with dead between the trenches at various points and after the day's work of burying estimates of 12,000 Turks killed have been made … Amongst this awful mass of dead Turks were some of our boys who had been killed on the 1st and 2nd days' fight and had lain there since … The bodies were horrible to look at being black and swelled up stretching out the clothing and in many cases when they were touched falling to pieces … It seems so strange, the quietness in the valley, no explosions and the men getting on the skyline and looking at the Turks through their glasses.'

Tuesday
25 May
DAY 31

The day after the truce, enemy submarines torpedoed the *Triumph* which 'rolled over and died' off Anzac Cove. As Corp. Rayment wrote in his diary. 'In the early afternoon we were startled by Jimmy Lane yelling out "look at the warship sinking". At first we thought he was joking as usual, but when we saw several small groups of men looking intently seaward we knew there was something untoward taking place ... Down towards Gaba Tepe, about a mile or so from shore, we saw a large cruiser with a list to starboard, the side on which the torpedo struck her ... I could see the men on deck calmly waiting to be taken off ... The destroyers were first on the scene and carried out rescue work until the boats arrived when they commenced hunting for the submarine.

'Once or twice we heard a gun boom but even with the aid of a couple of aeroplanes the destroyers were unable to locate the enemy boat which escaped. Meanwhile the rescue boats were hard at work and as soon as a pinnace or trawler was loaded up with men from the "Triumph" it sped away from the danger zone. Boats were working alongside picking up the struggling swimmers, risking everything in the attempt to save lives. Slowly but surely the big cruiser turned turtle, and as the rescuing boats crowded in to pick up the survivors the Turks commenced shelling.'

Wednesday
26 May
DAY 32

Lt Richards, a journalist in civilian life, commented on the many activities at Anzac Cove. 'Such multitude of momentous happenings crowd one upon the other day by day that it is really difficult to set down in a letter a complete or connected account of the doings of the Australian forces on the Gallipoli peninsula. Each succeeding twenty-four hours bring forth incidents of which columns of intensely absorbing readable matter might be written, but the very number and the frequency of these incidents give to each day a sameness which it would be difficult to imagine by the people of Australia, far removed from the scenes of conflict.

'Our primary objective of this campaign has been successfully accomplished, viz., the attainment of a sufficiently protected area of coastline and its commanding positions to enable the disembarkation of troops and the landing of supplies. Our next undertaking the improvement of our position in order to make it tenable against all attacks of the enemy — is almost completed, and we have no doubts as to the accomplishment of our third objective that of holding all our ground so as to be in a position to render effective assistance to our brother "The Tommies", when they have negotiated the intervening few miles between our right flank and their advancing front. Several attempts have been made by the enemy to break our lines, but the only result has been to thickly bestrew the ground between the opposing trenches with the dead bodies of hundreds of Turks ... There is not the slightest doubt that very many of the Turks have little heart in their work. "Finish Turk"! is usually the trite expression made by most of them who have given themselves up. Their pay books show that they have received no remuneration since the beginning of the war. Doubtless many more would surrender were it not for the fact that they gauge our treatment of prisoners by their own fiendish methods, and again the bonds of patriotism cannot but hold many to their cause no matter whether they consider it hopeful or forlorn, justifiable or evil.'

**Thursday
27 May**
DAY 33

Two days after he sank the *Triumph* on 25 May, German Naval commander Otto Hersing's *U21* then torpedoed the *Majestic* off Cape Helles, leaving the British feeling quite vulnerable. Naval support from the sea had dwindled down to a minimum. The British war correspondent who had worked alongside Bean, Ellis Ashmead-Bartlett, had watched the *Triumph* sink and was actually on the *Majestic* when it was hit. He noted that 'there came a sound as if the contents of every pantry in the world had fallen in the same moment'. Ashmead-Bartlett had taken the precaution of sleeping on deck and clambered over the side in his pajamas when the ship was hit and swam to a nearby cutter and safety. He was lucky since the *Majestic* sank within thirty minutes, taking 50 seamen to a watery grave.

Lt Col. John Corbin was among those at Anzac Cove who got the bad news on the same day. 'Off duty, just pottered some walking here and there. Heard *Majestic* was torpedoed at Helles this morning. All the battleships have been withdrawn to Imbros inside protection. They would doubtless come out if our flanks are threatened. Very little firing today. Some shrapnel on beach several bathers shot. Had a pleasant talk to Naval men tonight ... all good chaps.'

**Friday
28 May**
DAY 34

Apart from incessant firing from the heights, moments of peace could be found amidst the carnage. Trooper Ion Idriess noted that 'Snipers got 15 this morning, and a shrapnel got four of our own ... It is wretched to think so many men getting killed and maimed when they are not in the firing line. No matter on what peaceful errand we go there is death all about. We never know whether we will wake up alive. The enemy have been very quiet these last few days and nights.

I saw a man just now with his leg blown off. The doctors were working at it while it looked like a big red lump of beef. War is a sickening thing ... They are bombarding us with shrapnel. Their aim is getting fearfully close. They must have shifted their guns nearer during the armistice ... Tonight is the first night we have had no shrapnel. We are sitting by our dug outs on the hill side, smoking, the Colonels gramophone playing the Marseillaise, and the rest watching such a beautiful, peaceful scene. The sun is just sinking, a great ball of gold behind the island of Maidos. The sea is a beautiful blue, with the strong little destroyers just gliding through it, the hospital ships anchored with smaller craft in towards the shore. And as I write this one of our own guns has broken the peace, a bomb has burst in the trenches and now comes the isolated crackle of fire.'

End of Week 5

**Saturday
29 May
DAY 35**

The Turks stormed a forward position — Quinn's Post — during the small hours of 29 May 'with a wild outburst of firing', Bean noted and they captured the trench from the Anzacs. But with their blood up and determined not to give an inch of hard-won territory, the Anzacs fought back and after some heated exchanges, the Anzacs managed to finish the month of May by recapturing Quinn's Post.

The tenacity of the Australian soldiers certainly impressed Trooper Idriess, who would become a successful writer as a civilian. 'We have been under a hell of a bombardment ever since half past three this morning. Our own guns and an Indian mountain battery are replying. The shells are criss crossing just above our heads. The shrieking devils are kicking up a hell of a row. An hour ago when it was dark the shells were bursting in our little gully and illuminating our dugouts with vivid bursts of lightning.

'What men the Australians are. Under this fire plenty of them are crawling out and lighting their little fires. Breakfast against a big chance of death. They are calling out for stretcher bearers now. I don't know how many are hurt. The Indian stretcher bearers are going too. What marvelous escapes. A shell has burst right in front of me, just ten feet below two Infantry chaps who are cooking their breakfast. They were covered with smoke and dirt, but refuse to leave their cooking. As I write this another shell has burst beneath them, and still they will not move. Another has come, and this time they have grabbed their pots and ran. We all laughed loudly. By Caesar! It is about time they ran. A fourth shell has come, and where their fireplace was is now a cloud of

OPPOSITE: ALTHOUGH WOUNDED A COUPLE OF TIMES, MAJOR BRUDENELL WHITE, LEFT, DEVELOPED SUCH SKILLS AT GALLIPOLI THAT HE WAS APPOINTED TO COMMAND THE DECEMBER EVACUATION, CONSIDERED ONE OF THE MOST SUCCESSFUL ACHIEVEMENTS OF THE WHOLE CAMPAIGN. HE IS STANDING WITH LT COL. N.R. HOWSE VC. AWM G01329

smoke, ashes, earth and fragments of shell. By Jove! We are getting it hot … Half a stones throw from us are the Infantry … those poor devils are getting it far worse than us.'

Sunday 30 May
DAY 36

Things were also hotting up at Anzac Cove as Maj. White complained to his wife. 'In the middle of the day it is precious hot. I generally come back from my rounds bathed in perspiration. This is rather a nuisance as we can not get any washing done — except in salt water.'

Cleanliness may be next to godliness but Lt Cameron spent his Sunday reading the Bible. 'Last night's projected bayonet charge did not come off, the enemy evidently expecting something of the kind concentrated fire on the position. What a strange contrast is this day! Here I am comfortably lying in my dug-out, having had a shave, a wash and mouth cleaning all in one cup of water, and general change, and feel quite Sunday-like, while outside and all around is the thunder of guns, the whistle and scream of bullets and shells. Whistling Rufus gave us his usual pills this morning but did not get anyone, tho' two were wounded by stray rifle shots. The snipers are very accurate and dangerous; even in these rest places one is not safe to unnecessarily expose.

'Have been spending this couple of hours reading passages from my Bible, and a feeling of calm reassurance and confidence comes over me. Yesterday morning the Turks blew up our trenches held by the 10th Regt. and got them out, but the Australians rallied, charged and recaptured the position … This afternoon we lost our brave little officer, Lieut. S. McWilliam, than whom the Regt. boasted no better. He was on the observation post and just turned round to give an order when a bullet struck him in the left side of the head, coming out on the right. Mr Mac as he was familiarly called, died giving his orders — his last words were "Stand to arms, Twelve Hundred — Five Rounds — Oh God!" and fell back. It just required the word "Fire" to complete the order. I feel a great loss keenly.'

Monday 31 May
DAY 37

By the end of the month, Trooper Idriess was too sick to do his bit. He complained that 'Last night my troop and D troop were called out but only for trench digging. My knee was too stiff for me to go. If my troop go into the trench without me it will be horrible. I want to be in the first fight the 5th are in, I don't care so very much afterwards … Six of our fellows got shot yesterday. It is damned hard our getting picked off like

this and not being able to fire a shot in return ... Last night they buried a few of our fellows and a lot of the Turks killed yesterday afternoon ... There has been a big explosion out at sea. The destroyers are facing about with their sides awash with foam. I hope no more of our boats have been torpedoed ... We are detailed for the trenches this afternoon, and I am sick ... A few odd shells have been coming and going all through the day. Corporal Noisy was badly wounded yesterday. Poor Noisy ... The doctor is making me stay behind for a day or two. As the regiment is only sapping after all, I do not mind'.

THE BATTLE TO CAPTURE AND HOLD THE FRONTLINE TRENCH OF QUINN'S POST AT ANZAC COVE REQUIRED A CONSTANT SUPPLY OF TROOPS. THESE SUPPORT TROOPS OF COL. JOHN MONASH'S 4TH BRIGADE ARE WAITING TO TAKE THEIR TURN ON 29 MAY. AWM G01011

THE LANDING PLACE AT CAPE HELLES WAS VERY DIFFERENT TO ANZAC COVE AND MORE DIFFICULT BECAUSE THE EXPECTANT TURKS WERE INITIALLY SHOOTING DOWN FROM THEIR HIGH-WALLED FORTRESS AT THE BRITISH AND ALLIED FORCES LANDING ON AN OPEN BEACH WITHOUT THE PROTECTIVE CLIFFS AFFORDED BY ANZAC COVE. AWM A03076

CHAPTER 4
JUNE
All Hell Breaks Loose at Helles

Today a most deadly battle broke out. It was deafening to hear the French and British artillery commence the attack. This will be a memorable day for both the British, French and Turks more especially latter. French artillery fire swept the ground before them in a wicked manner ... British Artillery and Navy also attacked ... in a most furious and deadly conflict.

DRIVER E. BROWN,
1ST AUSTRALIAN LIGHT HORSE, AIF, DIARY

At Anzac Cove the stalemate continued with little change throughout June. Fewer Anzac offensives took place in June than May and even fewer Turkish counterattacks — although the constant firing from the heights continued. The Turks hoped to eventually demoralise 'the Australian bastards' who they vowed 'to push into the sea taking no prisoners'. The Anzacs spent the month holding their positions and improving their infrastructure with new landing piers and improved trenches.

At Helles the stubborn British — like bulldogs with a bone between their teeth — would not let go of their original plan. They still believed (after losing thousands in the first two battles for Krithia) that they could fight their way up the Gallipoli peninsula using 'frontal attacks' in broad daylight across open ground. But the Turks dug in, equally determined to stop them. Maj. Gen. Sir Aylmer Hunter-Weston (aka 'the butcher of Helles') had combined all British divisions as VIII Corps (29th Division, RND, 42nd Division and 29th Indian Infantry Brigade). He was convinced that with the help of the better-armed and highly skilled French troops, he could be third time lucky. He decided to attack again, even though his requested reinforcements from Britain had not yet arrived.

Successive attacks on the 4th, 21st and 28th June lacked heavy guns, shells and grenades and did not succeed in breaking through the well-armed Turkish defence — despite terrible loss of life. By the end of the month British Allied forces had suffered 40,000 casualties and the French 20,000 casualties. Not surprisingly the hospitals at Lemnos, Egypt, Malta and England were now stretched to the limit.

Anzac Cove, where Australians at least had some influence, was a much quieter place.

Tuesday 1 June
DAY 38

Having discussed the stalemate with planning officers, Charles Bean started the month worrying that 'our landing here will be very much discounted someday because we are content to hang on here and not push forward'.

Trooper Idriess noted 'I have just watched a poor devil of an infantryman being carried down on a stretcher. Half his face was shot away, and he was trying to sing Tipperary. And yet here I am lying in my dug out, in no pain, fretting like a great kid because I could not march off with the regiment. My blooming knee is now poisoned. The 7th L.H. occupied our dugouts during the early hours of the morning. I hobbled to the 7th doctor this morning, and when I returned someone had pinched my poor supply of jam. After a while I complained to the man in the next dugout that they might have left a sick mans jam alone. He has shared his dinner with me. He has two onions, I have a tin of beef. He is going to fry them to night and we are going halves. How I am looking forward to to-night. He is going to keep my water bottle filled. If he gets shot I think I will nearly cry. I cannot boil tea, and steel biscuits with water and salt tinned beef is no cure for a poisoned leg. Things are very quiet. Only a few odd shells passed today.'

Wednesday
2 June
DAY 39

In June, positions such as Quinn's Post (where there were still lots of spasmodic firing) needed to be defended. Officers delivered pep talks and moved among troops to keep up their spirits. 'We had a visit from Gen. Godley', B.C. Hobson noted 'and he thanked the 4th Infantry Brigade for the splendid work they had done within the past five weeks. We were all lined up the side of the hill when he made his speech and when he had finished, we gave three cheers for George of England, and, the sound of those cheers must have made the Turks do some thinking. I am beginning to think he must be doing a lot of thinking lately because he has not driven us into the sea and God only knows he has made enough attempts. Anyhow I will forgive him if he goes home, but if we have to drive him home, I will never forgive. While we are in Reserve Park we are being provided with new clothing which some of us needed greatly. I have been very busy since we arrived writing up requisitions and issuing clothing and fixing everyone in my company up with anything he was minus of.'

Thursday
3 June
DAY 40

After 40 days and 40 nights in this wilderness, regular supplies of food, water and clothing were hard to come by at Anzac Cove. To compensate, Chaplain E.N. Merrington made sure there was always plenty of comfort for the soul, not only on Sundays but also during the week. 'The line is still much quieter than before the recent battle. The water problem grows acute, and fresh wells are being sunk in the valley — some to a great depth, and with very little result. I saw one yesterday where the men were down to about 40 feet. On the windlass was posted a notice "To same foolish question, we have not yet struck water!" ... An order is necessary for each issue of water, and the total supply for each twenty-four hours is only half a gallon for all purposes. Strict orders have come out regarding the cleanliness of the area ... the flies about the whole place are indescribable ... I have established a little prayer meeting in my dugout on Pope's Hill. Each night some of the men gather there after tea, and as many as can get inside, while the others squat round the entrance. I read a chapter of scripture ... concluding with the Lord's Prayer ... It is very strange and beautiful in these grim surroundings, and we watch these lovely sunsets out at sea ... Sometimes we sing a well-known hymn, and the sound is wonderfully inspiring as it rolls down the valley. "Nearer, my God to Thee", and "Lead, Kindly Light" are so impressive here that I am sure we shall never hear them in time to come without thinking of these scenes'.

Friday 4 June
DAY 41

Maj. Gen. Sir Aylmer Hunter-Weston ordered a third attempt to take Krithia to begin on 4 June, even though reinforcements had not arrived. A diversionary attack was planned by the 1st Battalion at Anzac around Quinn's Post to deceive the Turks into thinking that was the main action of the day. However, this third offensive also failed to break through the Turkish lines. The attack was another costly failure, perhaps because the diversionary action at Anzac was a day late. By the end of a fierce day's fighting, the British suffered 4,500 casualties while the French lost approximately 2,000.

S/Sgt. Leslie Goldring provides a few insights into the Helles battles. 'At 11.30 a.m. there was a tremendous bombardment commenced and lasted all day. Our men advanced a good distance but in some instances they were compelled to retire. Whether the Artillery fire was good or bad one could not say as Krithia Hill was nothing but smoke. Sgt. Gitson was slightly wounded. There is very hard Infantry fighting in progress. We appear to have pretty heavy losses and the Turks must have suffered fearful losses caused by the Artillery fire alone.'

Driver E. Brown watched the fierce fighting at Helles through field glasses on 'Kings Birthday. On battlefield 11 a.m. Today a most deadly battle broke out. It was deafening to hear the French and British artillery commence the attack. This will be a memorable day for both the British, French and Turks more especially latter. French artillery fire swept the ground before them in a wicked manner. Theirs was on right flank. British Artillery and Navy also attacked from centre to left flank in a most furious and deadly conflict. Rifle fire was very heavy when able to hear. Saw about 100 Turk prisoners brought in. Was viewing today battle through glasses big part of time. Two Battle Ships Swiftfire and Exmouth were in the entrance and kept their end up. A blinding dust swept the battlefield all day. Airplanes were very busy six at one

time was seen moving above. This battle kept up to dark when things got to be a bit quiet.'

The diversionary attack took many of the Anzacs by surprise, including heavy sleepers like Lt Col. Carew Reynell of the 9th Light Horse. 'There was a Devil of a lot of firing going on in the neighbourhood of Quinn's Post and evidently a scrap of some dimention going on — they say there was heavy firing all night too but I never heard a sound.'

The normally reserved Sgt. A.S. Hutton described the battle as 'a bloody furnace' noting that 'The Turks made an attack last night but were repulsed. The Warships have been storming Achi Baba for about six hours the guns have been roaring all the time without a stop poor Turks. Afterward our people charged the hill, we could see them running about but do not know the results. Sgt. Paul and Cpl. Brown was shot dead today. The New Zealanders on our right flank are going to attack some trenches tonight. They are only a couple of hundred yards from us so we might get a fly too. Last night was like a bloody furnace with shrapnel flying about in the attack.'

BECAUSE OF HIS OUTDATED BELIEF THAT IF ENOUGH TROOPS CHARGED CAVALRY STYLE ACROSS OPEN GROUND AGAINST MACHINE GUNS THEY WOULD EVENTUALLY CAPTURE TURKISH TRENCHES, BRITAIN'S MAJ. GEN. AYLMER HUNTER-WESTON WAS NICKNAMED 'THE BUTCHER OF HELLES'.
AWM H10293

End of Week 6

The Turks suffered 9,000 casualties at Helles defending Achi Baba. The British and French began burying their own large number of dead as quickly as possible to avoid the spread of disease. One of those responsible for 'this ghastly business' was C.P.O. Johnston. He wrote that 'The flies crawled in their millions over the dead and rose in clouds when a corpse was lifted to the grave and then descended to their feast before the spadefull of earth was placed'.

Charles Bean pointed out that the diversionary action at Quinn's Post was meant to coordinate with the Helles attack, but it took place too late. 'The only thing was that the attack down south came first and our movement here afterwards'. Bean noted that the Anzacs still fought hard. In one action, eight men and two engineers tried to blow up a machine gun in the German officers' trench. The soldiers bombarded the Turks, pouring machine gun and rifle fire into enemy positions for some hours. The Turks were just too entrenched and well armed so the German officer's trench withstood the attack. Advancing at Anzac Cove was as difficult as the ordeal at Helles.

The ill-fated offensive against the Turks upset L/Corp. Langford. He recorded that the possibility of being killed inspired one of his comrades to shoot himself in the hand most probably to get out of the fighting. 'In trenches a fortnight. The time has passed very quickly. Last night we "stood to" for a considerable part of the night as eight of our men and an officer crept out to try to capture a machine gun. The attempt was unsuccessful so 100 men attacked but did not succeed as the Turkish fire was too hot. The Turks ran for their lives to the support trench however. Time — 5 a.m. I feel very sleepy as we were up most of the night. We expect to be relieved today. Very heavy bombardment with hand grenades this morning — Turkish trenches suffering severely. Time — 9 p.m. This morning the Turks have been giving us fits in the trenches. They have shelled repeatedly since about 7 with shrapnel until we are about sick of it. They killed one of our men, W. McGregor, with the third shot, and since then one man has been wounded ... The New Zealanders attacked and took some trenches last night, but they have their work cut out to hold them today ... this is the worst day so far ... This afternoon one of our troop shot himself in the hand, shattering it badly. This afternoon has been fairly quiet, and this evening you might be induced to think ... no war was on.'

When the Turks counterattacked at Helles, the British 29th Division retreated in large numbers. A British lieutenant, Dallas Moor, 18, who had ordered his men not to retreat actually shot four of them to keep the others from bolting. This desperate action won the officer a Victoria Cross but it also showed just how hopeless the British situation was in the offensive against Achi Baba.

At Anzac Cove the day started with a Church service. Pte. Pasini noted he had been wounded. 'I am not too bad. I stopped a bullet after fighting for four weeks. I got it in the back, below the kidney. It did not go right through; if it had, I might be a cold soldier now. Brother Peter is alright, as far as I know. He was in the trenches when I was hit on the 26th May. A big crowd of us were in the sea swimming, and the enemy started firing shrapnel. I escaped the bullets from the first shell, got out of the water fast, and sheltered under the bank of a hill. I was hit when the next shell burst. The Turks fire shells on the beach every day, and hit a lot of the boys. But we need to swim to wash off the lice! The day before I was hit, seven of us were lying on the side of the hill for a rest. We were dog-tired, having been in the trenches for 48 hours without any sleep. Well, a shell burst close by, and three of those on one side of me, and two on my other side, were wounded — some very badly — but I escaped ... A man's life is valued at nothing in this war! ... Our wounded men are well-looked after here. We all think of home as there is no place like Australia.'

It seems incongruous in this war setting to be enjoying 'an open air concert which was very good' but that is what Lt Col. Reynell observed. 'It was rather quaint to see a half-bearded ruffian stand up and sing a sentimental song to a lot of other disheveled ruffians with a lively obligato of musketry from above. We have a lot of fine voices here.'

**Sunday
6 June
DAY 43**

When summer came to Anzac Cove, the flies multiplied and dysentery brought down many officers and men. The first cases of enteric fever also appeared at the island of Lemnos. As if this was not enough, they also had spies to contend with. Because of the close stalemate, intelligence was a valuable asset. Bean noted the appearance of daring Turkish spies amongst the ranks of the Anzacs. Several were shot as soon as they were discovered. Trooper Quinane reported the first German spy discovered moving suspiciously in the trenches. 'A German spy was captured in our trenches today — or so said the 27th L. Horse'.

**Monday
7 June
DAY 44**

Tuesday
8 June
DAY 45

Charles Bean wanted the Anzacs to mount a serious offensive. He complained the Allies made no headway attacking the Turks again during the night in 'a half-hearted sideshow' of which the men 'were getting sick and tired'. Lt Col. Reynell agreed. 'We are still doing absolutely nothing. I can't understand this absolute inactivity while the Turks are surrounding us with a ring of fortifications'. Reynell wanted 'a general advance' because 'these little isolated attacks end in nothing'.

Pte. Fred Muir wrote to his mother about the varying health of soldiers in the trenches. 'Dear Mater, Have had several letters from you lately also a quantity of papers which were much appreciated by myself and the other boys here. We are looking forward to another mail during the next day or two. We have had a very lively time during the last six weeks but I am glad to say I have escaped injury up to the present. I sent you a cable saying I was well after the first couple of days we were here and hope you got same O.K. Your parcel arrived in good order a couple of weeks back and the socks in particular were most acceptable. We have been in the trenches for 5 weeks but are now having a weeks spell in the rear. We have got quite accustomed to life in the field now and find things fairly passable. We have not had our clothes off for 5 weeks and it

LT COL. CAREW REYNELL SPENT SOME TIME WITH HIS CHILDREN IN SOUTH AUSTRALIA BEFORE LEAVING FOR GALLIPOLI, WHERE HE COMMANDED THE 9TH LIGHT HORSE UNTIL HE WAS KILLED AGED 32 LEADING HIS MEN INTO BATTLE AT HILL 60 ON 28 AUGUST 1915.

was most pleasant to strip off on getting to rear and have a dip in the sea. The weather here is glorious just at present and I am in the best of health ... I was in the hospital for a few days with an attack of influenza on the "Afric" but nothing serious. That was six months ago ... I am very sorry to say that Duncan Brown (you remember me speaking of him) was shot dead the day of the landing. Alban Kirby is still alright but I have not heard any news of the other South Coast lads ... Best wishes to you all, and love from Yours affectionately Fred'. Muir, whose letters were published in the *South Coast Times,* Wollongong, died on the 28th November 1915 from wounds received at Gallipoli.

Wednesday 9 June DAY 46

Dashing off a sad but newsy letter, L/Sgt. C. Bosward included a weather report and confirmed he had sent a batch of post cards home. 'Rotten muggy and misty day. Very quiet. Flies have been very bad especially big blue blowflies. Saw a monitor a light battleship which can get into about 6 ft. water and shell away to her hearts content. Sent batch of service post cards to Australia. Capt. Magee returned to duty. Turks think periscope rifle is an awful weapon also the Jap. Bomb mortar. Canteen ship not a success so far, but should be when more stores arrive. Heard from Ted Sparke that Geo. Hill was wounded but refused to go away to hospital. Harold George and Thompson (of the Easts) reported by Ted to be killed. Harold was rescuing his wounded Sargt. when killed. Just got him on parapet of trench and was shot in head. Sargt. was saved.'

Thursday 10 June DAY 47

The main development at Anzac Cove was the construction of a new pier off Anzac Beach, replacing a temporary one built after the landing. Lt S.H. Watson supervised the construction of this permanent pier. He demonstrated some Anzac ingenuity when, after finding a large 8 inch Turkish shell, he decided to use the shell packed full of heavy shrapnel and sand as an innovative pile driver.

Pte. Gammage heard that the Turks threatened to drive the Anzacs into the sea. 'Stood to 3 to 5 a.m. Heavy firing all day ... one of our airplanes was brought down. Turks send over 50 shells after him 9 p.m. a Turkish prisoner used to try to draw them out they reply wanting to know when we will surrender also telling us if we don't they will drive us all in to the sea and take no prisoners that's nice to know. Our Artillery firing hard on left wing and Warships bombarding Achi Baba. Got a piece of bread (first piece) if fever or some disease does not break out here it is a miracle.'

As the temperatures rose, so did the number of flies as long-suffering Alf Guppy recorded. 'I had a bad night with cramps in the stomach last night. A great number of the boys are bad with dysentery many going away to Hosp the last few days. Also most of us are suffering from sceptic sores on our hands and arms. The flies are dreadful bad here; they are round you in swarms all day. We had to stand to arms from 3 a.m. to 4.30 a.m. Tonight a number of the boys had to go out, on a party sapping. Sgt. Gilbert; reinforcements has taken over my temporary place as platoon Sgt. I being only a Cpl. Cpl. Jones also reinforcements has joined my Coy. It is a bit rough on L/Cpls. Chubb and Huster and myself to have these men who have seen no fighting yet, put over us. An Australian casualty list, showing numbers since the landing, was posted today and our Brigade (4th) are the second heaviest loses as a Brigade and my Battn. the second heaviest in the Brigade ranging as follows 16th, 14th, 15th, 13th. Yet the men of one of the other Battns. (16th) has had the cheek to tell us we had done no fighting and called us the yellow streak Battn. There is only 1,500 of us left now in the Brigade of the original 4,000 who landed'.

The flies didn't distinguish between officers and men. Maj. White noted in his diary that the summer heat was sapping his strength especially as 'a lack of energy has always been my problem' but 'the flies are nearly driving me mad as I write'.

End of Week 7

Pte. N. Vallance finally got off a letter to his mother about the landing. 'I am in splendid health and would have written before but could not get any writing paper. I had a good supply in my pack when I came ashore, but it was a case of "Down with our packs!" as soon as we landed. Therefore, all our packs got mixed-up, and when we were relieved from the trenches we had to take any pack we could get hold of. We are having a good time generally. We get plenty of good food — the best since we joined up — and we have plenty of warm clothing. On the day we landed ... Our Lt Colonel was wounded while still on the destroyer, also two privates. With shrapnel and bullets falling all around us, our crew pulled ashore and luckily not one of our boat-load was hit ... We had a hard time entrenching the first fortnight after landing, but we did not mind as it was necessary. We have 24 hours in the firing-line trenches, then we are given 24 hours' rest, then we stand by for fatigues for another 24 hours, the

Friday
11 June
DAY 48

Saturday
12 June
DAY 49

OPPOSITE: ONE OF THE MOST IMPRESSIVE ENGINEERING FEATS AT GALLIPOLI WAS THE CONSTRUCTION OF WATSON'S PIER, THE COMPLETION OF WHICH WAS CELEBRATED WITH A SPECIAL DINNER, ALSO MARKING THE CENTENARY OF THE BATTLE OF WATERLOO. AWM G01046

next 24 hours we are in the support trenches, and then the firing-line again — and thus continues the routine'.

No one could really escape the firing line as Lt Col. Reynell noted. 'The Turks pitched a score of shells into our camp' and 'killed 3 Indians and half a dozen Mules before I ordered everyone into their dugouts'.

Sunday 13 June
DAY 50

Although he had now been on the beach for 50 days, Alan Treloar found it difficult to write unless he received letters himself. 'This was an uneventful day. During the day I was kept going very hard and I wanted as much as possible to leave my night free for letters home. We had expected to have some letters to answer this mail, but besides the newspapers we received but little. A mail did come in during the morning, but for the whole of DHQ, there were only about six letters; I was fortunate enough to get one from home. But everyone is feeling disappointed at the delay in the delivery of our letters. I think one of our chief weaknesses is the way we look forward to letters, or rather our inclination to be angry when they don't seem to come right. I expect it is partly because we are so far away from our homes. During the evening we found one of our tunnels had got within ten feet of an enemy one. Consequently a mine was tamped and laid ready to blow up the enemy. It was decided, however, to wait until he got within 2 feet before it was exploded. My word! There's a surprise in store for some Turks. In the afternoon one of our planes flew over and dropped some bombs. I managed to get a few letters fixed up, but they kept me very late. In fact, for the third night running I did not get to bed until considerably after midnight.'

Monday 14 June
DAY 51

A rough and windy day made life a little harder for Chaplain Dexter. 'During the morning several shells got near the hospital and one exploded in a hospital dugout. Killing one man and wounding 3 others. All the morning in the fire trenches (firing line) with the boys. Afternoon fairly warm and after tea at 7 p.m. went for a swim ... Most of the officers are "lousey". I got rid of mine on the "Clan MacGillivray" and up to the present the Doc and myself are free ... There was not much firing through the day. In the trenches only sniping was going on and several shells burst over our "humpies" but only dead shots fell around me. All the shrapnel bullets go over our heads. Whilst sitting writing up the diary a maxim gun got on to some idiot who was exposing himself and we got the benefit. As the bullets whistled the Doc and I ducked and jumped and got in our humpy. It just knocked up the dust on the graves ... To night I took the photo of these pathetic little crosses with boxes of ammunition in the foreground in the trenches. I rambled along to the 8th Headquarters our company ground is steep ... It would be impossible to make a steeper place than this habitable. Little dugouts have been made with the aid of fascines and these are the platforms which assist one to get to the bottom. In digging some of these "humpies" they came upon the bodies of several of our boys who had been killed in the first day and hastily buried ... One humpy has just by the entrance, a cross on the grave of a NSW. boy. The wind has gradually blown the soil away and some of his clothes are beginning to protrude from the ground.'

Staying inside his dugout during a second consecutive day of strong winds, Chaplain Gillison finally got up-to-date with his diary. He wrote of the heroic exploits of John Simpson Kirkpatrick who had been killed back on 19 May. 'I do not remember if I have mentioned a young fellow, Pvte. John Simpson, who used to take slightly wounded men down to the beach on a donkey. He made as many as 16 trips on one day, caring nothing for shrapnel or snipers. He seemed to have a charmed life, but one day he was shot dead. It can hardly have been an accident. We are willing to give the Turk in general the credit of not wishing to violate the accepted rules of warfare as regards those tending the wounded, but their snipers pay no attention to such delicacies'.

Later that day, Sgt. A.S. Hutton tried to find some reason for recent skirmishes around Quinn's Post. 'It is reported that the bombardment of 13th was directed on to 10,000 German troops who were coming to reinforce the Turks. They were annihilated. The Turks rushed two batteries up on our right flank and opened fire about 4 o'clock this morning without doing much damage. our destroyers and howitzers have been firing at them all day in fact the firing all round has been heavier all day. our mines are progressing favourably. we Sigs in a new position we have no protection from shell fire here.'

Tuesday
15 June
DAY 52

Wednesday 16 June
DAY 53

THE HIGHLY SKILLED 2ND AUSTRALIAN INFANTRY BRIGADE, WHO WERE SENT DOWN FROM ANZAC COVE TO CAPE HELLES TO HELP WITH OFFENSIVES, WERE ABLE TO LAND ON A PIER RATHER THAN A BEACH, WHEN THEIR VESSEL TIED UP ON THE PORT SIDE OF BRITAIN'S MIGHTY *RIVER CLYDE*. AWM G00957

Signaler R. Stanley could hear the sounds of battle taking place for control of the southern end of the peninsula. 'Something doing down Cape Helles all day, terrific bombardment, from our position we watch the fleet in action and huge shells bursting on Achi Baba. 10 a.m. A dummy landing is carried out a few miles below us, several man of war boats and a fleet of transport there. Turks hurry up forces and guns to stop the supposed landing, and get shelled for their trouble. In the afternoon Turks shell our position at Anzac, with every gun they have, our artillery replies vigorously, not much damage done by Turks terrific fire. 9 p.m. A force from the 12th Batt. goes out on the extreme right under cover of a destroyer. Destroyer puts search light on Turks trench and shells them, while the attacking force gives them the bayonet. Turks retire rather hurriedly, while our patrol damages their trenches and gets back with only a few casualties. Remainder of night fairly quiet.'

By contrast back at Anzac Cove, Chaplain Gillison was grateful for relative calm in his area. 'There has been comparatively little of note happening during the last three weeks. An attack by the Turks had ended so disastrously for them, that it became evident on Thursday May 20 through the showing of white and red crescent flags that they desired an armistice.'

All eyes turned to the beach, where bottles of wine suddenly washed ashore from the *Triumph*. It had been torpedoed in May. This wine would be drunk to celebrate the completion of the new pier. Thanks to the leadership of Lt S.H. Watson, the Royal Australian Engineers built 'Watson's Pier', adding a new facility for the watercraft unloading supplies and replacing the improvised landing stages.

Col. J. Dods noted events changed quickly that day as the Turks 'commenced to shell the beach and are doing so now … afternoon had a great shelling especially the beach and some of the trenches — few killed on beach. No news — except French have advanced some at the Cape … Health of troop so far good — though water still scarce. Food excellent'.

Thursday
17 June
DAY 54

To celebrate the completion of the piled jetty at Anzac Cove and also the centenary of the Battle of Waterloo (18 June 1815), the Royal Australian Engineers organised a special First Corps dinner which they turned into a 'gala' event. The Menu included Aperitifs: called Hors de Combat — Huitres au Naturel ('very much on the shell'); First Course: Consomme d' Autriche or Potage Allemande; Main Course: Poissons d'Avril (25th) or Boeuf Gelee d'Australie (salted bully beef); and Desert: Charlotte Russe avec Anzac bisquite especiale. The wine list included Hieland Toddy, Snakejuice, Worcestershire and Painkiller. The gala dinner was finished off with Café Turc and for Liqeurs the 'cordon bleu' chefs offered Submarine, Drymouth and Curacold. Wheelbarrows (rather than horse-drawn carriages) could be ordered to take drunken guests back to their dugouts. In reality, the engineers just ate tinned salmon and tinned turkey. But they did drink some of that recently rescued wine along with limited portions of 'medicinal' whisky and some secretly stored beer.

Friday
18 June
DAY 55

End of Week 8

After two months on the beach, some of the more impatient Anzacs, like Lt R.W. McHenry were pleased with any opportunity to have a go at the Turks. 'Slept part of the afternoon and during the evening, had the pleasure of laying the gun on the Turks. We put 16 rounds into their position before "Stop" — "Cease Fire" — "End of series" came through on the phone. The telephone systems have reached a good standard of efficiency and lines connect the observing stations with the

Saturday
19 June
DAY 56

various guns which are controlled therefrom. British aeroplanes are continually being used for purposes of reconnaissance and for bomb dropping on the Turks position which latter practice must cause a great amount of despondency and alarm to the recipients of these bombs. The trenches are ridiculously quiet considering war is on and often perfect quiet prevails to be broken by the pot of a single sniper or the dismal squeal of a shell. No mails have arrived for us yet which is sickening as one longs for a letter to bring news of home.'

Sunday
20 June
DAY 57

With no special offensives or counterattacks and just the usual firing from above, Bean said it was 'Quiet — quite like a Sunday today' with 'very few shells'. He 'counted 404 men bathing or sun-bathing on the beach and a lot more sitting down there half dressed, browning their back'. Despite the risks from snipers who had claimed so many lives, Lt McHenry was one of the many intrepid Anzacs to have his weekly Sunday wash. 'Had a bathe in the afternoon. During the evening sat outside on a terrace we built during the day on the slope overlooking the sea and had a sing song. At 2240 destroyer fired 2 rounds and immediately along the whole front we started firing at full speed to ascertain the strength of the enemy opposed to us at this position. Sounds of bombardment are continually heard from the British and French positions on our Right.'

The Turks were also taking risks, urinating and defecating in front of their trenches at the start of no-man's-land in full view of the Anzacs. Bean noted that 'The Turks are getting very cheeky — actually performing the offices of nature in front of their trenches'. He believed 'our men should stop this'. He also wrote 'as the Turkish prisoner's latrines are not far in front of our ridge' he had 'excellent grounds for saying that many Turks are as white as Europeans'.

Monday
21 June
DAY 58

At Helles, the life and death struggle dragged on intermittently. The French, who were better armed than the British, fought a well-planned battle for Haricot Redoubt, which they captured along with a series of Turkish trenches called Kereves Dere. The offensive cost the French 2,500 casualties but at last they could look down on the enemy. It was a great morale boost for the Allied forces.

Back at Anzac Cove, Lt McHenry enjoyed a major breakthrough of a more personal nature. 'A mail! and such a one arrived today after the countless rumors we have heard. I got no less than 23 letters and about 12 newspapers. A mail which had quite satisfied my voracious appetite and has put me in a good mood. A quiet day but was at E.E.O. this afternoon. Issue of tobacco and cigarettes. 2 chaps hit in the water by shrapnel including Jack Connors of my sub. They went bathing and the Turks started their old game.'

The supply of drinking water became a problem when two of the water barges sank. L/Cpl. P. Langford complained that this Monday was the 'Hottest day so far. Got mail from Australia dated about the middle of May — 12 letters from Mother, Dad, Vera, Rita, Orchard, Florrie, Rob, Nellie Roche, Art Law, Mith, Cis M. Hall, Miss Morrissey, Dorothy Atyeo and Mrs Hosie. Will try to answer them all by postcard this mail. Heard today that French had captured a couple of trenches, and that Turks were retreating from the Cape. Visit from Roy J. at night. Did some range finding. Saw Hydroplane set out on another trip. Did some more diving, and a little washing. A little shelling by Turks. Turks noisy at night. Great amount of firing at 11 o'clock. Got tin of jam from R.J. — god send. Bill fried onions for tea — they were great.'

OF ALL THE POSITIONS AT ANZAC, QUINN'S POST, AS CHARLES BEAN'S PHOTOGRAPH SHOWS, WAS ONE OF THE MOST SOPHISTICATED WITH A SERIES OF ROOFED SHELTERS LAID OUT ON DIFFERENT LEVELS DOWN THE SLOPE BEHIND THE TRENCH ITSELF. AWM G01026

THE CARTOONIST FOR *THE ANZAC BOOK* PRODUCED AT GALLIPOLI, DAVID BARKER, IMMORTALISED THE SOLDIERS' DEPENDENCE ON STRETCHER BEARERS TO TAKE THEM TO HOSPITAL, WATER CARRIERS TO QUENCH THEIR THIRST AND THE YMCA TO SUPPLY THOSE LITTLE NECESSITIES OF LIFE.

THE HOSPITAL CAMP

WATER CARRIERS

A YMCA CANTEEN QUEUE

Tuesday 22 June
DAY 59

Good news travelled fast at Gallipoli. Pte. A. Fricker saw the limited French advance as a real victory. 'At beach camp … Enemy and shrapnel on beach. Wrote to Doris and Father. French troops advancing between here and Cape Helles. Turks said to be retreating in a N.W. direction. Went to 2nd Engineers Camp and enquired for Billy Topp who I found was still away sick. Saw L. Birch.'

Sgt. A.S. Hutton also was encouraged by the French victory in his diary entry. 'We received a mail yesterday which was very cheering 1 letter from home for Reg & I (poor kid). We had a bit of "bluff stakes" attack yesterday. The French men are reported to be doing good work, they advanced about a mile last night (no news of Reg yet)'.

A disappointed Lt Col. Reynell noted 'When volunteers wanted to take out a few scouts to the front and to the Turkish lines, I volunteered and the Colonel recommended me but General Russell says I am "too valuable for the importance of the job". Personally I cannot imagine any more useful sphere than getting information especially as a general advance seems to be on the cards'.

The Turks struck gold when two of their shells hit the ammunition depot at the southern end of Anzac Beach damaging about fifty rifles and setting fire to two boxes of ammunition. They also 'hit a man in the water, and took off his arm — at least it was hanging by a thread', according to Bean. He was a bit shocked when 'he came out of the water holding it … bathing went on as usual'.

The shelling on land worried Maj. B.D. Jack, especially when the opposing trenches were so close. 'I have been moved again, this time I am "Intelligence officer of the Battn". It isn't a bad job consists mainly of sketching, map drawing and watching the movements of the enemy. We have been in the trenches for 12 days now and things are very quiet. Our observers use the periscope and the periscope rifle and we get some good shooting. Occasionally they shell our trenches but for the damage done it is waste ammunition. We are 15 yds from one trench and 200 from their main line. I used to laugh when I read in the papers that the trenches were only 50 yds apart but its only too true. We have them here just as close and we throw bombs at one another all day. Thank goodness they have no trench mortars. We have several that toss a 30 lb bomb of high explosive and it does some damage to their trenches. According to the "newspaper" we get, things are in a bad way in Constantinople and I think the Turks are pretty tired of it. I give the Turks credit for one thing and that is trenching. They dig very fast and large shovel fulls come over. When we fire at them and miss they signal a miss for us.'

Wednesday 23 June
DAY 60

When Maj. Gen. J.G. Legge replaced Gen. Bridges, Bean said some of the officers threatened to resign because of his reputation as a weak and feeble leader. Lt Gen. Birdwood told them they must stand loyally by their new commander. He cautioned them that 'if he was that weak there was all the more necessity to stand by him'.

L/Sgt. C. Bosward claimed the boys were busting for some action which had been put off too long by indecisive leaders. 'Another beautiful day. My cold coming on again. Have one handkerchief — the big red one Mother gave me at Randwick Camp. It has not been washed since last week in March. There is hardly a spot left now and one needs a handkie when he has a heavy cold. Things are awfully quiet and tiresome. Our boys are just dying to make a big attack (risk being cut up). The life of watching and waiting and sap sap tunnel, is the rottenest game out and will soon dishearten anybody. To be digging under the earth not knowing what moment Turks who may possibly be digging beneath you will blow

Thursday 24 June
DAY 61

BY MID-JUNE THE BRITISH AND
ALLIED FORCES HAD FINALLY
LANDED ENOUGH SUPPLIES AT
LANCASHIRE LANDING (W
BEACH) TO FEED AND SERVICE
THE FORCES FIGHTING THE
BLOODY BATTLES AT CAPE
HELLES. AWM G00313

one up. This watching and waiting game is worse than all the fighting and hills on earth. It is one constant fatigue and the weather and hills and conditions under which one works do not make it easier.

'My word! What the Austrnln papers are doing I don't know. We read of the casualties but the papers don't appear to be showing 1/20th of them. Why one paper said of the first 2 fighting days casualties 385. I saw myself at least 5,000. Think of all I didn't see … Tonight went with Lieut. Massie up to try a new bomb. He had one attached to a piece of string and was swinging it round. Just had a good swing up when string broke. She hit the ground and gee! What an explosion. Mr Massie was hit with chips in about a dozen places but very small punctures. Nobody else was hit. I went with him to the beach where he was kept for transfer to hospital ship next morning. Got back here about midnight. Some Scottish Territorials arrived with Howitzers.'

Friday
25 June
DAY 62

A keen-eyed Lt T.J. Richards noted some warships still managed to sail through Anzac waters if they took precautions. 'This afternoon the "Lord Nelson" came up from Cape Helles with seven torpedo boats as a guard against submarine attack. It seemed almost pathetic that a warship's existence depended almost upon the activeness of these small craft. The "Lord Nelson" fired some 10 big gun shots across the Peninsula and a lot of 6 in. shots and then went back again to Cape Helles. While the "Lord Nelson" was shelling the Turks poured in shrapnel which the warship never replied to. Flashes were seen with every shot coming from the top of a high hill and our men were quite indignant that we did not fire on them but this only rose the question as to whether they were false flashes or not, so intricate is this war business.'

End of Week 9

Chaplain E.N. Merrington was impressed with some Anzac ingenuity which he spotted on his pre-Sabbath day pastoral rounds. 'I made a tour of our firing trenches talking to the men from one end to the other, on Pope's Post. On Quinn's wire-netting has been set up to protect the trenches from bombs. The wire-netting serves to roll them off, so that they explode harmlessly in front of the trenches. The Turks are so close to our men there they are not likely to try to shell the wire-netting. The enemy's new gun positions seem to be increasing, and he shells Pope's, Walker's Ridge and the beach with high explosive ammunition. I must round the regiments in the afternoon.'

BELOW: ALTHOUGH JUST AS DANGEROUS, LANDING ONTO PIERS AT CAPE HELLES FROM LARGE TRANSPORT SHIPS LIKE THE *RIVER CLYDE* WAS A VERY DIFFERENT EXPERIENCE FOR BRITISH AND ALLIED FORCES, COMPARED TO ANZACS WHO OFTEN HAD TO WADE THROUGH THE WATER AS THEY SCRAMBLED ASHORE FROM OPEN BOATS AT ANZAC COVE.

Saturday
26 June
DAY 63

Sunday
27 June
DAY 64

It might have been Sunday and a day of worship for the Christians among the Anzacs, but 'The Turks concentrated about 10 guns of assorted sizes and from various directions on our trenches at day break'. Lt Col. Reynell wrote that they 'bombarded us solidly for two and a half hours. Maj. Gregory, the second in command of the 8th was killed' and 'most of us had headaches for hours and some were quite deaf and have remained so for days'.

The effect of this shelling reminded a Queensland chaplain of church services at home. Chaplain Merrington, of the Australian Light Horse, felt the service was stopped by shells in the same way it had been back home by coughing. 'The weather is simply roasting. I do not remember such trying heat, even in the Queensland summer. But of course, here we have no shelter. We live like rabbits in the ground, and there is no shade from trees. I was awakened this morning by a vicious bombardment on our trenches and dug-outs. The valley fairly shook with the battle-din. We had our service just the same at the foot of the hill, followed by Communion. It was a good service, and well attended. The extra noise made it more difficult than usual to speak so as to be heard; and a good many sentences had to be started over again, after being drowned in the crash of shells bursting close at hand. But one gets used to the premonitory scream of the shell, and is often able to pause, just as one stops speaking in church at home sometimes, when a person is coughing, and then goes on again.'

Monday
28 June
DAY 65

The British and Indian troops at Helles mounted yet another offensive on the western flank at Gully Spur. Perhaps inspired by the French success, they managed to secure a limited victory. After some ferocious fighting, they captured five lines of trenches advancing half a mile and then occupied Gully Spur. It cost 4,000 British casualties and as Lt Desmond O'Hara wrote to his fiancé, the battle was followed by 'A bloody red sunset that closed a day of bloodiness for us survivors were in a condition bordering on lunacy where it was all over'. The Turks counterattacked, forcing Allied troops to continue their offensive in a long drawn out fight that lasted until 5 July.

On the same day at Anzac Cove, the Australians mounted a diversionary attack in the Quinn's Post area pounding the Turks with punishing fire. Unlike the last diversionary action requested by the British, the Australians managed this time to attack before rather than after the main offensive at Helles. The Turks counterattacked at the Quinn's Post-Pope's Hill section of Anzac Cove and fighting continued for days after.

Albert Facey lost his brother Roy during this offensive. As Facey wrote in his autobiography, *A Fortunate Life*, 'the English were hard-pressed at Cape Helles a few miles right of our position, and we were to make an attack on the Turks in front of our trenches to draw them away. At some time in the afternoon we got an order to go over the top and attack the Turks. I was in the first lot to go. We had to run down hill as our trenches were on a higher position than the Turks. Below the hill there was a dry watercourse — it was some distance from our position but only about thirty yards from the Turk's trenches. Some twenty of us reached this watercourse and we were quite safe there from rifle-fire, but the Turks gave us a bad time with shelling. A lot of boys were killed and many wounded. We waited for the shelling to ease off before we charged the Turks' trenches. Just before we made our move we picked up a signal to retire back as we achieved our objective — the Turks had broken off the attack on the English at Cape Helles. We had to get back as best we could and were ordered not to take any unnecessary risks ... on arriving back I was told that Roy had been killed ... We had been through a lot together ... I helped to bury Roy and fifteen of our mates who had also been killed ... We put them in a grave side by side on the edge of a clearing we called Shell Green. Roy was in pieces when they found him. We put him together as best we could — I can remember carrying a leg — it was terrible'.

Maj. T.H. Redford recorded an account of the fighting at Quinn's Post in his diary. 'Heavy rifle fire during the evening, about midnight the Turks attacked our position in force creeping to within a few yards of the trenches. The left flank held by a Squadron of the 9th and B and C Sqdns of the 8th bore the brunt of the attack. We had splendid men in Tprs T.A. Wallace and G.A. Jeffries killed in the forward T sap and Tpr Brace, Hayball and Makeham were severely wounded and Deed had his thumb blown off. There were a couple of minor casualties. Two of C Sqdn were killed and two or three wounded. Our men, especially B Sqdn behaved splendidly. They held the forward saps where others failed. Tpr Sanderson, who was beside Wallace when he was killed, held the left flank of our No. 4 sap although Turks had got in on his left and fired on him. They probably accounted for poor Wallace. Sanderson shot two Turks and prevented others from coming on. The official estimate of the enemy killed and captured is 300. The casualties of the 9th were slight.' Maj. Redford was killed in action at Walker's Ridge on 7 July 1915.

Tuesday
29 June
DAY 66

Casualties at clearing hospitals on Anzac beach mounted. Charles Bean wondered 'if any big attack took place you might have 2,000 or 3,000 wounded on the beach and the hospital would be insufficient'. He noticed 'the seas washing almost up to the doors of their tents ... what will happen when it really gets rough and blows a S. pr S.W. gale I don't know'.

Wednesday 30 June
DAY 67

The day was windy with rough weather conditions building up to a fierce thunderstorm that evening. Sneaking a quiet moment while sheltering from the storm, Pte. George Irving wrote to his sweetheart of the horrors of the last few days and weeks. 'Dear Jeannie Just a few lines to let you know that I am well hoping this will find you all the same. I have been in the firing line since I came here. I was a bit timmid at first when they started to shell us but I have got used to it. I was sitting down having dinner in the trenches when a Turks shell came in and struck the trench and buried two fellows that was sitting beside me

Plugge's Plateau

Maclagan's Ridge.

ANZAC COVE

but we worked hard and got them out they were unconscious when we got them out — we are getting good food but the trenches are alive with lice and you would think we were monkeys … it is terrible to see the fellows that is killed by the shells some have their head and legs blown off. I seen one of the McPhearsons last night he was going away to the Base for a rest and he said that his brother was killed. I could not get any writing paper or invlopes some of the fellows was giving 5/- for a sheet of paper and invlope but I could not manage to get one … I wish the war was over so as a fellow could settle down in piece. I will draw to a close from your loving sweetheart George.'

Despite bad weather, Lt Col. Reynell says 'on Wednesday morning at 12.30 the Turks made a real attack on our trenches after they made two demonstrations' but 'the attack was easily repulsed and they left from two to three hundred dead in front of our trenches. About 15 prisoners were also captured who gave us a lot of interesting information. One of them was an Armenian'.

OPPOSITE: PLUGGE'S PLATEAU, STRAIGHT UP THE CLIFFS FROM ANZAC COVE AND THE FIRST CLIFF TOP REACHED ON 25 APRIL, WAS BY MAY STRONGLY DEFENDED AND VERY MUCH A PART OF THE ANZAC SETTLEMENT. MACLAGAN'S RIDGE WAS NAMED AFTER MAJ. SINCLAIR-MACLAGAN, THE COMMANDER OF THE 3RD BRIGADE, THE FIRST TO LAND AT GALLIPOLI.

AUSTRALIAN GUNNERS DEVELOPED A FORMIDABLE REPUTATION FOR SPEED AND ACCURACY AT GALLIPOLI, WHICH WAS CONFIRMED BY TURKISH PRISONERS OF WAR WHO SAID THE ANZACS' HIGH STRIKE RATE HAD PUT THE FEAR OF GOD INTO THEM.

CHAPTER 5
JULY
Talk of Mutiny

I would not care a rap if 75 per cent of our officers had a wooden cross over his head. Half of our duty men are taken up digging most secure dugouts for officers or washing shirts for them in half a bucket of water while other men are almost famished for a drink. By god if ever I am asked to dig a dugout for one or wash their shirts I will be shot at daybreak for refusing to obey an order on Active Service.

Pte. J.K. Gammage, 1st Battalion,
AIF, Diary, 25 July 1915

The hot month of July proved a turning point for the Gallipoli campaign. The latest Allied offensives at Helles had all failed with great loss of life. Not surprisingly, with so much blood on his hands, the 'Butcher of Helles', Maj. Gen. Hunter-Weston would break down and have to return to England before the end of July. Admitting defeat in the Helles theatre, the British War Council decided to concentrate on Anzac Cove for one last offensive. They aimed to dislodge the Turks from the heights and open the road to Constantinople and the Dardanelles. Although all the offensives at Anzac Cove had ended in stalemate because of the difficult terrain, the British high command still clung to the idea of victory at Gallipoli. Lord Kitchener sent a new Corps commander, the ageing Lt Gen. Sir Frederick Stopford, 61, along with three divisions of reinforcements. A force of 60,000 men, the cream of British youth, would bolster the troops at Anzac Cove in a new offensive on three fronts.

Gen. Hamilton had claimed that if he had enough troops he could capture the Gallipoli peninsula. When the 10th, 11th and 13th Divisions arrived, he would be proven right or wrong. If wrong, he would be recalled to London. Recruiting had also continued in Australia and New Zealand, which sent a contingent of 500 Maoris. In late July, plans for an August offensive were organised. However, the veteran Turkish army at Gallipoli had also built up their numbers from an inexhaustible local pool of men ready, willing and able to defend their homeland.

While the leaders were planning new offensives, ordinary soldiers — who could die in these new battles — were becoming discontented. With little to do during the long lull, they had time to think, criticise and complain. They had already seen thousands die in mismanaged, poorly led battles that achieved little or no results. They had lost respect for their officers — especially British officers. Some had heard of the British lieutenant who had been recommended for the Victoria Cross for shooting his own men at Helles when they tried to get out of harm's way.

The battlefields were littered with corpses which Corp. Alec Riley said 'looked like a midden and smelt like an opened cemetery'. As the weather turned hotter, the men also got sicker. Flies feasted on the unburied or half buried corpses and then landed on the food spreading disease through the hundreds of trenches and dugouts. The men, without proper toilets, had to empty their bowels and bladders in open pits. Of the 1,400 evacuated each week in July, 75 per cent were sick rather than wounded.

Lice were also a major irritation as a frustrated New Zealander wrote: 'They were beasts of prey and of a most voracious nature' because 'they moved with a certain cold, passionless persistence in quest of blood ... we itched and scratched until we were tired with scratching'. Maggots, according to Corp. Alec Riley, were also disgusting. 'We lived in a headquarters of maggots. Pale, wriggling, stinking, blasted things and as we sat on the ledge we watched the sandy trench floor heaving with them'.

July was also traditionally a rebellious month with memories of the successful American Revolution on 4 July in 1776, followed by the successful French Revolution on 14 July 1789. In fact, this 14 July a lot of disgruntled French soldiers down at Helles got so drunk they could not even turn up for duty.

Thursday
1 July
DAY 68

There was never a shortage of home thoughts from abroad, especially on anniversaries. Chaplain E.N. Merrington wrote that 'The weather is cooler after last night's storm. The rain did not last long, and this morning is bright and fresh. It is the anniversary of my wedding-day; and my thoughts are with my wife and children in far-off Australia. I know they will be thinking anxiously of me'.

Friday
2 July
DAY 69

Despite the stalemate at Anzac Cove, L/Sgt. C. Bosward remained optimistic about the future. 'Fine day. 12 noon. Sent up huge box kite which let drop a parachute which on opening let loose numbers of sheets of paper. Now very dull, sea choppy, air cool, likely to rain. Rumors of a mail further reports state that Turks casualties during advance at Cape Helles were enormous. Some rushed at the British and French lines with hands in the air (total Turkish casualties since commencement of fighting on Gallipoli are reported to be 90,000). The captured Turks or I should say the Turks who surrendered reckon that we are great shots. They are full of admiration for Austns and NZ's shooting and fighting generally and admit being terrified. They are ordered not to use loopholes at daytime as they are sure to be potted. They are told all sorts of lies to urge them on and when they attacked were told that only a few thousand Australians were in trenches whom they had to drive into the sea. (which they'll never do while there is an Austln. alive).'

End of Week 10

Saturday 3 July
DAY 70

After a photographic tour of strategic locations, Lt T.J. Richards was confident they had the upper hand over the Turks. 'We slept out last night but got no work to do. It started to rain and blow but did not come to much, though the weather has been cool of late and the sea fairly rough in the surf for our barges to land. I noticed while coming along the beach to-day that some 10–16 punts and large provision barges have been blown or washed ashore. We will miss them very much too, more so the water barges. There has been no fresh water on the beach for several days but the many deep wells along Shrapnel Gully now have good water in them, though it's a long wait to get the tins and cans filled. With the camera I started at 10.30 a.m. for Shrapnel Valley, taking a photo. of Fred Thompson's grave and going on past the water-holes up to Quinn's Post where great alterations have been made since the 15th Battalion first made the trenches and hung on to them for four weeks under bomb, rifle, machine gun and artillery fire without either sand-bags or shelters. Now the New Zealanders are holding it and have wood and iron bomb-proof shelters overhead, with steel loopholes to shoot through and where the trenches are open wire-netting bomb-screens are raised. The Turks' trenches opposite are terribly dilapidated and battered and instead of them commanding the position as of old we have it easily in hand. I took some four photos. in and around Quinn's and came back over Walker's Ridge and brought Jack Hynes back to dinner. A second swim at 9 p.m. was lovely. Photographed Quinn's grave and Indians watering mules.'

Sunday 4 July
DAY 71

Driver E. Brown noted the fighting in the harbour with British and French ships participating. 'Some old shells still coming over but very little damage done. British battleship came up and bombarded opposite side. While witnessing this engagement saw a French transport sinking when torpedoed, hit in stern and gradually reared straight up in air and sunk fairly quick. From when I first saw this to the end would be about 7 to 10 min. Shortly afterward a transport opened fire on water towards Tenders. Battleship left and went to Lemnos. Heavy shower of rain fell during night. Torpedoes scouting around. About 11 a.m. today a big explosion happened in French camp a magazine blew up.' With a journalist's eye, Charles Bean noted 'A shell landed in the dentist's dugout, and covered the hillside with false teeth'.

In Gully Ravine down at Helles, the Turks mounted their biggest counter offensive at dawn. It failed. The Turks were unable to push the British forces back. Over the eight days of this battle, they had lost 16,000 soldiers.

This last day of the Gully Ravine battle was the worst. Sgt. James Parker noted heavy enemy firing just before the British stopped their costly offensive. 'Base under heavy fire from 4 a.m. everyone there under shelter, no rations till evening. Turks gave us our heaviest shelling since landing, sending over thousands of shells, shrapnel and high explosive, from 10 pdrs., up to 11.2 from warships, both from Achi Baba and Asiatic side. Over 600 dropped around bty between 4 a.m. and 8 a.m. Trip for amm. to base 5.30 a.m., then to bty, shells dropping galore, plenty of unexploded ones to dodge, taking wagons up. Others dropping in gun pits and dug outs, one in Jim Fraser's but not exploding, and one smashing rifle in O Sul gun pit. Turks made 5 attacks on trenches, but were repulsed with heavy losses. Heavy bomb duels between front trenches, bty in action all the time, mowing enemy down in heaps ... Maj. again thanked us and complimented officers on our Batt.'s splendid shooting and beating the Turk's attacks ... Over 700 big shells in base during day. ASC wagon line suffering heavily,

ONE OF THE BEST INVENTIONS OF THE ANZACS WAS THE PERISCOPE RIFLE THROUGH WHICH SOLDIERS COULD SEARCH FOR THE ENEMY WITHOUT PUTTING THEIR HEADS OVER THE TOP. HAVING AIMED, THEY COULD 'BAG' ANOTHER TURK, ALL FROM THE SAFETY OF THE TRENCH.

several wagon lines smashed, also ordnance and hospital. 60 per bty. missed by feet several times. Trip to base 10 p.m., 2 wagon loads then to bty, and one load from dump to bty. French transport sunk by submarine early in afternoon, sinking in 3- minutes off base.'

When the fighting at Gully Ravine ended on 5 July, 10,000 Turks had been killed in the battle. Corpses littered the battlefield in the mid summer heat. The Turks asked for a truce to bury their dead. Though the Allies had their own dead lying in no-man's-land, the inhumane Maj. Gen. Hunter-Weston refused the request, hoping to demoralise the Turks. The result, however, was to increase the spread of disease for both armies dramatically.

At Anzac Cove where they had their share of unburied corpses, filth, flies and disease, Bean noted that 'we are now losing about 100 men a day — today in both Divisions it was about 150 — almost entirely by sickness.' Lt Col. Reynell calculated 'Our losses during the 6 weeks we have been here in killed and wounded amounted to 80, which is nearly 20 per cent of our strength on landing. We also have nearly a third of our strength away sick in hospital … we actually have 135 absent sick and they are going away every day faster than they come back'.

Tuesday 6 July
DAY 73

After weeks of constant shelling and firing, S/Sgt. Leslie Goldring suddenly found it 'Most horribly quiet, really unlike war'. But at least he was getting mail as he 'received a letter from Harold saying Eric has gone to England and he expects to go at any time'.

Later that day Sgt. McPherson confirmed the feeling of quiet. 'An exceptionally quiet day; have had Turkish "Orders" brought in by prisoners which say that they do not intend attacking us as when we attack them our losses are so great therefore Turks must win if they hold on and wait for us to take offensive.'

Wednesday 7 July
DAY 74

Charles Bean transferred to a new base for journalists on the nearby island of Imbros from where he had to commute to Anzac Cove. He says he sailed back on a warship's steamboat to the Anzac beach to gather more stories 'on a scorching hot day' but exhausted by the travel and heat 'was fit for little on arrival'. He was not the only one suffering from lassitude on this mid summer's day, as Ambulance man S/Sgt. Leslie Goldring described it as 'Quiet all day', saying he also 'went for swim.'

On 'another quiet day', Chaplain W.E. Dexter had a couple of lucky escapes from sniper fire. 'The day is rather hot and muggy and at 9 a.m. the Turks began shelling and making it hotter. Throughout the day shelling continued as far as we are concerned with no casualties. The monitor came over and fired a number of shells. In the afternoon I got sniped at twice. Just outside the dugout, so in the evening a fatigue party built up a bank to protect Headquarters. A few days ago I wrote that I thought a submarine had been caught just off us. Today the same phenomenon occurred and I have come to the conclusion that it is our trawlers experimenting with gas. The Turks have gas bombs on the way for us and possibly we are preparing to get in first. Each man has a respirator and these are kept close at hand in the trenches and wherever men are stationed so they can be got at a moments notice. It only wants the Turks to send some gas bombs at us and our boys will get that mad there will be no holiday then. They will simply go over the enemy trenches and not stop for anything ... At night time our flanks are guarded by two destroyers and to see them with their search lights shining on the hills reminds one of two unblinking eyes ever watching. As the search lights roam over the hills and gullies and those on board see any of the enemy they immediately fire and their guns go any hour of the night!'

Col. Monash noted —with some disappointment — the historic significance of the first post bringing reports of the 25 April landing. 'There is great excitement this evening. A mail from Australia has come in, the first bringing papers and letters since the news of the landing had reached Australia. This valley is now one fluttering mass of newspapers — a few of which I have had a peep at. The latest date is 9 May, and I notice that in the casualty lists published up to that date in Australia, practically only those names are given of wounded who died at sea or in hospital after leaving here. None of the names of those killed in action during 25–27 April appeared to have reached Australia ... I am afraid Australia will get a terrible shock when it gets the full lists later, and I grieve very much for the anxiety you must be feeling about me ... My own opinion is that the worst is now over, and that the rest of the fighting on the Gallipoli Peninsula will not be anything like so severe as what is past. The Turks have done their dash, and are now terribly frightened of us Australians. They have altogether given up their furious attack. As far as the dead, they have made their sacrifice and there is nothing to be done but to bury them in our little cemetery and reverently inscribe their names in the roll of Australia's fallen heroes. That Australia will honour the memory of all such, we are all well assured.'

Friday
9 July
DAY 76

With no plan of action and little to do, soldiers like Lt T.J. Richards felt increasingly rebellious and began challenging their superior officers. 'Captain Welch returned a letter to Father as being too big. I went and asked him what the damnable regulations say on the matter. He maintained that Maj. Stokes' orders were "one page only", and that he was sorry but would put it through the 4th Field Ambulance for me. I declined with thanks and told him that Major Stokes was both inconsiderate and mean, and acted as though he was a demi-god. We who in civil life were his equal were treated as low conscripts instead of free volunteers and men of reason. Seeing that we have nothing to read, and amidst such monotony we grow livery and dull-witted — so that it was in the interest of the Corps to encourage the fellows to write and exercise their minds in other ways than gossiping, cursing and swearing. I feel much hurt over this matter. If we were moving on and the censor officers had some work to do, I would be the last to complain, but they are all actually loafing and it does hurt me to think that we who are exposing ourselves to danger every day cannot get a decent letter through to our friends and relatives regardless of the subject dealt with. In this particular case I was dealing with a unique Church service, nothing else, and to Father who would much appreciate it, such being a purely religious topic. The gun enfilading us on the right flank is now called "Beachy Bill". It has done a lot of damage. On the left flank there is a nasty gun too. It is more silent than ours. The fellows call it "Lonely Liz".'

APART FROM SHOOTING ENEMY TURKS WITH THEIR RIFLES OR HEAVY ARTILLERY, THE ANZACS ATTACKED THEM WITH BOMBS WHICH THEY LEARNED TO THROW THROUGH PRACTICE SESSIONS HELD IN SHRAPNEL VALLEY.

End of Week 11

Others coped with the boredom by reading rather than writing. With so much time on their hands, Bean noted 'It is curious how men get back to simpler habits during a time like this. I have found one or two officers starting to read the bible — and one told me he found it extraordinarily interesting'.

S/Sgt. Leslie Goldring used the spare time he had that quiet Saturday to keep his hand and eye in practice with his 303 rifle saying, 'Fired a few rounds registration at a target — again very quiet'.

Saturday 10 July
DAY 77

Attending religious services in the outdoor churches on Sundays took a bit of courage. Chaplain Merrington noted 'A welcome Australian mail arrived. Were home letters ever so much appreciated as on Gallipoli, where we are shut off from the world, except the world at war? We had good services today … When dusk came on there were about 500 soldiers gathered in Pope's Reserve Gully … While the address was proceeding a rather amusing incident occurred … I was dimly conscious that enemy high-explosive shells were bursting near Courtney's Post … Suddenly I observed the whole of my congregation "duck" down flat on the ground, like a field of wheat struck by a heavy squall. I was nonplussed for the fraction of a second, thinking that the Turks must be coming down the ravine behind me, and the first law of nature asserted itself to such an extent that I "ducked" my head and half turned to look behind me. All in an instant it happened, although it takes so long to describe. A big fragment of high-explosive shell came tearing across the ravine; and it buried itself with a huge smack in the hillside. It passed just over the heads of the men sitting in the track. A laugh went up all around over the affair, and, of course, partly at the expense of the speaker'.

Sunday 11 July
DAY 78

The British and French mounted yet another offensive at Helles commanded by Maj. Gen. Hunter-Weston that this time was aimed at capturing Achi Baba Nullah. Inexperienced and newly arrived soldiers of the 155th Brigade led the attack. They were slaughtered by the veteran Turkish defenders. The 157th Brigade also inexperienced followed in the attack and they too were decimated. By nightfall the offensive had failed and survivors were sheltering alongside corpses

Monday 12 July
DAY 79

killed in earlier battles. The French did little better. This assault lasted two days before being called off.

Coping with the mounting death toll could be horrendous even for an experienced ambulance man like S/Sgt. Leslie Goldring. 'The Battery stood by at 4.30 a.m. at this time an attack was in full swing by the 29th Div. on the right flank at 6.30 a.m. the first shot was fired we fired during the day 1032 Rounds which is a long way in lead of the other days we have had we remained in action until 9 p.m., and I believe did excellent work. The Turks received an awful grueling and many prisoners were taken. Our infantry gained all that they set out for. The sight one sees are ungodly. To pass from one trench to another one must walk on the bodies of dead some instances 5 and 6 deep, though I am happy to say these corpses are mostly Turks who were killed by the violent Artillery bombardment preparatory to the advance of the Infantry. The stench from the bodies is unbearable. We had heavy casualties but not to be compared with the Turkish ... The French on the right did all that was asked for by them. Streams of wounded come past, and also prisoners in Batches of 20 or so. Some well provided for others far from it. German officers were also taken. Many other prisoners could have been taken had not the Turkish machine guns and Artillery mowed them down when coming to surrender. After these 14 hours hard going no one were sorry when the order came down to break off.'

Tuesday 13 July
DAY 80

The offensive at Helles aimed at capturing Achi Baba Nullah ended with only the smallest territorial gain. Maj. Gen. Hunter-Weston had learnt nothing. Even when the British sent in experienced Royal Naval Division troops they could not penetrate the Turkish front line. In this two-day battle the Turks sacrificed 9,600. The war-weary British foot soldiers advanced only 500 yards on the Helles front. In the three major battles in June and July the British suffered 12,300 casualties. The Turks lost 30,000 in the same bloody period. Although the Turks also lost 40,000 men overall, they were able to replace them quickly with reinforcements, being on their home ground and defending their homeland.

A meagre 500-yard gain seemed to please Maj. Gen. Hunter-Weston enormously, as Maj. R. Davidson revealed that 'the progress of the day had greatly satisfied him I could see and he was in great glee'. Fortunately, this battle was the last for the 'Butcher of Helles'. Maj. Gen. Hunter-Weston suffered a nervous breakdown soon after and was recalled to England. Despite his costly failures at Gallipoli, he was feted at home and received the highest military and civil honours including a subsequent appointment as Governor of Gibraltar.

An ordinary seaman like Joe Murray was aware of the costly price the soldiers paid for incompetent officers. 'It is pitiful to see men, not long ago strong and healthy, now with drawn faces and staring eyes, struggling towards the firing line. Most of them should be in hospital. They are cheating death but only just. They are walking corpses — the ghosts of Gallipoli'.

S/Sgt. Leslie Goldring revealed that some of the devastation from this conflict was so 'ungodly' he could not describe it. 'Stood by at 4.30 again this morning and fired 460 rounds in the afternoon when we made another attack in the centre. We hear that our Battery again did excellent work on the previous day which we were lucky enough to escape without a casualty but to-day we're far less fortunate and had 6 men wounded, during the last two days the bullets have been very thick around the Battery and have wounded at least 10 Tommies and Frenchmen. The Turkish Artillery fire has been deadly on our trenches, but our chaps appeared to go through it as it were a rain-storm. Again to-day we gained all that was set out for I understand that most of our casualties have been through the men being too eager to advance and went to far and had to retire. Capt. Callaghan and Cpl. Todd are in the front trenches and have done excellent work and necessarily had to advance with the Infantry. Their accounts of the trenches is not fit to write as some episodes I have learnt from them as I have said are ungodly. In action 6 hours'.

Optimists like Lt Col. Reynell still dreamed of a combined success through the Helles and Anzac campaigns. 'There is no doubt that a move will be made now before many weeks. I am tipping the idea is to make a crushing blow when our boys at Helles get the Turks on the run and collar Achi Baba after which we will push across to cut off their retreat by land' and 'we expect that at least another division will be landed here for the forward movement as we shall have such a long line to hold'.

In between the bloody battles, some of the disenchanted French soldiers managed to get some alcohol. They drank great quantities to drown their sorrows and celebrate their 14 July Bastille Day. After repeatedly toasting the success of their revolutionary past in overthrowing King Louis IV, their thoughts turned to overthrowing such British dictators as Maj. Gen. Hunter-Weston. There was a lot of rebellious talk and swearing but nothing came of it. By the next day, they had to prepare for the battlefield.

Wednesday
14 July
DAY 81

At Anzac Cove trying to bathe was still a precarious venture. E.N. Merrington noted that 'On returning to Anzac I went to Chaplain McPhee's dug-out, on the heights above the beach in Headquarters Gully. After tea we were sitting in front for some time, talking, and watching the bathers, who were very numerous on the Beach below. It was getting quite dark; when suddenly we saw the flash of a shell burst amid the forms of bathers who were dressing on a barge. Stretcher-bearers were called for at once; and we saw 4 of those that had been enjoying a bathe a few minutes before carried along the Beach towards the hospital. We went down, and found Capt. Campbell, a medical officer lying on the operating table, with his feet shot away … I understand there is no hope of his recovery. The other three who were standing by when the shell burst on the barge were also seriously wounded. When this tragic incident occurred the darkness was so far advanced that bathing might have been considered safe; but the Turks had evidently waited for this hour, and fired a high-explosive shell at the barge which they knew was patronised by bathers, and whose range they had ascertained with terrible precision.'

Thursday
15 July
DAY 82

The celebration of France's national day suddenly made S/Sgt. Leslie Goldring wonder about his own Jewish anniversaries. 'Practically the same as yesterday. The Frenchmen are walking around about with very sore heads as yesterday was there "Fete Nationale" and the majority imbibed too freely. I was wondering this morning how many "Jewish" holidays have passed as I have observed none at Gallipoli. The Jew is not catered for in any way which I think is a pity, certainly they are greatly in the minority here but still all other religions are catered for and I think the Jew is loyal to their country and why not have some little service for them. One no doubt learns here that he has a lot to thank the Almighty for and the only way one has is to say his prayers before retiring to rest. It is hardly the place for one to read his bible here as one is interrupted in many ways'.

Friday
16 July
DAY 83

Like many soldiers in the trenches, Lt R. Arnold was more interested in recording the minute details of his own personal routine. 'Up early got breakfast ready. Had breakfast then returned water tank and straightened up our camp. Moved out 10.30 and marched with kit to Headquarters and allotted to tents at new camp. Had dinner and about 4 o'clock went for swim. 18 of us went on guard tonight round camp'.

End of Week 12

After twelve weeks on the peninsula, Charles Bean decided to do a tour of the front line for his newspaper readers back home. 'Our front is pretty well protected now although we couldn't guarantee the front trenches everywhere. The mistake was that we did not begin with a regular plan — we only woke up to that necessity recently'. The model fortification was Quinn's Post which had been, 'absolutely transformed since my last visit. It is laid out in terraces, each with a shed on them with an iron roof, well sandbagged under which the supporters sleep'. Quinn's Post was also 'well bomb proofed by wires and our bomb throwers can throw their bombs from behind the wires'. The Anzacs at Quinn's Post had dug a series of tunnels in front of their position under Turkish trenches that they were systematically blowing up. 'The one we exploded opposite Johnson's Jolly today flung two Turks into the air and made a big crater so the Turkish trench must have been right above it.'

Corp. H. McKern was most impressed with the safety provided by these forward fortifications. 'Paid visit to left wing where I had been first days here. Position on left splendid especially No. 1 & 2 outposts. Indian mule transport etc all camped there in safety.' McKern was wounded at Lone Pine on 6 August and died 15 August 1915.

LANDING SOLDIERS AND SUPPLIES WAS ALWAYS DANGEROUS AT GALLIPOLI. ONCE A VESSEL, LIKE THE DESTROYER *LOUIS*, BECAME STRANDED IN SUVLA BAY, THE TURKS DID THEIR BEST TO FINISH IT OFF BY FIRING DOWN FROM THE HEIGHTS ABOVE.

Sunday
18 July
DAY 85

Despite distractions, Alan Treloar managed to sit through a Sunday morning church service. 'This morning I went to a divine service at 9.30 a.m. I have attended some strange services since I left Australia, but perhaps this one was the strangest of all. We met down in a gully below our HQ and there is the shelter of the cliffs we worshipped our God. On the top of the cliff a party of Maori soldiers were hard at work dragging iron tanks about and it was to the accompaniment of this noise we sang our hymns. For the address we "disposed ourselves as comfortably as possible", to use the words of the chaplain. Now and then through our midst men walked with their water cans and frequently we could hear the whistle of a bullet as it passed overhead. The text was from Rev. 21:5, "And He that sat upon the throne said, Behold I make all things new" … The address was helpful and altogether I felt it was good for me to have been there. During the morning we had many opportunities of watching the Maoris at work. They are fine men and seemed to get through a good deal of work, though loud yells seemed a necessary part of their work. In the afternoon our trenches were shelled fairly heavily and one piece of iron recovered points to the presence of something which throws an 11" spherical shell. However, it did no damage. We hoped the Turks might attack during the night, but our hopes were destined to be disappointed. As usual in the evening I devoted what little spare time I could afford to writing a letter home. I am not writing a good deal to friends in Australia at present for I feel unable to make the effort. I got to bed somewhere around 11.30 p.m. and fell immediately into a heavy sleep.'

Despite an unbearable toothache, 2nd Lt W.M. Cameron was having second thoughts about having visited the dentist. 'Last night was about the most agonising I have spent here. I had severe toothache and determined to have it drawn; this morning I held to my determination, and am wondering whether the cure is not as bad as the ache. It will be better when the gums heal, I suppose. Towards evening the Turks began shelling, but the shells went over our trenches to the reserves. We are holding an "easy" line just now. They threw several bombs last night also, one of which damaged a water barrel and wounded one man. The explosion threw two others out of their beds. All night long there was considerable restlessness, rockets and searchlights being used continuously, and quite a lot of rifle firing. We really expected an attack, but nothing of any consequence occurred. Tonight I have had a real good feed. Resoulles (can't spell it) well made by our men, sauce, jam, bread, and a lovely "Dixie" of tea.'

Artillery officers like Sgt. F.C. West kept the working guns in order. 'Arrived off Anzac (Gaba Tepe) about 2.30 a.m. sweeper dropped anchor about a mile from the shore … two horse boats came alongside and took off about 400 all told (mostly details). Arrived alongside jetty disembarked then made our way along the shore to the gully in which our Battery horses were. Had breakfast with the drivers and then went on up the hill to the guns where we reported to the O.C. He told us we should have to go back to Alex. Had a look at all our gun pits and over some of the Infantry Trenches. Saw gunfire about 30 rounds about 5.30 p.m. — Went down to beach with fatigue to get timber for roofing in gun pits. Camped in Warren's dugout — The day before our arrival a shell pierced A. gun shield, killed Leonard and Carter and wounded Sgt. Taylor in 19 places — Also heard of Buchanan's death.'

Monday
19 July
DAY 86

At Helles there was a respite in the fighting, as the mentally distraught Maj. Gen. Hunter-Weston was confined to his quarters awaiting transport back to England. Perhaps having seen so many dead and dying soldiers whom he had ordered to cross open ground (as if the machine gun had never been invented), Maj. Gen. Hunter-Weston had realised his errors. Gen. Hamilton said Maj. Gen. Hunter-Weston was now 'Suffering very much from his head' and had locked himself away refusing to see anyone.

Pte. R. Ward, expected the heavily reinforced Turks to carry out their earlier threat to 'push you Australian bastards into the sea — taking no prisoners … Up at 4 o'clock on 5 hours fatigue pulling tanks from the beach up the hill on the extreme right flank. Turks were sniping from Gala Tope. On sentry duty — at shrapnel point from 8 at night until 6 in the morning. Notices appear from G.H. 2 to the effect that the Turks have now brought up all their reserves that was possible for them to muster and they will make their final attack all along our front at any moment. They number 100,000 of trained and untrained men who are unwillingly fighting under German officers-ship and are only fighting because they do not want to see the downfall of Constantinople. Sickness, lack of food and proper sanitation is reported by the prisoners we have, to be very hard in the Turks lines. We have landed a number of 5 inch Howitzers to use against the Turks when they try to break through our lines. Our aero planes and nav. have been giving them soothing syrup these last few days. The weather remains awfully hot.'

Tuesday
20 July
DAY 87

ALTHOUGH THE TRENCHES
WERE ESSENTIAL FOR
SURVIVAL, WITH SO MANY MEN
CROWDED INTO THEM THEY
INEVITABLY BECAME BREEDING
GROUNDS FOR FLEAS, LICE,
FLIES AND DISEASE.

Wednesday
21 July
DAY 88

The latest rumour was that a poison gas attack was imminent. Sgt. R.L. Hampton made sure he was prepared for any Turkish attack using this deadly weapon. 'The whole of the troops on the Peninsula has been issued with respirators for use against poisonous gases. I have got two kinds. One a small pad of cotton waste with black attachment. The other is a flannel helmet with cellose eye piece.'

Thursday
22 July
DAY 89

Sgt. F.C. West, from the artillery, hoped the Turks would attack because it might get him out of a court case in Alexandria where he was to be tried for some unexplained breach of discipline. 'Went up to the guns. Was told to report to Corp. Brierly of A. Sub. as acting gunner together with Irvine and was told that that would be my job for good. Graham was put on the telephone and Fyfe with the horses. Brierly put us through some laying. Afternoon working on a gun pit in the infantry trenches for C Sub. Gun, — big attack expected tonight — evening got hold of a rifle bayonet and 2 doz rounds ammunition — going to have a go in with the Inf. if attack comes. Were told that the Provost Marshal at Alex. had ordered us to be sent back there to be dealt with by our O. C.'s there — have to go tomorrow. Capt. Rodgers took our statements of evidence. Maj. Brown told us that our only hope of remaining was for the expected attack to come off when we should probably be forgotten. Evening carrying ammunition to C. guns new pit — ready for attack. Turned in A. and B. gun pits.'

Given how long it had taken to build, Ambulanceman Lt Woods was disappointed that 'Turks damaged the pier'. But taking no chances with his health he had his '2nd inoc. agst. cholera'.

Not all casualties carted to the cemetery were buried, as Driver J.H. Turnbull noted in a packed diary entry. 'We have several tunnels leading from Stiches Post out towards the G.O. trench. We can hear the Turks sapping towards us. It is time then for us to cut a chamber to pack in the explosives, gun-cotton & ammonal & wait for the Turks to be close enough to fire the mine. We have mines now ready to blow up at a moments notice connected to switches in the front line. I have been working in the face. We have carrying parties who carry out the

Friday
23 July
DAY 90

THE MOST SOUGHT AFTER DUGOUTS AT GALLIPOLI WERE THOSE THAT FACED WEST ON THE HILLSIDE WITH A VIEW OF THE BAY OVER WHICH THE SUN SET, OFTEN WITH A BLAZE OF BEAUTIFUL COLOURS.

broken ground in sand bags and empty in the rear of our trenches. Today there was a man who emptied his bag and stood up and was shot in the head by a sniper. He rolled half way down the hill. His mates went down and thought he was dead and carried him to Shrapnel Gully below and laid him with the rest of the dead to be buried that night. Later he came to and was very upset at the company he was in and attracted the notice of passers by who took him to Dressing Station ... This tunneling is not a nice game. There are a lot of dead buried between the trenches and naturally you dive into these bodies. Niches are cut in the sides of our main tunnel and make good sleeping places for men in the line ... Fatigue to the beach to-day and had a look round ... Noticed the Headquarters Office of General Birdwood & Godly of the New Zealanders, with the board outside "A.N.Z.A.C. HQ" The Ceylon Planters Rifle Corps are Headquarters Guard. They seem a superior looking lot of johnnies. Our fellows in swimming as usual until hunted out by Beachy Bill. Birdwood was in swimming one morning. One of the men saw the bald headed man swimming round & promptly ducked him. But he did not know till later it was Birdy. He kept quiet for a day or two.'

End of Week 13

Saturday 24 July

DAY 91

Always searching for reassurance in an anti-semitic culture the Jewish Col. John Monash was pleased to tell his wife 'This morning Lt Gen. Birdwood came round into my section to congratulate me personally on my promotion. He spoke as if he were genuinely pleased and was good enough to say that if anybody deserved the honour I did. This confirms the information in your cable of 10 July, received a few days ago, and was the first local intimation I have had. It soon got about, and congratulations flowed in from all over Anzac. My staff set to work, and by some mysterious means managed to materialise for me a pair of new shoulder badges all ready to put on when the formal announcement is made'.

Monash also hoped for a Turkish attack so the Anzacs could teach the Turks a lesson. 'For the last two days we have been in a state of high expectation. Reliable secret intelligence is to hand that the Turks have assembled a new army of 100,000, and intend to make one supreme final effort to dislodge us. This is playing right into our hands, as we are more than ready for them; there is no possibility of their shifting us, as not only are our preparations complete in every particular, and we have ample guns and munitions, but also man for man we have obtained a remarkable ascendancy over them, in musketry, sharp-shooting, bomb attack, bayonet work and gunnery … So far as I can judge, the prospects of the war are daily becoming more satisfactory.'

The lack of Turkish attacks was actually bad for morale. With no offensives planned or attacks to repel, the more rebellious foot soldiers like Pte. J.K. Gammage started to talk of mutiny. 'Stood to 1 to 5. Still being shelled and starved and overworked. A bit sick and very weak. After doing 24 hours duty was allowed off for 4 hours rest and then put on digging for 6 hours, then was taken off that and given a post for 24 hours. I would like to do another 24 hours digging graves for our lazy mean cowardly officers. I would not care a rap if 75 per cent of our officers had a wooden cross over his head. Half of our duty men are taken up digging *most* secure dugouts for officers or washing shirts for them in half a bucket of water while other men are almost famished for a drink. By god if ever I am asked to dig a dugout for one or wash their shirts I will be shot at daybreak for refusing to obey an order on Active Service. There is one good point about them they can always be found — in their dugouts.'

While some thought of rebellion others, such as L/Cpl. S.R. Mills, thought of roses when writing a Sunday letter to his mother. 'Things are so quiet. Just the same old thing day after day. It is getting very monotonous I can tell you. Judging by the papers we receive here the people in Australia seem to be realising what war is now. There seems to be great difficulty in getting men to enlist. No doubt, there was a bit of a rush on when the casualties were first known but they seem to have slackened off now. You were suggesting in one of your letters to put red geraniums in the garden along the fence. I think that is a splendid idea. They would look just the thing. That is a good idea of Muriel's about the palms. Don't forget to keep George up to the mark in doing a little bit now & then. I wouldn't like to come home & see all my work gone for nothing. Now is the time for all those roses I was so anxious to put in. I don't think I explained to you about the bank book you sent me. I had to destroy it on account of not being able to post it back to you safely. Anyhow, if you keep the book I will always be able to get it when I return home. Well I will say good bye now Love to you all. Roley.'

Sunday 25 July
DAY 92

Monday
26 July

DAY 93

WITH JUST FLAT OPEN GROUND
BETWEEN THEM AND THE
TURKISH TRENCHES AT THE
HELLES FRONTLINE, BRITISH
AND ALLIED FORCES HAD TO
USE PERISCOPES FOR
MONITORING ENEMY ACTIVITIES
— BECAUSE IF THEY SHOWED
THEIR HEAD OVER THE TOP,
THEY RISKED GETTING SHOT.

The Turks may not have charged down the hill, but Pte. R. Ward noted they had moved a big gun into place. 'Turks have got a 75 gun into position close to our left flank and this afternoon they have been very busy with it. Several shells came very close to us bursting less than a chain away. Our howitzers opened fire but never got her. Turks roared out from their trench to the 16th Battalion yesterday "Come on you thieving bastards — we're waiting for you". German officers very likely have learnt them to say that. I made a watch chain out of mule hair.'

Charles Bean, a bookish man of letters, was asked if he would like to take a shot at 'a Turk with his black head and shoulders over the trench top'. He replied 'my job is not to shoot — I am not a combatant — and I will not do so'.

The mid summer heat, filth and flies took their toll as Charles Bean noted. 'About 250 men left Anzac yesterday — most of them men seriously sick with diarrhoea, but some influenza cases which may be typhoid. Our whole Division is living in an area much less than half a square mile and this illness is bound to come with the heat, dust and overwork ... The largest number of acute dysentery cases to date were in fact reported over the last week from 21 July to 27 July with 1,221 cases or nearly five per cent of the men fighting there.'

Finally, the Turks did attack which allowed the Anzacs a chance to test their latest techniques of tunnel warfare. According to Pte. John Henry Turnbull, 'Early last night we blew a mine in our sap, they were tunneling towards us. We heard the Turks groaning for 2 hours. We must have got a good few. We heard the Turks working towards us days before. We have listening tunnels with men who do nothing else but visit these tunnels. At dawn the Turks charged the N.Z. trenches on Pope's Hill. The N.Z. observers saw them climbing over their parapets. They gave them a cheer and blazed into them. The Turks never got halfway losing hundreds. The N.Z. had 27 casualties. It was all over in a few minutes. Our howizers have been busy lately ripping and tearing the Turks trenches to ruins'.

**Tuesday
27 July**
DAY 94

Capt. D.B.A. King tracked down one of the rarest commodities craved by soldiers with a sweet tooth. 'Very warm morning. Gaba Tepe gun firing at our beach and last night also. Got a new shirt and towel yesterday. Our detachment is on the gun to-day. Got some chocolate to-day and nuts and new stores from Hospital Ship. Went to bed early.'

**Wednesday
28 July**
DAY 95

Chaplain W.E. Dexter took care of the daily business of burying the dead. 'At 5 a.m. we shelled Johnston's Jolly and some of the pieces came flying back but nobody was hurt. In the morning I got wood from the beach sufficient to make 50 crosses for the cemetery and got to work on them. The days are very hot and one is constantly bathed in perspiration climbing the hills. 4 p.m. Abdul shelling the 4th Battn. Trenches. Had tea with Capt. Luxton in B coy. Headquarters. Dugout 7 p.m. our aero plane dropped a bomb and shortly afterwards a German Biplane came over lines. The two did not meet and the Germans went away immediately and then our guns save a few more shots at Abdul. This German plane is larger than ours and altogether more powerful.'

**Thursday
29 July**
DAY 96

Nobody was safe from the shelling as Driver F.A. Weeks explained. 'Our depot was again shelled last night and at 1 and 2 this morn. General Birdwood's A.D.C. was killed this morning just outside his dug-out. Capt. Anderson was also seriously wounded, also Major Gibbs. They were in charge of the depot here and both fine fellows. The "monitors" were again shelling the Turkish positions to-day. A German Taube aero plane came over our camp at tea time, and dropped a bomb on our ammun. stock. No damage was done. One of our chaps we left behind in "Alex." came over here on his accord on Wed. night. He is to stay with us till further notice. He said he was tired of Alex. so he cleared out and came over here.'

Friday
30 July
DAY 97

Enemy aeroplanes were the new menace in the skies. B. Hobson noted that they 'Had another visit from a hostile R.Q.M.S. plane, early this morning, but only just flew over our lines and went back again. We had some good news today. Our forces in the Persian Gulf on July 24th absolutely routed the Turks who left all the artillery, ammunition and baggage in our hands. The official list of the Turkish casualties was issued last night for the Gallipoli Peninsula. They have had 120,000 casualties and among these are 30,000 killed.'

Col. Monash wrote home with the best of news that 'Last night we got a cable announcing the grant of the Victoria Cross to Lance-Corporal Jacka of my 14th Battalion. This is the first V.C. in this brigade and this division, and I believe in the whole Army Corps. We are all very jubilant about it. Unfortunately Jacka is away ill, so we can't have a ceremony until he returns to duty'.

End of Week 14

Saturday
31 July
DAY 98

After a bloody struggle Anzac forward soldiers finally secured Leane's Trench, a position on Holly Ridge which they had been battling to capture from the Turks. Chaplain W.E. Dexter recorded details of the successful assault. 'Usual artillery dual, otherwise the day was quiet and nothing much doing. The German plane dropped two bombs in our valley but no harm done. Several isolated cases of wounding took place from fragments of shells. In the evening after sundown the weather looked a bit squally and Abdul got nervy and a little "unpleasantness" took place between him and the New Zealanders. However at 10 p.m.

we attacked on our right ... it was either a case of being blown up or taking the bull by the horns and charging. This the 3rd Brigade did and the casualties were about 12 killed and 70 wounded ... Things were very lively for a while all along the line and at the same time there was evidently fighting down at Achi Baba. Some shells were fired by the Turks and in our lines only one fatality occurred and that about midnight and in the 8th Battn. As the 8th have the worst section of the line when there is likely to be any shelling, they withdraw all their men into saps and trenches not yet opened up. As they are too close to the enemy lines for the Turks to fire upon they are comparatively safe and only a few men remain in the trench proper keeping a lookout, ready at any moment to call the men to their posts in case of a sudden attack. Night was fairly quiet after Abdul had settled down after the attack.'

AFTER MONTHS OF DIGGING AND BUILDING, THE HILLS OF ANZAC HAD BECOME AN ESTABLISHED SETTLEMENT HOUSING THOUSANDS OF 'DIGGERS' WHO LIVED IN A RANGE OF DUGOUTS ARRANGED IN DIFFERENT TERRACES UP THE SLOPE, ALL HOPEFULLY OUT OF RANGE OF TURKISH ARTILLERY. AWM C01734

THE LIGHT HORSE, WHICH PLAYED SUCH A KEY ROLE AT GALLIPOLI, INCLUDED NEW SOUTH WALES COUNTRY BOYS TROOPER COLIN BULL (LEFT), AND TROOPER GERALD DIGBY. ALTHOUGH TROOPER BULL WAS 'SHOT OUT OF THE SADDLE' WHEN THE 12TH LIGHT HORSE SUCCESSFULLY CHARGED BEERSHEBA IN 1917, TROOPER DIGBY SURVIVED THE WAR AND ON HIS RETURN WENT ONTO THE LAND WHERE HE RAISED A FAMILY.

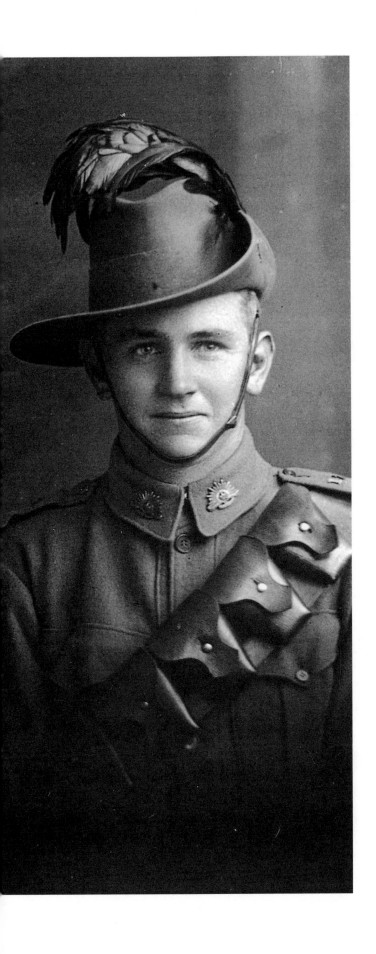

CHAPTER 6

AUGUST

Sending Lambs to Slaughter at Lone Pine & the Nek

LUXURIES FOR THE TURKS

No doubt today has been the fiercest battle in the history of the war.

The first Light Horse were absolutely cut up.

SGT. A.S. HUTTON, 3RD AUSTRALIAN LIGHT HORSE, AIF, DIARY

For the Anzacs, August was a month of killing and being killed. Big battles took place at Lone Pine and the Nek. By early August, plans were in place for the biggest Allied offensive against Turkish defenders at Gallipoli. The British War Council still believed the Allies could invade the peninsula successfully, if not from the south then from the west. Having failed on successive offensives at Helles, they decided to focus on Anzac Cove. Allied commanders, including Gen. Hamilton and his staff officer Lt Andrew Skeen, devised a bold but complicated strategy.

Their main objective was to capture the Sari Bair Range including the towering Hill 971, which at 971 feet was the commanding peak above Anzac Cove — the Mt Everest of the maze of surrounding hills on the Sari Bair range. From that vantage point, they would be looking down on the Turks. The British planned to capture these heights by landing about 20,000 reinforcements, under Lt Gen. Sir Frederick

MORE TROOPS WERE NEEDED DURING THE AUGUST OFFENSIVE THAN AT ANY OTHER TIME. THE ANZACS MOUNTED ATTACKS ON LONE PINE, THE NEK, CHUNUK BAIR AND HILL 971 AS PART OF THE STRATEGY TO TAKE THE HEIGHTS OF THE SARI BAIR RANGE. AWM P00188.014

Stopford, north of Anzac Cove at Suvla to secure the bay and foothills just inland. Described by Churchill as 'a placid, prudent, elderly English gentleman', many considered the 61-year-old Stopford too old, especially as he had never commanded troops in battle. His troops would then capture the Sari Bair Range from the northwest which the Turks would not expect. At the same time, Anzacs of the 4th Brigade under Col. Monash would capture Hill 971; and New Zealand troops would capture Chunuk Bair (which scouts claimed was poorly defended) with Baby 700 as a supplementary objective.

To achieve these ultimate goals, they had to distract the Turks with diversionary battles. The first would take place at Helles which, with all its unburied bodies and sickness combined with the extreme summer heat, 'smelt like an open cemetery' according to one infantryman. The other attack would be at Lone Pine opposite the Anzac Cove bridgehead. The Anzacs would succeed in capturing Lone Pine — a rare victory that won them seven Victoria Crosses but saw 2,000 men killed. Lone Pine would be one of the bloodiest battles of Gallipoli, as an anonymous soldier confirmed after the battle. 'The conditions are unspeakable. The dead, Turkish and Australians, are lying buried and half buried in the trench bottom, in the sides of the trench and even built into the parapet — of all the bastards of places this is the greatest bastard in the world.'

Another attack by the Light Horse, the cream of the Anzacs, on the strongly defended and unassailable Nek, would cost hundreds of lives. It was an ill-conceived and badly led assault directed by Lt Col. John Antill. Waves of young men were sent against machine gun fire to their certain death. Another attack would take place on Hill Q — the second highest peak at 900 feet — mainly by the tenacious Gurkhas. The whole August offensive would be a make or break attack with 100,000 Allied troops fighting in five different mini theatres.

However, the brilliant Turkish military leader, Mustafa Kemal, had predicted much of this strategy and had been getting ready for months with reinforcements and stronger defences. The Allies did not have a chance of succeeding. They gained very little ground and lost thousands more lives. Fortunately, the British War Council and Allied Commanders learnt their lesson. This was the last big life-wasting offensive of the Gallipoli campaign.

Nevertheless, in early August, an air of excitement could be noticed at Anzac Cove, where impatient soldiers were itching for action. At last something was about to happen. The Gallipoli campaign was now 100 days along and many of the soldiers believed the time had come for some action.

ALTHOUGH HE COULD SEE CLEARLY THAT MEN OF THE 8TH AND 10TH LIGHT HORSE WERE BEING SLAUGHTERED WHEN THEY CHARGED 'A WALL OF MACHINE GUN FIRE' AT THE NEK, BOER WAR VETERAN LT COL. JOHN 'BULL' ANTILL, THE HANDS-ON LEADER IN THE TRENCHES, CONTINUED TO ORDER SUCCESSIVE WAVES INTO ACTION, REFUSING TO CONSULT HIS SUPERIORS. AWM G01330

Sunday
1 August
DAY 99

With only five days to go till the big 'stunt', Lt J.E. Adlard complained about the extra workload, as he helped prepare for the 6 August offensive. 'Until 4.30 this morning since 8 last night we hauled guns on the beach to the New Zealanders positions. One has to work here at any time and all times. Mostly all night and sometimes day too. Shells bursting interfere with the work a bit but one must not notice them. One gets but little sleep, since our own guns fire over our heads and the concussion is rotten.'

As second in charge of the 9th Light Horse, Lt Col. Carew Reynell heard 'through the secret service that the Turks had been reinforced by upwards of 100,000 and intended to make a grand attack on us'. Reynell predicted 'our first job will be to take the trenches across the neck so that our casualties are bound to be very heavy indeed as we cross a confined space under fire of a half circle of Turk trenches'. Confident of his men, he claimed 'even if 75 per cent of us are knocked out I believe the other 25 per cent will get there … I must impress on them the necessity of getting there or dying in the attempt'. Having calculated that about 19 per cent of his men had become casualties and sensing the coming danger, he confided that 'All my pals wounded now and my turn next I suppose — damned nuisance if

ANZACS TAKING A BREAK
AFTER CAPTURING LONE PINE
AGAINST FORMIDABLE ODDS.

I have to provide the 20 per cent of the said casualties'. Reynell was killed on 27 August fighting at Lone Pine.

The Anzacs had been at Gallipoli for 100 days — too many of them, according to the more restless soldiers, spent idle. Unaware they would attack in four days, a frustrated Maj. B.D. Jack was still itching for a fight with an enemy apart from the small white wriggling ones bugging him. 'If you want to do us a really good turn send us lice proof clothes. I wear all cotton and I am as bad as the others. Every morning I run over the seams for them. Things have changed a good deal since I was away and we now occupy some of their trenches, these have overhead cover and are lousy just the same. In one spot the trenches are only 5 yards apart. It seems incredible but true and bombs are flying about all the time. The Tommies landed north of us and are getting on slowly. I think it is about time Mr Abdul turned it up. He ought to know we won't clear out until we've got him so he might just as well give up before he loses many more. My word, the recruiting over there is pretty lively and Australia must be just about run out. However the quicker they come the better. We are short of men and officers. I am doing 3 hrs on and 6 off by day and 1 on and 3 off at night so that all the spare time I get I sleep. It is very hard work.'

**Monday
2 August
DAY 100**

Reinforcements started coming ashore overnight. Although S/Sgt. Leslie Goldring didn't know about the diversionary offensive at Helles, he was still expecting something big. 'Spent a very interesting day, rode to the base with the Major and had a good view all around. There were only 2 hospital ships in the Bay ... 8 destroyers cruising around the Base had been shelled very thickly for the past few days but fortunately we escaped them. One cannot help but think of the main work that has been accomplished especially viewing our objective Achi Baba, a hill of some 750 feet, from one of the hills right in the rear. On returning we were lucky enough to see this hill being pasted by the Navy ... nothing could be seen but a mass of smoke. It was some time since I had been to the base, so fully appreciated the tour ... when back near Sidd-el-Bahi where the French head-quarters are has an excellent chance of viewing the Frenchmen's quaint ways. We are daily expecting a bombardment'.

**Tuesday
3 August
DAY 101**

Wednesday
4 August
DAY 102

With only two days to go, plans about the secret offensive started to emerge at Anzac Cove. Lt Col. C. Reynell revealed 'Our first definite orders about the attack last night. The attack is to be general and a big left flanking attack to be made in co-operation. Apparently the artillery support for the frontal attack will be good. Our 3rd L H. Brigade is to take the trenches on the neck with good covering fire by rifle machine and artillery fire after a very heavy and prolonged bombardment and so it should present no difficulties. However, there will be stacks of scrapings between here and the narrows 4 miles away, but from what I can guess of the plan of attack and the numbers we are to have I anticipate a great and glorious victory during the next few days with such a stunning blow to the Turks that it may end the Turkish hash in one hit. I have been busy all day with preliminary arrangements for the attack which is to start on the day after tomorrow either just before or after daylight. I feel I ought to be writing home sort of goodbye letters in case of a wash out ... I am looking forward to the attack very much as I am very hopeful that it may result in a glorious stroke.'

Thursday
5 August
DAY 103

The day before the big offensive, reinforcements arrived in the early hours of the morning, according to Lt Col. J. Corbin. 'Landed all troops last night — again one dead this time ... Arrangements not so good and delay in filling them in did not finish until 4.30 a.m. in daylight almost. Consequence being the usual. Stores have been coming in all day and the fire on the beach is hellish.'

If Petty Officer Bert Webster, 23rd Battalion, was any example of these reinforcements there would be no lack of enthusiasm. He wrote to his mother that 'both day and night we can hear & see bursting shells — which make us all the more anxious to get into the fun. I am more than pleased that this has at last fallen to my lot to participate in such a great and just cause. I am fully prepared for anything & fear nothing — this has been my hearts desire for months past'. All his money had been stolen on the way over on his ship, *Port Macquarie*, through 'a bit of bad luck'. He lamented to his mother that 'the belt you gave me, went for a walk with all my money in it — just after pay day too'.

Col. Monash was to lead the 4th Brigade up Hill 971 and Maj. H.G. Loughran attended his briefing. 'Colonel Monash assembled all officers and N.C.O.'s 4th Brigade and imparted to them the plan of operation for next day. He said that a feint attack would be made on Lone Pine on afternoon of 6th and during the night the 4th Brigade; Gurkhas, and New Zealanders, would turn the left flank of the Anzac position.

(This we had suspected for a good while.) He then mentioned the projected landing at Suvla (this was an eye opener — nobody had known anything about this). He detailed the plans for the night movement on the 6th, white patches to be worn on back and arms — no firing till daylight — bayonet to be the only weapon during the night … General comment that it was extraordinary of Monash to announce all this the day before the operation as a simple spy in communication with enemy could ruin whole thing. Many thought the whole tale was bluff and orders would be suddenly countermanded.'

The anonymous author of the official 14th Battalion diary, who listened to Lt Gen. Birdwood's briefing, confirmed his Battalion was working around the clock on tomorrow's attack. 'Work of preparing for offensive proceeded up to noon. 1430 C.O. Adj. Attended conferences of Maj. Gen. Birdwood who gave a brief description of coming operations their importance and why the offensive was taken, mainly to ensure a safe landing in case campaign was prolonged until rough weather set in. Received memo NZQ 486 dealing with the distribution of Force Rations water supply etc, 11th Bn. ordered to move up to head of gully, troops ordered to wear white Armlet Bands 6" deep on both arms and a white patch 8" x 8" on back.'

Friday 6 August
DAY 104

Finally, the big day arrived. Some felt it was going to be like the landing on 25th April all over again. That was 104 days ago and this was the biggest 'stunt' since then and long awaited.

The first diversionary battle started at 2.20 p.m. at Helles where 26,000 British 'rifles' of 29th Division and 13,000 French troops charged towards 40,000 well-entrenched Turkish defenders. Although they hoped to capture Krithia and Achi Baba, the Anglo-French forces faced an impossible task. Unbelievably, the Allied troops were even short of ammunition. They managed to capture a vineyard, which cost 3,490 casualties including nearly 2,000 soldiers killed out of 3,000 in the 88th Brigade alone. Military Landing Officer, Capt. Pawson wrote, 'It was a truly awful sight'. Corp. Alec Riley added that 'Once more the long procession of wounded, dirty, ragged, torn and bloody men came down to the dressing station … others lay just 25 yards in front of the trench in the hot sun not daring to move till night when some of them might be able to crawl slowly back to the lines'. Sadly, the attack proved to be a poor diversion, as the well-informed Turks knew the Allies were mounting their main offensive at Anzac.

The second diversionary action started at 4.30 p.m. at Anzac Cove when the 1st, 2nd and 3rd Brigades charged Lone Pine. A better planned attack, this time the Anzacs reached the Turkish trenches in seconds, surprising them. Although blocked by fences and ceilings, both made of logs, they just fired through gaps, tore the logs apart, jumped into the trenches and shot or bayoneted the Turks in hand-to-hand fighting. As Pte. J.K. Gammage reported, 'We felt like wild beasts but were calm and never fired reckless but were deliberate ... we rushed them out of their 2nd and 3rd line of trenches in half an hour'. Fortunately, he said 'bombs simply poured in and as fast as our men went down another would take his place' and soon 'the wounded were piled up three or four deep ... the moans of our own poor fellows and also the Turks we tramped on was awful'.

The Anzacs gained a foothold against all odds in the first series of trenches. With the help of reinforcements, they fought hard over the next few days to capture more trenches and eventually they held Lone Pine. The toll on both sides was in the thousands, according to Bean, who was wounded in 'the upper part of the right leg' while watching the battle that day. 'The dead lay so thick that the only respect which could be paid to them was to avoid treading on their faces ... you could not tell the difference between our dead and Turkish dead because their face went so black.'

Signaler R. Stanley believed the Anzacs were in Lone Pine to stay. 'More English troops landed during the night. Looks as if we are getting ready for a big push. Fairly quiet in the morning. At 4.30 p.m. we opened a terrific bombardment on Lone Pine, from 100 guns and Howitzers, 4 cruisers 3 monitors and several destroyers pour in a terrific fire. Lone Pine position is absolutely ploughed up. At 5.30 a signal is given, the firing ceases abruptly and the 2nd Brigade charge the position, and reached the Turks 3rd line of trenches — the Turks having to be bombed and bayoneted out of their trenches — The overhead covering having to be lifted off their trenches so as our men could get at them. I am on "O" station telephone all day and night and have great difficulty in hearing, owing to the terrific noise. Turks counterattacks and shell fire bravely stood by the remnants of the 2nd Brigade. All night the Turks try to regain their lost position, but fail their bomb attacks being exceptionally bad. While this is happening two divisions of Kitchener's Army are silently landed at Suvla Bay, and take the Turks by surprise and reach Hill 971. Our left flank swinging around and joining up.'

The third action of the day — the main thrust — started that evening when a series of troops began their coordinated night marches aimed at occupying different hill tops including Chunuk Bair and Hill 971. Their

ALTHOUGH CONSIDERED 'AN ACE CARD' BY THE BRITISH WAR COUNCIL, THE 61-YEAR-OLD LT GEN. SIR FREDERICK STOPFORD, WHO WAS APPOINTED FOR HIS HIGH SOCIAL STANDING AND WHO ARRIVED AS THE SAVIOUR OF SUVLA BAY IN EARLY AUGUST, HAD NEVER COMMANDED TROOPS IN ACTION AND WAS SUBSEQUENTLY SACKED FOR FAILING TO ADVANCE.

plans came unstuck when coordination collapsed as the different units lost contact with each other, fell behind or even stopped while others went on. They lost the intended impact of a mighty force attacking uphill at once. New Zealanders did reach Chunuk Bair by dawn, which seemed to be deserted. Unfortunately, the commander, Brig. Gen. Johnson, ordered them to wait for support units, which gave the Turks time to muster reinforcements. Other forces, including Monash's exhausted 4th Brigade, were so behind schedule as they approached Hill 971 that the overall attack failed.

The fourth and final action was the secret arrival that night of more than 20,000 British reinforcements at Suvla Bay. They got ashore successfully losing only one soldier killed by a sniper.

End of Week 15

As the second day of the August offensive unfolded, most of the Allied offensives had failed or were failing, especially the attempt to snatch the jewel in the crown from the Turks — Hill 971. Lone Pine was the exception, even though the Turks mounted counterattacks over the next four days. The New Zealanders got sick of waiting for supporting troops and attacked Chunuk Bair soon after daybreak. By now, however, the Turks were ready to repulse the attack. At Suvla, Lt Gen. Sir Frederick Stopford's 20,000 men also waited near the beach. Although the bulk of the army were ashore by morning, Stopford did not know what to do next, so they waited beside the beach. Anzac signaler, Corp. Ted Matthews, remembered that 'Those dam fool British just sat down had a picnic, drank cups of tea and played soccer for so long that the Turks were able to muster reinforcements — which means they lost any advantage of surprise'. Finally, realising he had to get off the exposed beach, Stopford ordered his men to attack inland. Once again, the enemy had time to mount reinforced opposition. The British could only capture the lowest hills held by the Turks, including Chocolate Hill, Green Hill and Hill 10 — but at the price of 1,700 casualties.

The original plan assumed the New Zealanders would have captured Chunuk Bair and so the coast would be clear for the Light Horse to mount their diversionary action at the Nek. The 'Kiwis' had not captured Chunuk Bair, but commanding officers at the Nek ordered an attack anyway. Anzacs were also meant to divert the Turks from the Nek by assaulting Pope's Hill and Quinn's Post, but their timing was also off. The officers in charge were the Boer War veteran, Maj. Gen.

Saturday 7 August

DAY 105

LIGHT HORSEMEN, READY WILLING AND ABLE, WAIT IN THEIR TRENCH FOR THE ORDER TO CHARGE ACROSS THE NEK INTO THE WALL OF MACHINE GUN FIRE FROM TURKISH TRENCHES ON THE OTHER SIDE OF 'THE TENNIS COURT OF DEATH.' AWM J02719

ONE OF THE LUCKY LIGHT HORSEMEN WAITING IN LINE TO GO OVER THE TOP AT THE NEK WAS TROOPER JOHN COX WHO WAS ORDERED TO 'STAND DOWN' AT THE LAST SECOND. AFTER THE CAPTURE OF BEERSHEBA IN 1917, HE RETURNED SAFELY TO AUSTRALIA WHERE HE SETTLED DOWN AND HAD A FAMILY.

Alexander John Godley, whose father fought in the Crimean War and who failed to realise that the invention of machine guns made the old fashioned cavalry charge obsolete, and his aging and sickly Australian subordinate, Brig. Gen. Fredrick Hughes, a civilian soldier who had direct command even though he had never commanded men before and who was sent back to Australia several weeks later. The hands-on leader in the trenches was Lt Col. John Macquarie 'Bull' Antill, 48, a Boer War veteran of cavalry charges and a controversial, intimidating, short-tempered professional soldier. They ordered the attack to proceed partly because it was already planned and they also hoped to divert the Turks away from Chunuk Bair and help the New Zealanders. The decision had disastrous consequences. The Anzacs had to cross open ground and faced a wall of Turkish machine guns that had never left their defending position and were waiting for them. Charles Bean said it was like asking men to run from the back line at one end of a tennis court towards the backline at the other end which was lined with Turks shoulder to shoulder with machine guns blazing.

One hundred and fifty men of the first wave of 8th Light Horse jumped out of the trench at 4.30 p.m. and were mown down within thirty seconds. One observer watched them 'sinking to the ground as though their limbs suddenly became string'. At 4.32 p.m., the 150 men of the second wave also from the 8th Light Horse jumped over the top. Only one man made it to the Turkish 'back line' waving a red and yellow flag before disappearing. An officer who, finding himself alone just short of the Turkish trench, flung himself to the ground in order to crawl back to safety later. Survivor, Capt. George Hore, recalled 'We bent low and ran as hard as we could. Ahead we could see the trench aflame with rifle fire. All around were smoke and dust kicked up by the bullets'.

Despite passionate pleas to Lt Col. Anthill from the officer in charge, Lt Col. Noel Brazier, the third wave of 150 men from the 10th Light Horse were also sent over the top and mown down as well. Survivor, Lt Andy Crawford recalled, 'I could see the Turks standing up two deep in their trench. I could see one soldier firing over another chap's shoulder'. Although commanding officers decided to call off the fourth wave, also from the 10th Light Horse, many did not hear the order and were mistakenly mown down. Fortunately others stayed back. Thinking he was going to die, Trooper Jack Cox of the fourth wave said he had been 'lost in my own thoughts, thinking about my wife with whom I had never really known the joys of married life and my time in similar battles in the Boer War'. But Cox had seen the phone ring and saw the officer doing a lot of talking. He saw the officer replace the receiver, look down the line and break into a smile shouting 'Stand Down, men!'.

Of 600 officers and men who charged the Turkish line of defence, 372 were killed or wounded, 300 of whose bodies were left on the battlefield where they stayed for weeks. The 8th Light Horse lost 234 killed or wounded from its 300 strong force and the 10th Light Horse lost 138 killed or wounded.

'I was in the first line to advance and we did not get ten yards' wrote Sgt. Cliff Pinnock who crawled back after being wounded. 'They were waiting ready for us and simply gave us a solid wall of lead. Everyone fell like lumps of meat ... all your pals who had you been with for months blown and shot out of all recognition'. When the roll was called afterwards, Pinnock said, 'I cried like a child'. Bean heard a 'tremendous fusillade break out' and said, 'God help anyone that was out in that tornado'.

Lt Col. Noel Braizer confirmed how he tried to stop the mass slaughter at the Nek. 'The Regiment took up position in trenches at 4 p.m. when bombardment commenced. Bombardment continued to 4.30 when a murderous machine gun and rifle fire upon our parapets commenced. At 4.40 Major Todd in charge of 3rd line, reported he could not advance as

AUSTRALIAN AND BRITISH TROOPS AT STORES STOCKPILE AMID DUGOUTS IN STEEP, DIFFICULT COUNTRY. ONE FALSE STEP AND A MAN COULD PLUNGE 100 METRES TO HIS DEATH. AWM P00516.002

8th Regt. was held up. Referred matter to Brigade HQ and informed them the task was impossible under such a fire. Was ordered to advance at once. Major Scott almost immediately reported he was held up; again referred matter to HQ and was told to advance. As the fire was murderous again referred matter personally to Brigadier who said to get what men I could and go round by BULLY BEEF Sap and MONASH GULLY. Meanwhile Majors Love and Todd had discussed matters in some dead ground in front of trenches, where to advance was impossible, and on returning received orders to go by BULLY BEEF Sap as above. The fire here was also deadly and as the casualties were then very heavy, were ordered to retire. Meanwhile I remained observing in No. 8 Sap, and at 5.35 Lieut. Lyall and 8 men of 10th and some men of 8th, returned to No. 8 Sap and reported that no one had reached the Turk's trenches. Reported at 5.40 after observing again, and held on here till relieved. The attack seemed premature and in view of the heavy machine gun fire, should have been held up — and many valuable lives saved.'

Meanwhile, Pte. Austin Fricker marched slowly with Col. Monash's troops towards Hill 971. He confirmed more heavy fighting. 'Called up last night just after turning in 9 p.m. and left with 4th Brigade who proceed along beach and to No. 3 Outpost where we encounted Turks. From here we drove them back some miles by the bayonet. Heavy battle all night and day with enormous bombardment from battleships. Division of Tommies and Gurkas took part and landed at Suvla Bay. Did very hard work amongst the wounded and felt exhausted.'

Sgt. A.S. Hutton landed at Gaba Tepe on his birthday. 'We arrived at Gaba Tepe about 3 a.m. As we were steaming into the Cove a steamer lying at anchor lay immediately in our track and we steamed straight into her. How it happened I don't know but we sunk her and knocked a hole in our bows large enough to admit a coach and four. We landed safely on a piquet boat and there was a fierce battle in progress. No doubt today has been the fiercest battle in the history of the war. The first Light Horse were absolutely cut up, the 1st and one squadron of the third regt. (B Squdn) held Popes hill and the 2nd regt. and 2 squadrons of the 3rd (A & C) held Quinn's Post. We had some fierce bayonet charges and we suffered rather heavy as did the Turks.

'The Turks evidently expected us to make a supreme attempt to drive them back from here, which resulted in them concentrating most of their troops to oppose us, this was what our Gen. wanted as he landed 29,000 English troops & Gurkhas higher up the coast with practically no opposition, the Gurkhas & Tommies swooped round our left flank and charged the big hill 971 and a few hours ago were reported to be within three hundred yards from the top, they must have it by now. The New

Zealanders also had wonderful success, they took three important trenches and our right flank came round and drove the Turks pell mell back and took their trenches. Altogether we had brilliant success but our first brigade paid the price heavily … the sights of mangled bodies has been sickening and the stench also. I have had quite a notable birthday'.

Sunday 8 August
DAY 106

After two days, the offensive seemed to be progressing too slowly. Short of a miracle, the offensive would fail. The 20,000 British troops had come ashore in Suvla and another two new Divisions would be safely ashore by 9 August. Anzacs still held Lone Pine despite the Turkish counterattacks. At Chunuk Bair, the New Zealanders had miraculously gained a temporary foothold assisted by a naval barrage. At Hill Q, the second highest peak, Gurkhas assisted by British troops were within striking distance. But at the Nek, wounded continued crawling back to safety while survivors tried to pull in the nearest bodies. Trooper Portman helped remove 'one of them who faced us on his hands and knees. Having started to crawl back when wounded another bullet killed him but a bush held him in position. As the sentry on this post had to look straight into his face … and his face always seemed to be asking a question … as sentries could not stand that for very long we had to remove him. Another dead man was found lying under a bush with his prayer book in his hand'.

At Hill 971, the Australians were still 'miles away' and pinned down by Turkish fire. Col. Monash's men also failed to capture Abdel Rahman. Lt T.J. Richards surveyed the battlefield and wrote that there was no chance of prayers that Sunday. 'It is 39 hours since we commenced the attack and it seems as unsettled as ever. The 1st Brigade made some 300 yards of ground and drove Turks out of three lines of trenches but John is still holding the fourth and knocking fair hell out of our men with bombs. A stream of stretcher and walking cases still continue to come down but, thank goodness, the ambulance units and dressing stations are able to avoid congestion … Information as to our exact position and what our fortune is scarce … The warships are crowded in around Suvla Bay and doing quite a lot of firing. The Turk is not doing much with his artillery … This battle has now been raging 48 hours, and though I still feel confident of a complete victory the news leaking through from all kinds of sources is not so glowing as it was yesterday … It is Sunday. I guess there will be no services held this day'.

Some soldiers amused themselves that Sunday by pouring a tin of kerosene over the ground laying a trail stretching into a wire compound containing Turkish and German prisoners of war. They lit this trail and

THE 'TOP BRASS' BEHIND THE IMPOSSIBLE CHARGE OF THE LIGHT HORSE AGAINST THE TURKISH MACHINE GUN FIRE AT THE NEK WAS THE UNAPPROACHABLE GENERAL SIR ALEXANDER GODLEY, WHO WAS TRAINED BY HIS FATHER (WHO HAD FOUGHT IN THE 1854 CRIMEAN WAR) AND WHO HAD ACQUIRED A TASTE FOR CAVALRY CHARGES IN THE BOER WAR LONG BEFORE MACHINE GUNS WERE INVENTED.
AWM 134755

'there was a huge flare of fire very uncomfortably close — if not dangerously — to the Turks'. Charles Bean noted that 'the wretched prisoners rushed to the other side of the pen like a flock of sheep rounded up by a dog and the fellows looked on and laughed'. This he thought was 'as caddish an act as I ever saw in my life'.

Monday 9 August
DAY 107

The third day after the big attack the Allies were in disarray. There were 18,000 casualties out of the 50,000 men fighting in Suvla and Anzac. Most strategic objectives like Hill 971 and Chunuk Bair had been abandoned. Little ground had been gained apart from Lone Pine and that had serious supply problems as Private Gammage explained. 'Since Friday food was turned off. All I had was taken from dead comrades haversacks but its all for a good cause.' However, the Turks were still determined to recapture Lone Pine and mounted a third counterattack. At the Nek, the flies moved in to feast on the dead soldiers. At Hill Q, although the unstoppable Gurkhas looked like closing on the enemy, at the last minute their own Allies shelled them. A ferocious barrage of friendly fire forced them to withdraw.

Ambulance men like Pte. A. Fricker had more than enough work to do. 'Fierce battle and terrific bombardment still going on. We are holding our position — advancing at great cost. Working increasingly carrying in wounded. Letter from Father (29th June). Duffy and reinforcement fellow hit, also 3 C. Section men. Our tent division moved higher up. Our aero plane chased German taube.'

Tuesday 10 August
DAY 108

Four days after the major offensive, events looked even more hopeless for the long-suffering Anzacs and their British supporters. Turkish commander, Mustafa Kemal, ordered a massive attack, which drove frontline Anzacs back down the heights towards the beach. Although this Turkish counterattack included Lone Pine, the Anzacs held on there.

Light Horseman Lt Col. Carew Reynell now tried to make sense of the senseless massacres. 'After 4 days continuous scrapping there has been a lull today and both sides seem fairly tired. Our Brigade made an attack on the trenches in front of us at 4.30 a.m. on the morning of the 7th. It failed and the 8th Regt. which found the first line was wiped out — all the officers on the spot with the exception of the 2nd in Command and a couple of subalterns being killed or wounded (mostly the former). The Regt. Lost 240 out of 400 and most of them were killed. The 10th Regt.

were to follow but when the first line were cut down they remained on the edge of the trenches and although their casualties were heavy they were light in comparison. We were to cover the attack on the first trenches with fire and then to attack the trenches further off which was really the worst job of the lot, but owing to the first failing our attack of course never came off and we have got off with only 30 killed and wounded in the 4 days … The Turks have counter attacked all our new front and we have been expecting a counter attack here but it hasn't come off yet. The 1st L.H. Brigade attacked from POPES and QUINNS and gained 4 lines but were driven out and their losses were very heavy — nearly 50 per cent. The 2nd L.H. Brigade attacked "German Officer"'s trench and failed and lost heavily … all now come to a fullstop some 5 or 600 yards below the ridge'. Reynell concluded 'the main cause of failure of our brigades attack was machine gun fire — some men's legs were completely severed by this fire'.

On the fifth day after the big offensive, both sides took stock. Lt Gen. Birdwood told Bean he feared his Anzacs were too exhausted to maintain any offensive. They were running short of ammunition and had problems getting supplies of food and water to the front line for the men who could be 'in a parlous way'.

Sadly, Gunner William Leonard Pacey made one of his last entries in his diary on this day. 'Things are fairly quiet this morning but this evening Br Dingwall let me go down for a swim and I was to bring up a couple of buckets of water. Well I got down and had a good swim and washed a couple of pairs of socks. Well I just got out of the water when the enemy started shelling and all round where I was swimming the bullets and shells were landing, then I nearly got knocked when I was coming up the hill. When I got up to the gun I found that our gun had opened on the enemys trenches and three of the Turks guns had concentrated on our gun and knocked four of the detachment out of five out. Br Dingwall was hit near the eye, Br McKinnon was severely wounded, Gr Moore was severely wounded and Gr Thurnhill slightly while the fifth man, Gr Hillback got off without a scratch. So going down for a swim saved me from getting knocked off as my No. on the Gun is 2. Our seaplane chased a German Taube that came over this afternoon and the old Taube went for the lick of his life down behind the enemys lines. Am a bit too busy to attend to the diary. When we get a land breeze the air is pretty thick from the dead which are lying out in front in thousands, both Turks and our own dead'. William Pacey died on the 25th August 1915 on the hospital ship *Arcadia* at sea as a consequence of wounds received on Gallipoli.

Wednesday 11 August
DAY 109

LT COL. NOEL BRAZIER, WHO COMMANDED THE 10TH LIGHT HORSE WHICH CHARGED THE NEK IN THE SECOND WAVE, TRIED UNSUCCESSFULLY TO STOP THE SLAUGHTER OF HIS MEN WHEN HE SAW THEY COULD NOT ADVANCE AGAINST MACHINE GUN FIRE.

Thursday
12 August
DAY 110

The battles continued on and off as the Allies attacked and Turks counterattacked at Suvla, on the heights above Anzac Cove and around Lone Pine. Lt Leslie Ward noted it was reassuring to have some support from offshore. 'The situation is about the same as yesterday. Our warboats are bombarding Cape Helles heavily also the Turks position on the other side of Hill 971. The ship has been sunk with our mail aboard so have not had any for 2 weeks.'

Friday
13 August
DAY 111

By now, a week after the 6 August offensive started, at least 22,000 wounded and sick casualties had been evacuated from Anzac, Suvla and Helles. Having started this offensive, the Allies could not stop the Turkish counterattacks at Helles, Lone Pine and at Suvla.

Although the suspicious may have feared things could get worse on Friday 13th, Petty Officer Bert Webster reported 'a narrow escape from death'. He was working outside his dugout when a shell 'screeched by my head less than six inches from my nose — the powder & dust blackening my face & the wind of it putting my hat back, it burst to the ground barely 4ft from where I stood. I was smothered with the dust & bricks flung about by the explosion'. He had not ducked he said because he wanted 'to crack hardy'. Although he was 'dazed by the shock', he still 'ran after the pieces of shell that nearly cost me my life to bring home with me & have engraved in remembrance of the occasion'. His superior officers 'treated it as a huge joke'. Thanks to his 'strong heart and nerves like iron', Webster survived and asked his mother to 'take a ticket in Tatts' for him because of his lucky streak, which ran out on the Somme where he was killed in 1916.

Sgt. A.S. Hutton noted a relative break in the fighting. 'Things have been pretty quiet today. We are still on Quinns Post. We set a mine of high explosives under the Turks trenches and blew them up at 9 p.m. the explosion was terrific and as we are only a dozen yards from the Turks we naturally were shaken up too. Big sleepers and pieces of timber and Turks and other things were hurled into the air and came down on top of us amid a shower of earth. We opened a brisk fire on them immediately after the explosion. The fighting has never stopped since we have been here (13 weeks now) so we are quite used to the thunder of guns etc.'

ONE OF THE MOST COLOURFUL AND OUTSPOKEN DIARIES KEPT AT SUVLA BAY WAS WRITTEN BY CHIEF PETTY OFFICER ALBERT 'BERT' WEBSTER OF MELBOURNE WHO SERVED WITH THE RAN BRIDGING TRAIN.

End of Week 16

Despite 'sounds of pretty heavy fighting down south', Charles Bean reported 'having a pretty quiet time here' as they only 'have a few new guns against us'. At least the Anzacs had finished burying the Turkish dead in Lone Pine and 'There seems to be less smell today', he said.

Aside from the horrors of war, Pte. P.R. Johanesen told his parents it was like an outback station. 'Well I am in the thick of it now. We have been giving "Allah" a bit of a bad time for a week or more, but things have quietened down a bit now. I am in the best of health at present and hope you are all the same at home. Bob Gay got crook and has gone back to the base. I will wonder where I am to get into a soft bed again. All the bed a man gets here is in the bottom of a trench or in a sap with everybody walking over him. Oh It's a great life, you can go along the trenches in the daytime when they are not shelling and see the chaps rounding up the herd and branding them. It is great branding when they kick and struggle. You get him between the two thumb nails and squeeze hard. I hear that Harry Rosewarne is in Egypt, he got there just after I left, so I never saw him. I lost my mate the other day. He was sitting in the trench talking when a shell lobbed right in the trench, killed one and wounded two. My mate got such a shock that he lost his speech, he couldn't even say goodbye when the stretcher bearers were taking him out. I have not had a wash for just on four weeks, that nice ain't it. How would you like to kiss my dirty dial now? "Not much" eh.'

War or no war, Pte. B.G. Thomson still had to help men respond to the call of nature. "Up early ready to go to Gully at 8. Things very slow in morning digging latrines. Archie and I sat up on cliff watching our 6 in howitzer putting shells on the "Olive Grove". Went up to 4th F.A. met the old boys. Pat Auld (WHC) and Tom English (WHC). Up the gully this evening. Slept. Bomb fight.'

Saturday
14 August
DAY 112

Gen. Hamilton sacked Lt Gen. Sir Frederick Stopford who failed in the 6 August offensive by not advancing quickly at Suvla and attacking Sari Bair from the north. Hamilton also sacked a number of other incompetent officers — which didn't make up for the many dead soldiers. Even with their new leader, Maj. Gen. Beauvoir De Lisle, the British at Suvla could not capture Turkish positions inland. As one British subaltern noted, this was because 'the bullets from rifles and machine guns were descending in a curtain over the ground we were covering'.

Sunday
15 August
DAY 113

Light Horseman Sgt. C.C. St. Pinnock tried to tell his family about the Nek. 'The General "Ian Hamilton", ordered that the whole line would advance on yesterday week. We all knew what that would mean to the poor 8th. They took all our kit, including our tunics, four days before the advance and simply left us with a shirt, pants, puttees and boots. Well, we simply perished those four nights ... Had very little sleep ... on the Friday we were told that the advance would take place on the following morning early at half past four ... but they were waiting ready for us ... we did not get ten yards ... The second line came on and got the same reception, and so on until the whole of the 8th and 10th were practically wiped out. Really too awful to write about. All your pals that had been with you for months and months blown and shot out of all recognition. There was no chance whatever of us gaining our point, but the roll call after was the saddest, just fancy only 47 answered their names out of close to 550 men. ... I simply cried like a child. It is really too awful. I got mine shortly after I got over the bank, and it felt like a million ton hammer falling on my shoulder. However, I managed to crawl back and got temporarily fixed up till they carried me to the Base Hospital.'

A frustrated Lt Col. Carew Reynell complained that 'We are still in these dirty damned dusty lousy trenches and no more prospect of getting out of them than flying to the moon. Our offensive has come to a stop everywhere and there is no sign of a revival. We were within an ace of victory and the New Zealanders were actually on the Sari Bair ridge at one point, entrenching on CHUNUK BAIR but were driven off and now our whole line had been driven down the hill some 60 ft or more'.

Monday
16 August
DAY 114

The fighting continued off and on and even those that were not wounded, like Lt J.E. Adlard, could still be very sick. 'Inside v.v. bad. Wonder how long I can hang out. All food ferments. Gastritis of course. After two trips had to give in. I fear that the weakness of my stomach has affected my old gland.'

The anonymous writer of the 14th Infantry Brigade diary noted, 'Very quiet all day. Enemy's snipers kept down by use of periscope rifles. Our 5" howitzers shelled enemy's trenches on our front but only a few ranging shots fired'.

Although writing about the battle at the Nek was difficult, Light Horsemen like 2nd Lt W.M. Cameron did his best to record the nightmare of war. 'It is twelve days since I saw this book; we had some severe fighting and it turns out that we have gained little in territory or position, yet sacrificed thousands of lives. On that eventful Friday when the advance was ordered, I was placed in charge of the Regtl. Sharp Shooters and took up position on the left at three o'clock in the morning and waited the rush forward of our comrades. The eighth Regt. was the first out. We saw them climb out and move forward about ten yards and lie flat. The second line did likewise; meantime the Turkish fire increased in intensity, and as they rose to charge the Turkish Machine Guns just poured out lead and our fellows went down like corn before a scythe'.

Lt Col. Carew Reynell warned that 'The weather will break in a month and the place will become a morass with our trenches on the clay hills just melting away [and with] continuous gales we shall be on half rations and short of ammunition. Into the bargain we are all ill to breaking point'. Even worse, Reynell wrote that the British reinforcements, the Leinsters were 'officered by a lot of bloody fools who can only make a mess well. The N.C.O.s are a lot of half trained ciphers and the men are harmless lambs and the Turks would probably just walk in and kick them out … one of the Leinsters is up before Court martial today for cowardice — ran away'.

Tuesday
17 August
DAY 115

Whenever soldiers like Pte. R. Ward got a moment off between fighting, their thoughts turned to basic necessities of life. 'We had a spell from the trenches in the daytime so a party of us walked back to Anzac Cove to get a change of clothing, overcoat, razors and above all to wash ourselves at the beach. This was the first wash we have had since August 6th. I brought two tins of condensed milk off some sailors and two tins of beef extract. Milk two shillings per tin; Beef one shilling. The beach presented a busy sight all day as artillery horses and mules were being landed in the Cove. A large number of transports were in the Cove. Our howitzers shelled Hill 971 for two hours in the afternoon and cut away the Turks barbed wire entanglements. On our way to the beach we came across one of the bivouacs of the Turks where they left from on the night of the 6th instant. They must have left hurriedly — as heaps of ammunition, gear and clothing was about everywhere. They must have been very comfortable as the dug outs had fresh straw for beds in them and food was scattered about. On the way to the beach (up and down over the hills) we came upon barbed wire entanglement

Wednesday
18 August
DAY 116

EXHAUSTED, WOUNDED AND
DEAD MEN AT THE DRESSING
STATION AT THE FOOT OF
POPE'S HILL AFTER FIGHTING
IN ONE OF THE MANY BATTLES
OF THE ILL-FATED AUGUST
OFFENSIVE. AWM CO2707

that were intended for us but the route we had taken at night took us in another direction.'

Petty Officer Bert Webster and his mates focused on their suntans, writing home that 'the heat here is terrific and the boys are all getting brown. My arms and legs are as brown as Waltons walnuts. I suffered a bit at first but have now hardened to it. … I am sending my watch home, I broke the glass & lost a hand, so if you will get it fixed up & look after it till I get back. Talking about coming home — I will lodge my first order: — a plate-ful of bacon & eggs, ox-tail soup & trifle with Union Dairy cream on it. (my mouth is watering now). What a change it will be after bully beef & biscuits'.

Thursday
19 August
DAY 117

Although Pte. A.J. Mychael put on a brave face, telling his sister battles were like sporting contests, losing comrades nevertheless cut him up. 'Well here I am still spared to write you a few lines … The first hundred and two hours I was here I only had seven hours sleep because of the battles. I am sorry to say the Scone lads had a very bad time. Will Pinkerton, Ted Keley, Sid Lee … were killed. Ken Dil, Joe Roe and Stan Thurlow were wounded. In my troop only Alf Harper, Walter Hudson one sargant and myself came back. It was just a living hell with a rain of bullets, bombs and shells … One doesn't feel afraid you dash in just the same as on a football field. Dill's was only a flesh wound in the leg but ugly, but Ken was hit in the knee. Billie P. was shot carrying one of our officers back to our trench. It is terribly lonely now such a lot of old mates gone. Alf and I are the only two Scone lads left in this camp … I heard Jim tried to enlist but couldn't pass the doctor. I am very glad he didn't three is enough from one family and it is not as nice as a picnic. It is quite a long time since I had a letter from home but of course we have shifted about such a lot … On no account put my letters in the paper. You can tell who you like but not that … I am your most affectionate brother Arch'. Mychael was subsequently killed.

Friday
20 August
DAY 118

Lt Leslie Ward's diary entry noted the increasing respect for Australians felt by the British. 'Fifth Inf. Bde. landed yesterday and they have gone to the centre left flank "Chanak Bair" where they will attack and take Hill 971, with the other Aust. and New Zealanders — Will our mail never come. Nearly four weeks now and not a letter and the biggest mail we would ever have got is the one that was sunk.

'I overheard an argument by two Tommies 1st T — "Your a liar it's not true who told you anyhow" 2nd T — "I'm not a liar its true, cos an Australian told me". This will just show the feeling they have for the Australians whom they think are wonderful — I heard a Tommie say one day with a very startled look and in his best Cockney accent "Why man! The Australians don't think there is a God"'.

End of Week 17

Saturday
21 August
DAY 119

The British, under their new leader Maj. Gen. De Lisle, finally mounted a major attack against the heights inland from Suvla Bay. British, Australian, New Zealand and Gurkha troops started attacking Hill 60 in the north west foothills of Sari Bair Range and tried in vain to capture it for the next ten days. The Allies were short of men as there had been 40,000 casualties overall since the 6 August.

The ferocious fighting of August left its mark on every soldier. 'I have been pretty bad this last couple of days. I am stone deaf in my left ear', Sgt. A.S. Hutton wrote. 'We have been landing a lot of troops lately, last night the 17' 18' 19' 20th Inf. landed and there are more following there is going to be another big attack today on the right flank and at

"Sarri Bair". a couple of our chaps were hit yesterday with our own shells. Our Submarines have sunk 50 odd coal ships in the Sea of Marmara and also wrecked the mining plant. Capt. Lewis A Squadn has gone away sick, fever I think.'

Sunday
22 August
DAY 120

Chaplains were not immune to the fortunes of war and were sorely missed when killed. Chaplain E.N. Merrington recorded the death of his colleague. 'After Divine Service this morning, I heard sad news ... Gillison ... was shot between the shoulders, where the bullet struck him as he crawled forwards. Dale, who had known him in Australia was with him to the last. His words were of his loved ones in Melbourne, and of the hope that never failed his courageous spirit. He died at 2 o'clock. Dale closed his eyes and straightened his limbs; and then walked over to tell me the news ... I had my Sunday evening service in Pope's Reserve Gully as usual, and then walked over in the moonlight to No. 2 Post, where the body lay waiting interment. The sergeant of No. 11 Casualty Clearing Station produced a Union Jack and placed it over the dead chaplain ... All denominations were represented by Chaplains and others, including many mourners of the 4th Infantry Brigade, by whom Chaplain Gillison was idolised. Chaplains Grant, Dale, King and I took part in the simple service, and then I reverently removed the flag. Chaplain Dale noticed a plain gold ring on his finger and we removed it for a last souvenir to be sent to his wife in Melbourne. The body was reverently laid in the stony grave by his brother chaplains. We saw his face with a slight smile lurking around the lips as he had often looked in life. A small wooden cross with his name on it marked the spot. He was a soldier and a friend to all. Full of high spirit and cheerfulness, knowing no fear, he led the men along the paths of their duty in this great campaign. He died for an unknown wounded man. What decoration, posthumous or in the time of life, can surpass the glory of his death in pure, unselfish heroism.'

Monday
23 August
DAY 121

On a day that was 'hazy with strong east winds' the author of the official diary for the 14th Battalion reported, 'Heavy firing and bomb throwing again in front of detached force, just after they had been relieved by 16th Bn. O150 Detached force under Major Dare returned to 14th Bn. Bivouac having been relieved by 16th Bn. Casulties of detached force during absence 3 officers 100 others. Strength: — 12 officers, 313 others. Capt. Chaplain Rev. A Gillison killed. Sick to hos. 18 others'.

As the death toll mounted from the abortive August offensives, Alfred Guppy, started to take it to heart on a day that was 'thundery with some rain'. Writing in his diary, he recounted that 'During last night Garcia and I obtained a few hours leave and walked across to our own Battn. The poor old Battn was mixed up in the fight last Saturday and lost heavily. Our much loved Padre, Captain Gillison, was killed, whilst trying to rescue a wounded man under machine gun fire. Lieut. Crabbe was killed and Lt's Coutie and Dadson wounded. Sgt. Gilbert was killed and Bob Lawson again wounded. In fact there seems to be hardly anyone of the old boys left, and there is less than 300 in the Battn again now. Garcia has been made a L/Cpl and myself a Sgt. We returned to our work at 3 p.m. A heavy shower fell today. There is an unpleasant job on hand for us tonight.'

Lt Col. Reynell claimed reinforcements from the British Leinsters were 'the absolute bally limit. A more miserable useless lot of Devils I can't imagine. They seem to have no spirit or pride of any sort ... one could do more with one battalion of Australians or New Zealanders than 5 battalions of these men whose officers are a wretchedly incompetent lot ... if we have a fair sample of Australians here then Australians are a damned sight better tribe than I ever thought'. Reynell

Tuesday
24 August
DAY 122

SUVLA BAY, WHERE THE BRITISH LANDED IN AUGUST, IS TO THE NORTH OF ANZAC COVE. IT HAS A LONG BEACH AND PLENTY OF WIDE OPEN FLAT LAND, WHICH WAS MOSTLY OUT OF RANGE OF TURKISH FIRE, WHERE HOSPITAL TENTS WERE ERECTED.

said the Australians had dash, pluck, initiative, resource, dogged determination, patience and cheerful fortitude.

The 14th Battalion historian, N. Wanliss, noted 'Chaplain Gillison was the first chaplain in the AIF to be killed during the war. He had a most engaging personality, and was the most popular man in the 4th Brigade. A man of exceptional courage, his kindness had endeared him to all ranks, and his death on an errand of mercy sent a cold chill through the hearts of the whole battalion. There was not any personal incident in the whole campaign which caused a greater sensation or gave rise to more sincere regret in the battalion'.

Wednesday 25 August
DAY 123

'Today was to be the beginning of the rainy season', Charles Bean announced 'and the weather has clearly changed. It was very muggy: a little rain fell'. Fortunately, according to Capt. D.B.A. King, the fighting was not as fierce today. 'Some Naval men visited our gun. Nothing much doing. Got some letters from home.'

Thursday 26 August
DAY 124

Charles Bean was recovering from light wounds received during the August offensives. He reported that 'our hardships will really begin with the winter'. Although after listening to the Tommies praising them, he thought Australians might have been 'greater heroes than we were inclined to think ourselves'. Despite this flattery, he also noted the Anzacs did not trust 'the Tommy'. The Anzacs did not have 'the slightest confidence in Kitchener's army — nor have our officers — nor have I'. Bean believed 'the truth is after 100 years of breeding in slums, the British race is not the same' as 'in the days of Waterloo' and 'the only hope is that those puncy narrow-chested little men, if they come out to Australia or N.Z. or Canada, within two generations breed men again'.

Friday 27 August
DAY 125

Led by Lt Gen. Birdwood, the Anzacs tried again to capture Hill 60 one last time. The nine battalions used included some of the best fighters from the 10th Light Horse. Although they captured some trenches, they failed to get anywhere near the summit and there were 2,500 casualties.

Pte. James Turnbull Grieve told his parents about his lucky escapes. 'It took us till nearly daylight to unload our Battalion and all our gear and ammunition, and it was the hardest bit of work I have done since I joined the army … At two o'clock on Sunday morning we were all roused out of bed and told that we had to make a charge … a good number of our boys were bowled right out … It was marvelous how I came out without a scratch, but I expect it was my luck … After the charge I got into a trench which about 60 of our Batt were in and there we had to stop for almost 35 hours … We were in such a cramped position … and I would have given all I possessed in this world for a real good drink of water … I never wish to have the same experience again. Since coming out of the trench we have only been sapping and digging trenches … it isn't too bad … give my best love to all the girls down at the Palace … From your ever loving son'.

In his last diary entry before being killed in action a few hours later, the popular Lt Col. Carew Reynell said, 'I hear we are to be withdrawn in a day or two … to be sent to Imbros or Lemnos for a few days rest. We can all do with a rest I think. Personally I am pretty run down and have had a cold for a long time and am lousy'. Col. Reynell had earlier seemed to predict his own death on 2 August when he wrote, 'Well some of us will be making room for others before long and it's all in the game'.

SUSPECTING HE MIGHT BE KILLED BUT VOLUNTEERING ANYWAY FOR A RISKY ATTACK ON HILL 60, THE BRAVE LT COL. CAREW REYNELL HAD REPORTED IN HIS DIARY THAT 19 PER CENT OF HIS UNIT HAD BEEN KILLED OR WOUNDED, ADDING, 'ALL MY PALS WOUNDED NOW AND MY TURN NEXT I SUPPOSE — DAMNED NUISANCE IF I AM TO PROVIDE THE 20 PER CENT KILLED OF THE SAID CASUALTIES'.

End of Week 18

The fighting went on until the end of the month. Maj. T.A. Kidd reported 'Heavy fighting on Hill 60. 800 yards from our present position. We meet quantities of wounded men as we move along to this position. Apparently operation ended in our favour. We carry our heavy packs and are favoured with un-aimed rifle fire throughout the route. We are subjected to shrapnel this morning directly after daybreak. Colonel Noel M. Brazier is struck near the eye with shrapnel. Olive trees grow wild and are now covered with unripe fruit. The thick tangled undergrowth consists mainly of dwarf oak covered with small acorns. It is quite a treat here in open country and fertile at that. What a change from the close … air of the trenches. Plenty of shrapnel flying about but one can breathe the pure air, hence the preference. We are associated with the famous 29th Division (Regulars) and are camped next to Connaught Rangers. Our 9th Regiment were heavily engaged last night … Their losses however were severe'.

**Saturday
28 August**
DAY 126

Sunday
29 August
DAY 127

Despite the odds, Lt Gen. Birdwood's Anzacs continued to attack Hill 60. The costs were indeed high, as Lt W.M. Cameron wrote a couple of days after one battle in which he lost his friend Lt Col. Carew Reynell. Cameron now noted 'At 6.30 p.m. the Colonel sent for me and gave me orders to report to Brigade Headquarters as Orderly Officer. I went round and reported to General Russell. Had not been there long when I got orders for our Regt. to supply 1 officer and 50 men for reinforcements on an important position which they had taken during the evening after a prolonged artillery bombardment. These were supplied and sent off. An hour later they called for 100 more and 2 officers and later for 25. These were duly sent along and I reported back to Bde. HQ I just got back when Colonel Reynell arrived behind me and asked the General to allow him to accompany his own Regt. This he was permitted to do, and after giving me some instructions for the 2nd in Command started off for the position; just as he left he turned to me and said "Goodnight Cameron".

'I do not know how it was but I felt a premonition that we would not meet again, and so it proved, for during the night, by some instructions received later, an attempt was made to take some more trenches. It was a gallant charge led by the Colonel and two Captains. On the command "The ninth Regiment will charge" they leaped over the parapet and raced for those lines of Turkish trenches on Hill 60. The fire, as always, was very furious, and men fell like flies. Col. Reynell and Capt. Jaffray were killed and Capt. Callary is missing, probably killed also. The hill and slopes are covered with dead and trenches are filled with bodies, friend and foe. We have thus lost two Colonels and 3 Captains in less than a month. We have had reinforcements since we came here which would bring us if there were no casualties up to 800 men, and out of all

AFTER CAPTURING THE LONE PINE TRENCHES, ANZACS HAD TO DEFEND THEM AROUND THE CLOCK AS THE TURKS REPEATEDLY COUNTER-ATTACKED, MAKING LONE PINE THE MOST DEARLY HELD OF ALL ANZAC POSITIONS. AWM AO4013

these I am sure this morning we cannot muster 200. In my troop I can only muster eight effectives out of forty-two'.

Despite continuing length of service, soldiers like Maj. T.A. Kidd remained proud of their achievements. 'Being the fittest I remained on duty last night. Men were very tired and some in a state of stupor. 2nd Lieut. Howard who rested during the day remained during night to help. We have a bomb fight practically from dusk to dawn but more than hold our own. Turks managed to hurl several bombs in our trench, but my bags on trench floor successfully stopped them and very little damage was done. I allowed three men only (2 Throwers 1 Observer) to remain in bomb throwing trench. ... Before daylight this morning a bomb prematurely exploded resulting in fatal injuries to Trooper Fletcher. Through faulty fuse bomb exploded in Fletcher's hand. His two hands and one leg were blown off, both eyes blown out and stomach pierced. He was conscious for an hour and calmly gave instruction re personal effects ... After beating yesterdays attack many Turks took refuge in a gully. We detected these yesterday afternoon crawling back to trenches ... In Sunday [29 August] morning fight we had no support from guns or M.G. Tonight I go down to bivouac to have a short rest weary but damned pleased with myself. We had letter of thanks and praise from General Godley during fight Sunday'.

The British forces finally gave up attempts to capture hills inland of Suvla Bay and Allied forces gave up trying to capture the heavily fortified Hill 60. After thousands of deaths, even the commanding officers realised they were wasting men's lives. As one imaginative participant remarked, 'even after all this fighting the Turks were still the forehead of the hills looking out over the sea while the Allies were just the eyebrows'.

After the heavy fighting, having a laugh was a relief, as Trooper I.L. Idriess revealed, 'Was on outpost duty last night. The Turks were very quiet. A destroyer would occasionally flash a search light on to the Turks trenches, fire a few shells, and then quieten down. I could feel my damned leg aching last night. I have just had the first wash for four days. It was delicious. As a sniper was pinging at us getting the water and running back to cover was a bit hurried. I did not know Gus Gaunt was such a sprinter before. To see him running naked from the beach with a bucket of water in his hand and a Turk bullet whistling merrily just overhead was very amusing. I was looking on'.

Although this 4th Brigade hospital, like most hospitals, was positioned as far away from the frontline as possible, because it only consisted of tents, patients were still killed or wounded in their beds whenever a long range shell lobbed from the Turkish guns fired from the hills above. AWM P01116.036

CHAPTER 7
SEPTEMBER
Murdoch Exposes the Disaster

It is undoubtedly one of the most terrible chapters in our history.

KEITH MURDOCH, JOURNALIST,
LETTER TO AUSTRALIAN PRIME MINISTER
ANDREW FISHER, 23 SEPTEMBER 1915

By September, the campaign had reached another stalemate. The Anzacs' attempt to break out of their trenches and capture the heights had failed. They captured Lone Pine but they had lost thousands of men killed or wounded and now many of the survivors were sick. The soldiers lived in the most unsanitary conditions surrounded by thousands of unburied bodies. Fleas, lice and a range of disease spread through the crowded trenches. More and more men were invalided away with dysentery, diarrhoea and enteric fever (cholera). Worse still, a troop ship ferrying reinforcements from the 2nd Australian Division towards Gallipoli was torpedoed. The poor soldiers of Anzac Cove were in no state to do anything but hold on.

It was a hopeless situation even though many of the officers and soldiers who had been fighting there for months could not see their dilemma. The visiting Australian journalist, Keith Murdoch, knew immediately that the Gallipoli campaign was a failure. Commissioned by the Australian government to review alleged irregularities in the troop's mail service, he also interviewed key players at Gallipoli about the campaign. He reviewed the progress or lack of it and wrote a critical report, which he sent back to the Australian Prime Minister, Andrew Fisher. Murdoch also visited London, briefing some of Britain's most influential political leaders. By the time he had finished alerting Australian and British leaders to his criticism of the battle, he had helped fast track an inevitable evacuation — which some of the more enlightened officers had been talking about since the day after the landing.

The ordinary Anzacs, however, put their energy into recovering from the defeat of the August offensives. They were intent on recuperating, improving their dugouts, trenches and 'quality of life' for the temperature had dropped and winter began to threaten the fragile seaside bivouac.

Wednesday 1 September
DAY 130

After the failures of August, Trooper Ion L. Idriess relished any chance at getting back at the enemy. 'It must be galling to Johnny Turk to have his parapets blown to dust while we joyously blaze at him and he dare not show up to fire back in return ... Another "stunt" to-night is rumoured. A "stunt" means a raid. A line of men with bombs dangling from their belts and armed otherwise with any lethal weapon they fancy, creep over the parapet and snake their way down the hill-slope, followed by more men with fixed bayonets. They creep over closer towards the Turkish trenches and if they do not run into an enemy patrol or meet a sudden volley of machine-gun fire they get right to the parapet and hurl in their bombs … they and the bayonet men, with mad yells, jump down into the fume-filled trench and kill every Turk they can. So any man due for a raid, cannot help wondering whether he will see another dawn.'

But the Anzacs were not the only ones attacking, as Trooper Ernest Pauls from the 12th Light Horse complained. 'There was a terrific fusillade of rifle, machine guns and bombs from 9.30 p.m. as the Turks kept things going after our boys started a stunt' and 'we were called to arms during this demonstration of fire, as a bayonet charge was anticipated.'

Thursday 2 September
DAY 131

Capt. Fay of 3rd Field Ambulance finally had a chance to write to the family of John Simpson Kirkpatrick, 'The man with the donkey' who was killed back in May. 'Dear Miss Simpson … Your brother landed with us … at daybreak on the 25th of April so taking part in the historic landing. He did excellent work during the day. He discovered a donkey in a deserted hut, took possession, and walked up and down a dangerous valley carrying wounded men to the beach on the donkey. His plan was a very great success, so he continued day by day from morning till night, and became one of the best known men in the division. Everyone from the general downwards seems to have known him and his donkey which he christened Murphy. The valley at the time was very dangerous as it was exposed to snipers, and was also continuously shelled. He scorned the danger, and always kept going whistling and singing, a universal favourite. So he worked for three weeks. On the night of the 18th May, as you will have read in the papers, the Turks made a heavy attack on our position. Early in the morning as usual your brother was at work, when a Turkish machine gun played on the track where he was passing, the day of his miraculous escapes were passed, for he fell on the spot shot thro' the heart. He truly died doing his duty. We buried him that night in a little hill near the seashore known as Queensland Point, Chaplain-Colonel Green of our Division reading the service.'

Meanwhile Trooper Ernest Pauls got a shock when digging a tunnel under Turkish positions. He came across a couple of Turks who, unlike Simpson, had never been properly buried. 'We unearthed two dead Turks while we were deepening the trench. They had to be removed. A view over the parapet with the periscope reveals a sight that is too gruesome to write of here — the remains of the charge in July.'

Friday
3 September
DAY 132

Charles Bean, although suffering from diarrhoea, took his fellow journalist, Keith Murdoch, who had just arrived to the top of a hill to see the view of the battlefield. Murdoch then investigated the situation on his own, interviewing officers and other journalists like Ellis Ashmead-Bartlett who also believed the campaign had been mismanaged.

Murdoch was lucky to get to Anzac safely, as the reinforcement ship *Southland* (with the 21st Battalion) sailing from Alexandria with the transport *Haverford* (carrying the 23rd Battalion) was torpedoed just hours from Lemnos by a German submarine on 2 September. As soon as the news reached Gallipoli, I.L. Idriess noted the disaster among the day's events. 'Was in the firing line again last night … working trenches to-day. There is much sickness. We have just received news that the Southland has been torpedoed. Brigadier Maj. Linton was drowned and a few men. They were of the 6th Brigade. The Southland eventually made port under her own steam.'

'Strike me pink if old Gus Gaunt hasn't been wounded in the arm', Trooper I.L. Idriess added. 'It does not look to be a very bad wound. One of our big sea planes is buzzing overhead and the Turks machine gun at Gaba Tepe is speaking a lightning tut-tut-tut-tut-tut-tut … There was very heavy firing towards Achi Baba … I with a few others, are detailed for the Lonesome Pine outpost this morning. There are plenty of bombs there, I believe … We have arrived at the Lonesome Pine, after a lumbersome walk through narrow saps. The stench is something awful, dead men, Turks and Australians, lying buried and half buried in and about the trenches. The flies are very thick and troublesome. No wonder they can only keep men in here for a 48 hours shift.'

Also at Lone Pine that night was Trooper Ernest Pauls who noted 'we received word at 9 p.m. to cease fire as a burial party was going out to bury some Turks that attempted to charge at 2 the previous night'.

End of Week 19

Saturday
4 September
DAY 133

Keith Murdoch went to see Brig. Gen. Harold Walker and inspected the front line outpost of Lone Pine, which was still being fired on by Turks. That was not the only target coming under fire, as Pte. E.G. King noted with alarm. 'We have been worried very much lately by a big gun, which the Turks got from the French and is called the French 75. She fires a shrapnel shell with terrific force and hardly ever fails to hit someone. In the last couple of days, we have had several men wounded and one killed outright by it. C Coy. has had the most casualties in the battalion, the number being now about 50 men. Rested all day.'

The Turks were just as worried as the Australians judging by a diary confiscated from a captured Turkish officer. Maj. Eric Hyman, who was in charge of the machine gun unit for the 12th Light Horse, recorded some of the Turkish soldier's notes. 'Our men have left everything to God and are all expecting to be killed any moment. After the flight of an enemy aeroplane four of the enemy ships began an unprecedented bombarding of our back trenches. In the meantime enemy machine guns firing from trenches only 30 metres away deprive us of many of our dear comrades. But with fixed bayonets we are waiting for the enemy'.

Bean reported that Murdoch interviewed Brig. Gen. Walker who he found 'was really expansive telling him how he had come to believe in and love his men and how he would not change his command for the world'. As the campaign dragged on, old mates became increasingly important as Capt. D.B.A. King noted. 'To-day I was sitting on the gun and who should walk in but Vernon looking darn well after an exciting trip from Alexandria; going up to see him to-night. Saw him and had a good yarn.'

The officer who ordered the hopeless attacks on the Nek to continue, Maj. Gen. J.M. Antill now attended to more domestic issues as he 'Spent all the morning supervising new area. There is an accumulation of all sorts of arms, equipment, ammunition used and unused tool clothing scattered everywhere. The place is filthy and covered with tins and rubbish'.

On arrival at Gallipoli, the survivors of the *Southland* began putting their lives back together as Capt. Ivor Williams explains. 'Today all the gear was brought over from the "Southland" and reissued. A Memorial Service was held in honor of those who lost their lives on the scrap. We lost our Brigadier — Colonel Linton who was drowned along with 32 others'.

Sunday
5 September
DAY 134

One of the most enthusiastic reinforcements arriving at Anzac Cove, Capt. Bill Knox of the 13th Australian Artillery Brigade, wrote to his wife Mim (aka Mildred), 'I will be in the party very soon now' after having had 'a very thrilling experience on the way across'. He believed 'a special providence must have been watching over me' because 'at the last moment before leaving I transferred from Southland to Haverford to join a cobber'.

Monday
6 September
DAY 135

Much to Pte. N.S. McLeod's disgust, many of the bodies from the August assaults remained unburied. 'We expected to be shifting first thing this morning but the other companies went first and left part of ours behind. I paid a visit to the trenches in the firing line and saw where some of the 8th Light Horse got badly cut up in a charge. You can only see this through a periscope as if it is not safe to look over the parapet. There were bodies and kit lying there unburied and had been in that state for a month. The trenches are that close together that you cannot bury the dead without coming under their fire at very close range. We shifted to the support trenches at Lone Pine this afternoon and found our packs very heavy when going up the hills and at night we got a taste of the noise of the firing line at close quarters.'

VISITING AUSTRALIAN JOURNALIST KEITH MURDOCH, WHO DESCRIBED THE CAMPAIGN AS 'UNDOUBTEDLY ONE OF THE MOST TERRIBLE CHAPTERS IN OUR HISTORY', LOBBIED THE AUSTRALIAN PRIME MINISTER AND POLITICAL LEADERS IN BRITAIN TO EVACUATE.
AWM A05396

Despite the August offensive, it seemed every hill was still a fortress. Lt Harry Briggs, wrote his mother 'Just a few lines, am still going along A1 and am pleased we are at least getting a spell, where we are going is not yet Public, but as long as its away from this Hole any old place will do … The weather still continues fine here never a sign of rain. I think they make up for it in the winter … I will have to see this job through I expect before they parade us in the Old Country. Things are going very satisfactory here its turning out rather a slower process than they thought, its a pity they gave the Turks all those months to prepare for us, every hill is a fortress. I think I mentioned in a previous letter that we captured Turko-German Machine Gun. You would have laughed when we first opened fire with it. At the first burst of lead there was absolute silence from the Enemies lines for about 5 minutes when they suddenly discovered they were receiving a dose of their own medicine. Then every rifle and M. Gun near by opened up without success.'

Tuesday 7 September
DAY 136

Although he rarely communicated with his troops, Gen. Hamilton now issued a Special order in which he 'formally recorded the fine feat of arms achieved by the troops under the command of Lt Gen. Sir W.R. Birdwood during the battle of Sari Bair. The fervent desire of all ranks to close with the enemy, the impetuosity of their onset and the steadfast valour with which they maintained the long struggle, these will surely make appeal to their fellow countrymen all over the world. The gallant capture of the almost impregnable Lone Pine trenches by the Australian Division and the equally gallant defence of the position against repeated counter attacks are exploits that will live in history'.

While in a writing mood, Gen. Hamilton also issued an order conveying 'admiration for the gallant behaviour of all ranks on board the transport Southland when that vessel was torpedoed'. Hamilton said he was proud 'of the courage and discipline shown at a moment when the nerves of the bravest were liable to be so highly tried'. Hamilton concluded 'The 2nd Australian Division knows well the high reputation it has to live up to, to carry on the brave deeds done by those who have been here earlier in the campaign, but with men like those on the Southland we are fully assured that our new comrades are going to prove themselves equal in all ways to the old hands who have fought so well.'

Despite Hamilton's fine words, it was clear Sapper V. Willey had had enough as he profiled a day in the life of an Anzac for the folks back home. 'It is very hard to give you any idea of what trench warfare is like, as the same thing occurs — day after day, night after night, and week after week. There is seldom a day goes by but we are under fire; with shells continuously bursting around us, flying machines dropping bombs and darts, and rifle fire, and men getting killed and wounded. Any amount of excitement, but of the wrong sort! It is enough to shatter the nerves of the strongest, and to make a man wish he was well out of this rotten place. We are fed up with this life, and the strain upon our constitution is terrible. In fact, some of us who have been in the trenches since 25th April are now as weak as cats, and no wonder! I will give you our "bill of fare" and you can see for yourselves that our luxuries are few and far between. In the morning we get a piece of bacon ... a pint of tea and hard biscuits. On rare occasions we also get a loaf of bread. For dinner, we have three courses — water, tea and sugar (lovely). For tea, we have bully-beef stew (done to perfection). This happens every day, barring the bread — but at times the bread is forgotten altogether ... Another trouble is the vermin, of which we also get a good supply — from the tiny red louse to the larger dog-fleas; as well as centipedes, flies and snakes ... I am beginning to feel like an old man! ... Have just received word that we are to be relieved from the trenches and sent to Lemnos for a spell; and we are now like a lot of school boys going on a holiday.'

Wednesday 8 September
DAY 137

Lone Pine remained the hot spot for most Anzacs as Pte. H.H. Abbott noted in his diary. 'We have just finished 24 hours sentry duty at Union Trench and are ready to march off to Lonesome Pine a pretty hot corner. We are in a Dugouts just behind the trenches, and have just been told that our Platoon is on fatigue duty for the next 48 hours.'

One of the reinforcements, Sgt. A.W. Bradley, told his family, 'we landed here about 3 o'clock Sunday morning, marched along about a mile to where we slept till daybreak. All Sunday we were making dugouts on the sides of the hill, got off for a little while in the afternoon for a swim but the shrapnel got a bit too thick so we took a move'. Bradley also reported his first lucky escape. 'We got orders Sunday night to be ready for the trenches by 8.30 next morning, when we would into support trenches, remaining there till next morning. Just after leaving they shelled it with shrapnel, were out just in time. These support trenches before mentioned are a network of trenches in rear of the firing line and connecting same. There are dugouts all along the walls for sleeping in. We went into the firing line first thing yesterday morning for 24 hours, came out into the supports again this morning. The trenches are about 80 yards apart where I'm posted ... Each post has a periscope — 2 men on each post at a time one man observing and one sniping, each man doing 2 hrs on and 4 off. Things are very quiet in the line, just shot for shot to show that the trenches are occupied, have a shot at their periscopes when they show, they hit one of ours yesterday and the glass cut one chap's face.'

These periscopes were essential as the Turks were becoming more accurate. 'One of the 11th Light Horse was sniped' Trooper Ernest Pauls wrote. 'It proved fatal and we buried him at night.'

Thursday 9 September DAY 138

With some excitement, Col. Darlington, a 'Tommie' serving with British forces reported the appearance of the first and only known visit of women at the front line. 'Yesterday afternoon when I was resting I saw a naval launch quite close to the shore and some handkerchiefs waving. I did not take much notice until one of the servants rushed in and said, 'There's women in that boat, Colonel'. I went out and sure enough there was a party of Australian nurses being shown round the shore to see how the wild soldier lives and sleeps. I got my glasses to see the unusual sight and much to all Tommies' annoyance, a young nut of a staff officer with much ostentation put his arm round one of the nurses' waists, struck an attitude and waved his hand at us. We all shook our fists at him, which caused great amusement on the launch ... they were the first women I have set eyes on since May 6th!'.

Although he had not seen any females, Sgt. A.S. Hutton was just happy to see signs of life outside Gallipoli. 'I went up on Table Top Hill today & got a fine view of our position all round. We have a pretty quiet time here up to now. I saw a village ... today it was quite nice to see civilization even in the distance'.

Trooper Ernest Pauls was 'relieved to see the last of Lonesome Pine as on first entering the trenches the stench is terrible and on looking through the periscope across the Turks trenches we see our gallant men laying there since July. Of course the Turks lay there in the majority, but our men are human beings and the thought is terrible and still nothing can be done'.

Friday
10 September
DAY 139

Now at Gallipoli, Capt. Bill Knox had helped pull survivors out of the water when his ship was torpedoed. He told his wife, 'We picked up many men from the water and all behaved with great coolness right through, a most cheery crowd even the ones hanging on the oars and deckchairs in the water did not seem to be worrying much ... I have had plenty of thrills as no place here is really free from Turkish fire and they sometimes put their explosive shells down in the most unexpected places' but 'they have done wonders here and it makes one wonder how many troops in the world could have landed that first day much less hung on and got their guns up. The men are well fed and cheery and nothing seems to worry them — all the British officers one meets unhesitatingly admit our fellows were magnificent'.

Stealing a quiet moment while his 'two mates are having a few mts sleep' Lt F. Burton said, 'I will drop you a few lines. We are in the firing line and my two mates are jolly fine fellows. We occupy No. 5 Post which is a very good one to sleep in and also to get a good view of the Turks trenches which are only 40 or 50 yds away from us. I think (Robertson) one of my mates shot a Turk this morning. The Turk was looking through the loop hole and Robby shifted him alright. The bullet went in the loophole so if the old Joe Bourke didn't get hit he was very lucky'. Although Turkish wounded could be reported, the Anzacs frowned upon reports about their own. 'I was round to see Jack O'Callaghan a few days ago and found him looking well and wishes to be remembered to all. He is very wild about Uncle putting his photo in the paper when he was wounded and wrote poor old Uncle a very stiff letter so I am afraid Uncle will not put it in again'.

Charles Bean claimed to have found the key issue of the campaign. 'Well, the problem of Gallipoli reduces itself to — why can't the British fight?' He came to the conclusion in his diary that 'The British social formula breeds very poor feeble specimens of men and makes sure they are kept in the place ... They have neither the nerve, the physique, nor the spirit and self-control to fit them for soldiers'.

Saturday
11 September
DAY 140

End of Week 20

Using his Saturday to catch up with overdue letters, Lance, Corporal H. Villers wrote the letter that families back home dreaded receiving. 'Dear Madam, I am taking the liberty of writing this short note being I think the last of the friends of poor Naish [Capt. P.I. Callary] to see him ... we are no ways certain of his death though there were a great number

THE CLIFFS RISING ABOVE
ANZAC COVE WERE SO STEEP
IN PLACES THE ANZACS HAD TO
BUILD STAIRS SO SOLDIERS,
WATER CARRIERS AND THOSE
CARRYING SUPPLIES COULD
SERVICE THE FRONTLINE.
AWM H15375

of bodies that were not recovered. There is just the bare possibility of his having been taken prisoner and we would know nothing about it. We got out of our trench first about the same time and I spoke to him just before we parted ... That is the last I saw of him ... he was actually seen to enter the Turkish trench, then nothing further. I would not yet grieve for him as lost, but hope for the best. I can assure you nobody misses him more than I am likely to do ... We had a pretty thorough search for Officers bodies ... but could find no trace of Naish and I can assure you I had a quiet search on my own ... We lost a lot of fine fellows that night, men who would have followed Naish anywhere and I am amongst the fortunate few that returned ... In conclusion I would like to tell you that your Brother proved himself one of the very bravest of men and also proved himself worthy of the position as Captain in our Squadron.'

Trooper Ernest Pauls spent most of his days digging and constructing tunnels under Turkish positions or *sapping*, as they called it, in order to blow Turks up from below. Writing by candlelight in his 'Sapper's Mansion', he said, 'It seems a strange game we are at. We are now 35 yards in front of our own firing line underground in the tunnel only 12 feet from the Turks. One day or night soon it will see either the Turks or us blowing one another up as they are playing the same game and sapping towards us.' Pauls noted they had to be prepared for anything. 'The idea now is to catch the Turks when they sap into our trenches and blow them up.'

On a lighter note, Capt. Bill Knox wrote to his wife that 'My dug out is known as the "bridal chamber" probably because I am the lucky possession of a bit of mosquito net which my man has hung out in front to keep out the flies — some blighter will pinch it soon I expect'.

Sunday 12 September
DAY 141

The big gun being used by the Turks continued to worry the Anzacs, as Lt H. Strangmar explained. 'A day of rest and gladness perhaps in some unmolested areas but not so with Mr Turk, as soon as daylight was well established the Turkish artillery gave us a fair sample of shell war and their shells, like ours contain no oysters, Beachy Bill throws what one might term a sea shell but it bursts above the water and is full of death not life. This gun has done an enormous amount of damage on the beach and it cannot be put out of action, try as our batteries will, she must have a wonderful position and many of our artillery men are anxious to examine the spot'. Shelling aside, he still had supper to look forward to. 'Our cooks made a bonzer plum pudding today for dinner, and I can say with full meaning it was very good and everyone did well on it. Our party was increased from six to nine today and now we are complete, and a very happy lot. I was told that Rickety Kate was put out of action during the shelling this morning. I hope that it is not a furphy she did not fire at all tonight. We have been here a week today and no damage done by us or to us.'

A proud Victorian, Sgt. A. Guppy, was pleased his home state was fuelling the recruitment so well. 'I received a letter from Bess today; she says that quite a number of the Benalla boys have enlisted. Nearly 40,000 enlisted in Aussie in a fortnight of July. Victoria contributing the largest percentage. I had a party of men on work carting the Battn. stores down to the beach. We are supposed to be going away tomorrow. All the 7th Brigade have landed and some of them came up to the trench today, and went in amongst our boys for instruction in front line routine and work.'

Monday 13 September
DAY 142

The great thing was to have some exercise outside the prison-like trenches, as Lt T. Miles explained. 'The 12th Battn are out of the trenches again, we have been out three days and are having a grand spell, we are right out in rear of the trenches and have good dugouts with plenty of room to stretch ones legs. we overlook the beach and are only 200 or 300 yards from the beach, there are generally some ships moving about, there are always at least two Hospital ships ... always several torpedo destroyers and small cruisers prowling about, before the 'Triumph' was sunk there used to be plenty of big warships up here, but now they run no risk, they remain in Lemnos Harbour.'

As Lt Miles noted, these water views came at a cost because, 'People who have not been here dont realise what a slender hold we have here what it has cost us. We talk of being "out of the firing line", whereas we are really in more danger from shells than we are in the trenches, we are never out of the firing line in Gallipoli. That is what makes it more trying than any of the other Campaigns even as I write shells go whistling overhead, most of them are meant for ANZAC Cove, but one often drops here. At first when you get among bursting shells you duck from them all, but you gradually get to know the sound so well, that you can judge almost to a yard where it is going to burst ... I wont be surprised if they put us back in the trenches again. The uncertainty is what knocks the heart out of a man here, if they would only tell us what we are to do we would be satisfied'.

Tuesday
14 September
DAY 143

Having now listened to comrades, it dawned on Capt. Bill Knox that 'we have to reckon this war may last another two or three years and what the outcome will be goodness knows ... I am getting used to it now for we are constantly getting shelled ... I was most awfully lucky not to be on the Southland when she was torpedoed — but that sort of luck can't happen twice running'.

There were, of course, financial compensations for the Anzacs as the author of the 12th Infantry Brigade Diary pointed out. 'Quiet day. arrangements made to relieve 9th Battalion. Pay drawn from Field Cashier for Battalion (705 pounds).'

Wednesday
15 September
DAY 144

A series of dreadful diseases now took an increasing toll among the troops. 'The general health is bad', the author of the 12th Infantry Brigade Diary reported. 'As 50 per cent of the men unfit for duty and unless relieved there will be to a certainty, a severe epidemic of Pneumonia, Dysentery and Enteric Fever as the resisting power to disease is practically nil.'

As torrential rains provided a mid-week break, Corp. Darnell, gave his 'Dear Little Mother' a portrait of his muddy life at Gallipoli. 'Well its beginning to get pretty cold here now don't know what it'll be in winter its trying to rain now as perhaps you can see by the unequal writing but its raining ... the whole of this place seems to be all hills and dales ... like at Kangaroo ground in rows one after another with a flat top on some of them its a great sight from the top of the hills ... its a devil of a game climbing up and rolling down the packs its easier to roll down than walk. We have to go on a long time without a wash its about 7 days since I had one before today' but with the rain 'I'm writing under my overcoat now ... if I'm not careful I'll be floating down the trench soon, at any rate I'm pretty well washed now. But the worst of it is that all my clothes get washed before me and the result is that all the mud off them runs on me. And when we crawl along, crouched down so as to keep below the top of the trench, we pick it up with every step, Oh well the main thing is I am contented. It's not all beer and skittles.'

The problem, Pte. E.G. King reported, was lack of shelter. 'Rained this morning for a while, making things very uncomfortable, as we are camped out in the open. The only shelter we can get when it rains is our waterproof sheets. This is the 2nd time it has rained in the few days we have been in the camp. The ground is clayey and when wet is very sticky and is heavy walking. We moved out about 2 p.m. and came up to the top of the Ridge (Pope's Post) where we have taken over the trenches.'

One of the recent reinforcements, Pte C.W. Schultze, wrote that he 'landed here on 7th September in the dark and went into the trenches next morning'. He told his family that 'It seems strange being under fire at the start, but you soon get used to it. The Turks' trenches are only 10 to 30 yards from us, and we can throw bombs into them by hand. The Turks are very fair fighters ... There are flying-machines over us at the present time, and guns and rifles going for all they are worth. It seemed strange at first to see men walking about as if nothing was going on. We stayed on Lemnos Island for four days to get equipped. This is a champion place for flies; and water is very scarce. I have not had a wash since I came here, and do not see any prospect of getting one. I am in good health and have so far escaped the shells, bullets and bombs. Several boys who came over in the same boat as I did from Australia have been wounded or killed ... I have had some narrow shaves, but seem to get myself out of the way in time ... It seems strange to be sitting down having your meals with bullets flying all around you. I am actually writing this a few yards from Courtney's Post ... I would just have to put my head up for a second and that would be the end of me'.

At Suvla Bay, Bert Webster said he had not ducked his head earlier when shells came over. In front of his mates, he 'took no notice of them but just stood still while everybody else nearby started to bob down and duck their heads' because he said he was still 'trying to crack hardy'. Having survived so far, he was as pleased as punch because he 'received a couple of papers two days ago and it was just like old times to sit down & read the "Age" after breakfast'.

Perhaps chaplains had special resilience because Chaplain W.E. Dexter survived even after being hit for the sixth time. 'In morning German plane came over and dropped 4 bombs but all dropped in the water. The 3rd Brigade Reinf. were sent to their Brigade and we have now in camp about 350 men. In am. went over to 3rd Brigade with a few parcels. On the road Abdul got on to the Reinforcements with "Beachy Bill". He did not get any but he got a sergeant of the 9th Bn. and whilst I was with him Beachy nearly got me. Then later when I was copying an inscription from a grave his shrapnel just went about 2 yards away. I stayed with Robertson (padre) to dinner and Abdul was shelling all the while. Apparently Abdul had been very busy all the morning and Robertson had several funerals. Abdul has started a new game now ... whilst the men were still in the trenches Abdul got his .75 to work on

Thursday
16 September
DAY 145

Friday
17 September
DAY 146

IN URGING THE EVACUATION
AFTER VISITING GALLIPOLI,
THE AUSTRALIAN JOURNALIST
KEITH MURDOCH, SHOWN HERE
SITTING BETWEEN HIS
BROTHERS IVON AND ALAN,
WARNED THE AUSTRALIAN
PRIME MINISTER ANDREW
FISHER, 'NOWHERE ARE WE
PROTECTED FROM THE TURKISH
SHELL. OUR HOLDINGS ARE SO
SMALL AND NARROW THAT WE
CANNOT HIDE FROM THE
TURKS'.

In urging the evacuation after visiting Gallipoli, the Australian journalist Keith Murdoch, shown here sitting between his brothers Ivon and Alan, warned the Australian prime minister Andrew Fisher, 'Nowhere are we protected from the Turkish shell. Our holdings are so small and narrow that we cannot hide from the Turks'.

our men and gave us a bad time. During the afternoon I dropped in to see Padre Bladeu (Melb.) and whilst in his dugout a shell burst close by and struck a man in the throat. It was only a graze but the fright knocked him out. I sent him away to the dressing station to get it painted and was just going away when another shell came and I got one bullet on the left elbow. Luckily no harm done but a lump. This is my 6th hit. I must be pretty thick skinned. A little iodine put things right. I saw a lot of Wonthaggi boys … In the evening went for a walk … Lovely moonlight night.'

Although not wounded, Lt T.E. Cozens, had his own cross to bear. 'Getting along as best I can but dysentery still bad. Can't eat. Don't want to go to Dr. if I can help it.'

End of Week 21

A homesick Capt. D.V. Mulholland received some reminders of home. 'I got the good old gum leaf and pretty sprig of wattle and to see the number of soldiers wearing all these little articles in their hats is most impressive. I also received the papers, bulletin and mails you also sent and unless anyone is actually in the front line of trenches with us they can't conceive how acceptable all these pages of news are to us. Even the items in the lost and found column are thoroughly digested. I felt proud to be an Australian when I read of the great work done by our people on Australia Day ... It is not much use sending much in the way of clothing as very often it appears somebody else usually gets them. Socks from what I hear are always acceptable as one has to throw away any that become worn at all simply because water cannot be spared to wash them. Knowing what the flies were like in Egypt, I took the precaution to purchase a fly net, and a good big piece of mosquito net to use over here. I wouldn't part with either for love or money. You can't imagine what the flies are like here. The usual thing is to eat with one hand and keep the other constantly waved over your tot of tea.'

The first cold weather began arriving towards the end of September. Pte. A. West recorded the weather as well as a death notice. 'Sent hospital Sergt. Foreman. Reported Corporal Clements died of wounds received at Lone Pine. Quiet day and night — becoming very cold towards morning. Ideal days and moonlight nights'.

Capt. Bill Knox also told his wife that although he was feeling 'splendid' he was 'shivering cold at this moment'. But he was not so anxious about the shelling as, 'I am getting used to it now for we are constantly getting shelled and familiarity breeds a certain amount of contempt with all here'.

Trooper Ernest Pauls, who was back in the firing line at Hollie Spur, complained his post was so bad 'we are more likely to be sniped at than do any successful sniping'. But as he said there were disadvantages to shooting across the ground as 'Turks get blown up out of shallow graves then we have to suffer with the smell and flies'.

Sunday
19 September
DAY 148

The death, casualty and sick list continued to mount, even during a month without any major battles. Maj. Gen. J.M. Antill reported the toll. 'One man killed, one wd. [wounded] 26th Battn. while working in Saps — The Brigadier sick to-day and to Hospital but Lt W.S.K. Hughes rejoins from sick. He states many men at Mudros well, who cannot get back to duty owing to no methods existing also Visited ANZAC and Beach to-day — first time for several weeks away from Section, and surprised to see the great changes — Terraces take the place of all our previous primitive dugouts — The tops of Hills razed, tents erected, a tramline from ANZAC to the old MULE GULLY —

Monday
20 September
DAY 149

thousands of tons of stores … Water laid on … Health of Bde. fair but usual number of sick chiefly "stomach" to Hospital also Diptheria case to-day.'

Tuesday 21 September
DAY 150

Although the Anzacs had been at Gallipoli for over four months, the parcel delivery system was still failing. Col. R.E. Roth couldn't even get some big items for the horses. He 'had settled everything before we left Egypt, by mistake some of the harness belonging to the 7 wagons instructed to leave behind was taken on with us. The shoemaker's tools which should have been sent to us at Heliopolis were sent to No. 1 Aust. General Hospital there. At present I have harness which ought to be at Heliopolis and equipment at Heliopolis which should be here. It seems to be impossible to allow me to send anyone to do this'.

On a day when Gen. Hamilton paid a rare visit to Anzac Cove, Lt W.H. Bertwistle 'Rigged up notice board and letter box perhaps to catch the great general's eye … Sir Ian Hamilton and staff came round line'. Despite falling temperatures, 'Party of us went to beach for a swim after dark. Mounted a gun in our new position. Fired a few shots out of it. Position sniped at'.

Wednesday 22 September
DAY 151

Anzacs were killed every day just going about their business. A philosophical Sgt. G. Hunter Rogers explained that it was par for the course. 'Sent up Scott's Creek 1st station for 24 hour shift. Just as we were moving of a taube flew overhead and dropped a bomb about 300 yards from the camp, it was quite close enough and sent us flying, in all directions (very high explosive shell used). I went up an took a photo of the hole made during the morning. About 3 p.m. we lost one of our boys Grimwade was on picquet at the water tank and a 75 burst at his feet. The shell (or piece of it) went in his back and through or close to the heart, he died immediately Thompson who was standing talking to Grimwade was wounded in the leg and saw the shell set fire to a pile of tents and smashed a bundle of poles up. We are all very sorry for both victims but they did their bit and someone has to go.'

While some were killed or wounded at Gallipoli, others celebrated lucky breaks. 'I suppose I am about the most popular man on the Peninsula at the moment' Capt. Bill Knox wrote to his wife 'as I just got — brought from Imbros — 30 dozen fresh eggs wonder of wonders'. Writing on, he said, 'You ought to see the — Anzac fleas, millions of them, and other things that crawl and stick closer than a brother. My blanket nearly walks by itself — however one can get used to anything ... post me a tin of powder for fleas and other things'.

Thursday 23 September
DAY 152

Having left Gallipoli for London, Keith Murdoch wrote a scathing report to the Australian Prime Minister, Andrew Fisher. This diatribe and his reports to British political leaders (corroborating critics like Ashmead-Bartlett) helped persuade the British War Council to evacuate Gallipoli. 'Dear Mr Fisher, The Cabinet will, ere this reaches you, have dealt with my report on AIF mails and wounded ... It is of bigger things I write to you now ... of the unfortunate Dardanelles expedition ... It is undoubtedly one of the most terrible chapters in our history ... Certainly there has been a series of disastrous under estimations ... Winter is on us, and it brings grave dangers. We have about 105,000 men ... on the peninsula ... Nowhere are we protected from Turkish shell. Our holdings are so small and narrow that we cannot hide from the Turks the positions of our guns, and repeatedly damage is done to them ... Already the flies are spreading dysentery to an alarming extent, and the sick-rate would astonish you. It cannot be less than 600 a day. We must be evacuating fully 1,000 sick and wounded men every day ... The spirit at Suvla is simply deplorable. The men have no confidence in the staff, and to tell the truth they have little confidence in London ... So badly shaken are they by their miserable defeats and by their surroundings; so physically affected are they by the lack of water and the monotony of a salt beef and rice diet, that they show an atrophy of mind and body ... At Anzac ... the men are thoroughly dispirited, weakened by dysentery and illness ... The men have great faith in Birdwood, Walker, and Legge — not much in Godley ... But for the General Staff, and I fear, for Hamilton, officers and men have nothing but contempt.'

Capt. Bill Knox had arrived just after Murdoch left and certainly agreed there was no safe place soldiers were protected from Turkish shells. 'We only have about 500 acres at Anzac and they can pump shells into any part of it ... we usually get a bit of morning and evening hate as a rule ... one gets some thrills up at the observing station as it is right in front of our front line trenches and plenty of odd shells come all around.'

ALTHOUGH HE HAD PROMISED BRITAIN SUPPORT 'TO THE LAST MAN AND THE LAST SHILLING' AT THE OUTBREAK OF WAR, AUSTRALIA'S LABOR PRIME MINISTER, ANDREW FISHER, HAD BEGUN TO DOUBT THE VIABILITY OF THIS CAMPAIGN BY SEPTEMBER.

Friday
24 September
DAY 153

Of all possible excuses for not doing the painstaking diary entries, Lt C. Dakin had the most compelling, although he did manage to describe yet another offensive. 'Owing to poisoned hand I have been unable to do any writing for 2 weeks. Most of the time has been fairly quiet with occasional outbursts on either side. Last week they landed on the beach in front of us a Battery of guns. There are I believe a lot more big guns still arriving so that there ought to be something doing shortly. Early this week the Turkish Artillery on our left gave a demonstration it lasted about 30 min in which they must have sent along a few hundred shells but from our position we could see them all sink out at sea some near the Battleships which began to reply … Big supplies of store are being stacked up at the foot of this Hill and around at Anzac; the small railway line extends now for about a mile and half around the beach … they also have 2 big motor lorries carrying supplies to our left, they only run during the night time as they have to cross ground exposed to the enemy's fire … this is the place where the dispatch rider crosses sometimes 4 or 5 times.'

At Hollie Spur, Trooper Ernest Pauls 'Had a sniping duel with a Turk for an hour today, but owing to his position couldn't catch him, although I was successful in making him cease fire. Weather very wintry now'.

End of Week 22

Saturday
25 September
DAY 154

Writing reassuringly to his mother, Sgt. R. Adam claimed it was now 'far safer, in fact it is very hard to realise we are "warring". Their is nothing doing up our end. — all the terrible fighting you read about is always at Cape Helas or on our left; up this end you might say there has been no real fighting (bar the one trench they took when I was away) since the day they landed. Our position is one maze of deep saps and tunnels (most bewildering at first) on the top of a steep ridge, as safe as any body on the east coast of England and about the safest position on the whole line (without exaggerating) If the powers that be allowed it, it would be perfectly safe to show people round, firing line inclusive. I simply tell you all this to prove I am not in a quarter of the danger I am afraid some suppose me to be in.'

Nevertheless, Sgt Adam could still use some special treats to supplement the menu. 'I will enclose 2 10/- notes so that when you feel inclined you can send along a cake or plum duff (not those nasty super rich black things you get at Xmas time or at Buzzards) all the same something which will stick to ones ribs as they say. Also stuff like … condensed milk, toffee, plain chocolate and such like. Please get them packed in air tight tins as it lessens chances of pilfering, and not in big lots at a time as such a small percentage of parcels turn up here, some unnamable brutes get them in between … It is generally agreed now that all parcels arriving for sick or wounded absent men are divided among his mates. That is fair but it is a different matter when parcels never reach here, and even then are often tampered with somewhere en route'. Not that Sgt Adam needed basics, as 'We get better food now too (to my mind) a bit of bacon for breakfast, tea with *milk* and sugar in it for all meals, fresh meat and bread odd times a week, otherwise, "dog" and hard biscuits, also jam. For tea we get rice, sometimes has currants in it, far better than cheese, and as we have platoon cooks it is all right. We also get desiccated vegetables in the daily tin dog stew … some times on the beach one can buy cigarettes and tobacco, tinned stuff, chocolate and eggs, but not often and v expensive … Don't send any more films as I have lost my camera, never having used it, which is a pity. R.W.W. Adam'.

ALTHOUGH SOME OF THE BODIES WERE BURIED IN HIGH CEMETERIES, DOWN NEAR THE BEACH AT ANZAC COVE, WHEN STORMS BATTERED THE LITTLE MILITARY SETTLEMENT IN NOVEMBER, VIOLENT SEAS UNCOVERED SOME OF THE BODIES. PHOTOGRAPHS BY CHARLES BEAN

Sunday
26 September
DAY 155

A religious Capt. Ivor Williams attended 'Church at 9 a.m. About the middle of it a German aero plane flew over. Just shortly after a shrapnel shell burst right in the middle of the Parade but did not hurt anyone. I am still feeling off colour'.

One hour later, Chaplain W.E. Dexter reported the same sort of distractions from the heavens which he averted. 'At 10 a.m. had a good service in the Reinf. camp followed by Communion (24). Just before Service a German plane was overhead but did not spot us for I forbade the men to look up. The human face is a most distinctive mark from an aero plane.' Undeterred, Dexter repeated his service that evening. 'At 6 p.m. had a good service followed by H.C. in the dark (22) … It was beautiful and moonlight when I got back and soon turned in.'

Although he complained 'all days are very much alike', Capt. Bill Knox acknowledged 'they do have church services at all places but so far I have not been able to go as one had one's job to do first'. He did receive some good news that he was 'Promoted to Staff Captain on Divisional Artillery HQ'. He also thought this had its disadvantages as 'the work is interesting but not the thrills of feeling you are actually killing a few of the blighters — but it has just as much chance of getting it oneself … it is bad luck now if anyone gets it as we are natural sort of fortress … a few poor beggars do get it every day'.

Using Sunday as a letter and report writing day, Maj. Gen. J.M. Antill recorded, 'Number of officers and other ranks absent, sick, wounded … colossal, representing two-thirds of the Bde. 55 officers and 1,209 others — many of them dating back as "fit" from June-July. The condition of affairs indicates an absence of system or control once an individual is evacuated for a trifling sickness such as, boils, cold diarrhoea or other. And from sufficient evidence it is clear, once a man gets away he can stay away or go to England or elsewhere … Ample evidence is rampant in regard to this great abuse which no representation has been able to alter or improve … if a serious attack were made we cannot hold our trenches … We hold about 550 to 500 yards with less than 400 bayonets'.

Monday
27 September
DAY 156

Lt T.E. Cozens thought another offensive was brewing and was happy to take it easy saying, 'Orderly Corporal today so had a very easy time. Took the sick in the morning, wrote seven letters, sewed the buttons on my trousers, had a lovely swim and fixed up my toe-nails and so forth. Big bombardment on the left in the evening. Something doing'.

The new Staff Capt. Bill Knox had been looking for action and was excited at last to be 'sitting in the Lone Pine trenches with the Turks only 20 yards away and the dammed shells coming in all around the place ... nobody pays any attention to rifle fire here except of course in the fire trenches but it is their blooming big Howitzer shells which don't give the boys much rest'.

Trooper Ernest Pauls who helped blow up a tunnel under the enemy now feared 'a death trap has been set for us by the Turks if we have to shift them from Hollie Spur and I will consider myself a lucky man if I am spared from death so that I can continue writing in this book'.

There had been some 'terrible bombardment at Achi Baba and Cape Helles' overnight and 'heavy cannonading on the Anzac's left flank' Trooper Ernest Pauls reported. However, things were looking up for Corp. A. Gunter, who was able to indulge in a couple of leisure activities. After a 'fine morning with heavy shelling at Turks trenches hitting barbed wire', he said 'Asia sent some big ones over near aerodrome'. Nevertheless, he took part in a 'Swimming parade with all hands' and observed a 'Great lot of gambling going on now'. The boys were gambling because it was payday.

Swimming days would soon come to an end Capt. Bill Knox predicted. 'We'll be here or here about over the winter and winter will be very cold and nasty and it will be hard to walk about up steep hills on wet clay.'

At Suvla, P.O. Bert Webster could not 'help but mention the good luck which seems to hang over our heads: — we have been working here for 6 weeks under this constant fire & have only had 8 casualties'. Webster was pleased to have helped build a pier at Suvla as 'Last Sunday morning, early, the Newfoundlanders (about 1,300 strong) landed at our pier'. But they were not as lucky as Webster's comrades because 'at daybreak the Turks sent over a few shells & injured 14 of their number before they have even made a start'.

Tuesday
28 September
DAY 157

Charles Bean returned to Anzac Cove after a break and bumped into Ellis Ashmead-Bartlett just in time. Bartlett had been expelled from Gallipoli for giving Murdoch a letter he had written to the British Prime Minister 'putting the state of things here in a somewhat crude light' which was 'brilliantly written' urging evacuation, Bean said. It was intercepted on route and Ashmead-Bartlett was accused of disloyalty and recalled. However, combined with Murdoch's letters, his criticism

Wednesday
29 September
DAY 158

helped start the discussion for evacuation, which would take place in a couple of months time.

An eager recruit, Pte. N. Wilson who 'Arrived at Anzac Bay at last', said he did not 'feel anyway nervous' as he wanted 'to get at them right away — brought ashore in a lighter and marched up to Shrapnel Gully. Demonstration held by the Turks as we arrived. very picturesque sight to see shells explosion of bombs and big guns and rifle fire. rifles made more din than anything else. several bullets came very close. one man slightly wounded two others hit bullet never penetrated. issued with more ammunition I have 280 rounds with full rations water bottle full packs with blankets waterproof. will never forget that march to Shrapnel Gully. arrived about 11 o'clock was told to rest for 3 hours needed no telling never took packs or equipment off. just fell down and slept'.

ONE OF THE MOST ENTHUSIASTIC RECRUITS TO ARRIVE IN SEPTEMBER WAS CAPTAIN BILL KNOX, 13TH AUSTRALIAN ARTILLERY BRIGADE, PICTURED WITH HIS WIFE MIM AND DAUGHTER DIANA (AKA 'BUBBYKINS').

The wide awake Trooper Ernest Pauls reported, 'The Turks erected a barbed-wire entanglement on our front last night, doing this right under our observers' noses, thereby having the laugh at us. Our bomb throwers and machine guns were not allowed to open fire for fear of bringing the Turkish artillery to play on us'.

'Your tin of cakes from Mutual Store turned up' Capt. Bill Knox told his wife 'and there was great joy. I bartered some for candles as the sun was so hot it used to melt them all before they got here. I was tremendously popular while it lasted'.

Thursday 30 September
DAY 159

Whether or not she wanted to hear such things, an optimistic Capt. Ron E. Smith told his 'Darling old Mother' of lucky escapes. 'Our battalion is in reserve while the other 3 are in the trenches. That doesn't mean we are doing nothing & escaping danger. We have had a fair number killed & wounded already. In particular we have been doing road making up the precipitous gullies and have lost men from the enemies' fire while doing this. I have had several bullets come within a yard of me but not been hit & don't expect to be. Just now the warships are shelling the Turks' trenches about 4 miles away & the rumble of the echoes amongst the hills is just like thunder. When they are closer to us & our guns fire as well the ground where we are shakes. Just now I had to stop to see one of my company. He was lying down in his dug out about 2 chains from mine, and had started to come out feet first, when a bullet went in the top of his instep & came out of the sole of his foot. It isn't dangerous but will take a good while to heal'.

There was always something new to report at Anzac Cove, especially with newfangled contraptions taking to the sky and eluding the enemy. An unnamed 20th Battalion soldier noted 'One of our Hydroplanes (they seem to be just an ordinary aero plane fitted with two big floats) flew along parallel to the Turks trenches. They were sending shells at it all the way, then, an aero plane flew right over the enemies position and they were shelling it. We counted as many as 20 shells, but they were all pretty wide of the mark. The heavy bombardment still continues on our right possibly our ships hammering at the Narrows'.

By October, the Anzac gunners had perfected their art and were knocking out Turkish gun emplacements and destroying trenches with great accuracy with this 18 pounder, which was operated in a sand-bagged gun pit by the members of the 9th Battery, 3rd Artillery Brigade. AWM P00046.041

CHAPTER 8
OCTOBER
Trading Tucker with the Turks

EACH ONE DOING HIS BIT
Drawn by W. OTHO HEWETT

*Extraordinary friendly exchanges between the
Turks and our fellows this morning early. Some
of our chaps ran right over to the enemy trenches
and exchanged bully, jam, cigarettes etc. The
whole business was wonderful and proves how
madly unnecessary this part of the war is.*

LT T.E. COZENS, AIF, DIARY, 19 OCTOBER

By October, the campaign at Gallipoli had ground to a halt. The Anzacs were not advancing nor were they retreating. They were in limbo — like the Turks on the other side of the no-man's-land between the trenches. In fact, front line soldiers had more in common with their enemy in the neighbouring trenches than they did with the superior officers back in comfortable quarters at the beach, or the generals out at sea on ships or the politicians directing the attack from London. So, although it was against orders, the soldiers from opposing trenches began to get together — swapping friendly notes, cigarettes, biscuits and bully beef (although, not surprisingly, the Turks often rejected the latter as it was so indigestible).

These unofficial friendships struck up with their Turkish opponents, (often just metres away in a facing trench) made a mockery of the ongoing attempts by both sides to kill each other. Many of the wounded were still recovering from the failed offensives in August against Lone Pine and the Nek and the Allies did not have enough momentum to mount any more attacks in the hope of a breakthrough. Their failed leader, Gen. Sir Ian Hamilton, was at last sacked and replaced by Gen. Sir Charles Munro. His mission was to assess the comparative feasibility of mounting new offensives, hanging on or effecting an

WITH WELL-ESTABLISHED WHARVES, UNLOADING AREAS, TIMBER YARDS, SUPPLY DEPOTS, 'STREETS' AND A WELL-LAID-OUT SERIES OF TENTS AND DUGOUTS, THE MILITARY SETTLEMENT AT ANZAC NESTLING UNDER THE FAMOUS SPHINX, SEEN HERE FROM NORTH BEACH, WAS LIKE A BUSY COUNTRY TOWN.

evacuation. The Anzacs still held onto their hard-won positions — especially Lone Pine, the pride of the front line trenches. To maintain their position, they had to withstand continual firing from the heights above which inevitably claimed lives.

Despite the relative safety, the Anzacs fell sick from the increasingly filthy conditions, surrounded as they were by poorly buried and decomposing bodies, lice, fleas and flies spreading diseases. Most could cope with the boredom but the worst thing was the uncertainty. After all, by late October some of them had been there six months without advancing against the Turks. So why were they still there?

Throughout October, the British did not change their official attitude toward the campaign. However, with no sustained attacks against the Turks, the diaries and letters now began to focus on smaller things that were closer to home — the weather, clothing, food and water. These mundane preoccupations held the soldiers' interest until the 'bombshell' that was dropped the following month — as a result of Gen. Munro's timely visit in late October.

OFTEN THE FRONTLINE TURKISH SOLDIERS BASED IN THEIR WELL-FORTIFIED TRENCHES WERE ONLY METRES AWAY FROM THE ANZACS IN THEIR FRONTLINE TRENCHES. THE SOLDIERS INEVITABLY GOT TALKING AND IN TIME THIS LED TO EXCHANGING NOTES, CIGARETTES AND FOOD, MUCH TO THEIR OFFICERS' ANNOYANCE.

Despite soldiers falling sick around him, the hard-hearted Maj. Gen. J.M. Antill, was always anxious to demonstrate progress, claiming in his official diary 'Generals Birdwood and Godley inspected trenches and expressed pleasure and surprise at the amount of work done and the excellent condition of lines and trenches. Enemy is now very consistent daily in shelling, in retaliation of our persistent worrying of his positions by day and night with M. Guns and R. fire'. He also noted 'An excellent Mule Road finished right up to Trenches and bridges built'.

The strain of building this excellent mule road now got to Light Horse Trooper Ernest Pauls, one of the gang who put it in place. 'Relieved from sapping tunnel, to go and widen another tunnel so that a mule train can take rations and water right up to the front line at Hollie Spur, so as to save carrying all the stuff. Shifted camp to old place overlooking Anzac Harbour with all its beauty and the warships and hospital ships and trawler fleet. Reported that Turks reinforcing heavily at Lone Pine, during which time Turkish batteries opened a terrific fire of shrapnel. Am feeling off colour and weak, I fancy it is the effects of the dysentery'.

Friday
1 October
DAY 160

End of Week 23

**Saturday
2 October
DAY 161**

Gallipoli lost one of its greatest war correspondents when the 'disgraced' Ellis Ashmead-Bartlett was informed that he was to be expelled from the front for attacking the war effort. It was his colourful reports of the landing that helped put Gallipoli and the Anzacs on the map. As Bean lamented, 'So Bartlett has gone' and the Anzacs have lost 'a friend of lost causes' who was always 'a rebel against the stupidity of the foreign office'. He was a correspondent, Bean claimed 'whose written dispatches are full of life and colour, hit hard, and give a brilliant idea which is remarkably true'.

The dreaded Beachy Bill continued to hit the mark as Corp. A. Gunter reported. 'Laid under guns all day, Beachy Bill fired about a dozen on the Beach got 5 or 6 men. About 10 p.m. took the Bty up to Shrapnel Gully past Casualty Point parked guns and wagons to bed about 3 a.m.'

Not that Beachy Bill was the only gun to watch out for, as an unnamed soldier from 20th Battalion noted, 'The Turks appear to have got a fresh gun up near Chunik Bear with which they shell the destroyers when they come in closer to shore to do some firing. It was rather amusing yesterday afternoon. We were all sitting watching the fun. The destroyer came in and commenced firing, then some high explosive landed very close, so she moved a little further, still they came close, so she turned around and made a big circle and came back to where she started, then tried again. This went on for some time. She always moved just in time for the shell to hit where she had just left. These little plays go on nearly every afternoon and it helps to pass the time nicely.'

**Sunday
3 October
DAY 162**

Maj. White informed his wife he had been promoted to General. 'Do not smile, for I am smiling still! I neither look nor feel like a General and I object to posing — so what am I to do?'

At the end of his first month, Captain Bill Knox revealed 'it really grows on you this place and the men in the Lonesome Pine area are really fond of their job'. That was by day, but at night things could be different as Knox revealed 'there is nothing so rotten as losing one's way and finding the bullets hitting pretty near and not knowing the way out … you can't show a light of course'. Knox complained he 'ended up in a blind tunnel in a particularly dark and lonely part and when I came back out a stray bullet glanced off the solid heel of my boot — not an Achilles Heel apparently'. He related that 'one poor beggar stopped one in the stomach' and 'one of the R.C. padres got his finish while swimming in the water, but the pleasure of a swim always seems to be worth the risk'.

That night Corp. A. Gunter paid a price as he helped with the unloading and delivery of newly arrived stores which always had to be done at night. 'To Beach with party of men to bring up stores. Beachy Bill got me in the back 1 p.m., to Hospital thence to Hospital ship, leg very painful.'

Monday
4 October
DAY 163

Having been relatively quiet for some time the Turks opened fire with vengeance as Captain Bill Knox reported. 'They have just started ripping in with all their guns on us from every side and there is the deuce of row going on — our fellows are now all opening and shells are everywhere up above and it is by no means healthy outside'. Dangerous though it was outside, Knox stayed indoors enjoying his mail. 'Thank you for your letter with the ripping photo of you and Bubbykins — what a lovely fine Kiddy she is and I am sure she is just as good as she looks'.

Unlike Knox, the youngest Australian soldier at Gallipoli, James Martin, who was only 14 years of age still hadn't received a letter from home. Yet he had written many times describing how he had survived the wreck of the *Southland* in early September and how he had 'been in the trenches for more than a month now so are used to it'. Although he reported, 'we have not had many casualties yet', he did reveal that 'one poor fellow of our old company been shot and killed and two or three wounded'. Even though he complained he was 'not seeing much of the fun', he did say 'now and again we give a few rounds of rapid fire and get them to waste their ammunitions for about twice as long'. But surrounded by death as he was, the youngster begged his parents for a letter. 'It is very disheartening to see all the others getting letters from home and me not even getting one. I have not received any since I left Melbourne on June 28th. So they must be going astray somewhere. I hope you are getting some of mine as I am writing pretty often'. The boy soldier added an urgent PS: 'Write soon as every letter is welcome here'.

Mail from home was not the only treat enjoyed by the Anzacs, as Capt. Ivor Williams noted. 'Some gift stores were distributed. They were in the way of biscuits, dates, sardines etc.'

AN OIL PAINTING BY TURKISH PAINTER ASKERI MUZESI DEPICTING THE TURKISH MISERY AT GALLIPOLI. (ISTANBUL MILITARY MUSEUM)

Tuesday
5 October
DAY 164

As the winter rains undermined accommodation, Charles Bean had his dugout moved and rebuilt because 'where it was it stopped a drain of water'. The assaults on Achi Baba had cost many thousands of Allied (and Turkish) lives. Capt. Ivor Williams was thrilled to see it at last. 'We saw the actual hill of Achi Baba today. It is not at all an imposing affair. We also had a good view of an enemy territory. One point we noticed where a fort used to be. It was blown right off by one of the Queen Lizzie's big guns.'

Yesterday's shelling by the Turks upset Capt. Bill Knox. 'Apparently they didn't mean any real attack but their shells got their toll of our chaps as every single gun has an allotted area to fire on and explosions were bursting all around my dugout but none came nearer than 30 or 40 yards although splinters fly all over the place but I saw some rather gruesome sights and that part I don't like much'. Sadly, Knox said 'just heard the little driver who got hit while unloading guns on the beach died today'. Despite early enthusiasm, he now admitted 'living in an atmosphere thick with dead Turks ain't the best thing going but I am still going strong old girl'.

Those who didn't get shot fell by the wayside through sickness. The hard working tunneller, Trooper Ernest Pauls, complained, 'I am now unable to work as I have a fever with a temperature of 102.2 degrees'.

Wednesday
6 October
DAY 165

While sheltering in his dugout during the constant shelling, Chaplain E.N. Merrington got a visit from a strange caller. 'The weather is warm again, like the "Indian Summer" in America. I went to divisional Headquarters in reference to obtaining Communion wine. Returning by the, 1st and 3rd Field Ambulances, I visited the patients. We observed Turkish bodies which have lain for some time in out of the way places being burnt by our men. After writing up the Burial Returns for the Division, I went for a swim. Sergeant Steel of the R.A.M.C. called on me at night. As I had no candle we talked in the darkness. My head was resting against the earth's wall dugout when I heard a scratching sound. Switching on an electric torch I saw a big centipede twisting and turning near where my head had been. He was soon dispatched. Dugout life knows many strange visitors. The vermin are the most persistent and are unspeakably awful when one sleeps in a crowded line, especially of old enemy trenches. My health is beginning to fail under the strain of the campaign.'

Capt. Knox reported a new flare up in the fighting. 'We are gunning again this morning but only in a very leisurely way, just like a light spar at boxing swapping shells with one another's vulnerable soft spots but the day may develop — that's the beauty of this business, when least expected we get some good shooting.'

Although the Anzacs held their own with conventional weapons, Lt H. Strangmar feared the arrival of a new and deadly weapon. 'A demonstration opened out about 8.30 from our Lone Pine trenches, it was a very fine effort and gave Mr Turk a hot time. The boats came to the party and gave a very helping hand with the pudding. This morning at about 2 a.m. orders were given that smoke helmets were to be held in readiness as some gas bombs had been sent from the Turkish Trenches it is said that some of our lads were damaged by the gas. Ye Gods and we were ordered not to fire the other night we have no word of movements on our flanks but are waiting very patiently they have given us some heavy shelling just lately.'

Nobody was safe, as Captain Bill Knox reported. 'Poor old Risdon Grimwade went out last week on the beach and a 75 went right through his chest. I believe he was Norton Grimwade's boy'. He also noted there was never a dull moment on the beach, thanks to false alarms. 'We just had great excitement for a few minutes as thought we saw a submarine periscope but that turned out to be only a buoy.'

Unable to walk, Trooper Ernest Pauls finally admitted defeat, but not without a fight. 'Doctor taking my temperature found out that I was trying to deceive him by cooling the thermometer so it showed only 98 degrees. But he took my temperature again and his correct reading showed 101.6 degrees. Besides giving me a severe overhauling he

Thursday
7 October
DAY 166

ONE OF THE MOST POPULAR CHAPLAINS AT GALLIPOLI WAS PADRE ERNEST NORTHCOTE MERRINGTON, SEEN HERE CONDUCTING A COMMUNION FOR MEMBERS OF THE 3RD LIGHT HORSE BRIGADE AT THE 'APEX' WHERE HE USED TWO BISCUIT BOXES AND A CLOTH AS AN ALTAR. AWM PO1875.004

decided to send me away at once.' As he was being shipped away, the reluctant patient heard 'heavy rifle fire opening up from our position at Hollie Spur, assisted by terrible number of star bombs. Fancy Turks have tried to attack. Just my rotten luck to be sent off the peninsula when something is doing'. After treatment for enteric fever in England, Trooper Pauls was sent to Palestine where he rode with the 12th Light Horse in their successful charge against Beersheba. Surviving the war he returned to New South Wales, married and started a family.

At Lemnos, Pte. F.W. Muir said they had a 'Concert in the Y.M.C.A. tent to-night. Quite a decent affair. Artists chiefly from the 3 A.G.H. The Dean presided and a number of nurses were present, was surprised to see Charlie D'Arcy Irvine among the singers'.

Friday
8 October
DAY 167

The Anzacs had been on the beach for 24 weeks and the weather had changed dramatically since that first spring day when they landed in their summer uniforms. Charles Bean noted approaching winter. Having said earlier he feared the settlement at Gallipoli could be washed away in torrential rains, he now recorded, 'A heavy storm tonight — the heaviest weather since we reached the Peninsula'.

Meanwhile, Pte. Wilson heard of the capture of an enemy officer. 'Very heavy rifle fire going on, Turks getting nervous, a Turkish officer has just passed under escort gave some valuable information. He gave himself up a few days ago, starting to rain naval guns going.'

End of Week 24

Saturday
9 October
DAY 168

Still waiting for letters that never came, the youngest soldier Jim Martin, continued writing home begging for letters. He said he hoped the chooks were laying eggs and that his parents had plenty of boarders. He also reassured them that he and his comrades were killing more Turks and looked like winning the battle at Gallipoli. 'According to an account of a Turkish Officer who gave himself up the other night, the Turks are getting badly treated by German officers and are only getting one meal a day'. Martin also reported that 'there was one Turk who tried to give himself up but got shot by the sentry. We dragged him into our trenches to bury him in the morning and you should have seen the state he was in. He had no boots on, an old pair of trousers all patched up and an old coat'. By comparison Martin said 'we are not doing bad for food we got that little present from Lady Ferguson that was 2 fancy biscuits, I half stick of chocolate and 2 sardines each'. He added another urgent PS saying, 'I have received no letters since I left Victoria and I have been writing often'. The baby of Anzac Cove never heard back in time because he died later that month.

Unlike Martin, Capt. Bill Knox did not think the enemy was beaten be any means. 'We have the Bulgarians against us now and from what we hear perhaps they will liven things up when they come down to help the Turks'. The Turks 'don't do much on the offensive but would be pretty difficult to shift when we attack them and they are on the defensive'. By now Knox was having second thoughts on the great Anzac achievement. 'Barring the bit at Suvla we hold no more ground now than they took on the first landing 6 months ago — however they can not shift us and that's a great thing … We had a nasty scare last night when it was reported the Turks were using gas in the Lone Pine although it turned out to be wrong. Any how we could blow them and their damned gas kits sky high with shells in a very few minutes after they started it so there is nothing to trouble us'. The alert Capt. Knox was right to worry about gas. Although the Turks never developed this deadly weapon, it was poison gas used by the Germans that eventually killed Capt. Knox in the Somme in 1917.

Enjoying a well-earned break, Pte. A.C. Trevena was relieved to have turned his back on exhausting fatigues. 'We have been relieved from the trenches for a spell which I can assure you was thoroughly earned … While in the trenches we had a fairly rough time. In over nine weeks we did not know what it was to get an hour's rest without having a corporal or sergeant ordering us to make up a fatigue-party. They would be after us before we could even get half an hour's sleep. Fatigue here is as hard on us as chopping Mallee-roots. The food we get is plentiful but not substantial; only bully-beef and cement biscuits. A fellow cannot do any work on such food, but we are still expected to do it. I will just give you an idea of what a fatigue party's work is like. One is told to do "water-fatigue" — which means walking a mile carrying two 2-gallon tins to a well, get them filled and hurry back. When nearing the end of the trip we have to climb up a steep gully, near straight up and down, and this pinch takes it out of us, especially working on empty stomachs. Then comes "drink-orderlies" which is one of the day-fatigues. To get our drink of tea we have the same caper again — down and up this blessed hill.'

As more rain fell and sickness increased, the Anzacs were in no fit state to do anything but hang on now as medico Lt Colonel R.E. Roth noted. 'Storm last night — rain and SW wind. 4 of the tents blew down

ALTHOUGH DESCRIBED AS A RABBIT WARREN BY SOME, GIVEN HOW DIFFICULT THE TERRAIN WAS RISING UP FROM THE BEACH AT ANZAC, THE DIGGERS STILL MANAGED TO PUT ALMOST EVERY INCH OF GROUND TO USE, CREATING AN ELABORATE SYSTEM OF DUGOUTS.

— the loose soil does not give the pegs a good grip. A case of mumps admitted yesterday, 2nd Reinf. of the 17th Bn. Was not in contact with the other cases. Notified that all cases for evacuation must be sent down to ACCS before 11 a.m. except emergencies. Cpl. Cook Edbrooke evacuated sick yesterday. Had a large hernia in the right side had it before the SC was transferred to 5th Field Amb. and was therefore not medically examined by us. Pte. Carruthers evacuated sick yesterday complained for some weeks about piles. On examination he was found to have two little piles about the size of half a pea. This condition made him very hypochondriacal — and as he was very unable to carry out his duties satisfactorily on account of this condition I evacuated him.'

Sunday
10 October
DAY 169

'Today is Sunday', P.O. Bert Webster announced to his mother '& it is a lovely day & as I lay basking in the sun, in the dinner hour, I think of you all at home dressed in your best & enjoying the rest after the weeks labor, but for us-well we have no holidays at all; Sundays being just the same as any other day. We have not had the opportunity of attending a church service since we landed here'.

Finally, Pte. E.G. King says the authorities made the connection between poor food and poor health. 'There have been so many men away sick with dysentery, that is has been found advisable to give us more substantial food. We now get fresh beef and bread 4 or 5 times a week and if that is kept up, it ought to improve the strength of the men. We also get plenty of rice, but we have always had that. The tinned beef isn't very appetising and the hard biscuits are little better.'

Accidental injuries added to evacuations. Sapper A. Nurse noted 'everything going on as usual. Only for a few bombardments by the Turks, but not much damage done. Turks' blow at D.26 but no one hurt. Our Lieut. Mr Thom gassed whilst trying to rescue Lieut. Bowra in C.2, which was entered too soon after the mine had been exploded, also three men killed through it. Bad day for us, for we had great respect for both Officers'.

Recruitment must have been going well in Australia. Corp. E. Magill reported that 'We got reinforcements a few days ago — young Rollo among them. The N.C.O. reverted to the ranks. We had every man in the firing line of a night and no supports so we needed them. C Squad. had 30 N.C.O.'s and men all told'. Corp. Magill was wounded on this day and died in Malta on 20 October 1915.

Before retreating to hospital with influenza later that day, the commander of the 12th Light Horse machine gun unit, Maj. Eric Hyman, reported some unusual observations. 'Found out this morning my orderly Saunders is a jew! Started gun in new position but hard to see with what effect. Fired 3,000 rounds with I think fair results. Attended at Divisional HQ and received pay for the unit. Corp. Malcolm reported for duty without any papers.' After Gallipoli, Maj. Hyman would lead the 12th Light Horse charge at Beersheba in 1917.

Fortunately one day's fighting was followed by another day's lull, as Capt. Ivor Williams noted there was 'Nothing doing. Very quiet'.

On this quiet Monday at the start of the week, an unnamed soldier, of the 20th Battalion exclaimed, 'Wonders will never cease. We got paid this morning, allowed to draw 30/-. We took it all then went searching for a canteen that might be open in a day or two. It worked up very stormy looking. We had a little rain then it cleared up again'.

Monday
11 October
DAY 170

Tuesday
12 October
DAY 171

Despite the general inactivity, the official diarist for the 20th Battalion reported some promising signs at last. 'We had all the Heads looking at our position today, Sir Ian Hamilton, Generals Birdwood and Holmes and about 15 Senior Officers'. The commanding officers may have used a lull in enemy firing to discuss their next move. 'Even the normal Turkish shelling from the heights had abated and there was very little doing. The heavy guns on the right have not been so noticeable the last few days. We have been on the third and half rations of water the past few days, but we got free rations today.'

At least the lull in fighting allowed some soldiers a chance to get over illnesses. Capt. Ivor Williams noted 'Am feeling very much better. Things are terribly quiet.' Over at Suvla, P.O. Bert Webster also noted, 'It is really marvellous how little damage the shells do compared to their large size and swiftness. The majority of them just seem to lob just where there is nothing'.

Capt. Bill Knox reported he still hoped they may 'have a stunt coming on at any moment, only a small show really but there will be some guns I expect and we want something to liven things up a bit especially as it is now obvious to all that we wont progress much from this base before the winter, if at all although there is any amount of the Turk chucking his hand in — but I doubt it very much'.

Wednesday
13 October
DAY 172

Even Generals could get hit by enemy fire. Chaplain W.E. Dexter described the incident. 'In the morning went for a ramble through the Lone Pine trench and found several boys I knew. When I was coming away I ran across General Walker who had just been wounded by a machine gun through the shoulder and a bullet still remaining in the thigh. He is very brave and went off to the Hospital ship where the bullet was taken out. He will not be back to us for at least a month. In the evening had 2 funerals at the beach cemetery. There is no padre on the beach now … It was very cold so wore my overcoat and went and had a yarn with Col. Marsh ASC for an hour of two. There is plenty of good stuff coming to hand now both clothing and eatables and it is at last reaching the men. Fine cold weather.'

Upset that Gen. Walker, who 'was a dear old chap and a gentleman', was wounded, a more philosophical Capt. Bill Knox decided that 'The more one sees of it the more one realises the rottenness and horror of the whole business. God knows I do want to do my bit and am far from having cold feet but any reasonable minded man must wonder what the outcome will be because to anyone gifted with any sort of imagination war is not a very pleasant thing, old girl'.

Things were improving for Corp. H. Billings who returned to Anzac Cove to find his fellow signallers had upgraded their accommodation. 'Left Suvla 11 a.m., got to Anzac about 12.30 a.m., had to wait long time and got to shore in horse boat 2 p.m., finally to Bde. H. Qrs. 5 p.m., after two mile walk through "saps" — Bds. HQ and 1sr Sig. Troop are now in a different position from where I left then two months before. They are now at "No. 3 Post" which is further North and just about adjoining the Suvla area which extends up to the extreme North flank of the Allied lines (That is just where we came back from) This is a fine position with the Signal Office and other offices cut out of solid very soft sand stone. We are in dugouts and shelters in a good sheltered position and quite well off.'

Good sheltered positions were important that day, as P.O. Bert Webster reported in the middle of writing a letter home. 'They have just piped "Hands get under cover"! and the shells are now flying over, my word how they whistle and hum'.

Capt. Knox also reported on a gun duel. 'We had a bit of a duel with the guns today as they lobbed a lot of iron mongery over here. I saw one poor lad who tried to stop a 75.mm with his head just outside here — but no use worrying my dearest, one just goes along from day to day'.

According to Charles Bean, advancing against the Turks was impossible because of worsening weather conditions, increasing sickness and enemy reinforcements. Bean confided that higher ranking officers now feared 'there were more Turks in front of us than since 6 August so tonight we have a demonstration planned to find out how many Turks there are in front of the whole line'.

That night Lt C. Dakin certainly reported that 'There was plenty of firing and Bomb throwing again last night the booming on our right has been very constant today, we now keep our guns mounted during the day'. Despite the shelling life went on. 'We drew each a packet and half of Woodbines presented by some firm; also we had 6 Cap Comforters 10 Cholera Belts, 3 pairs of Socks and 3 Flannel Shirts amongst 17 so we had to draw for them. I drew a Cap.' It was just as well there were some comforts as other moments still had their horrors. 'They have now opened up our new firing line in front of us and are now occupying it. It is a most gruesome sight to walk along it, as they have made it under where all the light horse bodies are laying and just on the parapet of the trench may be seen legs, heads and bodies of our men who died in the charge about the beginning of August and are still there.'

DRINKING WATER WAS A
PRECIOUS RESOURCE AT
GALLIPOLI, AS MOST OF IT HAD
TO BE BROUGHT BY BOAT AND
THEN CARRIED TO THE ANZACS
IN THEIR DIFFERENT POSITIONS
BY THE ALL-IMPORTANT WATER
CARRIERS. AWM G01241

To keep their spirits up against this background, Lt L.W. Sutherland noted the soldiers turned to sporting pastimes. 'Units were withdrawn out of the line for a period of rest, in the case of the Australian Light Horse ... fighting in connection with the Suvla Bay operations by the ALH had been extremely severe. October found the 1st and 3rd ALH on the Suvla Plain and as 'the Aussies were supposed to Rest so their thoughts naturally turned to Sport — Football and Cricket. Officers and men were sent to Lemnos to beg borrow or steal some kit — they, with Australian zeal produced it — various football matches were arranged and usually ran for about 20–30 minutes. Bully and biscuits doesn't build long winded forwards. The Cricket was much more successful — inter-regiments Matches were arranged between two Brigades and Brigade Teams were selected for the 1st Test — only one Test was played, the Brigades had to go into the line'.

End of Week 25

Saturday
16 October
DAY 175

The big news of the day was that Commander-in-chief, of the Mediterranean Expeditionary Force, Sir Ian Hamilton, was being withdrawn because the British War Council believed he was incompetent. They claimed he was too secretive, hopeless at communicating, explaining orders or briefing others and bad at planning. They alleged he sent misleadingly optimistic reports to Lord Kitchener and generally was unable to understand how badly his forces had performed. Having sent thousands of British, Australian and Allied troops to certain death, not many soldiers regretted his recall. Gen. Sir Charles Munro, 55, his replacement, would arrive soon to assess the merits of fighting on or evacuating the entire peninsula.

Hamilton's recall had no immediate impact on ordinary soldiers. Capt. Ivor Williams just had to get on with the daily routine. 'At 4 a.m. this morning we gave Abdul another demonstration, but somehow he did not take any notice of us. During the day the artillery on both sides was quite brisk. I had two very narrow escapes today. An Australian mail arrived'.

Gen. Hamilton's recall did little to lessen the dangers faced by Pte. E. King either. 'Shifted back to do our 8 days sentry in the trenches. The Turks have started to use a new bomb, which is thrown by a strong trench mortar. To-day was the first time it reached us and it did some damage, wounding about 10 of D. Company, who were camped in the place we had left at 1 p.m., today, so that our company just missed it. Our artillery were dropping shells over where the mortar was supposed to be and we heard that it had been smashed up, but it hasn't been confirmed yet.'

Sunday 17 October
DAY 176

After farewelling Hamilton, Charles Bean noted 'It is rather a fault of character than of intellect that has caused him to fail. He has not enough strength to command his staff — they command him'. His worst mistakes were the hopeless series of attacks on Achi Baba at Helles where, according to Bean, he 'did not have the strength either to give that plan up or to tell the War Office that the plan must be given up'.

There was nothing worse than a wet Sunday afternoon to depress idle troops. Lt T. Miles wrote in his diary 'Sunday afternoon, rain is falling steadily and it is a miserable sort of day altogether, it is twenty five weeks today since we landed here, only another week to go for six months of it.' Some of the duties were more interesting such as guarding prisoners for 'two hours on and four off, it is an easy job and as the temporary gaol is quite close to our dugout it is very convenient' and 'there are only two prisoners our men not Turks. One is a very sad case a chap in "C" Coy 12th Battn accidentally shot his mate dead while cleaning his rifle in the trenches the poor chap is only in the prison pending an enquiry and there is no doubt that he will be free from the blame but it is an awful thought to carry for the rest of his life. The other prisoner is a contemptible little cad waiting trial for stealing from his comrades, two extremes if you like, one deserves all pity and the other the extreme penalty that can be given for the crime, but such is life!'

In his Sunday letter to his mother, P.O. Bert Webster who had been building piers at Suvla announced his contempt for his duties. 'You don't know the conditions we have to contend with here — so *disgusted* have I been lately that I have handed in my resignation last week — I wanted to be reduced to A.B.D. (for they are having the best time) but it was not granted they would not hear of it at all, but I intend to put it through again, for this is an unthankful job and I tell you Ma, I know what I'm talking about. But never mind I am looking forward to a better day. Certainly the cash will be lessened but I will willingly forfeit all that is necessary.'

Amongst his domestic rounds, Maj. Eric Hyman of the the 12th Light Horse reported meeting the great general who would eventually give him command of the regiment for the charge at Beersheba. 'No

OPPOSITE: ALTHOUGH THE ANZACS HAD MANY NICKNAMES FOR THEIR ENEMY TURKS, THE FAVOURITE WAS ABDUL, WITH THE CLASSIC CARICATURE OF THEIR LONG-TIME FOE DRAWN HERE BY GALLIPOLI ARTIST TED COLLES FOR *THE ANZAC BOOK*.

parcels. Received letters also paper. Gave Baker ten shillings. Went around trenches and met General Chauvel. Heard from Capt. Hale that canteen stores had not all arrived. Seeton was issued with second blanket. Had dug-out made more comfortable.'

Monday
18 October
DAY 177

Rain and mud continued to dampen the soldiers' spirits. Pte. N. Wilson noted that it was 'Raining this morning and looks like keeping on. impossible to walk 2 yds to slippery being all clay saps'. This slipping and sliding would certainly have made Pte. N. McLeod's job more difficult, as he went 'Back to the trenches in the supports carting sandbags most of the day to ammunition guard at night'.

Although church services held yesterday could have been comforting amidst all the dangerous shelling, a newcomer, Pte. Caddy, pointed out you had to be able to hear them. 'Well we are here at last, and the first thing that strikes one is how the first troops that landed ever got over the hills and took up the position we now hold. Without seeing the country you could not realise the difficulty of the job ... The trenches are only about 20 yards apart in some places and bomb throwing is the great sport. They have special men trained as bomb throwers, and whenever there is a favourable opportunity they heave a bomb into the enemies trenches. There are not very many get killed at present, and I think one is just as dangerous outside the trenches as there are always stray bullets flying about from the snipers etc., and the shells from the big guns going over head, but after a few days one gets used to it and nobody worries or thinks about any danger, but goes on with their usual work. Yesterday we had church service — it seemed so peculiar — at times you could not hear the parson at all for the noise ... Water is not too plentiful. If you can get a wipe with a wet rag every second day you consider yourself lucky'.

Pte. Caddy then revealed the first of a series of unauthorised exchanges in which Anzacs started trading 'tucker' with the Turks, who initially even took a liking to the notorious bully beef. 'The Turk is not a bad sort of chap. A couple of days ago they sent a message across written in French and addressed to "heroic Australian comrades" asking for bully beef, which was given in exchange for cigarettes. The trenches are only about 20 yards apart in some places, so it is quite easy to communicate with each other'.

Now, amidst the boredom, this unexpected and most unofficial relationship between the lower ranking Australians and Turks developed further. They had shouted to each other across the narrow divide of no-man's-land for weeks but now they could not resist getting closer. This new friendship happened over a number of days in a number of different frontline trenches and Lt T.E. Cozens of 21st Battalion revealed the secret from his trench. 'Put in the day alternatively on the ledge and post. Extraordinary friendly exchanges between the Turks and our fellows this morning early. Some of our chaps ran right over to the enemy trenches and exchanged bully, jam, cigarettes etc. The whole business was wonderful and proves how madly unnecessary this part of the war is.'

Even as the opposing soldiers swapped goodies between their trenches, others fought on as Capt. Ivor Williams recorded. 'Again Abdul gave us a peppering with shrapnel, and had it not been for a sandbag hanging up and breaking force of the pellets I would have been down. All my shoulder was bruised where it hit me, and I have not been able to move my arm since.'

Other, smaller enemies in the trenches, Lt A. Eades said he could not befriend. 'Our dugouts are fairly comfortable and in pretty safe positions, the only thing I and many others have to complain about are the FLEAS in capital letters as there seem to be hundreds of them. You can just imagine what I looked like when I got up this morning. I was not able to sleep last night and so far this morning I have captured about ten in my blankets and half a dozen on my clothes. I am at present one mass of lumps or blisters due to flea bites, but we are trying hard to get rid of them and expect things to be better soon.'

Tuesday
19 October
DAY 178

Pte. E.G. King believed the Anzacs were making good progress with the settlement. 'I was down at Anzac Beach this morning where I haven't been for sometime. Everything seems altered since last I saw it. Great stacks of provisions are there for the winter. It put me in mind of some big industrial works. Mules carrying stuff and everybody busy running about, or toiling at something. On the way down I saw 4 Turks, a fatigue party, who were the first of the enemy I have seen alive. They, of course, were prisoners and were under armed guard, and were going to work with pick and shovel.'

The growing friendships between Turk and Australian were nurtured by quieter times. P.O. Bert Webster wrote 'We have not been disturbed greatly by the Turks of late, except for an occasional outburst of shelling now and then'.

Wednesday
20 October
DAY 179

There was a large Melbourne family who grieved for Gallipoli's youngest soldier, James Martin, 14, who died in October of heart failure after contracting enteritis (typhoid). Here he is shown with his five sisters, Annie, Alice, Millie, Esther and Mary.

Thursday 21 October
DAY 180

The main social news item of the day came to Anzac Cove by word of mouth from the island of Lemnos where the Anzacs went to rest and recuperate. A wedding ceremony was performed on the island in which Sgt. Ernest Lawrence (1st Light Horse Brig.) married Staff Nurse Clarice Daley (3rd Australian General Hospital).

In a letter home, Maj. P.J. Morgan, hoped for a fitting memorial for Gen. Bridges. 'That was terrible hard luck for the Scotts wasn't it, to lose two of their boys like that, they were two fine specimen of manhood. Poor old Theo Hill went west too. He was one of the best, old Theo … That makes nineteen Duntroon fellows so far killed in action. I believe they are going to take the old General's body [General Bridges] back to Duntroon and lay it in the Chapel Grounds they are now building the chapel on the hill, I think. I'm sure "Old Bill" would rest more quietly if he knew he was taking his last long spell by the place upon which he had stamped so deeply the force of that powerful personality, there must be fellows there now who must have seen the old fellow stalking round the barracks, the stooping shoulders and long stride always distinguishing him and it will bring home to them the fact that this old world is a queer place.'

Sgt. R. Adam, after writing 'Not much news this week, just the usual ordinary life', commented that 'Ian Hamilton has been withdrawn so I wonder how our new boss is going to shape up'. He thought the new boss might have to develop better weapons to deal with the growing menace in the skies. 'This morning a German aeroplane was very busy looking over the country up to our lines. The machine guns opened on him, but we

OCTOBER: *Trading Tucker with the Turks*

might just as well spat at him; except they may have kept him from coming too close.' Things were not better down at ground level. 'We had a new cook on recently — he blossomed forth into sort of pancake duffs etc. with raisins and currants in them … it was alright but proved too much for my constitution as I was violently ill that night and on sentry duty'.

The 20th Battalion diarist reported they 'had a treat this morning, that was the shelling of the neck just in front of us. Our trench was used as an observation post by the artillery officer, who had a phone laid on from his battery down on the beach to our left. All our section was standing well up over our own trench watching the 120lb shells containing Melinite burst. It was the closest we had been to our own shells bursting, and a fearful mess they made'.

Friday
22 October
DAY 181

'The men in the trenches are going wet', Charles Bean noted 'for the want of a single sheet of galvanised iron'. But the Anzacs were still taking scalps as Pte. E. King confirmed. 'Two Turks were shot last night at the end of A Company's lines. They had sneaked down and one had started to throw bombs, but did not damage. I saw one this morning and if he is a sample of their army, they must be in a bad way. His clothes were in rags and his boots worn out, so how they are to stand the winter in such a condition, is a wonder.'

Maj. Eric Hyman marked the end of his working week with a hot bath but this did little to ease his discomforts. He noted that he 'spent a miserable night in the trench, fleas notwithstanding but the hot bath with condy's fluid and vermin proof singlet, which were meant to help, were awlful. Raining all day spent most of day reading in dugout'.

End of Week 26

Saturday
23 October
DAY 182

'It is just possible', Capt. Bill Knox believed 'that since Sir Ian Hamilton has been sent home that the new General officer Commanding (Munro) might alter things here entirely and we might possibly find our way to Bulgaria via Salonica or be pulled out for a spell to refit and rest'. Knox hoped Munro would be better than his English predecessor because 'there are no English troops now that can hold a candle to the Australians, I am not skiting old girl it's just plain facts of the case. Poor old England some of the muck that they recruit now would make some of the old regulars blush and I personally would rather serve with the

Australians anytime. The Indians (natives) are splendid fellows and the little squat built Gurkhas are magnificent. The Gyppies cannot hold a candle to the Indians.'

International performance ratings aside, everybody was feeling the cold as Capt. Ivor Williams confirmed. 'We had a terrible night last night. It rained and blew the whole time and was bitterly cold. It cleared up considerably during the day. It was exceptionally quiet.'

Sunday 24 October
DAY 183

In announcing a change of boss to his wife, Gen. White also wondered 'whether or not that is going to do anything to force a decision, one can not tell although Munro has apparently been a great success in France'. But Munro would have to do something soon about supplies as officers and men alike were now getting short of clothing. Captain Bill Knox said that 'I wear a pair of socks till they are worn out (about 2 weeks) and then have to chuck them away or they'd walk about themselves'. The winter really was arriving. 'Yet another wet wintery day of rest'. Capt. Ivor Williams complained, 'Sunday. Bitterly cold, in fact it was cruel with a misty rain all day. Had another marvellous sunset'.

Bored by the routine at Suvla, P.O. Bert Webster complained to his mother that 'It is just a repetition, day after day. Our daily routine still remains the same; broken only by spasms when "Abdul" sends a few "eggs" over. They make you feel uncomfortable I tell you'. Webster still liked to watch, adding later 'There is an artillery duel going on down the ridge a bit — I must go and have a look at it; it is a wonderful sight, but more so at night when there is an attack and all the hills are ablaze with flashes from the guns & illumination rockets'.

Monday 25 October
DAY 184

On 25 October, which was 'a beautiful day, clear and cold', Charles Bean, with a keen sense of history, announced 'Six months today since we landed'. As the Anzacs faced another possible six months with winter fast advancing, he said Lt Gen. Birdwood planned to issue 'sheepskin jackets, cardigans, mits, 2 shirts and pants — mostly woollen clothing'. The troops had been sent to Gallipoli in khaki drill 'and who was responsible for this goodness knows?'. Even the hardy Captain Bill Knox admitted 'What would be a Godsend here would be a hot water bottle (rubber) one could use the water in the morning for washing so there would be no waste of water'.

Maj. Eric Hyman noted that he 'saw a man while up on Walker's Ridge get his foot blown off with a defective bomb. 85 reinforcements to the regiment arrived this morning. I hear Westgarth came over too'.

Patience was wearing thin over at Suvla where P.O. Bert Webster said he would 'be glad when this place is finished up. I hope we don't have to put the winter in here for I believe it will shake a few of us up'. The boredom was even getting to the later arrivals like Captain Bill Knox. 'All this business gets a bit weary at times not the amount of work one does but the sameness of it. We really want a jolly good scrap to shake us up, but no chance for the present'.

Tuesday
26 October
DAY 185

AFTER SEVERAL MONTHS, GALLIPOLI HAD BECOME A FAIRLY SELF-SUFFICIENT COMMUNITY COMPLETE WITH SHOPKEEPERS, CHAPLAINS, DOCTORS, DENTISTS AND OF COURSE THE TALKATIVE BARBER WHOSE 'SALON' THE ANZACS VISITED TO CATCH UP WITH THE LATEST GOSSIP AND HAVE A SHAVE AND A HAIRCUT. AWM PO2226.020

Without a weather bureau issuing forecasts, it was useful to have regular observation records from Capt. Ivor Williams. 'We had some heavy southerly winds, or gales, to be correct, today. Thank goodness they made it a bit warmer. Poor old Reg went to Hospital today.'

Wednesday 27 October
DAY 186

Gen. White was battling with his incompetent staff. 'My old servant is the funniest creature. I am an awful old fool to keep him. It drives me mad to see him doing any job, and he is worse than the smallest child with a spade or a hammer.' When White rebuked him, the servant replied 'Sir, give me pictures to paint or children to mind I can do them all day but I always get a carpenter in when I want such things done'.

Outside the comfort of officer's dugouts, the war went on, as the reliable diarist Capt. Ivor Williams reported: 'About midday Abdul heavily shelled our position. Little or no damage was done. The sunset tonight was most gorgeous'.

Thursday 28 October
DAY 187

Gen. Sir Charles Munro arrived at Imbros opposite Gallipoli where his general staff briefed him. They discussed whether the troops should stay or leave. His staff would need 400,000 troops for a successful offensive which could start the following April. They feared an evacuation could cost the lives of half of the men.

It was a warm day with 'a hot southerly half-gale blowing'. Charles Bean said 'They have brought in an old steamer (the Milo I think) and sunk her off Walker's Pier (at North beach) — with great success' as a breakwater because 'the beach is rough to the south of her but the water inside her is quite passable'.

Lt D. Campbell complained to his mother about approaching winter. 'I am still alive and kicking and am in good health but I think I spent the coldest night I ever spent the time before last night that we were in the trenches we were tramping up and down with overcoats on and warm clothing and we were shivering like leafs, but still that is not the worst, the Winter starts about the middle of January and there is to be cold snow blizzards for 7 days without stopping and the snow is on the ground for over 6 weeks ... I have been in charge of the platoon ever since I came to Gallipoli and pretty well since I came from Australia but I can tell you it doesn't put much heart in you if you see other Sgts. a lot junior to you, put over you and I can tell you it does make you want to get out of the rotten Coy. But I suppose everything comes to those that wait ... I wanted to get it permanent but I don't think our O.C. will allow me to, also he won't give me any chance to get a commission and he won't let me get out of the Coy.'

P.O. Bert Webster also told his mother that 'I am still in the land of the living — although I have not been able to keep up to my usual standard of health these last few days, having had a taste of "yellow jaundice", but am under treatment of our Staff Surgeon'.

Lord Kitchener cabled demanding to know whether Gen. Munro recommended staying or leaving. So Gen. Munro decided to get out and about and see for himself. Capt. Bill Knox reported that 'we are getting shelled a great deal more than customary lately, they got particularly lavish and gave us a very warm half hour the fiercest bombardment I have ever seen and literally hundreds of shells dropping all around and no living thing could go outside'. Knox also thought 'Some intelligent Hun has been teaching the Turks how to use guns more intelligently and now they are blazing away all the time with great efficiency, while we are building a regular rabbit warren below these dugouts about 20 feet down which then opens out into its own bullet proof "funk hole"'.

Meanwhile the 20th Battalion diarist spared a thought for the dead. 'We went down to Shrapnel Gully today and looked through the large graveyard there. It is a level piece of land about 3/4 of an acre in extent, and it is really kept in wonderful condition. Laid out so well and the graves with all their different headstones, crosses etc. Some are very artistically finished, done in some cases by the brothers of the dead, others have simply a bottle with a piece of paper with the name inside. It is very touching to see some of the graves intact, as it is with all of them. We walked down to the beach and passed the Turkish barbed wire entanglements which are very strong indeed. At this point we then came to a smaller cemetery. It is here that Colonel Braund is buried. This is right on the shore and a little further along is Hell Spit. All along the beach here is barbed wire fence.'

WITH ALL THE INFECTIONS IN THE TRENCHES AND DEAFENING FIRING DAY AFTER DAY, EAR PROBLEMS KEPT DOCTORS LIKE MAJOR CHARLES NAPIER FINN, OF THE 4TH AUSTRALIAN FIELD AMBULANCE, BUSY.

End of Week 27

Sir Charles Munro arrived at Anzac Cove and toured the battlefields to work out his plan of action. Towards the end of his tour Bean reported that Monro murmured 'It's just like Alice in Wonderland, curiouser and curiouser'. He interviewed all the commanders about the potential for

ALTHOUGH THEY WERE HAPPY
WITH MOST OFFERINGS,
THE ONE THING THE TURKS
REFUSED TO EAT WHEN THE
ANZACS TRADED 'TUCKER' WITH
THEM WAS THE NOTORIOUS
TINNED BEEF WHICH THEY
REJECTED OUT OF HAND AS
BEING INDIGESTIBLE.

further offensives and their ability to hang on. Then he returned to his headquarters to prepare a response for Lord Kitchener.

Capt. Ivor Williams reported, 'Turko threw some more shells at us today, but again did no damage.' In case his wife was worrying about newspaper reports exaggerating these Turkish attacks, Capt. Knox reassured her. 'Don't worry old girl, we have got the Germans well licked now and I feel confident the Turks will collapse soon.'

Sunday 31 October
DAY 190

Sir Charles Munro was a quick decision-maker. From his private headquarters, he recommended to Lord Kitchener that the British government evacuate all the troops from the Gallipoli peninsula. He said that 'We merely hold the fringe on the shore'. He wrote that the Turks had 'all the advantages of position and power of observation of our movements'. The recommendation had been made at last. All that was needed now was for Kitchener to come and see for himself and confirm it — which he would do in November.

The troops knew nothing of the recommendation. That Sunday, letter writing day, gave a refreshed Pte. G. Arnold a chance to ask his father about reported attacks of a new monster weapon over London. 'We are back at the Old Peninsula again after two months holiday, I feel a different man to what I did when I left it, I never felt so run down in all my life as I did then. I hear you have been having a few Zepplin attacks on London just lately; I wonder our aircraft can't cope with them a little better. We have had some rather cold windy weather just lately, I am not looking forward to the long night watches during winter too much; but I suppose it will have to be done otherwise I wish I could get hold of some interesting news to tell you, but everything is practically the same day after day. There is pretty heavy bombardment going on night and day here, with the big guns.'

ONE OF THE FACTORS THAT INFLUENCED THE DECISION TO EVACUATE GALLIPOLI WAS THE DETERIORATION IN THE WEATHER DURING NOVEMBER, WHEN FREEZING TEMPERATURES, RAIN AND SNOWSTORMS MADE SURVIVAL SO DIFFICULT FOR THE ANZACS, MANY OF WHOM LACKED WARM WINTER CLOTHING. AWM G01263

CHAPTER 9
NOVEMBER
Lord Kitchener Calls on the Boys

'Kitch'

To-day Lord Kitchener landed here. All the chaps on the beach gave him a cheer when he stepped ashore. He paid a visit to all the important posts around 'Anzac'. He addressed a small party of Colonials and told them he had a special message from the King. He was to thank them all on the King's behalf and to say he was more than proud of our doings.

F.A. Weeks, 5th AASC, AIF, Diary, 13 November

November was a turning point for the Gallipoli campaign. The new Commander-in-Chief, Gen. Sir Charles Munro, had already made the decision to evacuate. Now he was waiting for Britain's Minister for War, Lord Kitchener, to arrive and confirm it. That was the next step before the British government would authorise the evacuation. The game was up.

However, none of the officers or soldiers on Gallipoli knew this decision was imminent. In fact, the evacuation was the best kept secret on the peninsula and it stayed a secret for the rest of the month of November. The commander of Anzac forces, Lt Gen. Birdwood, was asked in early November 'in the utmost secrecy to complete a plan for evacuation if and when it should be decided upon'. Some of Lt Gen. Birdwood's inner circle of officers knew of the plan. Brudenell White, who had recently been promoted from Major to General, would eventually mastermind the evacuation.

November was also a turning point in other ways for the men in the trenches. The weather had turned and was terrible for most of the month. On 17 and also 27 November, fierce storms smashed into the flimsy military settlement. The cold temperatures, rain and snow of the approaching winter undermined the morale of the poorly clad soldiers. Their flimsy dugouts and trenches often filled with rainwater or were just washed away. Storms also battered the port, damaging piers, barges and lighters preventing the army from delivering food or fresh water supplies. Soldiers' rations dropped to half and in some cases they went hungry just when they needed to be fortified against the cold. Disease also increased as the storm deluge uncovered the decomposed human bodies and beasts of burden and water ran down the hill turning some trenches into open sewers.

Many soldiers were still wearing summer khaki uniforms as they waited for their winter woollies to arrive and they were unprepared for the storms. The shivering Anzacs caught colds, got influenza or frostbite and were generally miserable. At Suvla alone, in these bitter winter months, 200 died from hypothermia, influenza, or drowning and thousands also suffered the effects of frostbite.

November also saw the Turks, with a little help from their German officers, introduce a deadly new artillery weapon — the Howitzer which was heavier, more accurate and more efficient. These new guns blew Anzac trenches to smithereens and were the start of what Charles Bean called 'modern warfare'. The combination of weather and increased armament provided compelling reasons for evacuation.

When the Minister for War Lord Kitchener finally visited Gallipoli, inspecting the front line, he saw a hopeless situation facing his armies. The Allies were in a classic stalemate. The Turks knew they had the upper hand as they sent a note to Lone Pine saying 'We can not advance: you can not advance. What are you going to do?'

Unfortunately, Kitchener and the politicians in London dilly-dallied week after week trying to reach a face-saving solution for the failed campaign. In the meantime, many desperate soldiers on the peninsula died as a result. Ironically, when Lord Kitchener finally ordered the withdrawal from Gallipoli, it would be one of his last major decisions, as he died when his ship *HMS Hampshire* was sunk on 5 June the following year.

The high point during November after Kitchener's visit was the 19 November presentation of the Victoria Cross to Sgt. Albert Jacka by Col. Monash. Each individual also had moments of enjoyment from receiving bumper mails, getting food parcels, being paid at last or just having an extra day off.

Fed up with not being able to say what he really thought, Sgt. Maj. A.N. Macleod wrote a carefully coded letter to his girlfriend which she was to decipher should MacLeod be killed in action. The key word for deciphering the code was MARY but he said that 'if nothing happens to me I will read this to you when I get home'.

P.O. Bert Webster reminded his mother of the importance of letters. 'I was disappointed a couple of day ago when our mail came in and there was no word from you, but yesterday we had another big mail (nine bags) which did bring letters from you written in September.'

Monday
1 November
DAY 191

Remembering that the Melbourne Cup race was always the first Tuesday in November, a homesick Capt. Ivor Williams noted in his diary, 'Cup day in Melbourne. The day here was a lovely spring day. Abdul put some stick bombs near, in fact, too near to my dug-out. Am sending home a piece of one'.

The odds would have been pretty short for anybody placing a bet on how long the food would last in early November. Ambulance man, Pte. J. Lennie, noted an acute shortage on his return from holidays. 'Left the boat at 4 a.m. very quiet but found food very short now.'

On a more optimistic note, Charles Bean claimed 'Australians here can be picked out on the instant by their faces — a little hard, but the strong, lined, individual faces which men get who stand and think by themselves. The Australian discipline is for orderliness — to get an operation through

Tuesday
2 November
DAY 192

THE VISIT BY BRITAIN'S LEGENDARY MINISTER FOR WAR, LORD KITCHENER, PICTURED ON THE LEFT IN THE TRENCH AT RUSSELL'S TOP BESIDE LT GEN. BIRDWOOD, WAS BOTH A HIGHLIGHT FOR THE ANZACS AND A TURNING POINT BECAUSE KITCHENER RECOMMENDED EVACUATION.

Wednesday 3 November
DAY 193

in an organised manner'. He felt that 'British discipline … made men go forward because they are told to do so' whereas 'we rely on strong, independent willed men'. Bean also liked the Australian hatred of social class and the idea of 'giving a man a chance, a good, equal chance'.

Lt T.E. Cozens used a mid-week lull to dash off an impressive pile of letters in which he mentioned an optimistic rumour floating about. 'Q.M's fatigue in the morning. Otherwise a free and easy day in which I got a good rest. Did the usual amount of cooking and also wrote four letters so it was rather a satisfactory day. Rumours of early termination of war not credited but rather amusing to the fellows.'

P.O. Bert Webster asked his mother if she could 'send one of my photos to Percy Gow, at Fitchetts for he has again written asking me to send one. Now another one I want you to dispatch is to Ethel Sterling at Myers, she has also been asking for one. I don't care whether it's my naval or khaki uniform, just depends on what you have left'. Pte. J. Lennie also reported a changing of the guard. 'It was very quiet the 4th Brigade relieved the 7th Brigade.'

To impress Gen. Munro, his new boss, Lt Col. Braithwaite ordered gunners to improve strike rates by 'discussing, on the ground, the question of targets and methods of ensuring the best possible co-operation between the Artillery and the troops in the first line to achieve the closest co-operation facilitated by closer personal touch being kept between the Commanders of Artillery Units and the Brigades which they support'. To avoid friendly fire Braithwaite also stressed 'Commanders should let Brigades and Commanding Officers know the targets on which their particular batteries fire so all officers understand the direction and what support they may expect from their fire'.

Pte. J. Lennie 'moved camp from Taylor Gully to Cake Wake. The Australians made an attack and took 2 lines of trenches. Bill was in his dug out and a bullet hit the bushes above his head and buried him with leaves'.

Thursday
4 November
DAY 194

The Anzacs were fully established at Gallipoli when Alec Campbell arrived. At 16, he was the youngest member of the notorious 15th Battalion, which had the highest mortality rate of all Battalions. But he reassured his mother that he was safe, writing his first letter from, 'the bottom of the big hill 97, which I suppose you are reading a lot about in Tasy'. He wrote that 'We landed about 3 days ago, under fairly safe conditions all except one poor fellow who got shot through the head but then we were digging a new trench yesterday and there was a young New Zealander in charge of us he was talking to me when he lifted his head up above the trench only a few inches a (words blotted out by censor) through the head and after seeing that I can tell you I kept my own head pretty low'. Worried he may have alarmed her he continued 'but don't worry about my safety darling as it is quite safe as long as you don't pope your head up over the trench top'. Campbell, who survived the war and lived till May 2002, became the world's last survivor of the Gallipoli campaign.

Gallipoli's youngest soldier, James Martin, 14, who had been waiting in vain for his mother to write, had not been as lucky as Campbell. His mate, Cecil Hogan, wrote to Mrs Martin following Jim's death from heart failure in late October. 'Jim was in the firing line with us & he took bad but he stuck to his post till the last like the brave lad he was & made the greatest and noblest of sacrifices for his country.'

As if local fireworks were not enough, a mischievous Capt. Bill Knox announced 'Well its Guy Fawkes Day and we really ought to be having proper fireworks but we are not although there was a bit of a stunt last night and we took a trench … small interval there, as I thought our old friend "Beachy Bill" was going to lob one through my head cover but it

Friday
5 November
DAY 195

went about 20 yards down the hill — but I moved further under my wall all the same as Beachy's victims now amount to 1,500 casualties mainly on the beach which is why this gun is called Beachy Bill'.

Confirming these fireworks, Capt. Ivor Williams wrote that 'Abdul gave a very fierce demonstration. We had to stand to until about 10 p.m. Poor me, just my luck, lost all my sleep through him, and had to go on shift from 12 to 4 a.m.'. He added that the day 'ended in a gorgeous sunset, ranging from deepest scarlet to the palest pink, then to orange and green … tinting off to a deep blue sky'.

An unnamed 20th Battalion soldier was also woken by the fireworks. 'We had a little excitement last night. I was asleep at the time 9 o'clock, and had to be awakened and get into my boots, grab my rifle and bayonet and get up to the guns. There was a terrific rifle fire on our right, we think near Popes. Rockets were going up by the dozen, red, white and green. They give a splendid light floating for a mile or more. It kept up for about 1½ hours then died out so we went back to bed, and heard this morning that it was a Turk attack on Pine Ridge, but was repulsed.'

End of Week 28

**Saturday
6 November
DAY 196**

Capt. Bill Knox reported 'all our fellows are scheming at better ways of killing Turks trying new shooting techniques and new guns and new positions'. But, as Knox revealed, the Australian and New Zealand troops were not the only ones defending their precarious position. 'We have some Indian mountain men camped just below here, Sikhs and Pathams, splendid big fellows and game loyal chaps. One of them something Singh is his name and I have won his undying affection by giving him a sheet of iron to cover his dug out with.'

The fighting was getting worse according to an unnamed 4th Brigade officer because 'the enemy shelled FRANKLINS POST at 0900 and there were Two casualties in ARCHYL DERE from snipers both dangerously wounded'.

**Sunday
7 November
DAY 197**

While London newspapers predicted an evacuation from Gallipoli, the loyal Charles Bean claimed 'I believe Birdwood is strongly opposed to any idea of moving off; and certainly we are making preparations for staying. 40 bootmakers for example are due here'.

Sgt. Cyril Lawrence spent an unpleasant night in a new dugout and noted, 'of course we slept in our clothes'. He added that 'the only thing that worried me was the fact that the hole contained a smell. This morning I discovered that the place had been used for other purposes than sleeping. Anyhow, it won't kill us … Today is Sunday. The first thing I heard was a big howitzer shell going over the valley. Thank God it is one of ours. The next thing I heard was an explosion in the cook's fire. Someone had put a live cartridge in it and of course it went off. Where the bullet went to I don't know, but the Quartermaster who was down there getting my breakfast was wounded in the arm'.

Pte. J. Lennie who watched 'a fight in mid air with Aeropl. For ten minutes' said 'the Australians took two more trenches on the right.' Capt. Bill Knox 'got 150 cigarettes from Mrs McArthur, a ripping nice present and ever so welcome as we are all about out here and "cadging" all around the place'.

Monday 8 November
DAY 198

The battlefield seemed quiet for once. Charles Bean admitted 'For the first time I am beginning to feel it is a little difficult to keep up a supply of really good articles on the matter available'.

P.O. Bert Webster, told his mother, 'You satisfied my curiosity when you mention that you had read in the 'Age', of our landing with the British forces at Suvla Bay, for I have been wondering if you would have heard where we were and what we were doing'.

Pte. G. Arnold told his father he now had 'a different position in the trenches not subject to such heavy shell fire; and there is a very deep gully in between our trenches and the turks, called the Gully of Despair and very rightly too, as I think it would be very deadly for either side to attack in this particular position, unless it was done under cover of darkness, and then of course we are very much on the alert. We have patrols go out at night, creep up as near as possible to the Turks Lines,

TRANSPORTING SUPPLIES AND EQUIPMENT AROUND ANZAC BECAME A REAL PROBLEM AFTER THE FIRST BIG STORM WHICH HIT GALLIPOLI ON 17 NOVEMBER. MANY AREAS WERE TURNED INTO BOGGY QUAGMIRES, UNSETTLING THE HORSES. PHOTOGRAPH BY CHARLES BEAN.

to get as much information as possible, of course the Turks are up to the same game'. Before closing, Pte. Arnold wrote that he was 'Wishing you a very happy Xmas only wish I could be with you, it is a long time since we had the last Xmas together.'

Tuesday
9 November
DAY 199

An expectant and well-informed Charles Bean revealed that 'Lord Kitchener is in Mudros today'. Once he finished his work for the day, Lt B. Champion spotted a couple of old Gallipoli characters. He said he had been loading 'cheeses, bags and ammunition' on the beach and getting 'only a mug full of water for drinking purposes, because all the rest goes to the cooks for tea and cooking purposes' even though 'us new arrivals are now as dirty as the old hands and as lousey, too'. He said he was then introduced to 'Padre McKenzie (fighting Mac) who was behind the cookhouse, where he was stripped to his pants, chatting and examining his shirt and he called out his score at 47 lice for the morning's catch ... there is also another man here — an old hand named Clark — who has a most interesting dugout. It is stocked with Turkish souvenirs — rifles, letters, watches, personal belongings etc., all belonging to the Turks. He calls it his museum, and its quite a smelly one, too, but he has a mania for collection and it keeps him happy'.

Meanwhile the firing continued Pte. J. Lennie said, as there were 'plenty of shells flying over ... the 16th Batt. made a charge and succeeded but only one of our fellows was shot — it is the best we have had so far'.

Wednesday
10 November
DAY 200

Though the Anzacs held Lone Pine, by this the 200th day, the place was never totally secure. Sapper A. Nurse reported 'Everything going alright. Major Newcombe ordered us to dig in for they are expecting some big shells any day. No shells come, but snow does, and makes things a bit cold. Turks bombard Lone Pine with 11 in. 10 in. and 9.2 shells, wrecking our trenches completely. Casualties about 200 men, most of whom were buried whilst in the tunnels for shelter. Our Section is sent round to Lone Pine to help clear up the trenches. Had a very close call with bombs and machine gun whilst working there, but we came off safe'.

Having problems with a troubling tooth, Pte. N. McLeod 'Went to dentist first thing although he could not fill tooth. Went to canteen in afternoon could not purchase anything. Had a good nights rest'.

Updating his diary, Charles Bean commented on the changing friendship between Australians and Turks that started in October. 'There has been a good deal of communication with the Turks of late. We threw over some letters from prisoners saying they were well treated and some pictures of nice fat happy looking prisoners'. The Turks they threw back their answer. 'A man who lives by charity is a swine. We have plenty in our stomachs and something besides plenty. We have our hands on our bodies and our bayonets in our hands. The English may have plenty of munitions of war but we have our bayonet and our thoughts.'

The relationship had been better Bean wrote as 'three weeks ago Turks had a festival for three days. They threw over two packets of cigarettes with this inscription "*Prenez Femez avec plesir Notre herox ennemis*". We sent over bully beef. They threw back a message "Bully beef non". We threw some biscuits (good biscuits) and jam ... they called out "fini" and waved down with their hands — (all had heads up). Next morning same proceedings. Interpreter spoke to them from our lines. They were allowed to go over and get a pocket knife we had thrown over. Third morning we had orders not to carry on'.

Despite this communication, sporadic attacks continued as Pte. J. Lennie wrote in his diary. 'Very quiet, raining now again, very cold, not much doing tonight' but 'the turks attacked the Light Horse with failure, raining through the night'.

An unnamed 16th Battalion officer also recorded continuing attacks. 'Yesterday morning at 1130 the Turks shelled FRANKLINS POST heavily putting 25 shells into the position from W. HILLS no serious damage was done to the defence, and there were no casualties. Work was proceeded with in the communication trench to FRANKLINS during the night. A post of 3 men occupied SANDY KNOLL throughout the hours of darkness but no enemy movement was detected.'

The old hands might be exhausted but an enthusiastic recruit like Capt. B. Duggan wrote his father that 'At last we have reached the firing-line. I'm writing this in my dugout, by the light of a slush-lamp (a tobacco tin, filled with fat and a wick in it). The noise overhead is something terrible at times. Everything will seem to be at rest, when suddenly some of the big guns on the ships will open up — and talk about noise, it is enough to deafen one. One shell landed within 20 yards of our back sheds. They did rock it in. You can look over the parapet of your trench with the aid of a periscope and not see any movement; but if you put your hand up for a few seconds, you are lucky if you don't get a hole in it! As far inland as we can see, there are Turkish trenches; so it's going to be a long, weary way to Constantinople. The autumn weather here is "bonza". Every second day here I have a shave; and then with the same water, I clean my teeth and wash my face. Sometimes it is a cupful; but sometimes it is less! About every second time, I get enough to wash my ears and neck but something went wrong with the water-ship, so we are now on half-rations.' Capt. Duggan was pleased to be in this trench because he said it 'is where Jacka (of Wedderburn) won his Victoria Cross'.

End of Week 29

Saturday
13 November
DAY 203

ALTHOUGH HE KNEW THE BRITISH WOULD LOSE FACE, AFTER HE HAD SEEN HOW HOPELESS THE SITUATION WAS AT GALLIPOLI, BRITAIN'S MINISTER FOR WAR, LORD HERBERT HORATIO KITCHENER, MADE THE COURAGEOUS DECISION TO EVACUATE AND THEN SET ABOUT PERSUADING THE BRITISH WAR COUNCIL TO ENDORSE HIS DECISION.
AWM A03547

Saturday 13 November was an important moment for the Anzacs at Gallipoli as the Minister for War, Lord Kitchener, arrived to inspect the battlefield and assess the feasibility of evacuation, as recommended by Munro. The troops had been there 29 weeks but had not progressed much beyond the front line positions gained in the first few days. With no hope of breaking out of their entrenched positions by going up over the top, there was only one way out of their predicament.

Charles Bean noted Kitchener 'had scarcely reached the end of the pier when the men tumbled to it and down they came to the edge of the beach ... Men began to run from the dug outs above, hopping over intermediate scrub, holes and heaps of relics of old dug outs spontaneous cheering brought every Australian on the hill side out of his burrow and scuttling down like rabbits'.

Kitchener's 'tall red cap was rapidly closed in amongst them', Bean said, and 'It was purely a soldier's welcome with no officers leading the men who would not have cheered many men' and 'never have cheered Ian Hamilton'. Bean noted that Kitchener was 'the sort of man every Australian admires as a determined, uncompromising worker with no fancy display. Towering above the Anzacs, Kitchener said "The King asked me to tell you how splendidly he thinks you have done — you have done splendidly, better even than I thought you would"'. Later that day, perhaps inspired by Kitchener's fine words, Bean and others decided to produce a publication commemorating their experiences at Gallipoli. They started work on what would become *The Anzac Book* published in 1916, items from which are reproduced in this book.

Driver F.A. Weeks was there when the great man arrived and confirmed the ordinary soldier's respect for him. 'To-day Lord Kitchener landed here. All the chaps on the beach gave him a cheer when he stepped ashore. He paid a visit to all the important posts around

"Anzac". He addressed a small party of Colonials and told them he had a special message from the King. He was to thank them all on the King's behalf and to say he was more than proud of our doings. He left them here ("Anzac") at 5 in the afternoon for Imbros in a fast destroyer.'

Kitchener inspected Walkers Ridge, looked over Lone Pine, walked through the trenches, went through the firing line to Bully Beef Sap (which linked Russell's Top and Pope's Hill), looked at the Turks from observation posts and checked out Rest Gully, interviewing commanding officers along the way. Kitchener left after two and a half hours ready to report that the Gallipoli campaign was lost and to lay the ground work for evacuation.

Capt. Bill Knox who thought Kitchener 'went up our biggest hill like a two year old', said it was 'nice to know he is fit and well and is going to last the war out as we can not do without him'. Not everyone mentioned Kitchener's arrival. For Pte. J. Lennie it was pay day. 'Quiet again today nothing doing shell making the dressing station! About twenty shells landed all round us no one hit, pay day today and the best day of the lot.'

EVEN IF THE ANZACS HAD NOT BEEN GOING TO EVACUATE, THE BIG SNOW STORMS AND BLIZZARDS THAT STRUCK THE FLIMSY LITTLE GALLIPOLI SETTLEMENT ON 29 NOVEMBER WOULD HAVE FORCED THE DECISION. PHOTOGRAPH BY CHARLES BEAN.

Sunday 14 November
DAY 204

After Kitchener's exciting visit, Pte. F.W. Muir thought 'Everything now very quiet here. The Light Horse have advanced a little on the right without much opposition. The howitzers fire a good deal on the flank also the destroyer. The last few nights have been cold and wet, very miserable and depressing. Went along to the North beach a few days back — a great change everywhere. Big stacks of supplies, ammunition and shells, tents, hospitals, dug out etc. Some very elaborate places have been erected, large ordnance stores also field hospitals etc. The Y.M.C.A. have a tent there also a canteen where they sell cakes. Numbers of Maltese laborers are employed there. There were also a large number of Gurkhas dapper chaps, very like the Japs in features and stature and always smiling and skylarking themselves'.

Monday 15 November
DAY 205

Kitchener cabled home that 'The country is much more difficult than I imagined, and the Turkish positions' he said looked like 'natural fortresses, which if not taken by surprise at first could be held against very serious attacks by even larger forces than have been engaged'. He believed that 'To gain what we hold has been a most remarkable feat of arms ... everyone has done wonders'. Kitchener still hoped the Allies could try an attack on Turkey in another easier location. However, his report convinced Britain's War Cabinet to vote for evacuation, which Kitchener insisted was the only remedy.

It was business as usual at Anzac Cove, as Capt. Ivor Williams noted. 'Abdul gave us more than his usual quantity of shells today. The gales still continue and the view of the sea from my dug-out is just one mass of waves lashed into foam. It is a beautiful sight and I often wonder when it will be my luck to cross it again for home.'

Pte. J. Lennie described the ongoing clashes. 'The Navy started bombardment at 3 o'clock at Cape Helles and finish at 6.o'clock it was like a roar of thunder all the while and at 5 o'clock they started on the Hill 60 it lasted about 1 and 1/2 hours. tommy had five mines under it and when we blew it up we never lost a man.'

Tuesday 16 November
DAY 206

Capt. Bill Knox thanked his wife 'for sending the parcel of socks and gas respirators (the latter may possibly be useful later as we are worried that the Turk is preparing to use it against us and possibly he may get asphyxiating shells), aren't they swine, war is not the nice clean "death or glory" business it apparently was once but of course we are issued with anti-gas helmets as well — they are dirty swine and God help any Turk that falls into our hands if they use gas'.

Pte. Lennie reported on the uncertainty of each moment in the war zone. 'Still very quiet plenty of shells flying about, there was a mob of fellows standing near number 2 outposts and were going to Lemnos for a spell one of them said it would be funny if we don't go then a shell burst near them and cut one of them in half.'

Wednesday 17 November
DAY 207

The first really big storm struck the settlement without warning. Strong winds and rain battered Anzac Cove most of the day destroying some of the piers and littering the beach with debris. Heavy waves uncovered lightly buried donkeys and 'several bodies buried in shallow sand'. Charles Bean reported that 'Old barges half broken up were sawing and bumping about like elephants dancing some slow side step on the water's edge'. Bean waded along past a man who had just been shot with 'mud over my ankles' along inland gully's that became 'rushing streams three inches deep' and saw dugouts that were full of water.

Despite the rain, the settlement started running out of water because of problems with deliveries and the loss of piers and water containers.

Pte. A West, noted curtly they were 'Down to half issue water.' The shocking weather made things much worse for Pte. J. Lennie. 'Very cold and quiet. At about 7 p.m. the turks attack Walkers, with failure, but this was the worst night I have at the front — raining blowing all night.'

Getting supplies of sustaining food was also becoming a problem. Capt. Bill Knox wrote that 'We have not drawn enough meat or bread for some time as a result my innards are not behaving as nicely as they ought to but we always have tinned bully beef (muck) although I hear a rumour of a tin of sheep's tongues for tea — I never want to have a tin of anything when I leave here.'

WHEN LORD KITCHENER, CENTRE WITH STICK, ADDRESSED THE ANZACS ON 13 NOVEMBER HE SAID, 'THE KING ASKED ME TO TELL YOU HOW SPLENDIDLY HE THINKS YOU HAVE DONE — YOU HAVE DONE SPLENDIDLY, BETTER EVEN THAN I THOUGHT YOU WOULD'.

As November advanced so did the storms. The deluge uncovered decomposed bodies or washed body parts down the hill and some of the trenches became a combination of abandoned morgues and open sewers. It was certainly challenging for Capt. Ivor Williams. 'Had another storm last night. It was such as I have never in all my life seen before, and hope never to see again. The wind was something terrible — it was quite impossible to stand up in it. I tried it and lost my hat.

Thursday
18 November
DAY 208

It did not simply rain, but came down in one gallon drops — or something thereabouts. In about 6 minutes all the valleys were filled with rushing volumes of water, and the hillsides looked just like immense waterfalls. Everyone was flooded out. I know I was. Today I had to dig everything out from about 18 inches of slush. I was wet to the skin and had to stop so all day. The trenches are terrible and with all this it is bitterly cold and all the piers have been broken. We could see before the storm half a submerged trawler, but today it is no more. Abdul gave us some "hurry up"'.

Bean celebrated his 36th birthday today. When Commander Gipps revealed they only had 40 hours of drinking water remaining, Bean asked 'How do you think we are going to get on in the winter?' Gipps replied, 'The winter! I think we are within two days of disaster'. This prompted Bean to reflect in his diary that 'The Anzacs are being sacrificed to pure British incompetence … They haven't an idea beyond the present' and have no 'moral courage because the British nation has not the brains to make war. It is much better at manufacturing socks although by the same token our winter clothing is not yet landed'.

Friday
19 November
DAY 209

In between the storms, Col. Monash presented Sgt. Albert Jacka with his Victoria Cross complete with ribbon in a ceremony attended by many of the soldiers. Monash's citation reminded the crowd that Jacka had jumped into a Turkish trench at Courtney's Post on 19 May, shot five Turks, bayoneted two, taken two more prisoner and captured the trench on his own.

Capt. Bill Knox warned his wife that casualty reports weren't always accurate because of various scams. 'Although you may have heard "poor old so and so was killed at Gallipoli" don't you believe it as when you get over here you meet "poor old so and so" doing fine and as fit as a fiddle. It is a damned shame, but some kind friend may try the trick on you, it's still going on. So unless you ever here from someone you can trust or official sources don't ever believe what you hear'.

Although Pte. J. Lennie described the day as 'very quiet', nevertheless 'a shell landed right in the rally station and went off. then a German taube came over and dropped a bomb about 50 yards away from the station … no one hurt. very lucky'. There were also lighter moments that day as A. Guppy noted 'I accidentally made many of the boys about laugh some tonight, by falling and turning about three somersaults down a steep slope finishing up in a clump of bush'.

End of Week 30

Corp. R. Gardiner used his Saturday to catch up with overdue letters. 'Kitchener was here *last Saturday* for a few hours. I was only about 2 yds. away from him when he landed. He is very tall and broad, with bushy mustachios, and red face. He said about a dozen words to the crowd who had gathered round to the effect the King had told him to say he was proud of the Australians and all here. They then gave him three cheers.'

No matter how peaceful the day, some unsuspecting soldiers could easily come to harm especially if their own comrades did not recognise them. Pte. J. Lennie reported 'very quiet moved camp to Durrants Post. very cold. 3 men of the 16th Batt. went out to put a cross on one of the graves and when they got out in the open the Tommies opened fire and killed them — riddled them with bullets'.

**Saturday
20 November**
DAY 210

An unknown soldier of the 20th Battalion criticised authorities over their hopeless supply of provisions. 'Very cold weather and bad food. This morning one rasher of salty, stinking bacon and no tea. Midday, tea only, and at night we got fresh meat stew and nothing to drink. It is really awful to think that we have been established here for so long and are unable to get water and are being fed worse than in the hot weather. They have condensers lying on the beach for two months and they have just started to erect them, and at the rate they are going we might not get water in plenty before Christmas. One has only to reflect on the management of the affairs and he will soon conclude that the whole system is rotten to the core.'

This anonymous diarist was not alone. Capt. Bill Knox wrote 'I heard a cock crowing last night and risked my life by going out to investigate and found he was a mascot of some chaps down the hill a bit — they will be short of a mascot in a day or two. I am sure a bullet or something is bound to hit him — if I don't save him first'. Knox was developing his own skills. 'I am a champion pincher now and go about with an eye like a hawke for an odd piece of timber or galvanised iron. I have no conscience or pangs about pinching off the beach because the Heads do themselves mighty well down there and eat soup and things like that and I don't mean stew soup but the real McCoy with good stuff in it.'

**Sunday
21 November**
DAY 211

Monday
22 November
DAY 212

After long and involved discussions with the British War Committee, Kitchener finally recommended an unequivocal evacuation of Gallipoli. Now all that was needed was for the British Cabinet to say 'Yes'.

Hardly anybody at Gallipoli knew of the evacuation plan apart from Lt Gen. Birdwood. He was working with his most senior staff on plans that would now be fast tracked. Most of the soldiers would not find out about this until the following month. For the evacuation to succeed it had to be the best kept secret. After all some commanding officers at Gallipoli had predicted 50 per cent of those soldiers evacuating the beach would end up as casualties and 66 per cent of the guns would also be lost. A conference of senior leaders was held on 22 November to discuss the evacuation. Gen. White, now in charge of the evacuation, began developing a 'Silence Ruse' strategy. He planned to trick the Turks through a series of 'Silent Stunts' in which front line trenches stopped firing for longer and longer periods each day and did not fire back at the Turks even when attacked. This got the enemy accustomed to inactivity and quiet — which would enable Anzacs to maintain their presence with only a skeleton staff.

Blissfully unaware of any evacuation plans, a shivering Maj. B.D. Jack was already planning his Christmas dinner in between bombardments. 'If this is the beginning of winter, Lord help us in the middle of it. So far I've not taken off my cap, comforter, and scarf since I've been here and I only take my Great coat off for a couple of hours in the middle of the day'. He was not the only one rugging up, as Capt. Bill Knox said he had 'the most weird collection of cloths on, with my head and neck all wrapped up in three pairs of socks and sweaters like a Shackleton Expedition'.

They had to keep warm Maj. B.D. Jack said, because 'It was our turn to be noisy today. We got two cruisers and a destroyer plus a lot of our land batteries onto a section of his beloved country known to us as the "Olive Grove" and which contains several guns which annoy us. I don't think it was possible for any-one to live through that bombardment. Clouds of dust and trees flow about as salvoes from the boats hit it … We had scones and butter and tea at 1600 (4 p.m.) this afternoon so we get something homely at times (if we leave out the quality of the scone). We've also got a small hamper put by for Xmas of a bottle of wine and a box of almond raisins and biscuits and it makes our mouths water every time we look at it. If we work it properly we might get some chicken as there are two tied up outside a "Brass hats" dug-out.'

But time was dragging on for Pte J. Lennie as he wrote that it was 'a year ago since I left Adelaide South Australia'.

Although the bombardment was still going on with Turks attacking the Apex (considered by them the weakest front line point), at least the storms had stopped, enabling the first guns to be evacuated. Sgt. H. Affleck could now perform his arduous tasks. 'Fine. Turks charged "Apex" repulsed with heavy casualties, ours next to nil. On A sub act road. Our gun removed sent away to Mudros with others also waggons. Had to haul waggons over through gap near pinnacle to Williams pier. "Beachy Bill" active. Turks charged at Courtneys and were repulsed. Turks charged at Helles whole Division repulsed with heavy losses.'

Capt. Bill Knox complained that 'we don't even have the necessary timber and iron to roof the dug outs nor enough timber to cook a billy with (although timber is issued) let alone to warm up by. Someone will yet get himself hanged over the neglect of not fixing up winter quarters and quite rightly too — the boys can't keep warm in a hole in the hill when it's wet.'

Tuesday
23 November
DAY 213

Unaware that evacuation plans were being developed, an excited Capt. F.B. Stanton reported, 'After getting all ashore safely marched our Brigade men with the assistance of a guide up to the left (Not Lone Pine on the right as expected), nearly 4 miles, it was a drag, all were pretty tired, and had heavy loads, we were lucky, were not even sniped at, we camped in a gully in the open that night … my word it was cold that little nap, only from 3 a.m. to 6 a.m. my sleeping bag was invaluable … We are bivouacked in the gullies … I mean we imitate rabbits and dig and dig in, the dugouts are wonderful, I have just had a beauty completed for me … We are not far from the famous hill 971 and hill 60 which you may have read about. We feed pretty well too, bread sometimes and meat … It is wonderful the different understanding between officers and men here, quite chums, a lot better and the discipline is better. A. Jacka V.C. is my Coy. Sgt. Major, I am great pals with him. He is a particularly decent chap, knows the game, and very modest'.

Wednesday
24 November
DAY 214

AS THE SEAS WHIPPED UP BY THE NOVEMBER STORMS DAMAGED MOST OF THE PIERS AND MADE IT SO DIFFICULT TO LAND ESSENTIAL FOOD AND WATER, THE ARGUMENT FOR EVACUATION INCREASED — AS LONG AS THERE WOULD BE ENOUGH PIERS LEFT FOR THE SOLDIERS TO LEAVE FROM. PHOTOGRAPH BY CHARLES BEAN.

That night, Gen. White ordered all artillery and infantry fire to stop for two days unless the Turks mounted a major attack. This was the start of his 'Silent Stunts' getting the enemy used to periods of quiet which would eventually enable White to thin out the ranks but not alert the Turks to his exponential evacuation.

Thursday 25 November DAY 215

Charles Bean thought the Anzacs had stopped firing shots and also taken the artillery brigades away (both guns and gunners) 'just to give the Turks the impression that we are evacuating'.

Without knowing it, Pte. E.G. King began helping with the top secret evacuation. 'We are trying a new ruse to trick the Turks, and it is causing great amusement amongst the men. We are keeping low and the rations are being drawn at night, so as to make it appear that we have evacuated our positions. The men treat it as a huge joke, and think it will not have any effect on the cunning Turks or their German officers. The ruse is to keep it up till the Turks make an attack, and then give them a surprise. It started last night, so we are anxiously waiting developments. Things are very quiet, with no shots being fired by our own side, who usually do more firing by day, but the Turks fire a few occasionally and also throw a few bombs.'

As they were there to fight, a disappointed Pte. J. Lennie complained it was 'very quiet last night our lads had orders not to fire a shot for 48 hours it don't seem like a battlefield at all.' Bean said there was still fighting up at Quinn's Post where 'the Turks send a patrol right into the trench to see how strongly it was held and three men crept up to the trench — one was bayoneted but two got away'.

ONE OF THE MOST IMPORTANT PIERS, HOSPITAL PIER WAS SO BADLY DAMAGED BY THE STORMS IN NOVEMBER, THAT IT COULD NO LONGER BE USED — SHORT OF MAJOR REPAIRS AND THAT WAS PRESUMING THE SETTLEMENT STILL HAD ENOUGH TIMBER. AWM H00299

The 'Silent Stunt' continued at Quinn's Post as part of secret preparations for evacuation. The Turks managed to get past protective bombproof wire and tossed bombs into the Anzac trenches which they jumped into without being fired at. That was as far as they got because instead of being shot, they were silently bayoneted. 'Our fellows were splendid' Bean reported. 'Although bombed they didn't bomb back'.

The front line soldiers in the trenches had other concerns. 'The blooming north wind here seems to come right off the snow and ice on the hills of Imbros Island' Capt. Bill Knox wrote. 'But the poor infantry boys in the trenches can't even move about to keep warm'. Pte. J. Lennie provided accurate weather reports. 'The ships were firing all day long, it was like a roar of thunder all the while but although it was a nice day, in the night it changed, never seen a night so bad in all my life, the lightning was awful, it lighted the place up like day and the thunder worst than ever, than I have heard, raining too, it was that dark that you could not see your own hand in front of you, I have never seen a night like it in Aust., cold chilled you to the bone to be out in.'

Friday
26 November
DAY 216

End of Week 31

The biggest storm of the season now slammed into Gallipoli, battering the settlement at Anzac Cove for three days. Gale-force winds whipped up the seas, hail hit the hillsides and rain poured down the hills towards the beach. The howling winds built up to a cyclone that then turned into a snow storm. By the end of the three days, the settlement had been badly damaged and many of the earthen structures had been washed away. Trenches and dugouts filled up with filthy water carrying everything from bodies and body parts to assorted rubbish including human waste — capable of spreading disease. The storm seemed the final catastrophe for the troops.

Pte. John Henry Turnbull reported on the event. 'The first fall of snow fell to-night. We spent a cold, wet and miserable night. The ground was frozen. In our supports trenches we have no overhead cover. Our clothes and blanket wet through and our equipment frozen stiff. I had to stand at my post for my 2 hrs at the entrance of the communication trench. The wind cut through me whistling along the commun. trenches. My feet were very near frozen. The snow is a beautiful sight no doubt. We are past admiring scenery just now. We are on half rations, biscuits and cheese. How we hate the sight of those biscuits …

Saturday
27 November
DAY 217

'When we are not being frozen to death in the supports we are on Quartermasters fatigue making pack mules of ourselves carrying boxes of biscuits and petrol tins full of water and other stores ... On the way to the beach we have to pass over the Headquarters dugouts. They are very comfortable ... No wonder we common pack animals growl and use bad language. Of course on the return trip from the beach we are in a happy frame of mind when after packing sides of bacon, bags of bread (bread is unknown to us to eat) and perhaps a case of whisky' which he said they took to the front line.

Pte. J. Lennie had other reactions to the unpredictable weather. 'Got a big surprise of my life today it was snowing all last night and all day very cold, it was pretty to watch it fall, the hills look pretty, snow all around where ever you look, falling all day long.'

Meanwhile in the secrecy of his dugout Gen. White finalised his plans for the evacuation which he sent to the HQ for approval.

Sunday 28 November
DAY 218

Charles Bean was disgusted by the natural disaster of the storm. 'The authorities haven't prepared against the winter; they haven't made a harbour; they now find they can't expect to land water or stores as they would have wished (with piers and boats wrecked) their water condenser is holed and it is bitter tonight.' Bean wondered if they ever did plan to evacuate the Anzacs how would they get them off the beach 'without working piers let alone boats in which to ferry them away'.

These were tough times for the Anzacs, as Maj. P.J. Morgan told his mother. 'Our mail service has been very bad lately whether it is all due to boats being torpedoed or not I do not know. We have had a real taste of the Gallipoli winter at last. Last night it snowed for hours and it is still drifting down this morning. All the trenches round are deep in snow and you can scarcely pick up any landmarks owing to the drift. It is bitterly cold even in this comfortable dugout, what it will be like to people less comfortably placed I do not like to imagine. If we can only get timber & galvanised iron to fix the men up with descent shelters for the winter, everything should be all right, clothing will play a big part in the campaign during the winter.'

But to pass the time Morgan said, 'Our fellows have got a sort of "Beauty Queen" Carnival going. The pick of the battery will be the Gallipoli Queen of Beauty. At present a driver in A sub. heads the poll and it's doubtful if there are two uglier fellows in all Turkey than him. Isn't the time flying round, we will be at the end of the war before we know where we are ... In two weeks time we will have completed one year in the East'.

Maj. Eric Hyman of 12th Light Horse, who was the officer in charge of the machine gun unit, revealed that 'Six cases of rum were stolen last night, consequently several drunks about today. I woke up to find the whole country under snow and blowing a gale but I feel much better today although I fear the severe cold weather will play havoc with our boys — bitterly cold all day'.

Monday
29 November
DAY 219

Even as the great storm continued to punish the settlement, so did the Turks. An unnamed 20th Battalion soldier noted that it was 'freezing all night and all day. The coldest night and day I think most of us have experienced. Hostilities commenced afresh at midnight on the 27th, and has continued until this morning, when the Turkish artillery are very active. Indeed, they put some high explosive shells right against our A. Gun, only missing by feet. I was covered with earth and rubbish. I went down to the hospital to see one of our chaps who was being sent away to the beach to join the hospital ship. While there I saw where the large shell came through the tent roof and entered the ground in the middle of the tent, but did not explode. The tent was full of patients. There are a lot of tents with big holes in the roof from shells. The beach is in a terrible state, snow and ice on everything'.

Tuesday
30 November
DAY 220

By the end of the month the weather had calmed, with the sun now shining over the white world of Gallipoli. But for Lt Col. G. Murphy, the fighting never seemed to stop. 'At Lone Pine 3 officers and 18 men killed and 8 officers and 59 wounded. Mostly all buried but very cold snow still on the hard ground. Sea calm.'

Coming right after the storm as it did this attack demoralised the men. Capt. Ivor Williams wrote 'I feel very bad today. We got a terrible bombardment by the Turks. Casualties and damage are heavy'.

Charles Bean thought the Anzacs were much worse off than troops in Europe. 'Once wet our men can never get dry again — unlike the troops in Flanders where they go back after 4 days at the front to sleep in a house and get a warm bath and dry clothes'. The Anzacs made up for it he said, because 'They are clever at making the best of things and can make fires in a hole in the trench wall with a few sticks of broken biscuit box boiling a Billy, cooking food or warming themselves'.

It was a good thing these soldiers knew how to survive, because they would need every bit of their ingenuity in the make or break month ahead.

The evacuation of Gallipoli by stealth was so successful that approximately 80,000 Anzacs were secreted away from the peninsula during December under the cover of darkness and transported safely to Mediterranean bases like the island of Lemnos, where they rested before going on to fight in other theatres of war.

CHAPTER 10
DECEMBER
Retreating with Honour

Horror of horrors! We are to evacuate Anzac and Suvla. That is the movement that is taking place. If only fine weather lasts we are to be away by Saturday. I could cry. But what is the use? I must smile and cheer everybody up, but my heart is very sore, not for the evacuation itself, for I know this is best, but for all the valuable lives that have been lost here.

W. Dexter, Chaplain, Letter, in M. McKernan, *Padre, Australian Chaplains in Gallipoli and France*, Allen and Unwin, 1986

In December, the time finally came to evacuate Gallipoli. It was a momentous event — emotionally and logistically. The Anzacs would have to leave behind 8,709 Australians and 2,701 New Zealanders who died on the peninsula. They had failed to capture Gallipoli and now they had to transfer the largest number of people ever evacuated from a battle zone. Not until Dunkirk, 25 years later, would such a difficult retreat of Allied forces take place again. The evacuation of Gallipoli would test the logistics of the British command.

Eighty thousand troops encamped at Anzac Cove and Suvla Bay, with 5,000 horses and mules, 2,000 vehicles and 200 guns. Everybody and everything had to be evacuated at night so the Turks would not find out they were leaving and attack their diminishing garrison.

Remarkably, the Anzacs evacuated Gallipoli so skilfully, they turned this retreat into a victory. They got the 80,000 soldiers off the beaches with no losses. Lt Gen. Birdwood now gave the task of evacuation to the Australian, Gen. White, who masterminded the entire operation. White's strategy was to educate the Turks over time to expect silence from the Anzacs and to get used to seeing fewer soldiers while he sneaked men off the beach little by little and at night.

He planned to evacuate his troops in three stages: firstly, all troops, animals and munitions not required to maintain the bridgeheads would be withdrawn over the first weeks of December; secondly, the garrisons would be reduced to minimal strength during the third week of December; and thirdly, those troops remaining would be removed very quickly overnight on the weekend of 18 and 19 December. White hoped to have half the men off the beaches before that weekend of 18 December and by the morning of Monday 20 December, the entire garrison would be gone. His most important challenge was deceiving the Turks into thinking the Anzacs remained in their trenches in force. He named the operation 'Silence Ruse', ordering increasingly regular periods of silence and instructing troops not to retaliate when attacked in what they called 'Silent Stunts'.

ALTHOUGH VESSELS OF ALL SHAPES AND SIZES WERE USED DURING THIS MASSIVE TRANSPORTATION OPERATION, STEAM-POWERED NAVAL LAUNCHES ALSO PLAYED THEIR PART IN THE EVACUATION, OFTEN TOWING RAFTS CARRYING FIELD GUNS ALONG WITH THEIR CREW.

Not only did White and his staff get every one of the 80,000 troops away safely; they did not leave one soldier behind, although Capt. Nathaniel Barton of the 7th Light Horse reported it was touch and go for one sleepy fellow. 'A 13th Battalion man who was a sentry in a tunnel and fell asleep; he awoke with a pain in the tummy (only too common at Anzac) and on going out (to relieve himself) found the trenches deserted. He raced for the beach, and arrived without rifle or pack in time for one of the last boats. The tale he now tells himself is a very different addition, and much more heroic.'

Gen. White and his retreating Anzacs had luck on their side. The day after the last troops were evacuated, a violent storm as bad as the November storm hit the peninsula and would have made evacuation impossible. Even though the soldiers all got away safely, most of them did so reluctantly. The Anzacs regretted leaving in defeat and this confirmed their commitment to the cause and their grief at leaving their beloved comrades behind. Many soldiers cried as they sailed away, looking back at the graves of their mates. Nevertheless, as one of the most successful evacuation operations during warfare, the Gallipoli retreat is worth explaining in detail.

Charles Bean, who was not in the know this time, worked out his own plan for evacuation. 'If these troops could be got off with the loss of a third (of the men) and half the guns and nearly all the stores, is that the best? Staying on here we should be fighting the winter, which is Germany's game ... I doubt if we could evacuate from one pier and in this weather'. Although if they tried, he mused, 'we could leave the guns as late as possible (one gun for every three trenches) have sham camp fires; sham transport ... land big piles of empty boxes on the beach and keep up the appearance of men about the place with relief's marched in and around and out again and all men camped where the enemy sees our camps eg. Shrapnel Gully, Ari Burnu Point'. However, Bean concluded, 'If we stay on without a superhuman effort to back us, the result will be disaster'.

Not knowing he would be evacuated anyway within three weeks, 'Alex Robertson shot himself through the foot' Warrant Officer W.H. Garland reported. 'The general opinion is that he did it on purpose so as to get out of danger, he has broken the bones'. Robertson had good reason to fear death. Pte. J. Lennie revealed that 'the Turks blew up the trenches with 12 inch shells at Lone Pine killed about 100 officers and men and wounded 200 more of our fellows. Plenty of the men frost bitten the weather playing up with the mess — alright'.

Wednesday
1 December
DAY 221

Weather affected men differently. An optimistic Lt O. Law waxed lyrical that 'Old Winter has now taken a hand in the campaign in the Dardanelles. November was a cold wet month and December and the snow arrived together. It has been snowing all night and the ground between the trenches — a real no mans land held by neither Turk nor Australian — is covered with a beautiful mantle of white. The fantastically shaped hills are capped with snow with beautiful streaks of white running down their steep sides. Trees, bushes and shrubs are all weighed down with the weight of snow which has fallen on them. The floor of the trench and the tracks are covered with slush, the snow having been tramped into the ground but, despite the fact, that overcoats are wet, feet and hands are as cold as ice and boots covered with a thick mud everybody is wonderfully cheerful. "Keep smiling" is the motto of the battalion and everyone recognises that many hardships will have to be faced in a winter campaign and that we must make the best of things'.

Thursday 2 December
DAY 222

Not knowing about the 'Silent Stunts', Captain Bill Knox complained 'It is rotten to just take it all and do nothing in retaliation as we are getting pretty much hotted up lately by the Turks aggressive measures, but our tactics are defensive not offensive, they have bombed us heavily for days and blown up our communications tunnels with huge shells and pretty heavy losses'.

Maj. E. Brind reported the freak death of a dear friend. 'Dear Mum, Here's the weekly start for the home letter. It's astounding how the days go past and you are at the end of the week really before you know it has properly started. There has been a crowded week this week. First I'm awfully sorry to tell you our little Diggley Doc. Has gone to swell the number of Australians who have given their lives for the cause. It made a gloom over us all as he was a great favourite ... he was in the operating tent, and was just about to do an operation when a shrapnel shell burst just outside the tent and a bullet got him in the back and went into his heart. He made a motion as if to pluck it out and then just dropped. I could have howled when I heard as he was just the best pal I had in the Regiment ... it is a horrible waste of a good and useful life'. Sad though it was, Maj. Brind said reinforcements would fill the ranks. 'We just had a cable that Australia offering another 50, 000 men. Help! it's getting far too common and we won't be able to move without falling over Ballarat chaps here soon'.

With Silent Stunts preventing retaliation, the death toll rose as Pte. J. Lennie reported. 'Shells landed in the 1st A.S.H. and killed 2 lads and wounded 6 lads of the A.M.C. while having their meals'. Thirsting for revenge, Capt. Bill Knox claimed 'There are going to be some hideous noises made by us today as the Beachy Bill group of guns which have worried us for so long are set down for complete and final destruction. What oh for noise when the whole blooming army and navy concentrate on that spot'.

An unnamed 20th Battalion soldier recorded news of the latest market prices and post delivery at the front. 'Drizzling rain last night and all day. Still an awful shortage of water, men offering 5/- for a drink and unable to get it. The little drop of tea we get once or twice a day is delicious. We are still hearing rumours of mail, but it does not arrive. We have official news today that the tug Gaby foundered with 18 bags of mail from Australia, dated November 14th, 15th and 16th, and only 4 bags were saved.'

Friday
3 December
DAY 223

THE MASTERMIND BEHIND THE SUCCESSFUL EVACUATION OF ANZAC WAS GENERAL BRUDENELL WHITE, OF MELBOURNE, SEEN HERE IN HIS DUGOUT, COMPLETE WITH HIS EVER PRESENT PIPE, METICULOUSLY STUDYING PLANS.

End of Week 32

Saturday
4 December
DAY 224

With no knowledge of the bigger picture, Lt Col. G. Murphy continued to report developments in the one-sided conflict. 'Fine day. Turks again fired on us using about 100 shells — no damage. Very busy with trench orders'. For others, like Pte J. Lennie these Turkish attacks were more serious with 'plenty of shells kicking around doing plenty of damage too'.

An increasingly frustrated Capt. Bill Knox wrote 'This job gets so infernally dull and even being shot at soon loses interest for one as all the usual shell fire and stray bullets that lob around here fail to give one any thrills after a bit and it is extraordinary how callous one gets to seeing fellows hit'.

Sunday
5 December
DAY 225

Bored with the lack of action, Charles Bean retreated to his quarters where he spent the whole of Sunday 'Drawing and painting for the Anzac Magazine'. At Suvla Bay, P.O. Bert Webster, told his mother 'We have had a foresight of what it would be to put the winter in here as we had a torrential downpour of rain recently, it came down the hills as if a huge dam had been dug away & simply swamped the trenches & low lying ground.' Webster was relieved when it stopped raining but complained 'it was then awfully cold and then we had a fall of snow- how we appreciated the "stand-off" so thoughtfully given by our C.O.' He felt sorry for 'the poor "Tommies" in the trenches who suffered considerably as they presented some pitiful and heartbreaking sights as they were carried and helped to the Hospital'.

IN ORDER TO LULL THE TURKS INTO THINKING THEY WERE TAKING THINGS EASY AND HAD NO PLANS FOR EVACUATION WHATSOEVER, SOME OF THE ANZACS PLAYED CRICKET FROM TIME TO TIME ON 'PITCHES' LIKE SHELL GREEN, IGNORING INTERMITTENT SHELL FIRE FROM PERPLEXED TURKS FIRING FROM THE HILLS ABOVE.

The successes the Turks were having with their unopposed fire distressed Pte. Lennie who complained 'Shells flying around, Turks put them into the DHQ and blew the 16th C.C. Hospital to pieces and blew sick and wounded men to pieces while waiting to go on board the Hospital boat it was a awful sight to see. Legs and arms all over the place'.

British officers parading around in their 'Sunday best' finally got the better of Capt. Bill Knox. 'We have been on short water and tucker rations lately because of the problems landing supplies but what makes the men growl is seeing immaculately dressed British staff officers walking about washed and shaved asking silly damned questions — I am fairly convinced I am becoming a bit of a Socialist'.

Monday
6 December
DAY 226

Capt. Ivor Williams celebrated a 'heaven sent' addition to his collection. 'A German Taube flew over today and dropped two bombs — one in our Gully and one in the next. She also dropped numbers of steel darts (poisoned). I have grabbed one as a memento.' For his part, Capt. Bill Knox had a lucky break alleviating frustrating boredom when he 'got some Bovril Salmon biscuits last night, bottle of whiskey and a few candles but there is an ever present huge Supply problem here as all landing places are under never ceasing shell fire. I was down at the beach recently and saw 20 men get their finish in about an hour from Beachy Bill and still the work has to go on'.

'I have not had my clothes off for a week, only boots, it's far too cold' Knox continued. 'As one only has half a mug of water per man and this is how the "Three in One" is done: first you put some toothpaste in your mouth, then you dip your toothbrush in the mug and swill around, then you shave in the water not getting it any more soapy than you can help, then you get your sponge and dip a corner into what's left of the water and wipe your eyes and face and that's your toilet for the day'.

Tuesday
7 December
DAY 227

After long drawn out debates, the British Cabinet finally decided to endorse the evacuation of Gallipoli, ordering Gen. Munro to implement the plans. The government instructed Munro to evacuate both Anzac Cove and Suvla Bay but not Helles for the moment. Lt Gen. Birdwood, who had been reluctant to evacuate, now ordered Gen. White to fast track his secret plans. Now it was really on!

Evacuation could not have come sooner for the shivering Gurkhas, according to CQMS A. Guppy. 'A number of men, including about

200 Gurkhas, have been sent to Hosp. from the Peninsula suffering from frostbite. Two members of the R.N.A.S. were also killed here today. Their aeroplane turned turtle and crashed down.' Lt D. Caldwell worried that 'after it finished snowing we had it very cold and the snow froze and it caused a fair number of our men to get frost bitten feet and a couple of them are bound to lose their feet through it. I can tell you when the snow thawed and the sun started to shine they started to take the frost bitten ones aboard the Hospital boats their was a boat load of poor old Ghurka's with their feet badly frost bitten. In dozens of places men were also found in trenches sleeping but frozen stiff with cold. I can tell you it is pretty rotten to see some of them. The Turks also got on to our Hospitals and pretty well wiped it out of existence with one of their heavy guns. Tent fulls of wounded and sick were killed and maimed. Short of paper so I will finish'.

Desperate for writing paper, Trooper Gerald Digby, 1st Light Horse, sent a postcard home written on a piece of biscuit tin wrapping paper. 'Only a line to tell you that I am still alright. We are pegging along alright despite the cold weather. I might mention that I have not had a bath for three weeks — nearly a month. Water is pretty scarse over here and the same applies to writing paper. This card came out of a biscuit tin part of our rations'.

Wednesday 8 December
DAY 228

Now that it was 'official', Gen. White sped up the numbers leaving the beach every night. Officially, the soldiers were leaving for a rest on nearby islands before returning. The first of a series of daily orders said, 'Please take the necessary steps to prepare for embarking at short notice selected guns of your division'. The notice confirmed these selected guns 'will be accompanied by their proper proportion of personnel' and officers were ordered to 'send away any guns which can be spared'.

With only ten days to go until the first half of the final group was evacuated, White's team developed more tricks to fool the Turks. Their tactics included self-firing rifles which had a kerosene oil tin or bully beef tin filled with water above them with tiny holes punched in that allowed the water to slowly drip into an intact tin below tied to the trigger. When the lower tin got heavy enough from filling up with water this dropped, pulling the trigger firing the gun. This ruse made the Turks think Anzacs must still be in trenches. Bean said the self-firing rifles fired 20 minutes after soldiers left. Others fashioned explosives with long running fuses that took hours to reach the end before setting off.

ONE OF THE FIRST THINGS THE
ANZACS TOOK AWAY FROM
GALLIPOLI WAS THEIR HEAVY
GUNS. THEY WERE PULLED
DOWN TO NORTH BEACH NEAR
WILLIAMS PIER WHERE THEY
WERE LOADED ONTO VESSELS
AND TRANSPORTED TO OTHER
BATTLEFIELDS.
AWM PO1436.004

Remaining soldiers were ordered to gather in a 'smoking fatigue', that is, to lounge about smoking cigarettes in full view of the Turks. They also carried water about 'like stage soldiers' and conducted endless parades and marches with recycled animals over and over creating the impression of a crowd. Commanding officers also encouraged men to play cricket or Two Up as long as the Turks could see them. As most men had been ordered to keep out of sight for some time anyway, the Turks were getting used to seeing fewer men. Other soldiers staged fake daylight landings of reinforcements (only to leave again at night).

Lt C. Riddell had to blow up Turkish positions with the long running fuses that went off after the evacuation. 'The work was to charge our 4 longest tunnels under the enemy's trenches and to prepare a back line of defence to cover embarkation of main body if the Turks followed up — This meant a tremendous amount of work ... Also trenches could only be worked on at night so as not to be observed by enemy. Unfortunately I had no men I could trust to lay charges & to set detonators and connect up electric wires for firing so had to do whole thing myself ... it kept me going day & night for four days with from one to two hours sleep a day as I personally put in position every tin of explosive, 3,000 of them and connected up and did all jointing in the wires, so as to be sure. The defences were little lengths of trench well hidden and protected by good entanglements and all of them with a good back-door for the defenders ... The work was very secret & thorough many rumours & guesses were made, no one except a very few knew much, even my own brigadier knew hardly anything.'

PLAYING TWO UP TO DECEIVE THE TURKS ABOUT THEIR EVACUATION PLANS COULD BE COSTLY. FOUR MINUTES AFTER THIS PHOTOGRAPH WAS TAKEN OF PLAYERS ON BROWN'S DIP, A TURKISH SHELL BURST, KILLING FOUR OF THE ANZACS IN THE TWO UP CIRCLE AND SIX BYSTANDERS. AWM HO3557

At night, so they could leave silently, others made bags to cover soldier's noisy boots, or softened hard trench floors with picks and blankets which were laid on the track down to the beach progressively lined with white stones, salt and flour that could be seen in the dark. Bagging was also prepared to be laid along the piers.

Down the line, Sgt. Alan W. Bradley started celebrating Christmas with his newly arrived food parcel. 'We are not waiting for Xmas to put in an appearance but just bogging straight into the goodies before anyone else gets a chance' ... Old Abdul is still unchanged with the exception of a number of new inventions in the way of shells, of which he gives us a liberal issue each afternoon around the trenches, does little damage on the whole though we are now on quarter and half ration.' Others were not so lucky. 'Rather a tragedy', Capt. Bill Knox wrote to his wife. 'My Xmas pudding arrived unrecognisable, putrid and badly contaminated'.

Ignorant of evacuation plans, Lt J. Bourke criticised his leaders. 'I have not received any letters for a long time as a lot of mail sunk in the Mediterranean lately by the Kaiser's "Tin Fish" which accounts for it. But we now have good dug-outs, twenty feet below the surface. There has been very little fighting here this few weeks; through bad Generalship we have remained idle, while "Abdul" has consolidated his position so well that I think our opportunity of taking the Peninsula has been lost; we have the men to go through anything but lack competent leaders'. But to reassure his mother, Lt Bourke added 'Dear Mother I feel quite confident that I shall get through all right, but should my time come I am prepared to face it. I would like to write a lot but this letter is liable to Censor. I am certain the Allies will win eventually, thanks to Russia but it will probably be some years yet.'

Cpt. F.B. Stanton, who was responsible for censoring any references to evacuation along with other military secrets, finally found time to write his own self-censored letter. 'I didn't get up until 10 a.m. ... put in the afternoon with my head above the parapet and my glasses to my eyes just looking for a target, only had a couple of shots. Our Artillery had a little practice at Jacko's expense this afternoon'. Stanton thought it was 'amusing to see our chaps, head over parapet to see shells land, then when the bombardment ceased, Jacko had a few shots and of course down came all the heads but I have put in about an hour and a half this evening on the eternal job, censoring, not that the chaps know anything much that matters. This place is worse than even Broadmeadows for Furpheys ... I used to think fellows were exaggerating when they talked of the monotony of this life but there is no doubt about it, we take not the least bit of notice of the everlasting bang bang and I can tell you John Turk's index finger hangs on the trigger very lightly at night time, he wastes thousands of rounds of ammunition'.

A wounded Pte. N. Wilson managed to record being 'carried on a stretcher to clearing station on the beach' after being hit 'but feeling a little better, but still very weak. I see a lot of my mates here' he said and 'Turks are sending big howitzer shells very close destroyed a hospital tent and casualty 15 including a doctor.' Pte. J. Lennie was also nearly wounded as 'More shells landed and killed mules and wounded a couple of men. Our mules and 3 other fellows and myself just missed — we are very lucky so far. The Turks shell it day after day, but it is our job to draw rations every day at No. 2 outpost and shells are flying there every day'.

Guns, artillery personnel and animals were leaving secretly at night. Sgt. R. Gardiner confirmed that by day they were fooling the Turks. 'The battn moved up to trenches at the R. of Lone Pine at the top of Galway Road, they were great trenches all underground except the actual firing line which was reached by climbing a couple of steps up from the tunnel.'

Apart from evacuation rumours flying around, Capt. Ivor Williams also heard that he might be put back in a danger zone.

'Today a battleship, two cruisers, two monitors, three torpedo boats stood out opposite us and gave the extreme right flank a terrible doing with all the largest high explosive shells for about three quarters of an hour. They used about 800 rounds. The latest rumour is we are to man the Lonesome Pine trenches. It was here that I had two very narrow squeaks — one from a shell which blew the whole of the earth work from behind me and the other from a bomb which burst in front of me.'

Not realising the Anzacs were leaving, the Turks continued to drop propaganda leaflets aimed at demoralising front line soldiers. Capt. Bill Knox reported 'An aeroplane dropped a parachute at Lone Pine with a message telling us what fools we are to fight and inviting us to surrender claiming British and Australian prisoners of war were very well treated and live on roses in Persian gardens etc. very entrancing pictures'. Turkish prisoners, however, confessed they were sick of fighting and so they had surrendered. Knox wrote that 'the prisoners and deserters we have got lately are rather a miserable lot, mostly Asiatic Turks who feel the cold greatly although I think most are sent to pitch us tales, all utterly unreliable'.

End of Week 33

**Saturday
11 December
DAY 231**

On hearing that British politicians had recommended Anzacs 'take the bold course and withdraw', Capt. Bill Knox retorted 'the answer to that is it would be so dammed bold we couldn't do it because it was hard enough to get on and we couldn't get off if we wanted to. So we've just got to stay with it'.

With only one week to go, Lt S.H. Watson who supervised the pier building in June (now named after him) was brought into the secret operation by Gen. White. Watson said Gen. White informed him 'and Col. Newcombe and Maj. Blamey that 2nd Div. Sig. Coy. would be responsible for the laying, maintaining and operating the lines and communications, during final stages of evacuation of Anzac, which would take place on the nights of 17–18 and 19–20 December and the last troops would be those residue remaining after the major numbers had been withdrawn. This would be a gradual process, affecting the gradually contracting sector. Col. White also stressed this must be kept with absolute secrecy, and no steps taken which would be likely to give an indication of the intention to withdraw. Finally, he put his hand on my shoulder and looking me straight in the face, said "Watson, the communications must not fail. MUST NOT FAIL!! MUST NOT FAIL!!" Repeating it three times'.

Secrecy seemed to be working at the trench level because Pte. B.G. Thomson noted nothing of any importance that day. 'Up very early as 121 men to cook breakfast for. Had a very busy morning fixing up dinner and at it during the aft. Nothing of any importance happened during the day. Late to bed and had a very restless night. Headache.' Pte. J. Lennie reported 'we have had orders to have everything pack up ready to move in 24 hours'. He thought this transfer was just for a fortnight's well-earned rest.

Sunday 12 December
DAY 232

Only six more days to go from this last Sunday at Gallipoli. Chaplains who were 'in the know' held special services praying for the safe evacuation. Gen. White also brought some of his top brass into the secret, including Col. Monash who knew nothing of the operation to that point. 'Like a thunderbolt from a clear blue sky has come the stupendous and paralysing news that, after all, the Allied War Council has decided that the best and wisest course to take is to evacuate the Peninsula, and secret orders to carry out that operation have just reached here. The secret is known so far to only a small handful of men ... already we have stopped the further arrival of stores, mails, reinforcements, and munitions ... to secure as great a measure of secrecy as possible. The operation of withdrawal is going to be every bit as critical and dangerous an enterprise as the first landing, and if the Turks were to get the slightest inkling of what was intended, it would mean the sacrifice of at least half our men. As it is, it will mean the sacrifice of some men, and of vast quantities of munitions and stores.

'At a conference of the commanders it was decided to put up the bluff that, owing to the severe winter conditions, it is intended to form a winter rest-camp at Imbros, and take the brigades and battalions there by turn. In this way we should be able in two or three stages to remove about two-thirds of the total army, leaving the remaining third to man the defences very lightly, and then finally to make a bolt for the beach, in the dead of night and into boats which will be in waiting. It is of course an absolutely critical scheme, which may come off quite successfully or may end in a frightful disaster. But orders are orders. I need not say I feel very unhappy ... I am almost frightened to contemplate the howl of rage and disappointment there will be when the men find out what is afoot, and I am wondering what Australia will think at the desertion of her 6,000 dead and her 20,000 other casualties.'

Now the word had really passed around. Maj. Gen. J.M. Antill, who had ordered Light Horsemen to their deaths at the Nek on 7 August, suspected something. 'Indications point to evacuation — No stores being landed mules artillery and Hospitals being cleared — my appn. to visit Mudros to inspect rest details to be suspended etc. — 69th (D) Battery fired on Snipers Nest last night ... Conference at Div. HQrs. with G.O.C. Divn.' Even Capt. Bill Knox, who had been so opposed to leaving, told his wife, 'I can't say anything but there is something doing and we very much fancy we will spend winter in a warmer climate'.

Only the lowly privates in the trenches were still in the dark. Pte. E.G. King wrote that 'Every day is alike here, and one hardly knows when it is Sunday. Anyhow it isn't recognised as a day of rest, and the same old routine of war life is gone through, as on weekdays'.

Monday
13 December
DAY 233

With only five days to go, Chaplain W. Dexter revealed his feelings. 'Horror of horrors! We are to evacuate Anzac and Suvla. That is the movement that is taking place. If only fine weather lasts we are to be away by Saturday. I could cry. But what is the use? I must smile and cheer everybody up, but my heart is very sore, not for the evacuation itself, for I know this is best, but for all the valuable lives that have been lost here. The boys have done their job grandly and well. We are bound to leave many stores behind but nothing of any value in the way of munitions ... I do not know yet what part the Padres will take in this affair but I am shifting to the 1st Casualty Clearing Hospital for that will be the last to get away (if it gets away at all).

'The beach is very busy and everyone is packing up. All gear must be moved from the firing line at night so that Abdul does not get wind of anything unusual ... I could not sleep for thinking so at 1 a.m. I lit the lamp and read until about 6 a.m. and I have come to the conclusion that our evacuation is a wise move and that in military circles our getting away safely will take equal rank with our landing.'

With the clock ticking faster, Capt. Knox warned his wife (and daughter, Diana) of the worst. 'I am called upon to play a hard part in the evacuation and should I meet any bad luck I want you to feel I have done my best to play the game as gentlemen play ... I will be desperately sorry for both your sakes sweetheart ... you must be very brave and not let it matter too much.' By now even some privates like Pte. J. Lennie had found out and wrote that it was 'very quiet had orders to pack up things and be ready to move of in the night at 8 o'clock under sealed orders ... were waiting around the pier to embark, then left'.

ONCE OFF THE BEACH, THE EVACUATING ANZACS WERE TRANSPORTED TO ISLANDS SUCH AS LEMNOS ON VESSELS LIKE *HMS HORORATA*. SHOULD A SOLDIER DIE EN ROUTE, AS IN THIS PICTURE, THEY WERE BURIED AT SEA AFTER A SERVICE WAS PERFORMED ON THE DECK. AWM P00046.047

With only four days to go, Charles Bean also found out they were evacuating. He had spent his time editing *The Anzac Book* but the secret had been well kept. 'The idea', he noted in his diary 'is that on Friday night the trenches will be held by the smallest number of troops that can hold them — the rest will march off to the beach about nightfall. Whilst they are embarking the others will leave the trenches'.

The anonymous diarist for 20th Battalion painted the pre-evacuation picture. 'We have been busy all day getting rid of all the spare gear belonging to the different sections who have gone in a hurry, only taking the gun and tripod with them. We have here, 3 gun cases and rods, 4 spare parts boxes with lock and feed block in each and boxes upon boxes of belts etc. We had to get them over to the Q.M. Stores. Heavens knows what will happen to them if we are going as soon as rumour says we are. All our lines are undermined and a good lot of the Turkish trenches also, as our tunnels extend under all their front line, and enormous quantities of Amerol waiting to be touched off ... Large quantities of goods from Imbros are down on the beach being given away as they are unable to get them to their owners. There is also, I believe, a large mail for us, that is not going to be delivered to us for some reason or another. I suppose it will all be lost. We are not able to write and send letters away at present. Smaller boats are very active in the bay. We have no idea as to when we get out ... Troops are certainly going off every night ... Stores that have been brought over from Imbros were being resold to anyone

Tuesday
14 December
DAY 234

willing to have them. Cases upon cases of tunics, shirts and numerous other things were being broken open and everyone helping themselves … an officer put a stop to it … The prevailing opinion is that we are here for another week or more.'

Wednesday
15 December
DAY 235

Even though there were only three days to go, a highly critical Maj. Page still did not realise his brigade would be walking out of Gallipoli forever. 'We are at present living on the beach resting after 9 weeks continuous trench occupation. I say occupation because there is little fighting here except by artillery. We are still where we were on Aug. 6, 1915 and still have the methods that prevailed in times of the old Greeks or other ancients in almost all depts … a wash-out nearly describes the situation here and will still be without 50,000 troops at the best, UK's army men will not do it, even if they had 100,000 — I'd be glad to hear of your approach altho' there is talk of sending our Brigade away to either Salonika, Suez Canal or Bagdad being our destination and we have been packed awaiting transport about 10 days now.'

Fortunately, Pte. F. Corder's final posting passed off without incident. 'The last night I spent on the Gallipoli Peninsula … was put on guard over a lamp, it was a aiming point for one of our gun's, my duty was to see that the light did not go out, it was situated on a hill called Brighton knoll, all went well during the night the Turks did not attack as we expected.'

Thursday
16 December
DAY 236

With only two days to go, Lt J.G. Cosson 'tumbled to the plan' saying 'our people had us tricked, all sorts of reports were going round. However today, there is no doubt as to what is to be done, although not officially announced. Everything points to the early evacuation of the Peninsula. It will be a thunderbolt to Australia. This morning I went down to beach, and what a sight, guns broken, ammunition by cartloads, gun carriages, stores of biscuits, bully and clothing all being removed or sacrificed. There is no doubt this peninsula part of the war has been the greatest failure. I know not how our war office people will look at it. It looks as though we will be some of the last to leave'.

As the count down escalated, Maj. Eric Hyman, of the 12th Light Horse wondered if they would succeed. 'Still very quiet, the critical time is approaching. With what result I wonder? Everyone is cheerful though of course anxious. I hear that we will be amongst the last to leave. I hope for the best.'

With only one day to go before the first big night of evacuation, the Anzacs were acting normally in full view of the unsuspecting Turks. Charles Bean even 'found the Light Horse playing cricket on Shell Green (with Maj.Onslow batting) while the shells were flying overhead!'.

Like everybody else, Lt J.G. Cosson was now onto the ruse. 'Think we will be making a general retreat tonight, and when Jacko finds out, we are sure to get some hurry up in the way of shells ... Likely to move off at any time now. Twenty of my old Coy (C) have the honoured position of covering the retirement of machine guns. Jacko's plane or taube appeared this afternoon, but he kept at a great height, our machine guns rattled away. I have my pack ready, only taking one blanket, almost feel sorry to leave the dugout. All hospital tents are left standing, but empty, and work is going on just the same. This is all done to deceive the Turks who will get a shock in a few hours. It will indeed be a good piece of work if we get away without losing any men. It is ideal weather for the job, a fine calm sea and a lovely moonlight and nine of our chaps have been warned to be ready to move off at a minutes notice, so that is the start as far as our Company is concerned.'

Towards the end of the day, a fire started in a pile of the Anzacs stores embroiling 'a huge dump of MacConochie's rations and biscuits and a little oil'. Bean said 'the whole sky to the north was a great red glow'. So Gen. Leslie and 'as many Australians as were handy' started fighting the fire and after 'working very hard got it under control within an hour'.

That night a trial batch of just 200 men were evacuated to test out the piers and boats and other facilities put in place. As the system worked so well, the organisers had high hopes for the real thing. Overnight Charles Bean who had been there from the start and stuck it out to the end also left Gallipoli saying, 'So I have left old Anzac. In a way I was really fond of the place. I have certainly had some quite enjoyable times there in my old dugout — yarning to friends; or going around the lines'.

End of Week 34

As the sun rose slowly lighting up the famous beach on this last day, the men clutched their gear, held their breath and waited. Like the night before the landing, the Cove seemed to hold its breath. It was D Day — or rather D night. The large group of men who were selected to leave that night — about 20,000 the size of a well stocked Division — packed and repacked their gear, smoked, chatted and tried to fill in time that had never seemed to tick by so slowly. Once darkness fell, they would sneak across the beach and, assisted by moonlight, escape their prison of nine months. This would be the first of two parts of the main evacuation, with the last 20,000 men retreating the next night — if the Turks did not tumble to the plot before then.

Lt Gen. Birdwood issued his long-waited Special Army Order: 'In carrying out our present operations, we are undertaking what no soldier ever likes, viz., a withdrawal from the front of the enemy ... none of you will feel in the least disheartened, because we all know we have never been beaten ... we have prevented the Germans using the best fighting troops of the Turkish Army elsewhere ... we have fully played our part ... we can be better employed fighting elsewhere and I know how much you look forward to getting to grips with the enemy ... remember in the final retirement silence is essential ... this will be done steadily and without undue haste or scurry ... in the same soldierly manner in which the troops have affected their various magnificent landings during the last eight months. To withdraw in the face of the enemy in good order, and with hearts full of courage and

BELOW: MAJ. CHARLES NAPIER FINN, OF MELBOURNE, 4TH AUSTRALIAN FIELD AMBULANCE, WHO WAS ONE OF THE LEADING DOCTORS AT ANZAC COVE, VOLUNTEERED TO STAY TO THE LAST TO TREAT ANY SOLDIERS WOUNDED DURING THE EVACUATION.

BELOW RIGHT: HAVING WRITTEN A CONSTANT STREAM OF LETTERS AT GALLIPOLI TO HIS SWEETHEART, DOLLY CASTLES, A SINGER, MAJ. CHARLES NAPIER FINN, MARRIED HER AFTER THE WAR WHEN SHE ALSO ACHIEVED RECOGNITION FOR HER WONDERFUL VOICE ALONG WITH HER INTERNATIONALLY ACCLAIMED SISTER, AMY CASTLES.

confidence for the future, provides a test of which any soldiers in the world may be justly proud.'

During the day, Maj. Charles Napier Finn, of the 4th Australian Field Ambulance, who had stayed back to tend any wounded wrote that 'while most of the men all went away in little lots ... all the spare ammunition was put in a heap on the beach and painted white ready for the Navy to destroy'. He was pleased to be leaving because he said 'we are now all very short of water, down to ³/₄ of a breakfast cup full a day and no more. The food was alright but I had no tea as I used all my water for shaving and cleaning my teeth'.

As he got ready to leave, CQMS A. Guppy feared that if the Turks found out about it, the progressive evacuation might cause problems since it was a 'quiet night except for spasmodic bursts of rifle and No Gun fire. A large fire, visible for many miles, broke out, down at the beach last night; in a great heap of clothing, timber, and stores of all descriptions. We received orders at 1 p.m. that the 14th and 15th Battns are to move away tonight; the 13th and 16th Battns taking over the long sector of the line which the four Battns have been holding the last few days. Pity help the boys if Jacko discovers how lightly the line is held, there only being a man to about twenty yards'.

But once darkness fell, the careful plan was put in place as soldiers started leaving during the night of 18 December and kept on moving off the beach under cover of darkness until just before dawn on 19 December. One who got away that night was Corporal H. Wyatt who wrote that 'We fell in about 8.30 and given a lot of things to carry. I was staggering by the time we got to the beach, it was about 10 p.m. when we got on the barge. We were taken round to Suvla Bay to get on the boat. We are going to Lemnos'.

One of those still waiting for his turn, Lt N.E. McShane wrote 'I hope you in Australia are not ashamed of us; we have done our bit and no blame can fall on us. This is the night before the final evacuation. I go off tomorrow night'. Others were more nervous like Sgt. Pinnock hoping the Turks would not realise he was defending trenches with a skeleton staff and attack. 'You imagined wherever you fixed your eyes for a minute you saw a Turk. Unfortunately I was in an exposed position, pretty close up, and had instructions not to fire unless I was certain a Turk was there.'

Maj. Eric Hyman wrote his last entry before passing his diary on for safekeeping. 'Still waiting. I sent this book (diary) with a farewell letter addressed to Vee in case I did not get off, by Major Parsons.'

Sunday
19 December
DAY 239

The last day

When the sun rose over the sparsely populated beach on this last day, those soldiers still remaining held their breath for even longer than their predecessors, praying the Turks would not realise nearly all the Anzacs had deserted and only a skeleton army remained. This was a tense day at Anzac. Fortunately, Lt Gen. Birdwood came ashore to boost morale and check final details for the last batch of soldiers due to leave after dark.

Some anxious soldiers like Lt Howard Both started their preparations early. 'Was busy at 7 a.m. getting everything finally squared up. All lines seem perfect and I thought it was impossible to get out of communication, until "Jacky" started with 75's on what used to be a gun pit, but the gun had been removed days ago. He succeeded however, in blowing out a machine gun line and very nearly myself and offsider as well. While waiting in the head of the gully above the Signal Station YBA, Col. Paton and his staff came walking down the Gully about 4 p.m. He said cheerfully to my party, "Having your last meal, my lads?" I said without thinking, "By Christ I hope not!" It was however, my last on the Peninsula.'

Maj. Charles Finn was especially worried about their chances because 'at midday a Turkish plane flew over and we thought our game was up as they could see that most of the men had gone and the Turks would attack'. But for some reason the Turks did not act on this information and once darkness fell, Maj. Finn said he and 'the rest of the men were put into motorboats and taken onto trawlers', all except for '35 men from each brigade who were left behind to stop any rush from the Turks — brave men I can tell you.'

One of the earliest to get away that evening was Lt N.E. McShane who left just after dark on what was for him the day before his birthday. 'We left in small parties, I had 28 men and left the trenches at 5.15 p.m. each man, all ranks carried two match head grenades as well as ammunition and as we marched on to the pier we threw them into the water. It was a great success and I don't know yet whether the Turks know we have gone. We left at different times and marched in file down the tracks to the pier, old Beachy Bill who had been firing a great deal all day, did not trouble us; the embarkation arrangements were wonderful, carried out without delay. I have a few curios, 2 old Turkish caps which were probably worn by owners now deceased, a clip of cartridges in a reserve ammunition belt taken off a dead body, my gas helmet, the pouch got slightly blood stained when I was carrying a chap down who had been killed, some shrapnel bullets etc. I'll send them as soon as I get a chance. I shall be twenty three tomorrow.'

As this final group of men began moving off under the cover of darkness, Lt Both described the procedure. 'The "A" Party, the first of the last, came off about 10 p.m. with padded feet. They were the most fortunate I thought. We still had to stay until the "C" Party had gone and chance what "Jacky" Turk would do when he found the trenches empty. Everybody however, seemed light hearted trying to keep the real truth of the situation away from themselves. From midnight the trenches were almost empty, save for a few machine gunners and men in the line. "Jacky" would have had no trouble in getting through if he had only known. A message came in shortly after midnight saying in effect — "Forward line patrol reported to Battalion HQ that Lone Pine Turks appear to be putting in extra barbed wire and sand bags apparently anticipating attack!".'

One of the last off that night was Maj. Eric Hyman who said 'We left peninsula at 11.30 p.m. everything worked wonderfully and the Turks were completely surprised they were still improving their trenches the night we left'.

The last dawn

After the clock had struck midnight, ushering in Monday 20 December, the last of the final group sneaked away from both Anzac Cove and Suvla Bay. By daylight they had all gone. Pte. E.G. King said he left 'about midnight, and arrived at the beach about 1 a.m. this morning, and went on board a trawler (Alkahara) but the Colonel, an officer, and 10 men were left behind on Pope's Post after we left. The Colonel and 5 men left about 2 a.m. and the rest about 3 a.m. All getting off safely. The other battalions were all done the same way, and so far as we know all got off safely. Tunnelling under the Turk's trenches has been going on for months, and they were all charged ready to be blown up in case of attack. There was a good many battleships and cruisers standing in ready to shell the whole place, as soon as we were all safely away. We landed at Lemnos Island about 2 p.m., and marched about 4 miles to camp'.

One of the later departures was Capt. Ivor Williams who explained 'We rose at 2 a.m. and at 2.45 a.m. started for the pier. After passing through the deep saps which were carpeted with torn strips of blankets to deaden the sound arrived at the pier (likewise covered) at 3.45 a.m. At 4.45 a.m. we boarded a lighter which took us to the H.M.S.

"HEROIC" — a bonza and very fast boat. Harold and I made love to the stokers who shouted us a bonza breakfast. At 10.15 a.m. we arrived in Mudros Harbour, Lemnos, where we were transferred to the H.M.S. "RUSSELL" — a very large battleship carrying all 6 and 12" guns. It is a marvellous boat and the sailors could not do enough for us. They supplied us with big tubs of water and plenty to eat. 1.15 p.m. we were put ashore, our packs placed on a transport and taken to our new camp. We had a 3 and ½ mile march. Everyone is mixed up like chocolates in a box. We will all have to be sorted out and reorganised. The units are to have a rest here'.

One of the last to leave was Lt C. Riddell who, with his mate, had laid the charges for the explosives in the tunnels and trenches. 'On the last night we only had about one man to every 50 yards of trench, but he kept running about and firing to deceive the enemy, then after giving the last party a fair start we two — the only ones in half a mile of trenches at the front — came away after closing the entanglements and destroying the electric mine firing gear. We got down to the beach all right and got off in one of the last boats.'

Watching through binoculars from his ship, 'Grafton' Bean reported the final countdown. By 2.30 a.m. just as 'a thick mist has gone over the moon', Chatham's Post had been deserted, Charles Bean was told and 'the last lot left' were at the hard-won Quinn's Post and dearly-held Lone Pine. At 3.05 this last lot were 'now all alone' strung out along the front line. Bean could still hear 'a solitary rifle or two, no doubt the self-firing variety'. He said men 'were now hurrying down Chailak Dere down paths among the hills with the moon now too dark to see by'. By 3.15 a.m. the last men had left Lone Pine with 'very little firing now just the isolated rifle shots from our patent rifles set to fire after we have gone'. By 3.20 a.m. Quinn's Post and Popes now deserted. At 3.23 Beachy Bill fired shells down to the beach. At 3.25 Walker's Nek had been deserted — leaving the old Anzac Line now open to the Turks. At 3.26 the charges laid at the Nek blew it up (killing 70 Turks and wounding many more). This inspired 'tremendous firing' Bean said as angry 'Turks fired for all they were worth along the line. At 3.57 signal confirmed "Operations completed"'.

All troops had cleared the beach by 5.00 a.m. with the last men dousing the pile of stores on the beach with petrol and setting them alight. At 5.05 Turks were still firing but Bean said there was no one ashore. 'Machine guns were going every now and then he said and at 5.40 Turks were still firing at Anzac Cove and all the stores set alight at Suvla were burning brightly. At 7.05 our ships opened fire on our own stores and mule carts' (which must have been the final giveaway) as by

7.15 a.m. when the Anzacs stopped shelling their own beach Bean saw 'Turks running across our trenches' as they 'attacked' Lone Pine and other trenches — with needless to say surprisingly good results!

'Well, it's an extraordinary end to a fine history' Bean concluded as he left the deck to have his breakfast below. 'The Turks at last have got it — the place they never could take — by our quietly leaving it in the night. And in the end perhaps, the greatest success we have achieved there, is quietly giving it to them without their knowing it.'

As the sun now drenched the beach, it suddenly dawned on the watching Turks that the whole place was deserted. After firing testing shots they charged into trench after trench unopposed, guns at the ready. But all they found were empty trenches and dugouts with just the occasional notes and presents. At the official level Gen. Godley left a polite request for the Turkish leaders to preserve the Allied graves at Anzac. He hoped they would do this having already behaved so honourably during the fighting. At the unofficial level a larrikin Anzac's note read 'You didn't push us off Jacko, we just left'. Officers and privates left gramophones with classical records to teach the Turks some culture, as well as books, tables with meals set and souvenir photographs which they hoped the Turks might put in their albums. Not that anybody cared for they were now sailing over the horizon leaving Gallipoli behind them forever.

NOW snowflakes thickly falling in the winter breeze
  Have cloaked alike the hard, unbending ilex
And the grey, drooping branches of the olive trees,
  Transmitting into silver all their lead;
And, in between the winding lines, in No-Man's Land,
Have softly covered with a glittering shroud
    The unburied dead.

And in the silences of night, when winds are fair,
When shot and shard have ceased their wild surprising,
I hear a sound of music in the upper air,
  Rising and falling till it slowly dies—
It is the beating of the wings of migrant birds
Wafting the souls of these unburied heroes
    Into the skies.

                        M. R.,
                  N.Z. Headquarters.

AS THIS POEM FROM *THE ANZAC BOOK* REVEALS, ONE OF THE GREATEST REGRETS THE ANZACS HAD AS THEY EVACUATED GALLIPOLI WAS LEAVING BEHIND THEIR MATES, MANY OF WHOM THEY HAD BEEN UNABLE TO BURY.

Tuesday
21 December
DAY 241

All at sea

By now most of the Anzacs had landed at Lemnos or other staging posts or were still at sea heading for places like Alexandria. From today onwards they would be resting, recuperating and awaiting orders for their next battles — mostly the Western front.

Trooper Gerald Digby, 12th Light Horse, who celebrated his 21st birthday on the 21st December and had been in the rear guard and one of the last to leave, spoke for many when he told his family how bad he felt about the retreat. It was 'not a nice thing to know that we failed in our objective and having lost all those men as well ... still modern warfare nowadays demands many sacrifices and I suppose that is one of them but that was hard'. Digby continued 'The only good thing was the efficiency of the evacuation as 48,000 people were all evacuated and only about six casualties occurred and none of them fatal. Troops had been moving off all week and the Light Horse had to remain till last to cover the retreat of the others with machine guns'. Digby said 'The Turks were pretty quiet ... my squad was holding half a mile of front ... I was up on Camel's Hump on watch in case any Turks showed themselves.

'At last after silent waiting and watching the order came through to file out quietly with socks pulled over our boots we sneaked out through the bivouacs chucked on our packs and gear and stole quietly away through the saps down to the beach ... the only thing that we were frightened of was if old John Abdul had taken a tumble he would have poured shrapnel into us while we were embarking into the lighters. We had just got off and got going when Beachy Bill (the howitzer) dropped shrapnel on the beach but he only spoke once'. Before leaving Digby plucked a leaf from a tree as a 21st birthday present to himself and wrote on it with an indelible purple pencil "The last of Gallipoli evacuated 19 December 1915"'.

From his ship bound for Egypt, Col. Monash, who had been promoted to Brigadier General at Gallipoli, wrote 'And so ended the story of the Anzacs at Gallipoli'. The evacuation, he said was 'a most brilliant conception, brilliantly organised, and brilliantly executed — and will, I am sure, rank as the greatest joke in the whole range of military history'.

Even on this first day after the evacuation it was clear it had been a complete success. In fact, Maj. Gen. A. Lynden Bell, Chief of General Staff on behalf of the Commander-in-Chief, of the Mediterranean Expeditionary Force issued a Special order of the day expressing to all ranks 'his unreserved appreciation of the way in which recent operations ending in the evacuation of the "Anzac" and "Suvla" positions, have been carried to an issue beyond his hopes'. As the arrangement for secrecy and withdrawal 'could not have been improved' and the troops 'proved themselves more than equal to the most difficult task … It is no exaggeration to call this achievement one without parallel … one for which military history contains no precedent'.

Wednesday 22 December
DAY 242

Looking back now that it was over, the achievement seemed enormous as Capt. Nathaniel Dunbar Barton told his mother. 'I expect you know by now, Anzac and Suvla have been evacuated without a casualty. A few guns were left behind, but they were all old and of course were blown up before being deserted; most of the stores were burnt in an accidental fire a couple of nights before; a fire which we were very frightened might give the show away to the Turks, but which I think they must have thought was set alight by their shells. The rest of the supplies were to be shelled by our boats when the enemy discovered we were gone, which they did not do, till two o'clock the next afternoon at any rate, as up till then they were bombarding our trenches.

'The evacuation itself was carried out without a hitch but we can thank God for the weather, which was absolutely perfect for our plans … I knew for certain what was to be done four days before, and was at first told I was to be among the last party to leave. The night following the news I certainly felt excited and nervous, but I was all right after that till Saturday night, when the first big party left. I think everyone felt the strain a bit then just as the party was going off, and for about half an hour afterward … On Sunday night the rest of the regiment left, and was divided into three parties A, B and C. Each of these was again divided into three leaving a quarter of an hour after one another … It was bright moonlight marching down, and very impressive seeing parties coming from all directions in silence … out at sea the transports lay at anchor, with boats flying busily backwards and forwards to the shore and the brilliantly lighted hospital boats in deep contrast to the others which were without lights.

'You will probably here wild rumours of men left behind, but one case of a 13th Battalion man is true. He was a sentry in a tunnel and fell asleep; he awoke with a pain in the tummy (only too common at Anzac) and on going out (to relieve himself) found the trenches deserted. He raced for the beach, and arrived without rifle or pack in time for one of the last boats. The tale he now tells himself is a very different addition, and much more heroic, but I think this is right … I am afraid the

Australians haven't much of an opinion of a Tommy now. It is a pity but we have only seen second rate regiments, and the Australian seems much quicker at inventing things, which are useful for trench warfare. The English fought in France nine months before the Australians began, yet the later weren't at the front a month, before they invented the periscope rifle, a thing which has been invaluable to us, and which the enemy has not yet been able to make successfully.'

Lt Gen. Birdwood certainly recognised the achievement, writing to Gen. White that 'I must congratulate you most heartily on the very excellent results of all you did to ensure our withdrawal being the complete success it was. In our wildest dreams we could hardly have hoped to carry it off quite in this way'.

The British finally made the decision to evacuate Helles on 27 December 1915. The Turks mounted a massive assault on 7 January 1916 and all British troops were withdrawn on 9 January 1916. So, having sacrificed 21,255 lives, the British and their Allies also left that part of the Gallipoli peninsula which they could not capture. Britain's great dream of capturing the Dardanelles had been shattered. They had to admit defeat and move on to other battles.

The death toll was staggering. One million men had fought there from all armies. On the Allies side, the British had lost 21,255 dead; the French 10,000 dead; the Australians 8,709 dead; the New Zealanders 2,701 dead and the Turks lost 86,692 dead. Many were also wounded. The British suffered 73,485 wounded; the French 27,000; the Australians 19,441 and the New Zealanders 4,752. A massive 251,309 Turks were wounded. All the deaths and woundings on the Allied side were for no territorial gain. The Turks had lost most but they did manage to defend their country.

Although some then fought in Palestine most Anzacs went on to fight in Flanders and the Somme. In those battles, these brave volunteers put into practice all the skills they had developed at Gallipoli. By 1918, the Anzacs along with all the Australian volunteers who enlisted from 1916 onwards were brought together as five Divisions in Australia's first army. John Monash, by then a distinguished General, commanded this army which won many battles and went on to help win the war in France by November 1918. While they represented only nine per cent of the Allied forces, the Australian army captured nearly 25 per cent of German territory, prisoners of war and arms and ammunition. Gen. Monash claimed his soldiers were the best army in World War I. In France in August 1918, King George V also knighted Monash, who became the first warrior to be knighted in battle for over a century and history's last. Thus under their own steam the Anzacs and their

THE BONES OF TURKISH
SOLDIERS COLLECTED AT
GALLIPOLI IN 1919, PART
OF THEIR 86,692 DEAD.
AWM H11907

Australian commander achieved the victory they had been craving for since landing at Gallipoli on 25 April 1915.

As Capt. Bill Knox observed from the safety of Egypt in January 1916, having a final word on behalf of the Anzacs, 'The evacuation from Anzac was not by any means a defeat, but it became obvious we could do no good there and were getting HELL from the new bigger Turkish guns. Of course we left so many poor chaps buried there — splendid fellows and it all seems so sad but we had attempted the impossible at the Dardanelles and the Turks we now hear, are planning to make the Evacuation Day a special day of national feasting; and well they may, they fought well and very fairly and can make a very good story of their victory.'

FROM *THE ANZAC BOOK*
(1916)

263

References

The references are listed as they appear in the text, not alphabetically. A reference is only given once for each chapter even though the work might be quoted more than once in the chapter. If a quote is very short no reference is given. Most of the diaries and letters are in the Australian War Memorial (AWM) and can be located using the numbers given below.

Chapter 1: 25 April

An Anonymous Australian Soldier, AWM PR84/169.
Private No. 94, 9th Battalion, 3rd Brigade, *School Paper*, vol viii, Department of Public Instruction, Queensland, April 1916.
Perry, Pte. A.R., 10th Battalion, AIF, *The Anzac Book*, Cassell, London, 1916.
Hamilton, Pte. R.G., 9th Battalion, AIF, Letter, AWM PR85/151.
Suggett-Hagan, Pte. James, 3rd Battalion, AIF, Diary, AWM MSS1274.
Scobie, Robert, 2nd Battalion, Letter to wife, Scobie Family private collection, Maitland, NSW.
Turnbull, Driver J. H., Diary, AWM PR91/015.
Richards, Pte. T.J., 1st Field Ambulance, AIF, Diary, AWM 2DRL/0786.
Hamilton, Gen. Sir Ian, *The Anzac Book*, Cassell, London, 1916.
Rosenskjar, Lt Col. F.S., 26th Battalion, Records, AIF, AWM 2DRL/432.

Chapter 2: 26–30 April

Dawkins, Lt William Henry, Diary, in J.A. Ingle, *From Duntroon to the Dardanelles: A biography of Lieutenant William Dawkins*, Canberra, 1995.
Tiegs, Lt A.H., 28th Battalion, AIF, Diary, AWM 2DRL/0003.
French, Maj. David, Diary, in Robert Rhodes James, *Gallipoli*, Pimlico, London (first published 1965), 1999.
Treloar, W.O., John, Headquarters, First Division, AIF in J. L. Treloar, *An Anzac Diary*, Alan Treloar, Armidale, 1993.
Stanley, Signaler R., 10th Battalion, AIF, Diary, AWM 3DRL/3614.
Knaggs, Albert, on board Australian submarine *AE 2*, captured in the Sea of Marmara, Diary, in *First in Last Out: The Navy at Gallipoli*, Kangaroo Press, Kenthurst, 1990.
Monash, Col. John, Message to Maj. Gen. J. A. Godley, AWM 3DRL/2316(12).

Chapter 3: May

Dexter, Chaplain W.E., in Michael McKernan, *Padre, Australian Chaplains in Gallipoli and France*, Allen & Unwin, Sydney, 1986.

White, Maj. Brudenell in Rosemary Derham, *The Silent Ruse: Escape from Gallipoli*, Cliffe Books, Melbourne, 1998.

McHenry, Lt R.W., 2nd Field Artillery Brigade, AIF, Diary, AWM 2DRL/0136.

King, Cpt. D.B.A., 3 Battery, AFA, AIF, Diary, AWM 2DRL/0517.

Small, Lt F.T., 3rd and 5th Field Company, Australian Engineers, AIF, Diary, AWM 2DRL/0778.

Bean, Charles, Diary in Kevin Fewster, *Gallipoli Correspondent: the frontline diary of C.E.W. Bean*, Allen & Unwin, Sydney, 1983.

Parker, Saddler Sgt. James, 2nd Field Artillery Brigade, AIF, Diary, AWM PR01036.

McKern, Corp. H., 4th Battalion, AIF, Diary, AWM 2DRL/0465.

Taylor, Phil and Pam Cupper, *Gallipoli. A Battlefield Guide*, Kangaroo Press, Kenthurst, 1989.

Roberts, Corp. C., 8th Battalion, AIF, Diary, AWM 2DRL/0507.

McKenzie, William, Salvation Army Chaplain, Diary, in Michael McKernan, *Padre, Australian Chaplains in Gallipoli and France*, Allen & Unwin, Sydney, 1986.

Ward, Lt Leslie, 68 Squadron, AFC Diary, AWM PR83/230.

Monash, Col. John, Letter in F.M. Cutlack (ed.), *War Letters of General Monash*, Angus & Robertson, Sydney, 1934.

Spalding, Seaman A.L., Diary, AWM PR00563.

Treloar, W.O. John, Headquarters, First Division, AIF, in J. L Treloar, *An Anzac Diary*, Alan Treloar, Armidale, 1993.

Coulter, L/Corp. A.H. 4th Field Ambulance, AIF, Diary, AWM 2DRL/0507.

Smith, L/Corp. H.J.S., 3rd Battalion, AIF, Diary, AWM 2DRL/0318.

Lennie, Pte. J., 4th Field Ambulance Brigade, AIF, Diary AWM 3DRL/7681.

Reynell, Lt Col. C., 3rd Australian Light Horse Brigade, AIF, Diary, AWM PR86/388.

Hollis, Cpt. N.S., 2nd A.F.A Brigade, AIF, Letter, AWM 2DRL/0458.

Rayment, Cpt. George, 3rd Light Horse, Brigade, AIF, Diary, AWM PR91/042.

Richards, Lt E.J., 11th Battalion, AIF, Letter, AWM 2DRL/0301.

Corbin, Lt Colonel John. Diary, AWM PR00176.

Idriess, Trooper I.L., 5th Australian Light Horse Regiment, AIF, Diary AWM 1DRL/0373.

Cameron, 2nd Lt W.M., 9th Light Horse Regiment, AIF, Diary AWM 1DRL/0185.

Chapter 4: June

Idriess, Trooper I.L., 5th Australian Light Horse Regiment. Diary AWM 1DRL/0373.

Hobson, RQMS B.C., 13th Battalion, AIF, Diary, AWM 2DRL/694.

Merrington, Chaplain E.N., 1st Australian Light Horse Brigade, AIF, Diary, AWM 3DRL/3237.

Goldring, S/Sgt. Leslie, 12th Field Ambulance Brigade, AIF, Diary, AWM PR83/221.

Brown, Driver E, 1st Australian Light Horse, AIF, Diary, AWM 2DRL/1285.

Reynell, Lt Col. Carew, the 9th Light Horse, Diary, private collection, Mrs Anthony Caillard, Sydney.

Hutton, Sgt. A.S., 3rd Australian Light Horse, AIF, Diary, AWM 3DRL/3371.

Johnston, CPO. in Robert Rhodes James, *Gallipoli*, Pimlico, London (first published in 1965), 1999.

Langford, L/Corp. P., 4th Australian Light Horse, AIF, Diary, AWM 3DRL/7454.

Pasini, Pte. J, in Breed, C., *From Gallipoli With Love 1915 — Letters from the Anzacs of the Wimmera*, The History and Natural History Group of the M.L.A. Society, Donald, 1993.

Quinane, Trooper P.J., 7th Australian Light Horse, AIF, Diary, AWM 3DRL/3386.

Muir, Pte. FW., 1st Battalion, AIF, Letter to his mother, AWM 2DRL/0316. (Muir whose letters were published in the *South Coast Times*, Wollongong, died on 28 November 1915 from wounds received at Gallipoli).

Bosward, L/Sgt. C., 4th Battalion, AIF, Diary, AWM 3DRL/4104.

Gammage, Pte. J.K., 1st Battalion, AIF, Diary, AWM PR82/3.

Guppy, CQMS A., 14th Battalion, AIF, Diary, AWM 3DRL/1545.

Vallance Pte. N., Letter to his mother in C. Breed, *From Gallipoli With Love 1915 — Letters from the Anzacs of the Wimmera*, The History and Natural History Group of the M.L.A. Society, Donald, 1993.

Treloar , W. O. John, Headquarters First Division, Diary in J. L Treloar, *An Anzac Diary*, Alan Treloar, Armidale, 1993 (Treloar later became Lt Col. OBE).

Dexter, Chaplain W.E., 5th Battalion, AIF, Diary, AWM PR00248.

Gillison, Chaplain A., 14th Inf. Battalion and 4th Inf. Bde, AIF, Diary, AWM 3DRL/6277.

Stanley, Sig. R., 10th Battalion, AIF, Diary, AWM 3DRL/3614.

Dods, Col. J., Royal Australian Army Medical Corps, AIF, Diary, AWM PR86/034.

McNicoll, R., *The Royal Australian Engineers 1902 to 1919*, Corps Committee of the Royal Australian Engineers, Canberra, 1979.

McHenry, Lt R.W., 2nd Field Artillery Bgde., AIF, Diary, AWM 2DRL/0136.

Bean, Charles, Diary, in Kevin Fewster, *Gallipoli Corresponden: the frontline diary of C.E.W. Bean*, Allen & Unwin, Sydney, 1983.

Langford, L/Cpl. P., 4th Australian Light Horse, AIF, Diary, AWM 3DRL/7454.

Fricker, Pte. A., 4th Field Ambulance, AIF, Diary, AWM PR00956.

Jack, Major B.D. 54th Battalion, AIF, Letter, AWM 2DRL/0039.

Richards, Lt T.J., 1st Battalion, AIF, Diary, AWM 2DRL/0786.

Merrington, Chaplain E.N., 1st Australian Light Horse Brigade, AIF, Diary, AWM 3DRL/3237.

Merrington, E.N., 1st Australian Light Horse, AIF, Diary in Michael McKernan, *Padre, Australian Chaplains in Gallipoli and France*, Allen & Unwin, Sydney, 1986.

O'Hara, Lt Desmond, Letter in Robert Rhodes James, *Gallipoli*, Pimlico, London (first published in 1965), 1999.

Facey, A.B., *A Fortunate Life*, Fremantle Arts Centre Press, Fremantle, 1981.

Redford, Maj. T.H., B Sqn, 8th Light Horse Regiment, AIF, Diary, AWM PR85/064.

Irving, Pte. George, 3rd Battalion, AIF, Letter, AWM 3 DRL6547.

Chapter 5: July

Gammage, Pte. J.K., 1st Battalion, AIF. Diary, Sunday 25 July 1915, AWM PR82/3.

Riley, Corp. Alec, in Robert Rhodes James, *Gallipoli*, Pimlico, London (first published 1965), 1999.

Merrington, Chaplain E.N., 1st Australian Light Horse, AIF, Diary, in Michael McKernan, *Padre, Australian Chaplains in Gallipoli and France*, Allen & Unwin, Sydney, 1986.

Bosward, L/Sgt. C., 4th Battalion, AIF, Diary, AWM 3DRL/4104.

Richards, Lt T.J., 1st Battalion, AIF, Diary, AWM 2DRL/0786.

Brown, Driver E., 1st Australian Light Horse, AIF, Diary, AWM 2DRL/1285.

Parker, Saddler Sgt. James, 6th Royal Australian Field Artillery, AIF, Diary AWM PR01036.

Reynell, Lt Col. Carew, Diary, private collection, Mrs Anthony Caillard, Sydney.

Goldring, S/Sgt. Leslie, 12th Field Ambulance Brigade, AIF, Diary, AWM PR83/221

McPherson, from Sgt. D. 2nd Division Sigs, AIF, Diary, AWM 3DRL/7781.

Dexter, Chaplain W. E. 5th Battalion, AIF, Diary, AWM PR00248.

Monash, Col. John, in F.M. Cutlack (ed.), *War Letters of General Monash*, Angus & Robertson, Sydney, 1934.

Murray , Ordinary Seaman Joe, Diary, in Robert Rhodes James, *Gallipoli*, Pimlico, London (first published 1965), 1999.

Arnold, 2nd Lt R., 15th Battalion, AIF, Diary, AWM 3DRL/6430

Bean, Charles, Diary, in Kevin Fewster, *Gallipoli Correspondent: the frontline diary of C.E.W. Bean*, Allen & Unwin, Sydney, 1983.

McKern, Corp. H., 4th Battalion, Diary, AWM 3DRL/3906.

Treloar, Alan, Diary, in J.L. Treloar, *An Anzac Diary*, Alan Treloar, Armidale, 1993.

Cameron, 2nd Lt W.M., 9th Light Horse Regiment, AIF, Diary, AWM 1DRL/0185.

West, Sgt. F.C., 3rd Australian Field Artillery, AIF, Diary, AWM 3DRL/3969.

Ward, Pte. R, 13th Battalion, AIF, Diary, AWM PR00060.

Hampton, Sgt. R.L,. 5th Battalion, AIF AWM 3DRL/2310.

Woods, Lt H., 4th Field Ambulance, AIF AWM 3DRL/0358.

Turnbull, Driver J.H., 8th Battalion, AIF, Diary, AWM PR91/015.

Monash, Col., Commander 4th Brigade, Letter in F. M. Cutlack (ed.), *War Letters of General Monash*, Angus & Robertson, Sydney, 1934.

Mills, L/Corp. S.R., 1st Div. Sigs., AIF, Diary, AWM PR82/9.

Ward, Pte. R., 13th Battalion, AIF, Diary, AWM PROOO60.

Turnbull, Pte. John Henry, 8th Battalion, AIF, Diary AWM PR91/015.

King, Cpt. D.B.A., 3rd Battery, AFA, AIF, Diary, AWM 2DRL/0517.

Dexter, Chaplain W.E., 5th Battalion, AIF, Diary, AWM PR00248.

Weeks, Driver F.A., 5th AASC, AIF, Diary, AWM PR86/127.

Hobson, RQMS. B., 13th Battalion, AIF, Diary, AWM 2DRL/0694.

Chapter 6: August

Hutton Sgt. A.S., 3rd Australian Light Horse, AIF, Diary, 6 August 1915.

Adlard, Lt J.E., 1st Division Artillery, AIF, Diary AWM 2DRL/0020.

Reynell, Lt Col. Carew, 3rd Australian Light Horse Brigade, Diary, Private Collection, Mrs Anthony. Caillard, Sydney and AWM PR86/388.

Jack, Maj. B.D., 54th Battalion, AIF, Letter, AWM 2DRL/0039.

Goldring, S/Sgt. Leslie, 12th Field Ambulance Brig., AIF, Diary, AWM PR83/221.

Corbin, Lt Col. J., Diary, AWM PR00176.

Webster, P.O. Bert, Royal Australian Naval Bridging Train and 23rd Battalion, AIF, Letter to Mother, *Suvla to the Somme*, Helen Mitchell (ed.), Digital Solutions Press, Collingwood, Victoria.

Loughran, Maj. H.G., 14th Battalion, AIF, Diary, AWM 2DRL/0520.

Unit Diary, 14th Infantry Battalion, AIF, AWM AWM4 (Roll 46).

Pawson, Cpt. John, Military Landing Officer, in Robert Rhodes James, *Gallipoli*, Pimlico, London (first published 1965), 1999.

Gamage, Pte. J.K., in Les Carlyon, *Gallipoli*, Pan Macmillan, Sydney 2001.

Stanley, Sig. R. 10th Battalion, AIF, Diary, AWM 3DRL/3614.

Matthews, Corp. Ted, Author interview, Narrabean, 1997.

Hore, Cpt. G., Letter to mother, unattributed newspaper cutting, AWM (no number).

Crawford. Lt A., An interview with Ian Jones 25 April 1972, Transcript, Ian Jones private collection, Malvern, Victoria.

Pinnoch, Sgt. Cliff, in Les Carlyon, *Gallipoli*, Pan Macmillan, Sydney 2001.

Brazier, Lt Col. Noel, 10th Australian Light Horse Brigade, AIF Report on operations, AWM 1DRL/0147.

Fricker, Private Austin 4th Field Ambulance, AIF, Diary, AWM PR00956.

Portman, Trooper in Les Carlyon, *Gallipoli*, Pan Macmillan, Sydney 2001.

Richards, Lt T.J., 1st Battalion, AIF, Diary AWM 2DRL/0786.

Pacey, Gunner William Leonard, 3rd Australian Filed Artillery Brigade in William Pacey, *Anzac Diary*, transcribed from the original diary by Dallas Baker, compiled by Roslyn Nicol, 1993, AWM 3DRL/7681.

Ward, Lt Leslie, 68 Squadron, AIF, Diary AWM PR83/230.

Johanesen, Pte. P.R., 8th Battalion, AIF, Letter, AWM PR87/018.

Thomson, Pte. B.G., 3rd Field Ambulance, AIF, Diary, AWM PR88/001.

Pinnock, Sgt. C.C., St. 8th Light Horse Regiment, AIF, Letter, AWM 1DRL/0547.

Cameron, 2nd Lt W.M., 9th Light Horse Regiment, AIF, Diary, AWM 1DRL/0185.

Mychael, Pte. A.J., 1st Australian Light Horse, AIF, Letter, AWM 3DRL/6051.

McKernan, Michael, *Padre, Australian Chaplains in Gallipoli and France*, Allen & Unwin, Sydney, 1986.

Merrington, Chaplain E.N., 1st Australian Light Horse Brigade, AIF, Diary, in anonymous writer of the 14th Battalion, AIF, AWM4 (Roll 46).

Gupy, Alfred, Diary, AWM 3DRL/1545

Wanliss, N., *The History of the Fourteenth Battalion, A.I.F.*, the 14th Battalion and the 4th Brigade Association, Melbourne, 1929, p. 72.

King, Cpt. D.B.A. 3rd Battery, A.F.A., AIF, Diary, AWM 2DRL/0517.

Bean, Charles, Diary, in Kevin Fewster, *Gallipoli Correspondent: the frontline diary of C.E.W. Bean*, Allen & Unwin, Sydney 1983.

Grieve, Pte. James Turnbull Grieve, Letter to his parents on the day he died, AWM PR91/079.

Kidd, Maj. T.A., Diary, AWM PR82/137.

Idriess, Trooper I.L., 5th Australian Light Horse Regiment, AIF, Diary, AWM 1DRL/0373.

CHAPTER 7: SEPTEMBER

Murdoch, Keith, Journalist, Letter to prime minister Andrew Fisher, 23 September 1915, quoted in Les Carlyon, *Gallipoli*, Pan Macmillan, Sydney 2001.

Idriess, Trooper I.L., 5th Light Horse Regiment, AIF, Diary, AWM 1DRL/0373.

Pauls, Trooper Ernest, Diary, Private Collection Paul family, Raymond Terrace. (Pauls changed his name to Paul after the war).

Fay, Cpt., Letter to the sister of Pte. John Simpson, Kirkpatrick 3rd Field Ambulance, AIF, from the Captain, 3rd Field Ambulance regarding the death of her brother, AWM 3DRL/3424.

King, Pte. E.G., 19th Battalion, Diary, AIF AWM PR83/018.

Hyman, Maj. Eric, 12th Light Horse, Diary, private collection, Bob Hyman, Tamworth, NSW.

King, Cpt. D.B.A., 3 Battery, A.F.A., AIF, Diary, AWM 2DRL/0517.

Anthill, Maj. Gen. J. M., 3rd Australian Light Horse Brigade, AIF, Diary, AWM 3DRL/6458.

Williams, Cpt. Ivor Williams, 21ST Battalion, AIF, Diary AWM PR91/113.

Knox, Cpt. Bill, 13th Australian Artillery Brigade, Letter to wife Mim, Baillieu family private collection, Melbourne.

McLeod, Pte. N.S., 23rd Battalion, AIF, Diary, AWM PR91/047.

Briggs, Lt H., 14th Machine Gun Battalion, AIF, Letter, AWM 1DRL/0152.

Hamilton, Gen. Sir Ian, Special Orders, in *The Anzac Book*, Cassell, London, 1916.

Willey, Sapper V., Letter to parents quoted in C. Breed, *From Gallipoli With Love 1915 — Letters from the Anzacs of the Wimmera*, The History and Natural History Group of the M.L.A. Society, Donald, 1993.

Abbott, Pte. H.H., 24th Battalion, AIF, Diary, AWM 3DRL/3817.

Bradley, Sgt. A.W., 22nd Battalion, Letter from AIF, AWM 3DRL/3418.

Darlington, Col., Letter quoted in Sir Henry Darlington, *Letters From Helles*, Longmans, Green and Co. Ltd., London, 1936.

Hutton, Sgt. A.S., 3rd Australian Light Horse, AIF, Diary, AWM 3DRL/3371.

Burton, Lt F., 4th Light Horse Regiment, AIF, Letter, AWM 1DRL/0168.

Bean, Charles, Diary, in Kevin Fewster, *Gallipoli Correspondent: the frontline diary of C.E.W. Bean,* Allen & Unwin, Sydney, 1983.

Villers, L/Corp. H., 9th Light Horse, AIF, Letter to Miss G. Callary from AWM 1DRL/0178.

Strangmar, Lt H., 24th and 57th Battalions, AIF, Diary, AWM 2DRL/710.

Guppy, CQMS A., 14th Battalion, AIF, Diary, AWM 3DRL/1545.

Miles Lt T., 12th Battalion, AIF, Diary, AWM 2DRL/0554

12th Infantry Brigade, War Diary, AIF, AWM AWM 4.

Bleechmore, Sgt. D., 22nd Battalion, AIF, Letter, AWM 1DRL/131

Schultze Private C.W.letter quoted in C. Breed, *From Gallipoli With Love 1915— Letters from the Anzacs of the Wimmera*, The History and Natural History Group of the M.L.A. Society, Donald, 1993.

Webster, P.O. Bert, Letter to Aunt, in *Suvla to the Somme*, Helen Mitchell (ed.), Digital Solutions Press, Collingwood, Victoria.

Dexter, Chaplain W.E., 5th Battalion, AIF, Diary, AWM PR00248.

Cozens, Lt T.E., 21st Battalion, AIF, Diary, AWM 2DRL/0002.

Mulholland, Cpt. D.V., 1st Machine Gun Battalion, AIF. Letter AWM 2DRL/0040.

Roth, Lt Col. R.E., AAMC, AIF, Letter, AWM 2drl/1231.

Bertwistle, Lt W.H., 27th Battalion and 7th Machine Gun Company, AIF, Diary, AWM 2DRL/0428.

Hunter Rogers, Sgt. G., 6th Australian Army Medical Corps, AIF, Diary, AWM PR86/054.

Dakin, Lt C., 5th Machine Gun Company, AIF, Diary, AWM 3DRL/2272.

Adam Sgt. R., 11th Battalion, AIF, Letter, AWM 1DRL/0003.

Gunter, Corp. A., 1st AFA Brigade, AIF, Diary, AWM 1DRL/0327.

Wilson, Pte. N., 18th Battalion, AIF, Diary, AWM PR89/112.

Smith, Cpt. R.E., 26th Battalion, AIF, Letter, AWM 3DRL/3342.

An unnamed soldier, 20th Battalion, AIF, Diary, AWM PR01055.

Chapter 8: October

Cozens, Lt T.E., 21st Battalion, AIF, Diary, Sunday 19 October, AWM 2DRL/0002.

Antill, Maj. Gen. J.M., 3rd Australian Light Horse Brigade, AIF, Diary, AWM 3DRL/6458.

Pauls, Trooper Ernest, Diary, Private Collection, Paul Family, Raymond Terrace, NSW.

Gunter, Corp. A., 1st AFA Brigade, AIF, Diary, 1DRL/0327.

An unnamed soldier, 20th Battalion, AIF, Diary, AWM PR01055.

White, Maj. Brudenell, Letter by Rosemary Derham, *The Silent Ruse: Escape from Gallipoli*, Cliffe Books, Melbourne, 1919.

Knox, Cpt. Bill, 13th Australian Artillery Brigade, Letter to wife Mim, Baillieu family private collection, Melbourne.

Gunter, Corp. A., 1st AFA Brigade, AIF, Diary, 1DRL/0327.

Martin, James, 21st Battalion, AIF, Letter to Parents, AWM PR83/061 and/or 85/339.

Williams, Cpt. Ivor, 21st Battalion, AIF, Diary, AWM PR91/113.

Merrington, Chaplain E.N., 1st Australian Light Horse Brigade, AIF, Diary, AWM 3DRL/3237.

Strangmar, Lt H., 24th and 57th Battalions, AIF, Diary, AWM 2DRL/710.

Muir, Pte. F.W., 1st Battalion, AIF, Diary, AWM 2DRL/0316.

Wilson, Pte. N., 18th Battalion, AIF, Diary, AWM PR89/112.

Trevena, Pte. A.C., 8th Battalion, AIF, Letter to his friends in the Mallee, in C. Breed, *From Gallipoli With Love 1915— Letters from the Anzacs of the Wimmera*, The History and Natural History Group of the M.L.A. Society, Donald, 1993.

Roth, Lt Col. R.E., AAMC, AIF, Diary, AWM 2DRL/1231.

Webster, P.O. Bert, Letter to mother, *Suvla to Somme*, Helen Mitchell (ed.), Digital Solutions Press, Collingwood, Victoria, 2001.

King, Pte. E.G., 19th Battalion, AIF, Diary, AWM PR83/018.

Nurse, Sapper A., 4th Field Company, Australian Engineers, AIF, Diary, AWM PR85/398.

Magill, Cpl. E., 7th ALH Regt., AIF, AWM 2DRL/0212.

Hyman, Maj. Eric, 12th Light Horse, Diary, private collection, Bob Hyman, Tamworth, NSW.

An unnamed soldier, 20th Battalion, AIF, Diary, AWM PR01055.

Dexter, Chaplain W.E., 5th Battalion, AIF, Diary, AWM PR00248.

Billings, Cpl. H.R.A., Corps Sigs., AIF, Diary, AWM 3DRL/6060.

Bean, Charles, in Kevin Fewster, *Gallipoli Correspondent: the frontline diary of C.E.W. Bean,* Allen & Unwin, Sydney, 1983.

Dakin, Lt C., 5th Machine Gun Company, AIF, Diary, AWM 3DRL/2272.

Sutherland, Lt L.W., 1st Sqn. AFC Report on test cricket, AWM 2DRL/0988.

Miles, Lt T., 12th Battalion, AIF, Diary, AWM 2DRL/0554.

McLeod, Pte. N., 23rd Battalion, AIF, Diary, AWM PR91/047.

Caddy, Pte., Letter held within the papers of the Caddy family, AWM PR87/0177.

Eades, Lt A., 45th Battery, AFA, AIF, Letter, AWM 1DRL/0249.

Morgan, Maj. P.J., 17th Battery Field Artillery, AIF, Letter, AWM 1DRL/0510.

Adam, Sgt. R., 11th Battalion, AIF, Letter, AWM 1DRL/0003.

An unnamed soldier, 20th Battalion, AIF, Diary, AWM PR01055.

Campbell, Lt D., 27th Battalion, AIF, Letter, AWM 1DRL/0176.

An unnamed soldier, 20th Battalion, AIF, Diary, AWM PR01055. [REPEATED]

Arnold, Pte. G., 2nd Battalion, AIF, Letter, AWM 1DRL/0061.

Chapter 9: November

Weeks, Driver, F.A., 5th AASC, AIF, Diary, 13 November 1915, AWM PR86/127.

Macleod, Sgt. Maj. A.N., 27th Battalion, AIF, Letter, AWM PR87/232.

Webster, P.O. Bert, Letter to mother, *Suvla to the Somme*, Helen Mitchell (ed.), Digital Solutions Press, Collingwood, Victoria, 2001.

Williams, Captain Ivor, 21st Battalion, AIF, Diary, AWM PR91/113.

Lennie, Pte. J., 4th Field Ambulance, AIF, Diary AWM 3DRL/7681.

Cozens, Lt T.E., 21st Battalion, AIF, Diary, AWM 2DRL/0002.

Braithwaite, Lt Col., DHQ, N.Z. & A. Division Memorandum to the Brig. Gen., R.A. N.Z. & A. Division and all Brigadiers and O's C. Units, N.Z. & A. Division, AWM 3DRL/2316.

King, Jonathan, *Gallipoli, Our Last Man Standing: the extraordinary life of Alec Campbell*, John Wiley & Sons Australia, Brisbane, 2003.

Hogan, Cecil, Letter to Mrs. Martin, AWM, PR 83/061 and/or 85/339.

Knox, Cpt. Bill, 13th Australian Artillery Brigade, Letter to wife Mim, Baillieu family private collection, Melbourne.

An unnamed soldier, 20th Battalion, AIF, Diary, AWM PR01055

Commanding Officer, No. 2 Sub Section to the 4th Brigade, Message report for 24 hours ending 0500 AWM 3DRL/2316.

Lawrence, Sergeant Cyril, Diary, in Sir Ronald East (ed.), *The Gallipoli Diary of Sergeant Lawrence of the Australian Engineers-1st A.I.F. 1915*, Melbourne University Press, Carlton, 1981.

Arnold, Pte. G., 2nd Battalion, AIF, Letter, AWM 1DRL/0061.

Champion, Lt B., 1st Battalion, AIF, Diary, AWM 2DRL/0512.

Nurse, Sapper A., 4th Field Company, Australian, Engineers, AIF, Diary.

Bean, Charles, Diary, quoted in Kevin Fewster, *Gallipoli Correspondent: the frontline diary of C.E.W. Bean*, Allen & Unwin, Sydney, 1983.

Commanding Officer, No. 2 Sub Section, 16th Battalion, AIF, Report for the 24 hours ending 0530 11/11/15 AWM 3DRL/2316.

Duggan, Captain B. Letter to father in C. Breed, *From Gallipoli With Love 1915 — Letters from the Anzacs of the Wimmera*, The History and Natural History Group of the M.L.A. Society, Donald, 1993.

Weeks, Driver F.A., 5th AASC, AIF, Diary, AWMPR86/127.

Muir, Pte. F.W., 1st Battalion, AIF, Diary, AWM 2DRL/0316.

Guppy, CQMS A., 14th Battalion, AIF, Diary, AWM 3DRL/1545.

Gardiner, Corp. R., ADMS Branch, 1st Australian Div. HQ, AIF, Letter to mother, AWM 1DRL/0304.

An unknown soldier, 20th Battalion, AIF, Diary, AWM PR01055.

Jack, Maj. B.D., 54th Battalion, AIF, Letter, AWM 2DRL/0039.

Affleck, Sgt. H., 1st AFA Brigade, AIF, Diary, AWM 1DRL/0026.

Stanton, Cpt. F.B., 14th Battalion, AIF, Letter, AWM 2DRL/155.

King, Pte. E.G., 19th Battalion, AIF, Diary, AWM PR83/018.

Turnbull, Pte. John, Henry 8th Battalion, AIF, Diary, AWM PR91/015.

Morgan, Maj. P.J., 17th Battery Field Artillery, AIF, Letter, AWM 1DRL/0510.

Hyman, Maj. Eric, 12th Light Horse, Diary, private collection, Bob Hyman, Tamworth, NSW.

Murphy, Lt Col. G., 18th Battalion, AIF, Diary, AWM 1DRL/528.

Chapter 10: December

Dexter, Chaplain W.E., Diary, Saturday 13 December, 1915 in Michael McKernan, *Padre, Australian Chaplains in Gallipoli and France,* Allen & Unwin, Sydney, 1986.

Bean, Charles, Diary, quoted in Kevin Fewster, *Gallipoli Correspondent: the frontline diary of C.E.W. Bean,* Allen & Unwin, Sydney, 1983.

Garland, W.O. W.H., 4th Field Ambulance Brigade, AIF, Diary, AWM 3DRL/7681.

Lennie, Pte. J., 4th Field Ambulance, AIF, Diary, AWM 3DRL/7681.

Law, Lt O., 48th Battalion, AIF, Letter, AWM 1DRL/0408.

Knox, Cpt. Bill, 13th Australian Artillery Brigade, Letter to wife Mim, Baillieu family private collection, Melbourne.

Brind, Maj. E., 23rd Battalion, AIF, Letter from AWM 1DRL/0153. (Eric Brind was killed in action at Pozieres on 28/7/16)

An unnamed soldier, 20th Battalion, AIF, Diary AWM PR01055.

Murphy, Lt Col. G., 18th Battalion, AIF, Diary, AWM1DRL/528.

Webster, P.O. Bert, Letter to mother, *Suvla to the Somme,* Helen Mitchell (ed.), Digital Solutions Press, Collingwood, Victoria.

Williams, Cpt. Ivor, 21st Battalion, AIF, Diary, AWMPR91/113.

Guppy, CQMS A., 14th Battalion, AIF, Diary, AWM 3DRL/1545.

Caldwell, Lt D., 27th Battalion, AIF, Letter, AWM 1DRL/0176.

Digby, Trooper Gerald, No.2 Troop of A Squadron, 12th Light Horse, postcard to mother, private collection, Michael Digby, Glen Innes.

Riddell, Lieutenant C., Letter to sister in R. McNicoll, *The Royal Australian Engineers 1902 to 1919,* The Corps Committee of the Royal Australian Engineers, Canberra, 1979.

Bradley, Sgt. A.W., 22nd Battalion, AIF, Letter, AWM 3DRL/3418.

Bourke, Lt J., 2nd Australian Field Gun Company, AIF, Letter, AWM 1DRL/0140.

Stanton, Cpt. F.B., 14th Battalion, AIF, Letter, AWM 2DRL/155.

Wilson, Pte N., 18th Battalion, AIF, Diary, AWM PR89/112.

Gardiner, Sgt. R., 7th Battalion, AIF, Letter, AWM 1DRL/0305.

Watson, Lt Col. S.H., 2nd Div. Sigs, AIF, Diary, AWM 3DRL/3612.

Thomson, Pte. B.G., 3rd Field Ambulance, AIF, Diary, AWM PR88/001.

Monash, Col. John, Letter in F. M. Cutlack (ed.), *War Letters of General Monash,* Angus & Robertson, Sydney, 1934.

Anthill, Maj. Gen. J.M., 3rd Light Horse, AIF, Diary, AWM3DRL/6458.

King, Pte. E.G., 19th Battalion, AIF, Diary, AWM PR83/018.

Dexter, Chaplain W.E., Diary in Michael McKernan, *Padre, Australian Chaplains in Gallipoli and France,* Allen & Unwin, Sydney, 1986.

An unknown soldier, 20th Battalion, AIF, Diary, AWM PR0105.

Page, Maj. H.H., of the 25th Battalion, AIF, Letter to his brother, AWM 3DRL/6910.

Corder, F., Bombardier 7th Battery, AIF, Diary, AWM PR86/134.

Cosson, Lt J.G., 48th Battalion, AIF, Diary, AWM 1DRL/0216

Hyman, Maj. Eric, 12th Light Horse, Diary, private collection, Bob Hyman, Tamworth, NSW.

The Anzac Book, Cassell, London, 1916.

REFERENCES

Finn, Maj. Charles Napier, 4th Australian Field Ambulance, Letter to Dolly Castles, private collection Patti Finn, Melbourne.

Wyatt, Corp. H,. 2nd Battalion, AIF, Diary, AWM 1DRL/0608.

McShane, Lt N.E., 1st Battalion, AIF, Letter, AWM 2DRL/0005.

Pinnock, Sgt. Cliff, Letter, in Les Carlyon, *Gallipoli*, Pan Macmillan, Sydney, 2001.

Both, Lt Howard, Diary, in papers of Lt Col. S.H. Watson, 2nd Div., Sigs., AIF AWM 3DRL/3612.

King, Pte. E.G., 19th Battalion, AIF, Diary, AWM PR83/018.

Williams, Captain Ivor 21st Battalion, AIF, Diary, AWM PR91/113.

Monash, Col. John, in Les Carlyon, *Gallipoli,* Pan Macmillan, Sydney, 2001.

Bell, A. Lynden, Maj. Gen., Chief of the General Staff, MEF, Special Order, in Rosemary Derham, *The Silent Ruse: Escape from Gallipoli*, Cliff Books, Melbourne, 1998.

Barton, Cpt. Nathaniel Dunbar, 7th Light Horse Regiment, AIF, Letter, AWM 2DRL/55

Birdwood, Lt Gen. Sir William, in Rosemary Derham, *The Silent Ruse: Escape from Gallipoli*, Cliff Books, Melbourne, 1998.

APPENDIX 1

Army Ranks, Abbreviations and Glossary

ARMY RANKS

Army ranks used at Gallipoli compiled by military historian
Peter Bastick giving approximate numbers of men.

Other Ranks

Private, Bombardier, Gunner, Sapper, Trooper, Signaller

Non Commissioned Officers

Lance-Corporal
Corporal (commands a Section of 10 men)
Sergeant
Staff Sergeant
Warrant Officer Class 1
Warrant Officer Class 2

Commissioned Officers

Second Lieutenant		Commands a Platoon (made of 3 Sections each of 10 men)
Lieutenant		Assistant to the Captain.
Captain		Second in Charge of a Company (made up of 4 Platoons = 120 men)
Major		Commands a Company or a Squadron
Lieutenant Colonel		Commands a Battalion (made up of 4 rifle Companies or Squadrons and support Companies = 800–1,000 men))
Colonel		Interim rank
Brigadier General	1 Star	Commands a Brigade (made up of 4 Battalions = 4,000 men plus)
Major General	2 Stars	Commands a Division (made up of 4 Brigades = 16,000–20,000 men)
Lieutenant General	3 Stars	Commands a Corps (made up of 3 Divisions = 60,000 men)
General	4 Stars	Commands an Army (made up of 3 Corps = 180,000 men)
Field Marshal	5 Stars	Supreme Commander

ABBREVIATIONS

AAML	Australian Army Medical Corps
AANS Reserve	Australian Army Nursing Service Reserve
AASC	Australian Army Service Corps
ABD	Able-bodied driver
ADC	Australian Divisional Command
ADS	Advance Dressing Station
AFA	Australian Field Ambulance
AGH	Australian General Hospital
AIF	Australian Imperial Force
Am, Amm., Ammo.	ammunition
ASC	Australian Supply Corps
Austns.	Australians
AWM	Australian War Memorial
BEF	British Expeditionary Force
Br.	Bombardier
Bgde., Brig.	Brigade
Brig.	Brigadier
Brig. Gen.	Brigadier General
Btn., Bat., Batt., Battn.	Battalion
Bty.	Battery (artillery)
CCH	Casualty Clearing Hospital
C.O.	Commissioned officer
Co., Coy.	Company
Col.	Colonel
Cpl., Corp.	Corporal
C.P.O.	Chief Petty Officer
Cpt., Capt.	Captain
CQMS	Company Quarter Master's Sergeant
d.	dead
Div.	Division
DHQ.	Divisional headquarters
Gen.	General
GHQ	General headquarters (of whole army)
Gr.	Gunner
HC	Holy Communion
HQ	Headquarters (of Battalion)
Lght. Hse., L.H.	Light Horse
L/Corp.	Lance Corporal
Lt, Lieut.	Lieutenant
Lt Col.	Lieutenant Colonel
Lt Gen.	Lieutenant General
Maj.	Major
Maj. Gen.	Major General
MO	Medical Officer
NCO	Non commissioned officer

NZ, NZs	New Zealanders
OC	Officer commanding
Ops	Operations
Pds	pounds (imperial measurement)
Pltn.	Platoon
Pte., Pvte.	Private
RAFA	Royal Australian Field Artillery
RAMC	Royal Australian Medical Corps
RAP	Regimental Aid Post
Reg., Regt.	Regiment, Regimental
RNAS	Regimental Naval Air Service
RQMS	Regimental Quarter Master Staff
RSM	Regimental Sargeant Major
Spnl., Shrap.	shrapnel
Sgt.	Sergeant
S/Sgt.	Staff Sergeant
Sig., Sig.s	Signal/s
Squad.	Squadron
Sctn.	Section
TB	Torpedo boat
VC	Victoria Cross
Wd.	wounded
W.O.	Warrant Officer

GLOSSARY

Nicknames, acronyms and slang

Anzac	Australian and New Zealand Army Corps
Beachy Bill	Turkish heavy artillery mounted on hills above Anzac Cove
Billy	Tin for boiling water for cup of tea
Cadging	Borrowing with little intent to return items (especially cigarettes)
Digger	Australian soldier forced to dig in at Gallipoli — a name which stuck
Furphy	A rumour or lie
Lonely Liz	Turkish heavy artillery gun above Anzac Cove
Sapper/sapping	Trench digger/trench digging
Smoko	Morning or afternoon tea
Tommy or Tommie	English soldier at Gallipoli
Tucker	food

Turkish soldiers were given various nicknames, including
Abdul, Turko, Joe Burke, Asia, Jacko, Johnny, John, Johnny Turk

APPENDIX 2

Gallipoli Timeline

1914

June   28: Assassination of Archduke Franz Ferdinand, heir to Austro-Hungarian Empire, by a Serb separatist at Sarajevo, the spark that ignited World War I.

July   28: War declared.
Austro-Hungarian Empire declares war on Serbia, then Russia.
31: Australia joins in the war.
Australian government pledges support to Britain if war widens 'to the last man and the last shilling'.

August   1: Fighting starts.
Germany declares war on Russia then invades Luxembourg.
3: Germany declares war on France.
Australia offers 20,000 troops to fight Germany.
4: Britain joins in the war.
Germany invades Belgium. Britain declares war on Germany, then on the Austro-Hungarian Empire and sends troops to France.
5: Australia declares war on Germany.
10: Australian Imperial Force starts recruiting volunteers.

October   31: Turkey declares war on Britain and her Allies.

November   1: First Australian troops sail for Europe.
9: Australia's *HMAS Sydney* destroys German raider *Emden* off Cocos Island.

December   3: Australians arrive in Egypt and establish training camp at Mena near pyramids of Giza, combining with New Zealanders to form Anzacs.
21: Lt Gen. Sir William Birdwood takes command of Anzacs.

1915

February   1: Second Australian convoy arrives in Egypt.
19: Anglo-French fleet tries to capture Dardanelles sea canal.

March   18: Allies defeated in Dardanelles.

April   25: Campaign to capture Gallipoli peninsula opens as first Anzacs land at Anzac Cove led by 3rd Brigade followed by 2nd and 1st Brigades.
Anglo-French troops also land at Helles.

April	**26**: Gen. Hamilton orders Anzacs to dig in rather than retreat.
	Body count confirms 2,000 Australians killed in first 24 hours.
	28: First battle of Krithia aims at capturing Achi Baba hill (Helles).
	Royal Naval Division reinforcements arrive at Anzac Cove.
	30: Australia's *AE2* submarine is sunk in Sea of Marmara off Turkish coast.
May	**1**: Turks counterattack at Helles until 4 May.
	2: Col. John Monash leads Anzacs in new offensives against Baby 700 hill but fails.
	6: Second battle of Krithia until 8 May also fails to gain new ground at Helles.
	19: Turks launch a massive counterattack along front line aimed at pushing the 'Australian bastards' back in to the sea but Anzacs stand firm.
	Private Albert Jacka wins the first Victoria Cross at Anzac Cove.
	John Simpson Kirkpatrick 'the man with the donkey' killed at Anzac Cove.
	24: Truce held at Anzac Cove to bury the dead.
June	**4**: Third battle of Krithia fails to gain more ground at Helles.
	21: Battle for Haricot Redoubt at Helles won by French who capture trenches at Kereves Dere.
	28: Battle for Gully Ravine (aka Gully Spur) at Helles until 5 July in which British gain a little ground at cost of 4,000 casualties.
July	**12**: Battle for Achi Baba Nullah till 13 July fails to achieve any worthwhile gains.
August	**6**: 'August Offensive' mounted to capture the Sari Bair range of hills above Anzac Cove by a series of battles.
	Anglo-French forces are defeated at Helles.
	Anzacs capture Lone Pine at Anzac winning seven Victoria Crosses but losing 2,000 dead.
	First of 20,000 British reinforcements arrive Suvla Bay under Lt Gen. Sir Frederick Stopford who fails to advance.
	7: New Zealanders and Gurkhas gain ground attacking Chunuk Bair, above Anzac Cove.
	Anzacs fail to capture Hill 971 'the Mt Everest' of the hills above Anzac Cove.
	The 8th and 10th Australian Light Horse Regiments are massacred while attacking the Nek.
	Anzacs fail to capture German Officer's Ridge but win, lose, then regain Quinn's Post.
	9: Turks counterattack at Suvla Bay.
	British 'friendly fire' drives Anzacs from Hill Q which they had captured.
	10: Mustafa Kemal personally leads Turkish counterattack driving New Zealanders and Gurkhas from Chunuk Bair.
	15: Gen. Hamilton sacks Sir Fredrick Stopford commander of Suvla Bay troops.
	21: British offensive against Turkish positions in hills above Suvla Bay fails
	Anzacs fail to capture Hill 60.
	29: Anzacs abandon further offensives, admitting stalemate.
September	**2**: Troop reinforcement ship *Southland* is torpedoed en route to Gallipoli.
	3: Journalist Keith Murdoch visits Gallipoli gathering material for report advocating evacuation.
	23: Murdoch sends letter to Australian Prime Minister and lobbies British political leaders to evacuate Gallipoli.

October   **15**: Gen. Sir Ian Hamilton, Commander in Chief of the Mediterranean Expeditionary Force, is sacked.
30: Hamilton's replacement, Gen. Sir Charles Munro, visits Gallipoli and recommends evacuation.

November   **13**: British Minister for War, Lord Kitchener, visits Gallipoli to assess evacuation proposal.
17: First big storm batters Anzac Cove military settlement.
19: Col. Monash presents Victoria Cross to Sgt. Albert Jacka.
22: Lord Kitchener advises evacuation and Birdwood appoints Gen. White to develop plans.
27: Massive storm with galeforce winds, rain, sleet and snow devastates Anzac Cove settlement.

December   **7**: British War Cabinet endorses evacuation.
18: The main evacuation of Anzacs starts after nightfall.
19: The remainder of the Anzac troops evacuated after nightfall.
20: All Anzacs evacuated from Gallipoli, sailing away but leaving behind 8,709 Australians dead and 2,701 New Zealanders dead.
25: Christmas Day celebrated away from Gallipoli at Lemnos or Egypt or on board ships in the Mediterranean Sea.

1916

January   **9**: All British and French troops evacuated from Helles.

March   **7**: First Anzac troops reach European theatre of war.

APPENDIX 3

Who Was Who

PECKING ORDER

British Prime Minister	Herbert **Asquith**
Head of Admiralty First Lord of Admiralty	Winston **Churchill** (discredited and resigned during campaign)
British Minister for War	Lord Herbert Horatio **Kitchener**
Commander-in-Chief Mediterranean Expeditionary Force	General Sir Ian **Hamilton** GCB DSO ADC (dismissed during campaign)
Commander-in-Chief Mediterranean Expeditionary Force	General Sir Charles **Munro** (replaced Hamilton)
Commander Australian and New Zealand Army Corps (Anzacs)	Lt General Sir William R. **Birdwood**
Commander New Zealand and Australian Division NZ Infantry Brigade Australian 4th Brigade First Aust. Light Horse NZ Mounted Rifles	Major General Alexander John **Godley** (in charge of disastrous battle at the Nek)
Admiral in charge of British Naval Squadron	Admiral C.F. **Thursby** (recommended against evacuation in April)
Commander, 29th Division (British) British Forces at Helles Aka 'Hunter Bunter' or 'The Butcher of Helles' (returned to England with nervous breakdown)	Major General Aylmer **Hunter-Weston**, 50 (Former Boer War Cavalry Commander in charge of Helles)
Commander 1st Australian Division	Major General William Throsby **Bridges** Australia's permanent army (former Inspector General, killed in May 1915)

Commander 1st Australian Division	Brigadier General Harold B. **Walker**, DSO, (acting replacement for Bridges)
Commander 1st Australian Division	Major General J.G. **Legge** (arrived June 1915, permanent replacement for Bridges)
Chief of Staff for General Bridges	Major Cyril Brudenell Bingham **White** (later promoted to General, organised evacuation)
Commander, 3rd Brigade	Major E.G. **Sinclair-MacLagan** (the first to land at Gallipoli, all Australian brigade)
Commander, 2nd Brigade	Brigadier-General James W. **McCay**
Commander, 1st Brigade	Colonel H.N. **MacLaurin** (shot dead 27 April)
Commander, 4th Brigade	Colonel John **Monash** (attacked Baby 700 and Hill 971, later promoted to General, AIF)
Corps Commander IX Corps (British)	Lt General Sir Frederick **Stopford** (directed August landing and failed offensive at Suvla, sacked in August)
Commander New Zealand Infantry Brigade	Brig. General Francis **Johnston** (reported to be a heavy drinker)
Commander New Zealand Mounted Rifles Brigade	Brig. General Andrew **Russell**
Staff Officer to Lt General Birdwood	Lt Colonel Andrew **Skeen** (conceived August offensive plan)
Commander 3rd Light Horse	Brig. General Frederick **Hughes** (helped direct battle at the Nek)
Brigade-Major 3rd Light Horse	Lt Colonel John **Antill** (helped direct battle at the Nek)
Commander 10th Light Horse Regiment (which was massacred at the Nek)	Lt Colonel Noel **Braizer** (helped direct battle at the Nek)

Commander 8th Light Horse Regiment (which were massacred at the Nek)	Lt Colonel Alexander **White**
Commander 1st Australian Light Horse	Colonel Harry **Chauvel** (later led successful charge at Beersheba in 1917)
War Correspondent *Sydney Morning Herald*	Charles **Bean** (aka C.E.W. Bean, later: Official Historian WWI)
War Correspondent *Daily Telegraph* (London) & other Fleet Street newspapers	Ellis **Ashmead-Bartlett**
Australian journalist	Keith **Murdoch** (recommended evacuation)
Australian Prime Minister	Andrew **Fisher** (Labor Party)

TURKS & GERMANS

Divisional Commander of forces at Gallipoli	Mustafa **Kemal** (aka Kemal Ataturk, later President of Turkey)
Commander of German officers fighting in Turkey	General Liman **von Sanders**

APPENDIX 4

The Roll of Honour

The following names have been extracted from the Australian War Memorial's Roll of Honour database. They represent those who died in 1915 or early 1916 and are known to be buried or commemorated at Gallipoli or on the nearby island of Lemnos. It is not a definitive list of those who died during the Gallipoli campaign. More detail about these individuals is available on the Roll of Honour database which can be found on the Memorial's web site (www.awm.gov.au).

A'BECKETT, Frank Leigh
AARONS, Harold
AARONS, Maurice Lewis
ABBEY, Harold Claude
ABBOTT, Claude Walter
ABBOTT, Harold Henry
ABBOTT, James Ellaby
ABEL, Arthur Edward
ABERDEEN, Norman Edward
ABERNETHY, Arthur
ADAM, Charles Robert
ADAM, John
ADAMS, Arthur John
ADAMS, Douglas Bernard Matthew
ADAMS, Edgar Robert Colbeck
ADAMS, Frederick James
ADAMS, Jack Adrian Finlayson
ADAMS, John Albert
ADAMS, John Henry
ADAMS, John Knox
ADAMS, Lindsay Thomas
ADAMS, Sidney James
ADAMS, Vivian Douglas
ADAMS, William Henry
ADAMS, William James
ADAMS, William Thomas
ADAMSON, Charles Wesley
ADCOCK, Frank Henry Burton
ADCOCK, Frederick Brenchley
ADDISON, Arthur Jack
ADDISON, George Albert
ADDISON, Wilfred Emmott
ADELT, Carl
AH TUCK, Charles
AICHER, William Ludwig
AINSWORTH, Jack
AIRD, Robert
AIREY, James Valentine
AITCHISON, Alexander Walker
AITCHISON, Angus Campbell
AITKEN, Albert
AITKEN, Arthur
AITKEN, James Tod
AITKIN, Frank Keith
AKEHURST, Charles Frederick John
ALBAN, Rollo Charles Stacpole
ALBON, George William
ALDERSON, Lancelot Reginald
ALDERSON, Percy
ALDOUS, Percival John
ALDRED, Herbert Wright
ALDRIDGE, Thomas Henry
ALEXANDER, Archibald
ALEXANDER, David Gibson
ALEXANDER, Donald

ALEXANDER, James Cyril
ALEXANDER, Robert Osborne
ALEXANDER, Thomas
ALFORD, Gordon James
ALFORD, Thomas William Barker
ALLAN, David Thomson
ALLAN, Jacob
ALLAN, Walter Graham
ALLARD, Alfred Donald Macallister
ALLDRITT, Francis Ralph
ALLEN, Charles Henry
ALLEN, Con Harold
ALLEN, Edgar
ALLEN, Frederick Charles
ALLEN, George Herbert
ALLEN, Henry
ALLEN, John Arthur
ALLEN, Millington John
ALLEN, Percy Bartholomew
ALLEN, Richard William
ALLEN, Sidney Torrington
ALLEN, William Vincent
ALLEN, William Wallace Bentley
ALLERDICE, Charles Stewart
ALLERY, Henry Thomas
ALLISON, Frederick
ALLISON, John
ALLISON, John Malcolm
ALLISON, Lloyd Samuel
ALLISON, William Smith
ALLOM, Owen Bertram
ALSOPE, Charles Arthur
ALSTON, Harry
ALTMANN, Charles
ALTREE, William
AMINDE, John Bernard Conrad
AMOLIN, John
AMOR, Patrick Joseph
AMOS, Carl
AMOS, Clarence Cawtan
AMOS, Harry Oswald
ANDERSEN, Edward John Martin
ANDERSEN, Peter William
ANDERSEN, William Herbert
ANDERSON, Albert Howard
ANDERSON, Andrew Ernest
ANDERSON, Andrew Frederick
ANDERSON, Arthur
ANDERSON, Arthur Andreas
ANDERSON, Arthur Ernest
ANDERSON, Arthur Frederick
ANDERSON, Arthur Leslie
ANDERSON, David John
ANDERSON, Enderby Gordon
ANDERSON, Frederick Alexander

ANDERSON, Frederick Signor
ANDERSON, George John Stewart
ANDERSON, James
ANDERSON, James
ANDERSON, James
ANDERSON, James Alfred
ANDERSON, James McKenzie
ANDERSON, John
ANDERSON, John Edward
ANDERSON, John Shaw
ANDERSON, Kenneth Henry
ANDERSON, Kieran Leopold
ANDERSON, Leo William Hall
ANDERSON, Neville Otho Cockburn
ANDERSON, Robert
ANDERSON, Roice Campbell
ANDERSON, Samuel
ANDERSON, Thomas Bonner
ANDERSON, Victor George
ANDERSON, William
ANDERSON, William Fleming
ANDERSON, William Keith
ANDERSON, William Stowell
ANDERSON, William Walter
ANDREW, John
ANDREW, Thomas
ANDREW, William
ANDREWARTHA, Frederick
ANDREWS, David
ANDREWS, Henry
ANDREWS, Percy
ANDREWS, Sydney
ANGELL, Harry
ANGUS, John Sinclair
ANGUS, Robert Laurence
ANNAND, Victor William Joseph
ANNEAR, Paul Dalton
ANNEAR, Robert Loton
ANNEAR, William Richard
ANNESLEY, Reginald Roy
ANNONI, Joseph
ANSELL, Albert Harold
ANSELL, Allan
ANSELL, Allan Lingham
ANSTEE, William
ANSTIS, John
ANTHONEY, Henry
ANTONIO, Jack
ANTRAM, Harry
ANTROBUS, Ernest
APPLEQVIST, Frank
ARBUCKLE, Beresford
ARBUTHNOT, Stephen
ARCHER, Bruce Charles Curtis
ARCHER, Edward

ARMFIELD, Lionel
ARMITAGE, Walter
ARMSTRONG, Alexander
ARMSTRONG, Alexander Murray
ARMSTRONG, Benjamin Harrison
ARMSTRONG, Charles
ARMSTRONG, Eric Boyd
ARMSTRONG, Francis Leofric
ARMSTRONG, Hutton Perkins
ARMSTRONG, Percival William
ARMSTRONG, Reginald Edward
ARMSTRONG, Robert
ARMSTRONG, Victor Seymour
ARMSTRONG, William
ARMSTRONG, William
ARNOLD, Alfred
ARNOLD, John Peter
ARNOLD, Jonas Price
ARNOLD, William Arden Egerton
ARNTZEN, Louis
ARTHUR, Charles Edmund Perriam
ARTHUR, Leslie Raymond
ARTHUR-MASON, William Norman
ARUNDALE, Rupert Louis
ASHBY, Albert
ASHFORD, Leonard Joseph
ASHLEY, James Alfred
ASHMORE, Archibald Alfred
ASHTON, Benjamin
ASHTON, Isaac
ASHTON, James Richard
ASHTON, John
ASPIN, James
ASPINALL, Alfred
ASPINALL, Bernard Frederick
ASTLES, Jack Western
ATKINS, Frederick Allan
ATKINS, Herbert Joseph
ATKINS, Thomas
ATKINSON, Bertram
ATKINSON, Clarence Anthony Etheridge
ATKINSON, John Hall
ATKINSON, Raymond Harold
ATKINSON, Thomas Christopher
ATTRIDGE, Arthur Sydney
ATTWOOD, Charles Neville
ATWILL, Percy Gerard
ATWILL, Thomas Alfred
AUBIN, Albert Louis
AUBREY, Sydney Ellis
AUCHINACHIE, William
AUCHTERLONIE, Archibald Vivian

AUCHTERLONIE, Bertrand Innes
AULT, Edwin Joseph
AUSTIN, Colin Douglas
AUSTIN, George
AUSTIN, James Keith
AUSTIN, William Lewis
AVERY, Harold McLean
AVES, Henry George
AXTENS, Alec Luffman
AYERS, William Bruce
AYRES, Arthur Henry
AYSCOUGH, George
BACK, Herbert Stanley
BACKMAN, Charles James
BACON, David Oran
BACON, Lester Sidney
BADGER, Walter Henry
BAGE, Edward Frederick Robert
BAGGARLEY, William Charles
BAGLEY, Arthur Davies
BAGOT, Charles Ernest
BAILE, Ernest Arthur
BAILES, Alfred
BAILEY, Alfred
BAILEY, Ben Harold
BAILEY, Frank
BAILEY, Henry John
BAILEY, John Arthur Alexander
BAILEY, Leslie Charles
BAILEY, Michael James
BAILEY, Ralph Ernest
BAILLIE, James
BAILLIE, Robert Hamilton
BAIN, Duncan Farquhar Grant
BAINBRIDGE, Joseph Stanley
BAIRD, David
BAIRD, William George
BAIRD, William Henry
BAKER, Alexander John
BAKER, Arthur Alexander
BAKER, Arthur Edward
BAKER, Cyril George
BAKER, Douglas Gibbs
BAKER, Edward Hazle
BAKER, Frederick
BAKER, Frederick Ernest
BAKER, Harold Louis
BAKER, Herbert William Alfred
BAKER, Horatio Harold Roberts
BAKER, Richard Hamilton
BAKER, Thomas
BAKER, Thomas Vincent
BAKER, Walter Edward
BAKER, Walter George
BAKER, William Albert
BAKER, William Robert

BALDERSON, Arthur Gordon
BALDERSON, John
BALDIE, David William
BALDIE, Robert Douglas
BALDWIN, Alfred
BALDWIN, Charles Robert
BALDWIN, Edward Miller
BALDWIN, Harry
BALE, Charles
BALE, Harry
BALFE, Joseph Rupert
BALL, Frank
BALL, Frederick Worlledge
BALL, William George
BALL, William George
BALLANTYNE, David
BALLARD, Abe
BALSTON, Harry Love
BAMBERY, George Sweeten
BAMBERY, Timothy Richard
BANCROFT, Frank Osborn
BANCROFT, William
BANES, George
BANFIELD, George Henry
BANFIELD, Leonard John
BANGLE, Harold Edward
BANKS, Charles Elliot
BANN, Thomas
BANNER, Sydney Alfred
BANNISTER, Alfred George
BANWELL, William John
BAPTIE, Alexander
BARBER, Alexander Watt Andrew
BARBER, Charles Victor
BARBER, Henry John
BARBER, Vernon Henry
BARCLAY, Alexander
BARCLAY, John Edward
BARCLAY, Roy Austin
BARDEN, John
BARDON, Frank
BARKER, Charles
BARKER, Frank
BARKER, William Thomas
BARKLEY, Victor
BARLING, Frederick Stanley
BARLOW, Frank Clifford
BARLOW, John Edgar
BARLOW, Stanley Neville
BARNARD, Clement Aubrey John
BARNES, Arthur
BARNES, Charles Albert
BARNES, George
BARNES, Herbert
BARNES, John Russell
BARNES, Joseph George
BARNES, Thomas
BARNES, Thomas Albert
BARNES, William
BARNES, William
BARNETT, Alexander
BARNETT, Allan Robert
BARNETT, Charles
BARNETT, Kenneth Knight
BARNETT, Stirling Ferguson
BARNETT, Victor Charles
BARNSLEY, William
BARNWELL, Stephen James
BARR, Alfred Irwin
BARR, Andrew
BARR, George Herbert
BARR, Robert Wright
BARRACK, Cecil Thomas
BARRACLOUGH, Harold
BARRATT, Thomas Leslie
BARRETT, Rupert Sunderland
BARRETT-LENNARD, Douglas
BARRON, William Talbot

BARRY, Harold Joseph
BARRY, William John
BARTLEM, Frank John
BARTLETT, Donald McLarty
BARTLETT, Norman James
BARTON, Harold Eric Getting
BARTON, Harold Pryor
BARTON, Horace Albert
BARTON, Walter Ernest
BARTROP, Henry Herbert
BARWICK, Arthur Thomas Lewis
BASS, Charles Ernest
BASSAN, Reginald Albert
BASSETT, Jack Frederick
BASTO, John Leo Patrick
BATCH, Oliver Arnold
BATEMAN, Claude John
BATEMAN, William Horace
BATES, John
BATES, John Hugh
BATES, Walter George
BATES, Warren Francis
BATES, Wilfred Froud
BATES, William Holdsworth
BATES, William James
BATT, Frank
BATT, Thomas
BATTILANA, Bert
BATTY, Percival
BATTY, William Kingsley
BATTYE, Crispin Kenworthy
BAUER, Francis Charles
BAULDERSTONE, Percy Harold
BAX, Alec Hartly
BAXTER, Harold Evelyn
BAXTER, Hugh
BAXTER, John Robertson
BAXTER, Leslie Percy
BAXTER, Neil
BAYER, John Hutchinson
BAYLES, Frederick
BAYLIS, Charles Henry
BAYLIS, Oswald Cecil Jeffrey
BAYLISS, Frederick Joseph
BAYLY, William Henry
BAYNES, Edgar
BAYNHAM, George
BAZIN, Rupert Charles
BEACHLEY, Hubert Godfrey
BEADLE, Ernest John
BEADLE, Jesse
BEAL, William
BEALIN, William Thomas
BEARD, Edward Frank
BEASLEY, William Robert Clive
BEASTON, Reginald George
BEATH, Thomas Herbert
BEATON, Neil
BEATON, William John
BEATTIE, Edward Leslie
BEATTY, Walter Cusack
BEAUMONT, Harold George
BEAVIS, Edward Bathurst
BEBBINGTON, William
BECHERVAISE, Noel Edward
BECK, Ferdinand
BECKENSALL, Walter Herbert
BECKER, Frederick William
BECKETT, Percy Hamlin
BEDFORD, Charles Leslie
BEDFORD, James Charles
BEECHAM, Ted Jack
BEEKEN, William Christian
BEER, Ernest Wills
BEER, Stanley Havelock
BEESLEY, Ernest George
BEHAN, William Walter Bernard
BEHENNA, Harry

BEHM, Benjamin
BEHR, Willen Broudus Peterns
BEILBY, Robert
BEITH, John Humphry
BELL, Andrew
BELL, Bertie
BELL, Edgar Watson
BELL, Edward
BELL, Edward James
BELL, Eric Chalcroft
BELL, Frederick
BELL, George
BELL, Harry
BELL, James Alexander
BELL, James Joseph Thomas
BELL, John Charles
BELL, John George
BELL, Laurie George
BELL, Richard Turner
BELL, Thomas George
BELL, Walter Cyril
BELL, Willoughby George
BELLESINI, Harry
BELLINGER, Burt
BELLINGHAM, Frederick George
BELSEY, John Robert
BELSON, William Charles
BELTON, Robert William
BENBOW, Mervin Albert
BENDLE, John Clarence
BENDREY, Ronald Wall
BENNET, Thomas
BENNETT, Cyril Arthur
BENNETT, Ernest
BENNETT, Frederick Arthur
BENNETT, George Brian
BENNETT, Godfrey Arthur
BENNETT, James Dunn
BENNETT, Leonard Spencer
BENNETT, Raymond Charles
BENNETT, Robert
BENNETT, William George
BENNETTS, Edward James
BENSON, Alfred Ernest
BENSON, Charles
BENSON, Henry
BENSON, Samuel Ernest William
BENSON, William Haywood
BENT, Albert Alfred
BENTLEY, Lionel Samuel
BENTLEY, Thorburn
BENTZON, Sydney Malcolm
BEPLATE, Ernest Herbert
BERGIN, Walter
BERKIS, Arvid
BERNAYS, Roy Marr
BERRIMAN, Joseph William
BERRY, John
BERRYMAN, Ralph
BERTRAM, Andrew
BESANVALLE, Albert
BEST, Albert
BEST, George
BEST, John William
BESWICK, Leslie James
BETHEL, Robert
BETHUNE, Alexander Douglas
BETTLES, Howard Williams
BETTS, Arthur
BETTS, Harry
BEULKE, Dudley Charles
BEVAN, Ernest Victor
BEVAN, Lawrence Charles
BEVAN, Reginald James
BEVERLEY, Thomas
BEWICKE, Sydney John Fleming
BEYERS, James Albert
BICK, Harry

BIDDLE, Arthur Edwin
BIDEN, Noel Ernest
BIDGOOD, Harold George
BIGGS, Archibald
BIGGS, Edward James
BIGGS, Richard Henry
BIGGSLEY, Herbert Alexander
BIGNELL, Edwin Allen
BIGNELL, Gordon Albert
BILBEY, William Henry
BIMSON, Herbert
BINGE, Charles Leslie
BINKS, Frederick
BINKS, Thomas William
BINNIE, George Webster
BINNS, Arthur
BINNS, Frank Southam
BINYON, Harry Hickman
BIRCHETT, Arthur Leonard
BIRD, Charles Arthur
BIRD, Cuthbert Periston
BIRD, Edgar Ernest
BIRD, Edward Cyril
BIRD, Eric James
BIRD, Frederick Arthur
BIRD, Frederick George
BIRD, George Harrington
BIRD, Jeremiah
BIRD, Samuel Nathaniel
BIRKILL, Edward Archibald
BIRKMYRE, Byron Wrixon
BIRMINGHAM, John Patrick
BIRT, Herbert Henry
BISHOP, Samuel Richard
BISHOP, Stanley Howard
BISHOP, Thomas Stephen Sydney
BISHOP, William Robert
BLACK, Frederick
BLACK, Harrold Frederick
BLACK, Harry Daly
BLACK, James
BLACKBURN, Jack
BLACKETT, Howard
BLACKETT, James Colville
BLACKETT, John Carruthers
BLACKIE, Norman Robertson
BLACKLEY, James
BLACKLOCK, Herbert John
BLACKLOCK, John Douglas
BLACKMORE, Alfred Penrose
BLACKMORE, Frederick Spencer
BLACKMORE, Henry
BLACKSTOCK, Wilfred Lawson
BLACKWELL, Harry Frederick
BLACKWELL, Henry Albert
BLACKWELL, John Milton Roy
BLAIR, David Knox
BLAIR, Walter Bell
BLAIR, William
BLAIR, William Henry Stewart
  Simm
BLAKE, Athol Clyde
BLAKE, Ernest Samuel
BLAKE, Frederick
BLAKE, Walter Henry
BLAKE, William
BLAKE, William
BLAKELEY, Harry
BLAKENEY, Victor Eric
BLAMEY, Norman Henry
BLANCH, Ernest Victor
BLANCH, John Dudley
BLANCHFIELD, William
BLANDFORD, Leslie Charles
BLANN-HAY, Henry James
BLANNIN-FERGUSON, Daryl
  Gardner

BLANNIN-FERGUSON, Lance
  Sisca
BLENCOWE, Lewis
BLIGHT, James Henry
BLOCK, Norman Samuel
BLOMQVIST, Eric Gustav Alfred
BLOOM, Julius Sydney
BLOOM, Louis Robert
BLOOMFIELD, Alex
BLOXAM, Joseph
BLUNDELL, John
BLUNT, Harry James
BLYTHE, Drummond James
BLYTHEN, Duncan
BOAL, William David
BOARD, George
BOARDMAN, Henry Edward
BOASE, Colin Arthur
BOASE, William Vernon
BODDY, Douglas
BODEN, Frederick Augustus
BODGER, Thomas Edward Ralph
BODILLY, John Stephen
BOGGS, John
BOGIE, Robert Brackenberry
  Dickson
BOHLSEN, Henry
BOLAN, Ernest
BOLAND, Percival James
BOLDEN, Cyril Alfred
BOLDEN, Horace Stanley
BOLGER, Arthur Ernest
BOLLE, Cyril
BOLTON, Percy Roy
BOLTON, Wilfred
BONAVIA, Charles Emanuel
BOND, Albert Henry
BOND, Charles Joseph
BOND, Frederick William
BOND, James Henry
BOND, Reginald Rupert
BONE, Frederick Anthony
BONHAM, Roy
BONNAR, William
BONNEFIN, Charles
BOOKER, Harold
BOOKER, Herbert Edward
BOOLEY, James
BOON, John Richard
BOOT, Arthur
BOOTH, Clarence
BOOTH, Ernest
BOOTH, James Edward
BOOTH, John Lionel Calvert
BOOTH, Thomas
BOOTH, William Thomas
BORE, John Everett
BORMANN, Stanley Thomas
BORTHWICK, Keith Allan
BOSEMAN, John
BOSSENCE, Francis
BOSTON, Percy Walter
BOSWARD, Charles Frederick
  Richmond
BOSWELL, John
BOTTOMLEY, Oswald George
BOUCHER, Joseph William
  Alexander
BOUCHER, William
BOUCHER, William Joseph
BOUGHEN, Edward
BOULTON, Reginald George
BOUNDY, Albert Henry
BOUNSELL, William
BOURKE, Edward William
BOURKE, James
BOURKE, James Archibald
BOURKE, John Joseph

BOURNE, Harry Cyril
BOUSFIELD, Thomas Victor
BOWDEN, Alfred Richard
BOWDEN, John Stirling
BOWDEN, William
BOWEN, Henry William
BOWEN, Herbert
BOWEN, James
BOWEN, William Reymond
BOWER, Horace
BOWERING, Richard
BOWERMAN, George
BOWERS, Archibald William
BOWIE, Harold Harcourt
BOWKER, Alwynne Stanley
BOWKER, William Charles
BOWLER, Valentine Fennell
BOWLEY, Wilhemy
BOWMAKER, John Montague
BOWMAN, George Franklin
BOWMAN, Percy Algernon St George
BOWMAN, Vincent
BOWRA, Frederick Douglas Atlee
BOWSER, Harry Laughlan
BOYCE, Harold Paul
BOYD, David
BOYD, William
BOYDLE, John
BOYER, Brinley Richard
BOYLE, Austin Walter
BOYLE, Owen Dunigan
BRACE, Samuel Britian
BRADDOCK, Charles Thomas
BRADFORD, Arthur Jesse George
BRADFORD, George Edward
BRADLEY, George Fenick
BRADLEY, Jack Keith
BRADLEY, Patrick
BRADLEY, Robert Cleveland
BRADLEY, William John
BRADSHAW, Alfred Edward
BRADSHAW, William
BRADSHAW, William George Mason
BRADY, Charles
BRADY, Edgar Vernon
BRADY, George
BRADY, Samuel
BRADY, William Harold
BRAGG, Edmund Aelen
BRAGG, Reginald Arthur
BRAIN, Edward George
BRAITHWAITE, Joseph
BRAMLEY, Frank Albert
BRAMMY, George Howard
BRAND, Benjamin Newton
BRANLEY, Arthur Joseph Lavery
BRANSON, William
BRASHAW, Joseph Arthur
BRAUND, George Frederick
BRAY, John Joseph
BRAY, Robert Henry
BREADY, William John
BREBBER, John George
BREEN, James Francis
BREM, Frederick Thomas
BREMEN, William George
BREMNER, Henry Sadler
BRENNAN, Francis Patrick
BRENNAN, John
BRENNAN, Phillip Joseph
BRENNAN, William
BRENNAN, William Gregory
BRENNEN, Ernest George
BRERETON, William Robert
BRETT, Charles
BREWER, John Harold

BREWER, Percival James
BREWSTER, William
BRIANT, Alfred Charles Campbell
BRIANT, Reginald Stuart
BRICE, Jonathan Walter
BRIDESON, John Thomas
BRIDESON, Wesley Stanley
BRIDGELAND, Frederick Charles Lionel
BRIDGER, Frederick
BRIDGES, James Clyde
BRIERLEY, Alwyn Huard
BRIERLEY, Richard
BRIGGS, Francis
BRIGGS, Guy Alfred
BRIGGS, James Walter
BRIGGS, John
BRIGHT, George Henry
BRIGHT, Thomas Henry
BRINKMAN, Vincent Erle
BRISBIN, Lowry Mc Clelland
BRISTOW, John Trotman
BRITT, Isaac Reay
BRITTENDEN, Charles Sclater
BROADHURST, Maurice
BROADWAY, Percy John
BROCK, Halcombe Ferrier
BROCK, James Earl
BROCK, John Alexander
BROCKMAN, Frederick Locke
BROCKMAN, Hubert Howden
BRODERICK, Hilary John
BROKENSHIRE, William James
BROMLEY, John Henry
BROOKE, Vivian Cyril
BROOKES, Vernon Thomas
BROOKS, Ernest George
BROOKS, Garnet Albert Roy
BROOKS, Harold Johnson
BROOKS, Herbert John
BROOKS, William Edward
BROOKSBANK, William
BROOME, Geoffrey George
BROOME, Hilder Stanley Filmer
BROOMHALL, John
BROUGHTON, Frederick John
BROUGHTON, Thomas
BROUGHTON, Thomas George
BROUGHTON, Travers Robert Rhys
BROWN, Allan Clare
BROWN, Allan Daniel
BROWN, Arthur Benjamin
BROWN, Charles George
BROWN, Clarence
BROWN, Donald Arthur Henry Edward
BROWN, Duncan Napier
BROWN, Duncan Sinclair
BROWN, Ernest
BROWN, Ernest
BROWN, Ernest Samuel
BROWN, Frederick
BROWN, Frederick Clarence
BROWN, Frederick John
BROWN, Frederick Newman
BROWN, Garnet Wollesley
BROWN, George
BROWN, Harold Baylie
BROWN, Henry Sangster
BROWN, James
BROWN, John
BROWN, John
BROWN, John
BROWN, John William
BROWN, Joseph
BROWN, Joseph William
BROWN, Kenneth Roy

BROWN, Malcolm
BROWN, Malcolm Horace
BROWN, Michael
BROWN, Oliver
BROWN, Richard Thomas
BROWN, Sydney Bunten
BROWN, Thomas
BROWN, William Alder
BROWNE, Alfred Benjamin
BROWNE, George
BROWNE, George Vernon
BROWNE, Roderic Stawell
BROWNELL, Reginald Clive
BROWNING, Harold Osborne
BROWNING, Joseph
BROWNING, Thomas
BROWNING, William
BRUCE, George Hamilton
BRUCE, John
BRUCE, Robert John
BRUCE, Wyndle James
BRUNDRIT, Thomas Joseph
BRUNS, Ernest Otto Alfred
BRUSHETT, Percy Sydney
BRUTON, Bernard Joseph
BRUTON, James
BRYAN, Edmund Thomas
BRYANT, Frederick James
BRYANT, James Henry
BRYCE, Peter Boyce
BRYDEN, Edward Carruthers Bingham
BUCHAN, Archibald
BUCHANAN, Archibald John
BUCHANAN, Donald Spencer
BUCHANAN, Frank Cuthbert
BUCHANAN, William
BUCHANAN, William
BUCHER, Leslie
BUCK, Thomas Walter
BUCKERIDGE, Charles Stanley
BUCKINGHAM, Thomas
BUCKINGHAM, William John
BUCKLEY, Charles
BUCKLEY, Charles Edward
BUCKLEY, David
BUCKLEY, Henry Francis
BUCKLEY, Jeremiah
BUCKLEY, Sydney John
BUCKLEY, Sylvester
BUCKPITT, George Kenny
BUFFETT, Allen Fletcher
BUGBIRD, Alexander Miller
BUGDEN, Stanley
BUICK, James
BULL, Frederick Angus
BULL, Thomas Henry
BULLEN, Henry Ernest
BULLEN, Marcus Charles
BULMER, Albert
BULMER, Robert Henry
BUNCE, Frederick John
BUNN, George
BUNWORTH, Joseph Francis
BURCH, George Charles
BURDEKIN, James Vivian
BURDEU, Cyril Andrew
BURDON, Francis Roy
BURGE, Joseph
BURGE, William
BURGES, Thomas Francis
BURGESS, Andrew
BURGESS, Joseph
BURGESS, Nathaniel Strafford
BURGESS, William Henry
BURKE, Charles
BURKE, George Harman
BURKE, John Joseph

BURKE, Robert
BURKE, Thomas
BURKE, Thomas Duffy
BURKE, William
BURLEY, Leslie James
BURN, Albert Ernest
BURN, Arthur Sowerby
BURNE, Rainald Knightly
BURNELL, Frederick Joseph
BURNET, Thomas
BURNETT, Richard William
BURNICLE, Henry Edgar
BURNS, David
BURNS, Henry Moore
BURNS, Jack
BURNS, James Drummond
BURNS, Patrick James
BURNS, Peter Robert
BURNS, Ronald
BURNS, William Henry
BURRELL, John William
BURRIDGE, Albert Dennis
BURRILL, Arthur
BURROUGH, James Andrew
BURROWS, Albert Frederick
BURROWS, Alexander
BURROWS, Alfred
BURTON, Albert Arthur
BURTON, Harry James
BURTON, Henry
BURTON, Henry James
BURTON, Richard Harvey
BURTON, Stephen Henry David
BURVETT, Herbert Henry
BURVILL, Herbert Henry
BUSBY, George Cyril
BUSH, Thomas
BUSKIN, Alexander Frank
BUTCHER, Ernest Henry Alex
BUTLER, Albert James
BUTLER, Edgar Henry
BUTLER, Edwin Mac Mullen Everitt
BUTLER, Ernest Rupert
BUTLER, Herbert Augustus Kingsbury
BUTT, Ernest
BUTT, Richard
BUTTERFIELD, Ernest
BUTTERS, Cyril Roy Allen
BUTTERWORTH, James
BUTTON, Frederick
BYARD, Douglas Austin
BYCROFT, Samuel Russell
BYERLEY, Arthur Leslie
BYRAM, James
BYRNE, Albert John
BYRNE, Henry Francis
BYRNE, Herbert Horan
BYRNE, James
BYRNE, John Henry
BYRNE, Michael
BYRNE, Reginald John Murray
BYRNE, Thomas Edward
BYRNE, William
BYRON, John
BYRT, Frederick George
CABLE, Arthur
CADDELL, James
CADELL, Thomas Leonard
CADMAN, Edwin Albert
CADOUX, Donald Neville
CADY, Horace Leman Churchman
CAHILL, David Daniel
CAHILL, Edward Augustine
CAHILL, Vincent Patrick
CAIN, Sydney Alexander
CAIRNCROSS, Jack

CAIRNS, Edward John
CAIRNS, Reuben
CAIRNS, William Burridge
CAKEBREAD, Alfred
CAKEBREAD, Morton Alfred
CALCUTT, Gerald
CALDERBANK, Hugh
CALDERWOOD, William
CALDWELL, Henry Charles Hope
CALDWELL, Robert Arthur
CALLAGHAN, Benjamin
CALLAN, James Henry
CALLARY, Philip Ignatius
CAMERON, Angus
CAMERON, Colin Henry
CAMERON, Donald
CAMERON, Donald
CAMERON, Gordon Peter
CAMERON, James Pullar
CAMERON, John
CAMERON, Kenneth Roderick
CAMERON, Percival James
CAMERON, Richard
CAMERON, Thomas Waddell
CAMERON, William
CAMERON, William
CAMERON, William Ernest
CAMM, James
CAMMACK, William
CAMP, John
CAMPBELL, Alan
CAMPBELL, Alexander
CAMPBELL, Arthur
CAMPBELL, Arthur John
CAMPBELL, Augustus
CAMPBELL, Charles
CAMPBELL, Donald
CAMPBELL, Donald Alexander Russell
CAMPBELL, Fredrick
CAMPBELL, Harold
CAMPBELL, Henry Alexander
CAMPBELL, Irvine Fleming
CAMPBELL, James
CAMPBELL, John
CAMPBELL, Patrick Joseph
CAMPBELL, Robert
CAMPBELL, Robert
CAMPBELL, Sydney James
CAMPBELL, Warren McAllister
CANE, Charles Herbert
CANE, George Allan
CANNAN, Douglas Herman
CANNAN, Frederick Wallace
CANNELL, Reginald Ramsey
CANNING, Francis Arnold
CANNING, Frank Hill
CANNON, Sidney James
CANNONS, Edward Wilfred
CANT, Robert Sutherland
CANTOR, Benjamin
CANTWELL, William Richard
CAPERN, Percival
CAPORN, Harold de Causey
CAPPER, William Ross
CAPPS, Arthur
CARDWELL, Rupert Edgar
CAREW, James
CAREY, Richard
CAREY, Thomas
CAREY, Thomas James
CAREY, William Reginald
CARGEEG, Albert Victor Selway
CARGILL, William
CARL, William
CARLAND, Leslie Thomas
CARLESS, James Neville
CARLSEN, Arthur

CARLSON, Douglas
CARLSON, Herbert Clarence
CARMALT, Edward
CARMICHAEL, Alexander
CARMICHAEL, David
CARMICHAEL, John Henry
CARMICHAEL, Thomas McLeod
CARNE, John Charles
CARNELL, Arthur James
CARNELL, Francis George
CARNEY, Frank
CARNEY, James Maxwell
CARNEY, Mervyn
CARNOCHAN, Alexander
CARPENTER, Alfred Ernest
CARPENTER, Frederick Thomas
CARR, Francis Sidney
CARR, James
CARR, Maurice Frederick
CARR, Reginald Ivan Cooper
CARR, Roland Mansfield
CARR, Thomas John
CARRE, Maurice Tennant
CARRICK, Esmond Richard John
CARRINGTON, Frederick Deacon
CARRINGTON, James Edward
CARRINGTON, John
CARROLL, James Joseph Robert
CARROLL, John Charles
CARROLL, John Thomas
CARROLL, Joseph John
CARROLL, Michael Francis
CARROLL, Thomas George
CARSELDINE, Harold Edwin
CARSON, Theodore Ronald
CARSTAIRS, William Cleave
CARTER, Cyril Keith
CARTER, Francis Bird
CARTER, Francis Thomas
CARTER, Frederick
CARTER, George Frederick Walter
CARTER, Harold Reginald
CARTER, Hugh Creagh Massy
CARTER, John
CARTER, John Oswald
CARTER, Robert
CARTER, Stanley Grant
CARTER, Strutten John
CARTER, Thomas
CARTER, William
CARTER, William Watson
CARTHEW, Charles
CARTWRIGHT, Bernard Ray
CARTWRIGHT, John Henry
CARWARDINE, Frederick William
CASEY, Michael
CASEY, Patrick
CASH, William Charles
CASLICK, John Percy
CASTLE, George Philip
CATLIN, Robert Henry
CATLOW, Thomas Norris
CATO, Vincent Arthur
CATTO, Frederick
CAVANAGH, Alfred
CAVANAGH, George Clarence
CAVEY, Sidney
CAVILL, Walter William
CAWLEY, William
CAWSEY, Charles Ernest
CAWTHORN, Edwin
CAWTHORNE, Cyril Leslie
CEREZO, Joseph Francis
CHABREL, Francis George
CHADDERTON, George
CHADWICK, Harry
CHALLENGER, Arthur William
CHALLENOR, Albert

CHALLINOR, William
CHALMERS, James Hynd
CHAMBERLAIN, John
CHAMBERS, Charles Todd Crompton
CHAMBERS, Frederick Henry
CHAMBERS, Harold Heathcote Hayes
CHAMBERS, James Robert
CHAMBERS, Keith
CHAMBERS, Robert Laing
CHAMBERS, Stanley
CHAMBERS, Thomas
CHAMBERS, William Nelson
CHAMLEY, Rupert Robert
CHAMPION, Thomas George Roy
CHANDLER, Cecil Herbert
CHANDLER, Charles Frederick
CHANDLER, Cornelius
CHANDLER, Henry Norman
CHANDLER, Richard Charles James
CHANDLER, William
CHANT, John Henry James
CHAPLAIN, Thomas Alfred
CHAPLIN, George Charles
CHAPMAN, Alfred George
CHAPMAN, Charles Percy
CHAPMAN, Earl Haddon Simpson
CHAPMAN, George
CHAPMAN, Harold Thomas Arthur
CHAPMAN, John
CHAPMAN, Morrice
CHAPPELL, Stanley James
CHARITY, Alfred Adren
CHARLES, Frank
CHARLES, William Henry
CHARLESWORTH, Stanley George
CHARLTON, Albert Thomas
CHARLTON, Francis Alexander
CHARLTON, Henry Arthur
CHARLTON, Matthew Mark
CHARMAN, Percival Edward Francis
CHARNOCK, John Herbert Alfred
CHASE, Richard Henry
CHATTERTON, Stanley Vine
CHEAL, Edwin Harold
CHEAPE, Alexander Caird
CHEETHAM, Albert Middleton
CHEETHAM, John Henry Alexander
CHESTNUT, David
CHETTLE, Thomas
CHIDLEY, Edward
CHILLINGSWORTH, Leonard Worrall
CHIMES, George Henry
CHINCHI, Alfred John
CHIPPER, Henry Thomas
CHIPPER, Lindsay Lewis Stirling
CHIPPER, Ross Richard Vivian
CHIPPINDALL, Henry Dawson
CHISHOLM, Charles
CHISHOLM, Cyril Roy
CHISHOLM, Donald Alexander Gordon
CHIVERTON, Alfred
CHIVERTON, William Henry
CHOPPING, Charles
CHRISTIAN, Andrew George
CHRISTIANSEN, John
CHRISTIE, Alfred Bembrick
CHRISTIE, Andrew

CHRISTIE, Henry
CHRISTOPHER, Charles Leslie
CHRISTOPHER, James
CHURCHILL, Lionel
CHURCHILL, William Ernest
CHUTE, Eric Cecil
CINQUEGRANA, Francis Ernest
CIZZIO, Joseph William
CLANCY, John Charles
CLANCY, John Henry
CLANCY, Victor Clarence
CLAPHAM, George Roy
CLAPHAM, William Henry
CLARK, Albert
CLARK, Albert
CLARK, Albert Edward
CLARK, Alexander Cullen
CLARK, Alfred James
CLARK, Eric Gordon
CLARK, George
CLARK, Harry Corben
CLARK, Harry Maxwell
CLARK, Hugh
CLARK, Hugh Dufaur
CLARK, James
CLARK, John Carlton
CLARK, John Watsford
CLARK, Matthew
CLARK, Norman
CLARK, Phillip
CLARK, Victor
CLARK, William John
CLARKE, Cyril
CLARKE, Francis Andrew
CLARKE, Frank Gordon
CLARKE, George Thomas Mitchell
CLARKE, Henry John Thomas
CLARKE, James Morrison Forsyth
CLARKE, John Joseph
CLARKE, John Joyce
CLARKE, Lancelot Fox
CLARKE, Norman Windsor
CLARKE, Percival Michael
CLARKE, Raymond
CLARKE, Reginald Charles
CLARKE, William Edward
CLARKE, William Isaac
CLASSEN, Alfred Ernest
CLAXTON, Herbert Frederick
CLAYDEN, Norman Albert
CLAYTON, John Henry
CLAYTON, Lawrence
CLAYTON, Norman
CLAYTON, Simon Fraser
CLEARY, Errol Vincent
CLEGG, Thomas Arthur
CLEMENT, David Purdie
CLEMENT, Ebeneger David
CLEMENT, Sydney Reynold
CLEMENTS, Robert William
CLEVELAND, Francis Edward
CLIFFE, John Robert
CLIFFORD, Leslie
CLIFTON, Ferdinand William
CLIFTON, Frederick Charles
CLIFTON, Percival Edgar
CLIFTON, Roy Kimberley
CLOSE, Frederick Laurence
CLOSE, Stanley Robert
CLOUGH, Edward Charles
CLOUGH, Richard Henry
CLOUGH, Walter
CLOVER, Hector Albert
CLUES, Charles Edwin Joseph
CLUES, Robert Josiah
CLUETT, Edward Frank
CLUETT, Ernest Randolph

CLYDE, Frederick
CLYDESDALE, William Dyson
COAD, Edward Harold
COATES, George Bernard
COATES, Ronald Ernest
COATES, Thomas George
COBB, Albert George
COBBE, Henry Clermont
COBURN, Hugh
COCHRANE, Andrew Downie
COCHRANE, Herbert
COCKERALL, William John
COCKIN, George Bernard
COCKING, Leonard Francis
COCKS, William
COE, Charles Burton
COFFEE, Frank Mathew
COFFEY, Ernest Ivey Robisson
COFFIN, Carl Douglas
COGHILL, Sinclair
COHEN, William
COLBERT, Sydney James
COLBORNE, William Hector
COLBORNE-VEEL, Geoffrey Colborne
COLBURT, Edward Charles
COLDHAM-FUSSELL, Vernon
COLE, Charles William
COLE, Dyson Frederick
COLE, Eldon Torel Trevor
COLE, Herbert Daniel
COLE, Lionel Nelson
COLEMAN, Charles Jenkin
COLEMAN, Claude Hamilton
COLEMAN, Edward John James
COLEMAN, James George
COLEMAN, Thomas
COLEMAN, William Shedrock
COLES, George William
COLES, William
COLGATE, Oscar
COLK, George
COLL, James
COLLETT, Henry
COLLIE, John Alexander
COLLIER, John
COLLIN, Leslie Norman
COLLINGS, Mervyn Dane
COLLINS, Alfred James
COLLINS, Arthur Turner
COLLINS, Charles William
COLLINS, Harry
COLLINS, Henry Edward
COLLINS, Herbert Alfred
COLLINS, John
COLLINS, Leslie
COLLINS, William
COLLINSON, Richard Albert
COLLINSON, William Rushton
COLLISTER, George Francis
COLLS, Lisle Bertram Dinniss
COLLYER, John
COLQUHOUN, Harold Robert Lyne
COLQUHOUN, Hugh
COMBLEY, Tom
COMBS, Walter
COMINS, Percival Richards
COMPTON, Reginald Clyde
COMPTON, Stanley
COMTE, Albert Edward
CONCANON, George Lewis Blake
CONDELL, John Joseph
CONDON, Austin James
CONDON, William Joseph
CONLAN, Percival Thomas
CONLEN, John

CONN, William Galloway
CONNEL, Thomas
CONNELL, John Mc Millan
CONNELL, Matthew
CONNELLY, Clive Emerson
CONNELLY, Frederick
CONNELLY, John Joseph
CONNELLY, Thomas Henry
CONNETT, Herman Oswald
CONNOLLY, Alfred Henry
CONNOLLY, Mark
CONNOR, John Leslie
CONNOR, Joseph
CONRAD, Herbert Selmar
CONROY, Thomas
CONSIDINE, John
CONSTABLE, Charlie
CONSTABLE, Herbert Leslie
CONVILLE, Thomas
CONWAY, James
CONYERS, Alfred Edgar
COOGAN, Thomas Patrick
COOK, Douglas
COOK, Frederick Harry
COOK, John Thomas
COOK, John William
COOK, Reginald Hastings
COOKE, Donald Walter
COOKE, Frank Newton
COOKE, Harold
COOKE, Herbert William
COOKE, Joseph Henry
COOKE, Roy Egerton
COOKE, Sydney Stevenson
COOLEY, Frederick James
COOLING, John
COOLING, William Henry
COOMBES, Arthur Robert
COOMBS, Edward James
COOMBS, Robert George
COOMBS, Tressilian Herbert
COONAN, William Michael
COOP, Reuben
COOPER, Albert John
COOPER, Archibald
COOPER, Clive Sedgwick
COOPER, Collingwood Thomas
COOPER, George James Sydney
COOPER, George William Lawson
COOPER, Hugh
COOPER, Ivan William
COOPER, Volney Leonard
COOTES, William Edward
COPELAND, William
COPLAND, John
COPLEY, Norman
COPPINS, William Thomas Angus Horace Valentine
COPSON, George Norman
CORBLET, Leopold Alfred
CORBY, Eugene Joseph
CORDNER, Joseph Alan
CORKER, Harry
CORLEY, Anthony Purden Hagarty
CORMICK, Leslie
CORNELL, Walter Goulburn
CORNISH, James Dudley
CORNISH, Lawrence
CORNWALL, Clifford Gordon
CORRIE, William Henry
CORRY, Thomas Edison Spurgeon
CORSER, Percy
COSGRAVE, Francis Michael
COSGROVE, Harry Edward
COSGROVE, Nicholas Thomas
COSTA, Ernest
COSTELLO, James Albert

COSTELLO, Kenneth
COSTELLO, Thomas
COSTIN, Joseph William
COTT, Reginald
COTTER, Augustine
COTTER, Joseph
COTTERILL, Eric Roland
COTTRELL, Fothergill William Swinfen
COUGHLAN, Thomas
COULSON, John Herbert
COULSTOCK, Walter George
COULTHARD, Roland Claude
COURTIS, Harry
COURTNEY, Thomas Joseph
COUSENS, Norman
COUSINS, Daniel Thomas
COUTTS, James Alexander Ramsden
COUVE, Alan Crawford
COUVE, Henry Thomas Ladson
COVERDALE, Robert William
COVERLID, James
COVEY, Percy
COWARD, Thomas Roy
COWDERY, Francis Reynolds
COWELL, Harry Stephen
COWELL, Henry Lennox
COWELL, John William
COWELL, Sidney Lewis
COX, Alan Birchenall
COX, Charles George
COX, Ernest Sydney
COX, Frank
COX, Frederic John
COX, Henry James
COX, Herbert James
COX, John
COX, John William Eric
COX, Leslie George
COX, Rodger
COX, Sydney Douglas
COX, Wallace
COX, William
COYNE, Patrick Paul
COYNE, Thaddeus
CRABBE, Keith George Wallace
CRADICK, William Rupert
CRAIG, Guthrie
CRAIG, Harold Gordon
CRAIG, John
CRAIG, Roy Mackenzie
CRAIG, Thomas Johnson
CRAKE, George Cecil
CRAMER, Albert
CRAMOND, Colin Hearder
CRANE, John Thornhill
CRANE, Wilfred John
CRANSTON, Alexander Charles
CRAPPER, Oliver
CRAVEN, George Fulwar Llewellyn
CRAVEN, Norman
CRAVEN, Walter Hiram
CRAW, Harry
CRAWFORD, David
CRAWFORD, Ronald
CRAWFORTH, Louis Stephen
CREER, Errol Joseph Hart
CREES, Henry Victor
CREGAN, Clarence Theodore Augustus
CREIGHTON, Alexander
CRELLIN, Norman Colvin
CRERAR, David Knox
CRERAR, Duncan Robertson
CRESSWELL, Sydney
CRIBB, Keith Norman

CRICHTON, Gerald Edgecombe
CRICHTON, Joseph Michael Smith
CRICHTON, William Donald
CRISP, David Harold
CRISP, Frederick Gordon
CRITCHER, Thomas Alfred
CRITCHLEY, William
CROCKER, George Evered
CROCKER, Gordon
CROCKER, Robert Clive
CROCKFORD, Cyril Grove
CROFT, James Henry
CROKER, Alexander John
CRONIN, Arthur Joseph Dennis
CROSS, Claude Malcolm
CROSS, Russell Douglas
CROSS, Sydney Robert
CROTHERS, James
CROUCH, John Lewis
CROUCHER, Harold
CROUD, Alfred George
CROW, Robert Harold
CROWE, Phillip William Archibald
CROWHURST, Frank Samuel
CROWL, Claude Terrell
CROWL, Joseph Terrell
CROWLE, Thomas
CROWLEY, Matthew Nicholas
CROWTHER, Alfred
CROWTHER, Kenneth Singleton
CROWTHER, Percy William
CROWTHER, Samuel
CUBITT, Albert
CUDDEFORD, Frederick George
CULLEN, Edward Henry
CULLEN, George Frederick
CULLEN, Hedley Elbert
CULLEN, Hugo James
CULLEN, James
CULLINAN, Henry Maxwell
CULLING, John William
CULPH, Thomas Wilson
CUMBERLAND, Oliver James
CUMMING, Alexander George
CUMMING, Andrew Thomas Gordon
CUMMING, Gordon Knight
CUMMING, Herbert Harold
CUMMING, Norman
CUMMING, Richard Edward
CUMMINGS, Allan
CUMMINGS, Edward James
CUNNINGHAM, David William
CUNNINGHAM, James
CUNNINGHAM, Royston Kingsborough
CURLEWIS, Gordon Levason
CURLEWIS, Kenneth
CURLEWIS, Selwyn Lord
CURLEY, John
CURLIS, Roland Hall
CURNOW, John Herbert
CURPHEY, Alfred Albert
CURRAN, John
CURRAN, John Patrick
CURRIE, Charles Chetwynd
CURRIE, Francis Moore
CURRIE, Harry
CURRIE, Hubert Roulstone Clifford
CURRIE, James
CURRIE, Thomas
CURRINGTON, Frederick John Harold
CURRY, George John
CURTIS, Frank

CURTIS, Frederick Henry
CURTIS, Reginald Johnston
CURTIS, William Rufus
CURWEN, Frederick Edward
CURWEN-WALKER, Arthur Herbert
CUSACK, Eric Athanasius
CUSSION, Christian Walter
CUTHBERT, Albert Edwin
CUTTRISS, Fredric William
CUTTS, Lawrence Henry
D'ALTON, Charles Edward
D'ALTON, Henry St Eloy
DA-COSTA, Alfred Edwin
DACK, Frank
DAEMEN, Alfred
DALE, Charles Coning
DALE, Edwin John
DALE, George Frederick
DALE, George Thomas
DALLING, George
DALMAIN, Herbert Clarence
DALSON, Andrew Anderson
DALTON, James
DALY, Ernest Robert
DALY, Frank
DALY, James Henry
DALY, John
DALY, John Edward Joseph
DALY, William
DALZELL, Douglas Pulteney
DALZIELL, Charles
DAMEN, Charles
DANAHER, Edmond Butterworth
DANES, Harold Edward
DANGERFIELD, Albert Victor
DANGERFIELD, Joseph Garnet
DANIEL, Claude Arthur
DANIELS, James
DANN, Frederick
DANNEFAERD, William Jacob
DANSON, Herbert Francis
DARBY, William Gladstone
DARGAN, William Robert
DARGIN, Sydney Norman
DARLING, Joseph William
DARLINGTON, George Brockwell
DARRAGH, George Edmond
DARRAGH, Joseph William
DARTON, Henry Theodore
DARVILL, Joseph Alfred
DASH, Frank Noel
DASHWOOD, Frank Leopold
DAVENPORT, Charles
DAVEY, Albert Henry
DAVEY, Charles Basil Trevor
DAVEY, John
DAVEY, Ronald George
DAVIDGE, Alfred James
DAVIDSON, Allan Mc Kinnon
DAVIDSON, Richard
DAVIDSON, William
DAVIES, David Mancel
DAVIES, Edric Albert
DAVIES, Frank
DAVIES, Frederick
DAVIES, Frederick James
DAVIES, Henry
DAVIES, James Albert
DAVIES, Thomas
DAVIS, Alfred
DAVIS, Arthur George
DAVIS, Charles
DAVIS, Charles Berte Montague
DAVIS, Charles Lindsay
DAVIS, David John Reginald
DAVIS, Emanuel Percival

DAVIS, Eric James Victor
DAVIS, Ewatt William
DAVIS, Frank Edgar
DAVIS, Frederick James
DAVIS, George
DAVIS, Gordon Edgerton
DAVIS, Harry Herbert
DAVIS, Horace Alfred
DAVIS, John
DAVIS, John Henry
DAVIS, Norman Ernest
DAVIS, Percy Charles
DAVIS, Richard Roy
DAVIS, Roland Dudley
DAVIS, Roland Herbert
DAVIS, Thomas Ernest
DAVIS, William Edwin
DAVISON, Cuthbert Glen
DAVISON, Frank Sinclair
DAVY, John Edward
DAW, Sidney Frank
DAWES, George
DAWKINS, William Henry
DAWSON, Alan Douglas Gibb
DAWSON, Albert Robert
DAWSON, Bernard Patrick
DAWSON, Edward
DAWSON, George William
DAWSON, Herbert Selwyn
DAWSON, John Mitchell
DAWSON, Leslie James
DAWSON, Martin Russell McDonald
DAWSON, Vivian Gwynne
DAWSON, Walter
DAWSON, Wilfred Yelverton
DAY, Albert Howard
DAY, Albert Thomas
DAY, Alfred Ernest
DAY, Charles Edward
DAY, Ernest
DAY, George Thomas
DAY, Sylvester Sydney
DAY, William Alfred
DE BROUGHE, Arthur Benjamin
DE LAUTOUR, Edgar Frederick
DE LEPERVANCHE, Reginald Charles
DE WILLIMOFF, Norman Julius
DEACON, Henry
DEACON, John George
DEACON, Reginald
DEAKIN, Alec Bertram
DEAM, William
DEAN, Alexander Valentine
DEAN, Arthur Stewart
DEAN, John Francis
DEAN, Joseph
DEAN, Owen Francis
DEAN, William Knight
DEARLOVE, William John
DEAZELEY, John Firmin
DEBNAM, George Parkman
DEE, David William
DEE, John Patrick
DEEPROSE, William
DELAHUNTY, Daniel
DELANEY, Michael
DELAPORTE, Richard
DELLAR, Frederick
DEMEL, George Blake
DEMPSEY, Kevin Claude
DEMPSTER, Reginald Garry
DENDTLER, Robert
DENFORD, Dustin Lee
DENHOLM, John Hughes
DENNEHY, William John
DENNEY, James Arthur

DENNEY, John
DENNIEN, Francis Joseph
DENNIS, Roderick George
DENNISON, Bertie
DENNISON, Charles
DENSLEY, Benjamin
DENSLOW, Edward
DENSTON, Harold
DENTON, Victor
DERRETT, Vincent Harrigan
DERRICK, Cecil Reginald
DERRICK, John
DERRICK, John Scott
DETMAR, Arthur August Charles
DEUCHAR, Erlf
DEVENISH, Arthur Lancelot
DEVINE, Henry
DEVLIN, James Lawrence
DEWAR, Douglas
DEWAR, Henry Gordon
DEWATER, John
DEWELL, William Scoones
DEWHURST, Percy George
DEWS, William
DEY, Charles Henry Calder
DICK, James
DICKER, Arthur Seymour
DICKERSON, James
DICKIE, Albert Andrew
DICKINSON, Avery Benjamin
DICKINSON, Thomas
DICKSON, Frank Kirkpatrick
DICKSON, Murray John
DICKSON, Norman
DICKSON, Robert Lang
DIDCOTE, Wilfred Bartlett
DIEDRICH, Harold
DIGBY, John Alexander
DIGGES-LA TOUCHE, Everard
DIGNAM, Percy Lionel
DILLISTONE, William Jacob
DILLON, Francis William
DILLON, Herbert
DILLON, Leslie Frank
DILLON, Martin Michael
DINGWALL, Ernest William
DITCHBURN, Campbell James
DIXON, Alexander
DIXON, George William
DIXON, Ralph Taylor
DIXON, William George
DIXON, William Robert
DOBBIE, Leslie Oswald
DOBBIE, Vernon Robert
DOBINSON, Patrick William
DOBSON, George Edward
DOBSON, James
DOBSON, William Anthony
DOCKER, Norman
DOCKERY, Lester Frederick
DOCTER, Francis Joseph
DODD, Charles
DODD, Howard George
DODD, William
DODDS, Clarence
DODWELL, Malby George Crofton
DOLLA, Carl
DONAGHER, James
DONALD, Henry Alexander
DONALD, Horace Francis
DONALD, John Gordon
DONALD, Vivian De Burgh
DONALDSON, Charles Bernard
DONALDSON, Joseph Kenneth
DONALDSON, Oliver Ernest
DONALDSON, Robert Coventry
DONALDSON, Robert Henry

DONEHUE, Archie Victor
DONKIN, Reginald Lyons
DONNELLAN, Thomas
DONNELLY, George William
DONNELLY, James Patrick
DONNELLY, Patrick
DONNELLY, Robert Raymond
DONNELLY, William
DONOHOE, William Henry
DONOHUE, Joseph
DONOVAN, James
DONOVAN, John William
DOOHAN, John Theodore
DORIS, Arthur Denis
DOUGHERTY, Robert
DOUGHTY, Albert Percy
DOUGLAS, Claude Campbell
    Telford
DOUGLAS, Colin Langslow
DOUGLAS, John Andrew
DOUGLAS, Morton Osborne
DOUGLAS, Percy
DOUGLAS, William Bowman
DOUGLASS, Horace Surry
DOUST, Amos Leonard
DOVETON, Robert Trevelyan
DOW, John
DOW, William
DOWLING, Edward Allan
DOWN, Cecil Vernon
DOWNEY, William
DOWNIE, David Norman Hedley
DOWNIE, Frederick Ernest
    Michael
DOWNIE, John Jabez
DOWNING, George Patrick
DOWNING, Llewellyn Samuel
DOWNTON, Archibald
DOWNWARD, Thomas Leonard
DOWTON, Edward Richard
DOYLE, Christopher Thomas
DOYLE, Joseph
DOYLE, Kenneth Herbert
DOYLE, Thomas
DOYLE, William James
DRAIN, Edward
DRAPER, George Noel
DRAPER, Hubert James
DRAPER, Percy Smedley
DRAPER, William
DRAY, Thomas William
DREVES, Arthur Wellesley
DREW, Frank Napier
DREW, George Edward
DRISCOLL, Alfred
DRISCOLL, Rowland Edward
DRIVER, Clement Claude
DRIVER, Ernest Edward
DRUMMOND, John Albert
DRYSDALE, William Willis
DU VAL, Denis
DUBOIS, Fernand George Jules
    Marie
DUCHESNE, William Sydney
DUCKWORTH, John Curry
DUDDERIDGE, Thomas Alfred
DUDLEY, Clarence Murchicent
DUFF, Robert
DUFF, Sidney John
DUFFETT, Richard Thomas
DUFFIELD, Frank
DUFFIN, Benjamin
DUFFIN, George William
DUFFY, James
DUGGAN, John Robert
DUKE, Reginald Herbert
DUKELOW, William Henry
DUNBAR, Tom Park

DUNCAN, Gordon Clifford
DUNCAN, Harry
DUNCAN, James Francis
DUNCAN, John James
DUNCAN, Joseph Daniel
DUNHAM, William
DUNKINSON, Richmond
    Valentine
DUNKLEY, Arthur Henry
DUNKLEY, Henry Edward
DUNLEAVY, Edward Singleton
DUNLEAVY, James Bourke
DUNLOP, George Alfred
DUNLOP, John Edgar
DUNLOP, Norman James
DUNN, Alfred William George
DUNN, Arthur Sylvester
DUNN, David Henry
DUNN, Oscar Thomas
DUNN, Ray Wilfred
DUNN, Thomas
DUNN, William
DUNNE, Ernest Bryant
DUNNICLIFF, Ernest Albert
    Francis
DUNPHY, Cecil Annesley
DUNSDON, Richard George
DUNSTAN, Stanley Oliver
DUNSTAN, William Joseph
DUNT, Frank Ulrie
DUPEN, Cuthbert John Ernest
DUPUY, James Gordon
DURACK, Fergus James
DURACK, Thomas John
DURANCE, Eric William John
DURAND, Havilland Montague
DURHAM, Edward Pearce
DURIE, Edward
DURSTON, Norman Henry
DUTHIE, Rudley Ernest
DWAN, William
DWYER, Albert Valentine
DWYER, Francis Edward
DWYER, Jack
DWYER, John Francis
DWYER, Thomas Leo
DWYER, Thomas Michael
DYER, Frank Gordon
DYER, Gilbert Beresford
DYER, Norman Charles
DYER, Stephen John
DYER, Walter Samuel
DYMOND, John Joseph
EADIE, Allan Keith
EADY, John
EARL, Albert
EARL, William Robert
EARLL, Robin Bevian
EARLY, Walter Edward
EAST, Herbert Harold
EAST, Walter Leonard
EASTHAM, William
EASTON, Frederick William
EASTON, Robert Inglis
EASTWOOD, George Douglas
EATHER, Athol Bert
EATHER, Cecil George
EATHER, John
EATON, Arthur Ernest Wilson
ECCLES, Alfred Frederick
EDDY, James Henry
EDGAR, Edgar James
EDGAR, Frederick
EDGAR, James
EDGAR, Stuart Halbert
EDGAR, Wolverton Mason
EDGCUMBE, James Adolphus
EDGE, James

EDGE, Randolph Edward
EDGELEY, Adolphus Bert
EDGEWORTH, Charles Henry
EDGINGTON, Albert Henry
EDGINGTON, William Alfred
EDGLEY, Edward James
EDMENDS, William Herbert
EDMISTON, Percy William
EDMISTON, Stanley
EDMONDS, Thomas
EDMONDSON, Ernest
EDMONDSON, James Whittaker
EDMUNDS, Ernest Arthur
EDMUNDS, Lemuel Henry
EDNEY, Thomas Alfred
EDWARDS, Alfred
EDWARDS, Alfred Outtrim
EDWARDS, Arthur
EDWARDS, Arthur Louis
EDWARDS, Benjamin Noel
    William
EDWARDS, Ernest Irving
EDWARDS, Francis William
EDWARDS, Frederick
EDWARDS, Harold Eustace
EDWARDS, Henry
EDWARDS, Jack
EDWARDS, James
EDWARDS, Joseph Thomas
EDWARDS, Lawrence
EDWARDS, Robert
EDWARDS, Walter
EDWARDS, William Albert
EELES, William Stanley
EGAN, Alfred Edward
EGAN, John Raymond
EGAN, Patrick
EGAN, Thomas
EGGINS, Harold James
EGGINS, Roy Hamilton
EHRENBERG, Samuel Morris
ELDER, Howard Thomas
ELDRIDGE, Charles Edward
ELDRIDGE, George
ELKINGTON, Arthur Francis
    Gordon
ELLEFSEN, Thomas Elevious
ELLEM, David Harold
ELLIOT, John Amyand
ELLIOT, William Walter Highton
ELLIOTT, Arthur Massey
ELLIOTT, Augustus John
ELLIOTT, John William
ELLIOTT, Sidney Harold Richards
ELLIOTT, Walter Vivian
ELLIOTT, William Henry
ELLIS, Frederick George
ELLIS, Leicester George
ELLIS, Owen John
ELLIS, Ralph Louis
ELLIS, Raymond Stanley
ELLIS, Walter Whyte
ELLISON, James Leslie
ELLISS, Baizel Dudley
ELLISTON, Harry Mills
ELPHICK, Arthur Thomas
ELSEN, John Thomas
ELSO, Leslie Charles Thomas
ELSTOB, Robert Leonard
ELWOOD, Alfred Terah
EMERY, John James
EMERY, Robert Norman
EMERY, Walter Sydney
EMMETT, John
EMMETT, Verner Allen
EMSLIE, Alexander
ENGELMANN, Walter Hector
ENGLEY, Walter Alfred

ENGLISH, George
ENGLISH, George Charles
ENNIS, John Archibald
ENRIGHT, Daniel
EPTHORP, Reginald James
EREKSON, Herbert Henry
ERICKSON, Percival
ERSKINE, Frederick William
ESSAY, Wallace
EUGARDE, Stephen Francis
EUSTACE, William Williamson
EVANS, Abraham
EVANS, Albert Lacey
EVANS, Alexander George
EVANS, Allan Samuel Joseph
EVANS, Arthur Cecil
EVANS, Charles Richard
    Hargraves
EVANS, Cyril Eisle
EVANS, David
EVANS, Francis Raymond
EVANS, Frank Hubert
EVANS, Frank Norman
EVANS, Henry
EVANS, John
EVANS, John David
EVANS, Nevill Gordon Gwynne
EVANS, Thomas Hatfield
EVANS, Thomas Henry
EVANS, Thomas Robert
EVANS, Walter Eric
EVANS, William Roy
EVERITT, Avenal Leonard
EVERS, Henry
EVISTON, John Martin
EWERT, Ewen Charles
EWIN, Walter Seccombe
EWING, Frederick
EWINGTON, Frederick William
EXTON, Harry
EYDEN, Leslie William
EYERS, Herbert Ernest
EYLES, John William
EYRE, John Charles
EZZY, Urtle Hilton
FABIAN, William Albert
FACEY, Joseph Thomas
FACEY, Roy Barker
FADDY, Francis Horatio
FAHEY, Harry
FAHEY, James
FAHY, Edward
FAIRBEARD, Charles Henry
FAIRCLOUGH, Robert
    Twentyman
FAIRHALL, Samuel
FAIRLIE, Ernest Robert
FAIRNHAM, Henry Harnam
FALCONBRIDGE, John William
FALCONER, Lake
FALCONER, Norman Frederick
    Napier
FALK, Charles John
FALK, George Edward
FALKNER, Reginald
FALLON, John
FANNING, John Ritchie
FARDELL, Edwin Hercules
FARISH, Robert Turner
FARMER, Aubrey
FARNCOMBE, Jesse Knight
FARNELL, Stanley Squire
FARNHAM, Leslie
FARNSWORTH, John
FARQUHAR, Mure Robertson
FARR, Victor Emanuel
FARRANTS, Arthur George
    William

FARRAR, Alan Francis
FARRAR, Albert Victor
FARRAR, Arthur
FARRELL, Andrew
FARRELL, Basil Albert
FARRELL, Ernest Martin
FARRELL, Frederick Stanley
FARRELL, Harold Alexander
FARRELL, John Thomas
FARRELL, Thomas Ince
FARRELL, Thomas Patrick
FARRELL, William
FARRER, Allen Bertram
FARRIER, Charles Percy
FATHERS, Ormond
FAULDS, Thomas Barclay
FAWCETT, William Charles
FAWKNER, Albert Ernest
FAWLEY, Henry Wilfred
FEAGAN, Alexander Thomas
FEAKIN, James
FEATONBY, George James
FEENEY, Richard
FEENEY, William
FEETAM, Joseph Henry
FEGAN, Don
FEGAN, Hugh Robert
FELL, Charles Frederick Roy
FELL, John
FELSTEAD, Walter
FENN, Samuel James
FENTON, Stanley
FENWICK, Basil Middleton
FENWICK, Sydney
FEREDAY, Daniel
FERGUSON, Archibald
FERGUSON, Hugh Valentine
FERGUSON, John James
FERGUSON, Logie
FERGUSON, Robert William
FERGUSSON, Edward James
FERGUSSON, Maurice Cameron
FERRES, Sydney Eversley
FERRETT, George Clement
FERRIER, Albert
FERRIER, Sutton Henry
FERRIS, William Thomas Chilton
FETHERS, Erle Finlayson Denton
FIANDER, Louis Godfrey
FIELDING, James
FIELDING, John Howard
FIELDING, Joseph Vincent
FIELDS, George William
FIGGIS, Samuel Douglas
    Johnstone
FILGATE, Bertie Edward
FILIPPI, Albert
FINCH, Herbert Lionel Ingle
FINCH, John Henry
FINCH, William Albert
FINCHER, Charles
FINDLAY, David Henry
FINDLAY, John
FINDLEY, Charles Etherington
FINDON, Richard
FINK, Gordon
FINLAY, William Seymour
FINN, Laurence Gerald
FINNING, Leonard John
FIRNS, Hobart Douglas
FISH, Walter
FISHER, Athol Hugh
FISHER, David
FISHER, Edward Theophilus
FISHER, Frank Norman
FISHER, John Byers
FISHER, John Martin
FISHER, Joseph William

FISHER, Thomas
FISHER, Vivian William
FISK, Newton
FITCHER, John Matthews
FITZGERALD, Edgar Lewis
FITZGERALD, Edward William
FITZGERALD, Thomas Joseph
FITZGERALD, William George
  Gladstone
FITZGIBBON, John
FITZGIBBON, Michael
FITZHANNAM, Charles Edgar
FITZHERBERT, Charles Edward
FITZHUGH, Harold Alfred
FITZPATRICK, Joseph Michael
FLACK, Walter Robert
FLAHERTY, Herbert Walter
FLAHERTY, Thomas Patrick
FLANAGAN, Gordon
FLANAGAN, James
FLAVELL, Thomas Wright
FLEMING, David Archibald
FLEMING, Edward Richard
FLEMING, John
FLEMMING, Geoffrey Lionel
FLEMMING, Valentine
FLETCHER, Walter Bell
FLINTOFF, Arthur John
FLOCKART, Robert Pearce
FLOWER, Hedley Vickers
FLOWER, James Herbert
FLUX, Jack
FLYNN, Joseph Thomas
FOARD, Nelson Alfred
FOAT, Arthur James
FODDY, Harry
FOGARTY, Andrew Christopher
FOGARTY, Edward
FOGARTY, Mervyn
FOLEY, Michael Vincent
FOLEY, Morris
FOLEY, Patrick
FOLEY, Patrick
FOLEY, Thomas
FOLEY, Thomas Francis
FOLEY, Victor Joseph
FOLKS, Norman Wakefield
FOLLENT, James Martin
FOOT, Alexander Madden
FOOT, Henry Daintree
FOOTE, John Thomas
FOOTE, Reginald Vivian
FORBES, Benjamin
FORBES, Duncan
FORBES, Fergus Decimus
FORBES, Finlay
FORBES, James
FORBES, Richard Andrew
FORD, Arthur
FORD, Ernest
FORD, Michael Joseph
FORD, Thomas Walter
FORDE, Thomas Charles
FOREMAN, Samuel John
FORNACHON, Paul Charles
  Albert
FORREST, Christopher Frank
FORREST, William Clarence
FORRESTER, Percy Vivian
FORSTER, Andrew Forrester
FORSTER, Charles Stanley
FORSTER, Victor
FORSYTH, James
FORSYTH, William Henry
FORWARD, Thomas
FOSSEY, Hurtle
FOSTER, Arthur John
FOSTER, Ernest Harold

FOSTER, Fred Burnett
FOSTER, Frederick
FOSTER, James Henry
FOSTER, John
FOSTER, John Henry
FOSTER, Lionel
FOSTER, Reginald William
FOTHERGILL, John
FOWLER, George Charles Cecil
  Compton
FOWLER, Herbert Leopold Arthur
FOWLER, Lawrie Joseph D'Arcy
FOWLER, William
FOWLES, Herbert Arthur George
FOWLES, Herbert Howard
  Kentwell
FOWLES, Walter Ernest
FOWLIE, Alexander John
FOX, Albert Henry
FOX, Charles Edward
FOX, George
FOX, Marshall Tregellis
FRAHER, Philip
FRANCIS, John Richard
FRANCIS, Thomas
FRANCISCO, George Hillman
FRANKCOMBE, Vernon Egbert
FRANKLIN, Albert Edward
FRANKLIN, Frank
FRANKLIN, James Leonard
FRANKLYN, John William
FRAPPELL, Jack
FRASER, Bromley Campbell
  Cadogan
FRASER, Donald Alexander
FRASER, Donald Duncan
FRASER, Frederick Leopold
FRASER, Henry Victor Roy
FRASER, Herbert Henry
FRASER, James O'Neill
FRASER, John
FRASER, Norman Byron
FRASER, Robert James
FRASER, Robert Reid
FRASER, Robert William
FRASER, Walter Warwick
FRASER, William
FRASER, William
FRAWLEY, John
FRAYNE, William Stanley
FRAZER, Thomas Michael
FREDERICKS, Charles
FREEBAIRN, Walter
FREEMAN, Alfred Garnett
FREEMAN, Arthur Ernest
FREEMAN, Arthur Henry
FREEMAN, Douglas Stephen
FREEMAN, William James
  Gordon
FREEMAN, William Joseph
FREER, Percy William
FREESTONE, Albert Edward
FRENCH, Vivian Ambrose
FRENZEN, Henry Pierce
FRETWELL, Stephen Robert
  Austin
FREW, Robert John
FRITH, Albert Hector
FRITH, Harry
FRUIN, Charles
FRY, Henry Philip
FRY, John George
FRY, Reginald Jack
FULLAGAR, Edwin
FULLAGAR, Josephus
FULLER, Charles Alan
FULLER, Charles Upton
FULLER, Godfrey Archibald

FULLER, Henry
FULLER, William Jacob
FULTON, John Alexander James
FULTON, William Henry
FUNKENSTEIN, Henry
FURNESS, Joseph Maultby
FURNIVAL, James Richey
FYFE, Hugh Brown
FYFE, James
FYFFE, Arthur William
FYVIE, Edgar Henry
GABBETT, Norcliffe Esca
GABEL, Benhart Alfred
GABITES, Eric Briggs
GABRIEL, Frederick George
GAGINO, Harry
GAILLARD, Lucien D'Estainville
GAILLE, Edward
GAIN, George
GALAGHER, Frederick Alfred
GALE, Frederick George
GALE, Noel William Howard
GALE, William Henry
GALLACHER, James
GALLARD, Bertram Stuart
GALLOWAY, John
GALVIN, Allan St Clair
GALVIN, John Joseph
GAMBETTA, Noel
GAMBLE, Archibald
GAMMIE, Alexander
GAMMONE, Henry William
GANNON, Francis Joseph
GARDEN, John
GARDINER, Alfred John
GARDINER, William Thomas
  Briggs
GARDNER, Douglas Charles
GARDNER, John Archibald
GARDNER, Joseph Roy
GARDNER, Leonard Norman
GARGET, Edward
GARLAKE, Rayner
GARLAND, Herbert Frederick
  Edward
GARLAND, William John
GARNER, Albert
GARNER, Alexander Francis
GARNER, George Godfrey
GARNETT, Gladwyn O'Brien
GARNHAM, Stanley Millwood
GARRATT, John Clarence
GARRETT, Daniel
GARRETT, James
GARTON, William Arthur
GARTSIDE, Robert
GARVEY, Lawrence Patrick
GARWES, Frederick James
GASCOYNE, George Francis
  James
GASKELL, William
GATTY, Leonard James
GAUNT, Percival
GAVIN, Charles
GAYNOR, Dennis Edward
  William
GEDDES, Cyril Arthur
GEDDES, James Arthur
GEDDES, William Longfield
GEE, David
GEE, Edward
GEE, Harold
GELL, John
GELL, Walter
GELLATLY, William
GELLON, Percival James Garfield
GEMMELL, Robert
GENERY, Walter John

GENT, Percy Lionel
GEOGHEGAN, Arthur Michael
  Creagh
GEORGE, Frank Alderley Charles
GEORGE, Harold Leslie
GEORGE, Harold Wesley
GEORGE, Harold William Burn
GEORGE, Henry
GEORGE, John
GEORGE, John Lock
GEORGE, Percy Edward
GEORGE, Richard
GEORGE, William Charles
GERBER, Frederick William
GERRANS, David
GERRETS, Harry Nicholas
GERRY, John
GERVASI, Joseph James
GIBAUD, Henry James
GIBB, William David
GIBBONS, Clarence Gordon
GIBBONS, Thomas Bell
GIBBONS, William James
GIBBS, Alexander Frederick
GIBBS, Edward Buckley
GIBBS, Francis Worton
GIBBS, George Henry
GIBBS, Percy Lennie
GIBLIN, William David
GIBNEY, James
GIBSON, Arthur Gordon
GIBSON, Benjamin Paul
GIBSON, Charles William
GIBSON, Edwin Robert
GIBSON, Francis Walter
GIBSON, Frederick William
GIBSON, James Raymond
GIBSON, John Woodside
GIBSON, Matthew Rae
GIBSON, Peter
GIBSON, Russell William
GIBSON, Sydney Walter
GIBSON, Walter John Box
GIBSON, William Alexander
GILBERT, John Frederick
GILBERT, Thomas
GILCHRIST, Edward William
GILCHRIST, Horace William
GILES, Arthur Mckellar
GILES, Dudley Frederick Lionel
GILES, George Leslie
GILL, Frank Morley
GILL, Henry Albert
GILL, John William
GILL, Thomas Richard
GILLAM, Hubert Evelyn
GILLAM, Sydney Harry
  Davenport
GILLAM, William Albert
GILLANDERS, James Gordon
GILLATT, Charles Frederick
GILLESPIE, Robert
GILLESPIE, Robert Macgregor
GILLETT, Arthur Samuel Thomas
GILLIES, David Martin
GILLIES, Ernest
GILLIES, James
GILLIES, Kenneth
GILLIES, Neil
GILLISON, Andrew
GILLISON, Thomas Andrew
GILLMAN, Charles
GILMORE, Edward John
GILMOUR, James Campbell
GILMOUR, Joseph
GILPIN, Anthony Simpson
GILROY, Charles William
GIOTTI, Joseph Stephen

GIPPS, Frederick Gilbert Young
GIRLING, Frederick Horace
GIST, Charles
GLADING, Walter Daniel
GLANVILLE, Leigh George John
GLASGOW, Colin
GLASGOW, Robert
GLASSON, Alfred Bertram
GLATZ, Albert
GLEASON, Raymond Desmond
GLEESON, John Bernard
GLEESON, Samuel James
GLENNIE, David
GLITHRO, Arthur
GLOVER, Alfred Percy
GLOVER, William Stanley
GLUCK, Leopold Joel
GOBLE, William
GODDARD, Reginald
GODFREY, Frederick William
GODFREY, Noel George
GOLDEN, Thomas
GOLDRING, Gordon
GOLDSMITH, Raymond Leslie
GOLDTHORPE, Arthur
GOMBERT, France
GOOCH, Herbert Sherlock
GOOCH, Hugh Loudon
GOOD, William Barrett Silk
GOODALL, Thomas Edward
GOODALL, Thomas Lowden
GOODALL, Walter
GOODCHILD, Rupert Arthur
  Kent
GOODE, Eric Ralf
GOODE, Lynton
GOODIER, Walter
GOODLAD, Oliver
GOODWIN, Arthur Willoughby
GOODWIN, George Victor
GOOLD, Pierce Arthur
GOOLEY, Wilfred
GORDON, Alexander
GORDON, Charles George
GORDON, Hugh Garfield
GORDON, James Leslie
GORDON, Kenneth Douglas
GORDON, Louis Clive
GORDON, Reginald Charles
GORDON, S E
GORHAM, Edward Henry
GORMAN, Francis Gordon
GORMAN, John Christopher
GORMAN, Joseph
GORMAN, Maurice Edwin
GORMAN, Patrick
GORMAN, Thomas Ernest
  Tasman
GORRIE, Edward
GORRIE, James
GOSDEN, Robert Patterson
GOSS, Gerald Harry
GOSTELOW, Frederick Cecil
GOUGH, James
GOUGH, John Joseph
GOULD, Bruce
GOULDEN, Ernest Samuel
GOW, William
GOWER, Frederick Stephen
GOWER, John Lewes Davison
GOWER, Wilfred Rotherham
GOYNE, John George Letcher
GRACE, Hugh
GRACEY, George Charles
GRAFFUNDER, Albert
  Christopher Julius
GRAHAM, Dugald Maxwell
  Lockwood

GRAHAM, Gerald Lawrence
GRAHAM, Harry John
GRAHAM, Hugh Barclay
GRAHAM, Percy
GRAHAM, Percy
GRAHAM, Percy Eric
GRAHAM, Percy George
GRAHAM, Robert Charlens
GRAHAM, Robert William
GRAHAM, Thomas Anthony
GRAHAM, William Henry
GRANGER, Wilfred Bert
GRANT, Alexander
GRANT, Alexander
GRANT, Donald Robinson
GRANT, Ernest
GRANT, Geoffrey Treacher
GRANT, George Muir
GRANT, Henry
GRANT, James Joseph
GRANT, John Bede
GRANT, Leslie William
GRANT, Lewis Leonard
GRANT, Peter
GRANT, Thomas Watt
GRAVES, Frederick
GRAY, Albert
GRAY, Clarence Brownlie
GRAY, Frank
GRAY, George Alexander Hutton
GRAY, Gerald Francis
GRAY, Horace William Herbert
GRAY, John
GRAY, Mervyn William
GRAY, Robert Henry
GRAY-BUCHANAN, Cecil
  Gordon
GREAR, James
GREAVES, Charles
GREEDY, William Ernest
GREEN, Bertie George
GREEN, Francis Henry
GREEN, Frederick Benjamin
GREEN, George David
GREEN, George Henry
GREEN, George Henry
GREEN, George Reuben Robert
GREEN, Harry Franklyn
GREEN, Herbert Arthur
GREEN, James
GREEN, Joseph Watkin
GREEN, Keith Eddowes
GREEN, Robert George
GREEN, William Harry
GREEN, William Lionel
GREENAWAY, Harold John
GREENAWAY, Robert Cooper
GREENFIELD, Robert
GREENGRASS, George William
GREENHAM, Charles Gustus
GREENHAM, William Frederick
GREENHILL, Percival Charles
GREENLAND, Fred A V G
GREENLEES, James Alexander
GREENWELL, Thomas William
GREENWOOD, Ernest Edward
  Robert
GREENWOOD, Frederick William
GREENWOOD, George Herbert
GREGORY, Clive Winchcombe
GREGORY, Ernest Albert Edward
GREGORY, Hubert
GREIG, George Fergus
GREIG, Norman James
GREIG, Oswald Wilkie
GRENFELL, Clifton
GRIBBLE, Norman Arthur
GRIBBLE, William James

GRICE, Edward
GRIEVE, James Turnbull
GRIEVE, John
GRIEVES, Herbert George
GRIFFIN, Edward
GRIFFIN, Edward Denis
GRIFFIN, James Edward
GRIFFIN, Louis Gerald
GRIFFIN, William
GRIFFITH, Gerald Redmond
GRIFFITHS, Ainslie Arthur Hope
GRIFFITHS, Alfred Henry
GRIFFITHS, George Henry
GRIFFITHS, Hugh
GRIFFITHS, Lewis Owen
GRIFFITHS, Mansel David
GRIFFITHS, Rhys Emlyn
GRIFFITHS, Samuel
GRIFFITHS, Thomas
GRIFFITHS, William Halsall
GRIMES, John
GRIMES, John
GRIMES, Martin Patrick
GRIMSHAW, Charles Edward
GRIMSLEY, Stephen
GRIMWADE, George Risdon
GROESSLER, William Jacob
  Henry
GROOM, Frederick George
GROOM, George
GROOM, William Edward
GROSE, Joseph Donald
GROVE, Leslie Rowley
GROVES, James Hubert
GRUNDSTROM, Victor
GUEST, Arthur Percy
GUILFOYLE, Joseph Patrick
GUILFOYLE, William Luke
GULLIVER, William Gordon
GULLOFSEN, Rubin Henry
GUNN, Charles Edward
GUNN, William
GUNNELSON, Percy Oscar
GUNNING, Edward
GUNNING, George
GUNNING, James Sidney
GUNTHER, Harold Emslie
GUPPY, Edward Charles
GURNEY, Frank Bernard
GURR, Alfred Edward
GURRY, Joseph
GUTHRIE, Alexander Richard
GUTHRIE, Graham Buchanan
GUTHRIE, Norman Bruce
GUTHRIE, William Earle
GUTTRIDGE, Henry Charles
GUY, Harry Charles
GUYATT, Herbert Arthur
GWYNNE, John
GWYNNE, Sackville Wyndham
  Napier
HABBLETT, Harold
HADDON, Arthur Henry
HADDOW, David Eastwood
  Sydney
HADDRICK, Ethelbert
HADLEY, Samuel William
HAFFENDEN, Frank
HAGAN, Edgar Charles
HAGUE, Henry
HAHN, William
HAILSTONE, Arthur John
HAILWOOD, Charles William
HAINS, Morris
HALE, Edward Godfrey
HALES, William
HALL, Albert
HALL, Allen Lyle

HALL, Anthony Basil McKellar
HALL, Charles Arthur Jocelyn
HALL, Daniel James
HALL, Frederick Dugard
HALL, Frederick George
HALL, Frederick James
HALL, George William
HALL, Harold
HALL, Jack
HALL, Richard
HALL, Robert Bates
HALL, Sydney Gordon Leslie
HALL, Sydney Raymond
HALL, Tom
HALL, Vernon Charles
HALL, William James
HALLAM, Arthur
HALLAM, Edmund John
HALLAM, Hector Leslie
HALLETT, Albert
HALLETT, Herbert
HALLETT, James
HALLETT, John
HALLIDAY, Robert Michael
HALLIGAN, Michael
HAMILTON, Charles Vere
HAMILTON, George Fullard
HAMILTON, Herbert Percival
HAMILTON, James
HAMILTON, John
HAMILTON, John
HAMILTON, John
HAMILTON, John Harvy Grant
HAMILTON, John William
HAMILTON, William Hugh
HAMLYN, Arthur Franklin
HAMMOND, Alfred Henry
HAMMOND, George Lewis
HAMMOND, Henry
HAMMOND, John
HAMMOND, Leonard
HAMMOND, Leonard Charles
HAMMOND, William
HAMP, Stuart Samson
HAMPSON, Charles George
  Hubbard
HAMPSON, James Armistead
HAMPTON, Henry Cyril Percival
HANCHER, John Thomas
HANCOCK, Arthur
HANCOCK, Charles Evan
HANCOCK, Herbert William
HANCOCK, John
HANCOCK, Thomas Valentine
HANCOCK, Vivian Richard
  Claude
HANCOX, John
HANDCOCK, Albert John
HANDFORD, Douglas Frederick
HANDFORD, Robert
HANIGAN, Cecil Herbert
HANLEY, Charles Stewart Parnell
HANLEY, Frank Raymond
HANLEY, Maxwell
HANLEY, Patrick
HANLON, Edward James
HANLY, John Matthew
HANNA, Robert Alex
HANNA, Thomas
HANNAFORD, Lancelot Ramsay
HANNAH, George
HANNAH, James
HANNANT, Frederick
HANRAHAN, Thomas Frederick
HANSEN, Claude Hilfred
HANSEN, Frederick Nicholas
HANSEN, Henry Christian
HANSEN, Herbert Walter

HANSEN, Rasmus Robinson
HANSEN, Walter
HANSLOW, George
HANSON, Cecil Bertram
HANSON, Joseph Edward
HARBER, Horace
HARBOTTLE, David Thomas
HARCUS, James Logie
HARDAKER, Charles William
HARDIE, Peter
HARDIE, William
HARDIE, William Robertson
HARDING, Barker Orielly
HARDING, Bertie
HARDING, Claude
HARDING, George Ernest
HARDING, James Arthur
HARDMAN, Roy
HARDWICK, Herbert
HARDWICKE, Aubrey Charles
  Julian
HARDY, Edward Caro
HARDY, Harry Linton
HARDY, Nelson Albert
HARGRAVE, Geoffrey Lewis
HARKEN, Martin Theodore
HARKNESS, Edward George John
HARMAN, Henry
HARMER, John
HARNESS, Tom
HARNEY, John William
HARPER, David James
HARPER, Gresley Tatlock
HARPER, Wilfred Lukin
HARREX, Albert
HARRIES, Thomas Owen
HARRINGTON, Keith
HARRINGTON, Maxwell David
HARRINGTON, Sydney Arnold
HARRIS, Albert John Barclay
HARRIS, Bertram Page
HARRIS, Charles
HARRIS, David
HARRIS, Ernest Clarence
HARRIS, Frederick Carlton
HARRIS, Harold Robert
HARRIS, Harry Mitchell
HARRIS, Herbert Ernest
HARRIS, Hubert Jennings Imrie
HARRIS, Jack Bolton
HARRIS, John Auguste Emile
HARRIS, Langdon Albert
HARRIS, Lovell Poulett
HARRIS, Norman Elton
HARRIS, Oliver
HARRIS, Percival
HARRIS, Reginald Desmond
HARRIS, William John
HARRIS, William Locke
HARRIS, William Patrick
HARRIS, William Reginald
HARRISON, Allan
HARRISON, Arthur Frederick
HARRISON, Barnard Gregory
HARRISON, David
HARRISON, Henry Christopher
HARRISON, Herbert Victor
HARRISON, John Henry
HARRISON, Neville Mackersey
HARRISON, Philip Harry
HARRISON, Thomas Hodgson
HARRISON, William
HARRY, Samuel William
HARSANT, Herbert Charles
HART, Christodas Frederick
HART, Harry Oliver
HART, Henry
HART, Horace Arthur

HART, John
HART, Leslie
HARTLAND, Leslie Richard
HARTLAND, William Bullen
HARTNELL-SINCLAIR, Hubert
HARTON, Horace Carl
HARTRIDGE, Herbert Wilfrid
HARVEY, Frederick
HARVEY, Jack
HARVEY, James Henry
HARVEY, Percy Robert
HARVEY, Reuben Arthur
HARVEY, William Edward
HARWOOD, David Frederick
HARWOOD, Ralph Osborne
HASSELBACH, Edward Peter
HASSELL, Oscar Donald Humfray
HASTINGS, Alfred James Hedley
HASTINGS, Arthur George
  Howard
HASTINGS, Frederick John
HATCH, Clement Alphonso
  William
HATRICK, Robert Ellis
HAUA, Andrew Charles
HAVARD, Stephen Ebenezer
HAWKES, George John
HAWKES, George William
HAWKINS, David
HAWKINS, Gordon Gray
  Carruthers
HAWKINS, Leonard
HAWKINS, Leonard
HAWKINS, William Frank
HAWLEY, Clayton Kenrick
HAWORTH, Benjamin
HAWSON, Alexander Lincoln
HAWTHORNE, Edward
HAY, John
HAYBALL, Herbert Frederick
HAYDOCK, Ralph
HAYES, Alan Melrose
HAYES, Charles Henry
HAYES, Harold
HAYES, Henry Harold
HAYES, Herbert Richard
HAYES, James Lawrence
HAYES, Monaghan Raymond
HAYES, Robert James
HAYES, Wallace
HAYLES, Noel Alfred Douglas
HAYLOCK, Thomas Enoch
HAYMAN, Spencer Alexander
HAYMEN, Frank Granville
HAYNES, Henry Aguilar
HAYNES, Thomas William
HAYNES, William Francis
HAYWARD, Frederick
HAYWARD, George Leslie
HAZLETT, James Holmes
HEAD, Colin Wilfrid
HEAD, John
HEAD, William Arthur
HEAD, William Walter James
HEAGNEY, Herbert Spencer
HEALEY, Henry Percival
HEALEY, William Roberts
HEALY, Arthur Leslie
HEALY, Maurice
HEAP, Albert Edward
HEAP, Walter
HEARD, Albert Jack
HEARLE, Ernest Alfred
HEARSEY, Harold Garnet
HEASLIP, Robert Herbert
HEATH, Thomas Lloyd
HEATHER, Charles Alfred
HEATON, John Edward

HEAWOOD, James Charles
HECHLE, George
HEDLEY, Charles
HEFFERAN, Thomas Patrick
HEFFERNAN, George Vincent
HEGARTY, Walter James
HEIGHT, Horace Letcher
HELLER, Thomas James
HELLIER, Stuart
HELSHAM, John George Douglas
HEMING, Leslie Duncan
HEMINGWAY, Herbert
HEMMINGS, Benjamin
HENDEN, Alfred
HENDERSON, Albert Edward
HENDERSON, Alexander John
HENDERSON, David
HENDERSON, David Alexander
HENDERSON, George
HENDERSON, Henry Ernest
HENDERSON, Peter
HENDERSON, Robert Charles
    Neil
HENDERSON, Rupert Howard
HENDERSON, Sydney Gordon
HENDRICK, John
HENDRY, William Thomas
HENDY, Edward Percival
HENKEL, James Joseph
HENKERS, William George
HENLEY, Albert Edward
HENLEY, Henry
HENNELL, Harold Benjamin
HENNELL, Victor Edmund John
HENNESSY, Clifford James
HENRY, William Gladstone
HENSLER, Charles
HENSON, Fred
HENSTOCK, Frederick Walter
HENTY, Edward Ellis
HEPBURN, Rupert Osric
HEPBURN, William David
HEPBURN, William Nathan
HERBERT, Jack
HERBERT, John Charles
HERMAN, Harold Ellis
HERON, John
HERON, William
HERRING, Edward Edgar
HESTON, John
HETHERTON, Arthur
HETT, George
HEUGH, David McNeil
HEWET, George Frederick
HEWETT, Frank Bennett
HEWITT, Brian Charles
HEWITT, Frederick Charles
HEWITT, George
HEWITT, John
HEWITT, Walter
HEYES, Herbert
HEYLEN, Walter John
HEYMAN, James Andrew Herbert
HEYWOOD, Albert Paul
HIBBERD, John Augustus
HIBBERT, John
HIBBOTTSON, Thomas Alfred
HICK, Stanley
HICKEY, Herbert James
HICKEY, John Joseph
HICKEY, Patrick
HICKLING, Edgar William
HICKS, Colin
HICKS, Frederick Anthony Allan
HICKS, Frederick Arthur
HICKS, Wallace
HIDE, William Albert
HIDES, Ernest

HIDES, John Gordon
HIGGINBOTTOM, Joseph
    Broome
HIGGINBOTTOM, Thomas
HIGGINS, Richard Robert
HIGGINS, Thomas John
HIGGINS, Tom Roberts Louis
HIGGINS, William James
HIGGINS, William Joseph
HIGGINSON, Ernest Everard
    Chester
HIGGS, John
HIGGS, William Arthur Vernon
HIGSON, William Clarence
HILDEBRAND, John Henry
HILDER, Basil Richard
HILL, Alexander McPherson
HILL, Arthur Henry
HILL, Arthur John
HILL, Ashworth
HILL, Bertie
HILL, Frank Edwin
HILL, Frederick
HILL, Frederick William
HILL, Henry George
HILL, John Leo
HILL, John Thomas
HILL, Joseph Issac
HILL, Otto Gordon
HILL, Raymond Davenport
HILL, Stanley George
HILL, Thomas Charles Whitfield
HILL, Thomas Ninian Wardrop
HILL, Wilfred Carl
HILL, William Corbett
HILL, William Eric
HILL, William Kenneth
HILLIEAR, Edward Francis
    Patrick
HILLIER, Albert Edward
HILLIER, Arthur
HILLIER, Arthur John
HILLIER, Herbert Fred
HILLS, George
HILLS, William
HILTON, Victor George
HINCHCLIFF, Norman Alfred
HIND, William Arthur
HINDE, Kenneth John
HINDHAUGH, Russell George
HINDS, James Alexander
HINE, Alfred William
HINMAN, Arthur Gurr
HINMAN, James Thomas
HINSLEY, Joseph Charles
HINSLEY, Reginald John
HINTON, Herbert Gerald
HINTZE, Spensley John
HIRD, Henry
HISLOP, John
HITCH, William Thomas
HITCHINGS, John
HOAR, Norman Archibald
HOARE, Joseph Andrew
HOBBS, Alfred
HOBBS, Edwin
HOBBS, Henry George
HOBBS, William
HOBDEN, Douglas Clive
HOBDEN, Raymond Robert
    George
HOBSON, William Albert
HOCKEY, Edwin Percy
HOCKIN, Stuart Roy Luxmoore
HOCKING, John Percival
HOCKRIDGE, Robert Charles
HODDER, George
HODDER, Henry

HODGE, Francis Stephen
HODGE, James De Orbet
HODGES, Albert Henry
HODGES, Arthur John
HODGKINSON, Arthur Herbert
HODGKINSON, Eric
HODGMAN, Harry
HODGSON, Henry
HODGSON, Joseph
HODGSON, William Frederick
HOEY, James Francis
HOGAN, Hugh
HOGAN, James Henry
HOGAN, John Patrick
HOGAN, Michael John
HOGARTH, George Alexander
HOGBEN, Harold David
HOGBEN, Richard Hubert
HOGBEN, William James Aushen
HOGGARD, Francis Edwin
HOGGART, William Ross
HOJEIN, Lauritz
HOKIN, Harold Stanley
HOLBUT, Thomas James
HOLCOMBE, Cuthbert Oliver
HOLDAWAY, William James
HOLDEN, Ernest Henry
HOLDEN, Hugh Cyprian
HOLDEN, James
HOLDEN, John
HOLDER, William James
HOLDSWORTH, Edwin
HOLDSWORTH, Ernest Brook
HOLLAND, Archibald
HOLLAND, Thomas Edwin
HOLLAND, Vernon
HOLLAND, William
HOLLANDS, Bertie Frank
HOLLANDS, Thomas George
HOLLICK, Albert George
HOLLINGSWORTH, Joseph
    Victor
HOLLINGWORTH, Thomas
    Henry Montague
HOLLOWAY, Alfred John
HOLLOWAY, James Richard
HOLMAN, Albert Philip
HOLMBERG, Carl
HOLMES, Alfred Thomas
HOLMES, Evan
HOLMES, Frederick Nicholas
HOLMES, George William
HOLMES, Louis Gordon
HOLMES, Oliver Aitken
HOLT, Sydney Brooks
HOLTON, Clifford Lionel
HOMER, Arthur Charles
HOMER, Harry Raymond
HONEYCHURCH, Henry
HOOD, Archibald
HOOD, David Lowson
HOOK, Alfred Arthur
HOOKE, John Huon
HOOKER, Claude
HOOPER, Andrew Archibald
HOOPER, Basil John
HOOPER, Francis Herbert
HOOPER, Henry
HOOPER, Jack Richard
HOOPER, Robert James Mansfield
HOOPER, Robert Murdoch
    Finlayson
HOOPPELL, Percy Samuel
HOPE, Edward Somerville
HOPE, George Reuben
HOPE, Thomas Frank
HOPKINS, Charles
HOPKINS, Douglas Walter

HOPKINS, Frederick Lisbon
HOPPER, Walter
HOPPING, John Leslie
HORAN, Charles Thomas
HORAN, George Richard
HORAN, Richard Joseph
HORNBY, William Robert
HORNE, Robert Bulmer
HORNE, Wilfred L'Estrange
HORROCKS, Edwin James
HORROCKS, Joseph
HORSBURGH, John Henry
HORSBURGH, William Brown
HORSFALL, Geoffrey Garnett
HORTON, Cyril Aubrey
HORTON, Robert
HOSKIN, Harry
HOSKING, Leslie Gordon
HOTHAM, Arthur John
HOTSON, John Edward
HOUGH, James
HOUGH, James
HOVENDEN, William
HOWARD, Alfred
HOWARD, Cecil John
HOWARD, Frank Rodney
HOWARD, George
HOWARD, Herbert Richard
HOWARD, Robert
HOWARD, Thomas Spencer
HOWARTH, Henry Joseph
HOWARTH, John
HOWAT, Alfred Charles
HOWCROFT, Robert
HOWDEN, George Thomas
HOWE, Thomas Henry
HOWELL, Geoffrey Castell
HOWELL, Raymond
HOWES, George
HOWES, Joseph Charles
HOWIESON, David
HOWITZ, Maxwell
HOWLETT, Cecil William Robert
HOWLETT, Herbert Gladstone
HOWLEY, Roger Francis
HOYNES, Nicholas
HUBBARD, Albert Charles
HUDSON, Bertram Lennox
HUDSON, Charles Forster
HUDSON, Frank
HUDSON, Frederick Arthur
HUDSON, Frederick George
HUDSON, Herbert Thomas
HUDSON, James
HUDSON, Richard
HUDSON, Vincent
HUGHES, Alfred Thomas
HUGHES, Arthur Edward
HUGHES, Arthur Samuel
HUGHES, Arthur Walker Joseph
HUGHES, George Thomas
HUGHES, George Thomas
HUGHES, Griffith Roy
HUGHES, Harold Gwynne
HUGHES, Harrison
HUGHES, John
HUGHES, John Henry
HUGHES, Joseph
HUGHES, Thomas
HUGHES, Vincent Williams
HUGHES, William
HUGHES, William John
HULBERT, Patrick Ravenhill
HULME, Alfred Lloyd
HUME, James
HUME, William Henry Hampton
HUMPHREY, Jesse
HUMPHREYS, Alfred Ernest

HUMPHREYS, Cyril
HUMPHREYS, Leonard Hugh
HUMPHREYS, Thomas Owen
HUMPHRYS, Reginald Angus
HUNDLEY, Walter
HUNGERFORD, Harold Aubrey
HUNGERFORD, William
HUNT, Arthur George
HUNT, Charles Lawrence
HUNT, Frederick William
HUNT, George Albury
HUNT, Leonard Leslie
HUNT, Maurice Alan
HUNT, Robert Edward
HUNT, Victor Frederick
HUNT, William Herbert
HUNTER, Frederick Emerton
HUNTER, Hector Norman
HUNTER, Herbert Humphreys
HUNTER, James Graham
HUNTER, John George
HUNTER, Maurice James
    Emerton
HUNTER, William
HUNTER, William
HUNTLEY, Clive Neilson
    Reynolds
HUNTLEY, George Henry Stuart
HURLEY, Andrew Edward Albert
HURLEY, Robert
HURLSTONE, George Henry
HURNE, Albert Edward
HURRY, Robert
HURST, Herbert Edward
HURST, William Macleod
HUSK, Hugh Herbert
HUTCHINS, Thomas Arthur
HUTCHINSON, John
HUTCHINSON, Lewis
HUTCHINSON, Lorenzo
HUTCHISON, Archibald James
HUTCHISON, James William
HUTCHISON, William
HUTHWAITE, George James
HUTTON, Clarence Edward
HUTTON, Reginald Alex
HYDE, Leslie
HYDE, Norman Cropley
HYDE, Walter
HYLAND, Laurence
HYLAND, Thomas Benedict
HYNES, Nicholas Patrick
ILETT, Ernest Campbell
INCE, Arthur John
INGLIS, Thomas Gordon
INGRAM, Edward George
INGRAM, William Bradley
INMAN, John William
INNES, Peter
INNES, William
IREDALE, John
IRELAND, Edmund George
IRELAND, George
IRVINE, Ernest Norton
IRVINE, Francis Duncan
IRVINE, Geoffry Ransom
IRVING, Sydney Clark
IRWIN, George Roy
IRWIN, Joseph Alfred
ISAAC, Robert Luff
ISON, Adolphus George
IVISON, James Miller
IVISON, John
IZATT, John
JACK, Alfred Lachlan
JACKA, Leslie Harold Newton
JACKSON, Alfred Charles Harrop

291

JACKSON, Arthur William
  Panchand
JACKSON, Daniel Joseph
JACKSON, David Alexander
JACKSON, Ernest
JACKSON, Ernest
JACKSON, George
JACKSON, George Albert
JACKSON, George Stanley
JACKSON, Henry Reginald
JACKSON, James
JACKSON, James William Lewis
JACKSON, John
JACKSON, John
JACKSON, Kenneth Halstead
JACOB, Herbert Gordon
JACOBS, Henry
JACOBS, Leslie Gordon
JACOBS, Louis William
JACOBSON, Thomas Godfrey
JACOMB, Robert Arthur
JACOMBS, David Matthew
JAENSCH, Ernest Arthur
JAFFRAY, Alfred John
JAHNS, William Theodore Henry
JAKEMAN, Charles James
JAMES, Claude Beresford
JAMES, Cyril
JAMES, David
JAMES, Jonathan Albert
JAMES, Joseph
JAMES, Percival Clarence Rodda
JAMES, Reginald
JAMES, Samuel
JAMES, Stanley
JAMES, Trevor
JAMES, William Royal
JAMIESON, Alexander
JAMIESON, Douglas
JAMIESON, John Edwin
JAMIESON, John Henry
JAMIESON, Thomas
JAMIESON, William
JANES, Frederick Walter
JANSSEN, Carl Wilhelm
JANSSEN, Ernek Valdemar
JARMAN, Harry Henry
JARMAN, Richard Alexander
JARRETT, Harold Norman
JARVEY, James
JARVIS, Alfred Henry
JARVIS, Richard George
JARVIS, Tasman
JASPER, Thomas John
JEAL, Ernest John
JEFFERY, Harold
JEFFERY, Harold Anchor
JEFFERY, Percy
JEFFREY, John
JEFFREY, John
JEFFREY, Norman Stanley
JEFFRIES, George Allan
JELLETT, Frederick
JENKINS, Chester Royal
JENKINS, Richard Lewis Hay
  Blake
JENKINS, Roy
JENKINS, William Benjamin
JENNINGS, Harry Jarvis
JENNINGS, John Ernest
JENNINGS, Thomas
JENNINGS, William Thomas
JENSEN, Francis Ernest
JENSEN, Henry
JENSEN, Karl Alfred
JENSEN, Lawrence Francis
JETSON, Ernest John
JEWELL, Richard Greenwood

JIFFKINS, Herbert Harry Victor
JINNETTE, Herbert
JOB, Leslie
JOFS, Jacob Lamtan
JOHNS, Benjamin Davies
JOHNS, Henry Louis
JOHNS, John Benjamin
JOHNS, William Thomas
JOHNSON, Albert
JOHNSON, Albert
JOHNSON, Amos Samuel
JOHNSON, Andrew
JOHNSON, Andrew Nathaniel
JOHNSON, Arthur
JOHNSON, Arthur Chaplin
JOHNSON, Arthur Sydney
JOHNSON, Aubert Richard
JOHNSON, Cedric
JOHNSON, Charles Frederick
JOHNSON, Cyril Allen
JOHNSON, Donald Mathieson
  McGregor
JOHNSON, Edward Victor
JOHNSON, Ernest Napoleon
JOHNSON, Francis
JOHNSON, Francis Charles
JOHNSON, Frank Thomas
JOHNSON, Frederick Aloysius
JOHNSON, Frederick Miller
JOHNSON, George
JOHNSON, George Albert
JOHNSON, George Blatchford
  Fay
JOHNSON, James Clarence
JOHNSON, James Leonard
JOHNSON, John
JOHNSON, John Frederick
JOHNSON, Louis Victor
JOHNSON, Oscar Edward
JOHNSON, Stanley
JOHNSON, Thomas
JOHNSON, William James
JOHNSTON, Alexander Thomas
JOHNSTON, Alfred Ernest
JOHNSTON, Allan
JOHNSTON, Arthur
JOHNSTON, David Norman
JOHNSTON, Donald William
JOHNSTON, Frederick William
JOHNSTON, George Richard
  Somerville
JOHNSTON, James
JOHNSTON, John
JOHNSTON, Leslie William
JOHNSTON, Leybourne
JOHNSTON, Norman
JOHNSTON, Reginald
JOHNSTON, Roy Victor
JOHNSTON, Sydney Tasman
JOHNSTON, William
JOHNSTONE, Alfred James
JOHNSTONE, Hugh
JOHNSTONE, Miller
JOHNSTONE, Thomas Valentine
JOLLY, Arthur
JOLLY, John Joshua
JONAS, Charles
JONES, Alexander Cecil Turner
JONES, Alfred Robert
JONES, Arthur M
JONES, Bernard Ashford
JONES, Charles Edward
JONES, Edward George Rooke
JONES, Edward Victor
JONES, Edwin Sydney
JONES, Ernest
JONES, Frederick
JONES, Frederick Blondon

JONES, Frederick Harold
JONES, Garnet David Victor
JONES, George
JONES, George James
JONES, Herman Hill
JONES, Hubert Cromwell
  Warwick
JONES, Ivor
JONES, James Henry
JONES, John Wilson
JONES, Laidley Edward Elbert
JONES, Leslie Theophilus
JONES, Leslie Thomas
JONES, Michael
JONES, Octavious
JONES, Philip Vivian
JONES, Reginald Steven
JONES, Richard Henry Phillip
JONES, Robert David
JONES, Roger Montgomery
JONES, Stanley Herbert
JONES, Sydney Fisher
JONES, Sydney Victor
JONES, Theophilus
JONES, Thomas
JONES, Thomas Christopher
JONES, Thomas Leonard
JONES, Thomas Pickworth
JONES, Walter Nelson
JONES, Wilfred Walter
JONES, William Frederick
JONES, William Henry
JONES, William John
JONES, William Rees
JORDAN, Harold Vernon
JORDAN, Robert
JOSE, William Graham
JOSH, Frank
JOY, Ivo Brian
JOY, Robert Sizer
JOYCE, Edward William
JOYCE, Joshua James
JUBY, Henry James
JUDE, David Harold
JUDELL, Elias
JUNIER, Edward Wilfred
JURY, Henry William
KAIN, Reginald Harrington
KAIZER, Stanley Ivan
KALMAN, Maurice
KANE, Francis William
KANE, John
KANE, Patrick
KANE, William James
KARNEY, William James
KAU, Lewis Paul
KAUFMANN, Cuthbert
KAVANAGH, Joseph
KAWELMACHER, Otto James
KAY, Francis Lawrence
KAY, James Ronald
KEAIRNS, Victor Roy
KEALY, Reginald
KEAM, Herbert M
KEAN, Thomas
KEARNEY, Ernest
KEARNEY, John Nicholas
KEAST, Thomas Eric Carter
KEEFFE, Joseph Patrick
KEEGAN, Joseph
KEELING, Samuel Arthur
KEENAN, Cyril Patrick
KEENAN, John
KEENAN, William Joseph
KEENS, Archibald Joseph
KEEPENCE, Herbert Spencer
KEERS, Harold
KEID, William

KEIGHERY, Frank
KEIGHLEY, John
KEIRAN, Richard Clement
KELAHER, James Joseph
KELCEY, Frederick Henry
KELLE, Leonard Jean
KELLER, Frank
KELLY, Charles
KELLY, Charles Oswald
KELLY, Ernest
KELLY, Frederick
KELLY, George Edward Eccleston
KELLY, Herbert
KELLY, James
KELLY, John Thomas Henry
KELLY, Manus John
KELLY, Michael James
KELLY, Patrick
KELLY, Patrick
KELLY, Patrick Joseph
KELLY, Thomas James
KELLY, William
KELLY, William
KELSALL, William Joseph
KELSO, Norman
KEMMIS, John Russell
KEMP, Alexander
KEMP, Frank Winterburn
KEMP, George
KEMP, William
KEMP, William Henry
KEMPE, Russell Stacey
KEMPSON, Sydney Thomas
KEMSLEY, George
KENDRICK, Alfred
KENDRICK, Edward Francis
KENNANE, Leslie Augustine
KENNEDY, Alexander
KENNEDY, Allen Edgar
KENNEDY, Arthur Charles
  Valentine
KENNEDY, Edward Kittrick
KENNEDY, Ernest Thomas John
KENNEDY, Frederick R
KENNEDY, George Henry
KENNEDY, John
KENNEDY, John Michael
KENNEDY, Kerion
KENNEDY, Martin
KENNEDY-TAYLOR, Derrick
  William
KENNELLY, Leon Patrick
KENNERICK, William
KENNERLEY, Thomas Frederick
KENNETT, Archibald
KENNEY, William Harold
KENNON, Alexander
KENNY, Arthur Vincent
KENNY, Charles
KENT, Francis Burwood
KENT, James
KENT, John Scott
KENT, William
KENYON, Arthur Leslie
KENYON, Claude Septimus
  Selborne
KENYON, Thomas William
  Hoyles
KEPPIE, Arthur Ernest
KER, Henry George
KERBY, Norman Vivian Gladstone
KERR, Daniel
KERR, Harold Younger
KERR, James
KERR, Robert
KERR, Ronald George
KERR, William Buchanan
KERRIDGE, Robert

KERRIGAN, James
KERSHAW, Ernest Abraham
KERSHAW, George
KERSWILL, Leo James
KEWLEY, Frederick Hugh
KEYS, Charles
KIBBEY, Frederick
KIDD, Ernest
KIDD, Neil
KIDD, Sidney John Claud
KIDMAN, William John Cyril
KIDSON, Edric Doyle
KIEHL, Anton
KIELLERUP, Frederick Charles
KIELY, Frank
KIELY, Patrick
KIERNAN, Albert Arthur
KIERNAN, James
KILEY, Edmund
KILLEN, Peter
KILLICOAT, Philip Darby
KILMINSTER, Erol Rutter
KILPATRICK, Edward Richard
KIMBER, Henry Robert
KIMBER, James Henry
KIMPTON, Frank
KING, Alexander
KING, Charles
KING, Charles Leslie
KING, Charles Trethowan
KING, Charles Wesley
KING, Frank
KING, George Austin
KING, Hainsworth
KING, Henry John
KING, Herbert Henry
KING, Herbert John
KING, John Leonard
KING, John Talbot
KING, Martin Frederick
KING, Roy Holcombe
KING, Thomas Alfred
KING, Thomas Nathaniel
KING, Walter Macintosh
KING, William
KING, William Ernest
KINGSLAND, Sydney John
KINGSTON, Herbert James
KINGSTON, John Seabrook
KINGSTON, William Joseph
KINNAIRD, Allan Bruce
KINSELLA, Richard Alphonsus
KIPPING, Frederick George
KIPPING, Ralph Ezekiah
KIRBY, Alfred
KIRBY, Edmond
KIRBY, Edward Ashton
KIRBY, Frank
KIRBY, John Hopkins
KIRBY, Thomas
KIRK, Eric
KIRK, John Frederick
KIRKLAND, James Gordon
KIRKPATRICK, James
KIRKPATRICK, John Simpson
KIRKWOOD, Athol MacGregor
KIRKWOOD, Phillip Barton
KIRSCH, Frederick William
KISSICK, John
KITCHENER, Frederick George
KITCHENER, Thomas Edgar
KITCHIN, Hedley Vernon George
KITSON, Arthur Frederick
KLOPP, Arthur
KLOPPER, Louis Alfred
KLUGLEIN, Carl Herman
KLUMP, John Charles
KNEALE, Edward Gerald

KNIBBS, William John
KNIGHT, Archibald John
KNIGHT, Archibald Roland
KNIGHT, Edward Luke
KNIGHT, George Finlay
KNIGHT, James Taylor
KNIGHT, Joseph James
KNIGHT, Peter
KNIGHT, Wilfred Victor
KNOTT, Edward George
KNOWLES, Arthur Willie
KNOX, Archibald Henry Richard
KNOX, Arthur Herbert
KOLTS, Henry Frederick
KOSAKOWSCHENEK, Blas
KRETCHMAR, Edmund Herman
KRUMMEL, Oscar Otto
KUJALA, Antti
KYDD, George
LA NAUZE, Charles Andrew
LADLAY, Edgar
LAFALAISE, Louise Edward
    Archie Menzyes
LAFFERTY, James David
LAHZ, Roy
LAIDLAW, John
LAILEY, John Charles
LAILEY, William Henry
LAING, David
LAING, James
LAKE, Gordon
LAKELAND, Thomas Victor
LAKEMAN, Allen
LAKER, Christopher Joseph
LAKER, Percy Bernard
LAKEY, Ernest Thomas
LALLY, Malcolm Almore
LALOR, Joseph Peter
LAMB, Joseph
LAMBAHIRT, Theodor Hugo
LAMBERT, Claude Wand
LAMBERT, Harry
LAMBERT, Henry Alfred
LAMBERT, Leonard Clement
LAMBERT, William
LAMBERT, William Joseph
LAMBETH, Reginald Walter
LAMBORNE, George St Clair
LAMBOURN, Frederick George
LAMOND, Alexander
LAMOND, David
LAMOND, Thomas Bede
LAMONT, Charles Robert
LAMPAN, William George
LAMPARD, John
LANCASTER, George Albert
LANCASTER, William Henry
LANDQUIST, Thorsten Eric
LANE, Charles Henry
LANE, Clement Frederick Wills
LANE, Cyril Herbert Dodson
LANG, William
LANG, William
LANGDON, Leslie John
LANGE, Frederick Einar
LANGFORD, Arthur
LANGFORD, Stroud Lincoln
LANGLANDS, Robert Whitton
LANGSTON, Albert Charles
LANYON, Vernon Clifford
LAPTHORNE, Victor Walter
    Athelstone
LAREDO, Donald
LARKIN, Edward Rennix
LARKIN, Martin Joseph
LARKIN, Michael Edward
LARKING, Cyril Frederick
LARTER, George

LASHMAR, Allan John
LAST, Joseph
LATHAM, Harold
LATHAM, Walter Martin
LATIMER, George Edward
LAUDER, John
LAUGHER, James Edgar
LAUNDER, Joseph
LAUNT, Leslie Claude
LAURENCE, Stanley Rupert
LAURIE, Bertram
LAVELLE, Anthony
LAVELLE, Michael
LAVER, Arthur John
LAVERCOMBE, John
LAVERY, William
LAW, Frederick Charles
LAWLER, Richard James
LAWLOR, Leonard Joseph
LAWRENCE, Frank
LAWRENCE, Jack Warren
LAWRENCE, Sydney
LAWRIE, James
LAWS, Frank Albert
LAWSON, Martial
LAWSON, Robert
LAWSON, Robert Henry
LAWTON, James Herbert
LAYCOCK, Harold
LAYH, Cyril Keith
LAYTHER, William John
LAYTON, Arthur
LAYTON, Norman Stanley
LAZARUS, Isaac
LE MASURIER, John Edward
LEA, Charles Henry
LEA, Thomas
LEACH, William Henry
LEAHEY, John
LEAKE, George Arthur
LEAR, William Edward
LEARY, Charles
LEAVER, Louis Arthur Stanley
LEDINGHAM, Walter Greig
LEDWIDGE, Arthur
LEE, Alec Lionel
LEE, Charles
LEE, Charles James
LEE, David
LEE, Frank Edward
LEE, George Frederick
LEE, Henry Robert
LEE, John Charles
LEE, Robert Augustus
LEE, Sidney
LEE, Thomas
LEE, Thomas
LEE, William H
LEECH, Samuel
LEEDEN, William Henry
LEER, Charles Edward
LEER, Sidney Cecil
LEES, David
LEES, Ernest Leonard
LEES, James Barker
LEES, Ralph
LEES, Vere Lionel
LEESON, Cecil George
LEESON, William Herbert Charles
LEGGETT, David Mackay
LEGGO, Frederick William
LEHFELDT, William Robert
LEISHMAN, Cyril Thomas
LEISHMAN, Robert
LEMKE, Albert Walter
LEMON, Henry David
LEMON, Joseph Royal Surrige
LEMON, William

LENAN, George
LENNIE, James
LENNON, Hugh
LENNON, Richard
LENNOX, Horace Gilchrist
LENTON, James Henry
LEO, John Bernard
LEONARD, John Thomas
LESLIE, Edward
LESLIE, Valentine
LESLIE, Walter Aland
LESLIE, William Leichhardt
LESTER, Harold
LEVENE, Abraham
LEVENS, George Hill
LEVETT, Henry Reginald Donald
LEVEY, Ernest Charles
LEVI, Keith Maurice
LEVIEN, Cyril Benjamin
LEVINE, Michael
LEWIN, Reginald Arthur
LEWIS, Alexander
LEWIS, Alfred Henry
LEWIS, Arthur Dudley
LEWIS, Arthur Harold
LEWIS, David
LEWIS, Edwin Thomas
LEWIS, Ernest Vivian
LEWIS, George Barret
LEWIS, Harold Walters
LEWIS, Henry Robert
LEWIS, James
LEWIS, James Llewellyn
LEWIS, John
LEWIS, John Percival
LEWIS, Mervyn Clive
LEYDIN, John
LEYLAND, Ralph Elvas
LEYON, Carl William
LIBBIS, William Thomas
LICKFOLD, Edward
LIDSTER, Cecil Reginald John
LIESCHKE, George Albert
LIGHT, Frederick Augustus
LILBURNE, James Thomas
LILLIE, George
LILLIE, James
LILLIS, Patrick
LIMEROCK, John Grieve
LIND, Robert Houston
LINDELL, Ernest
LINDLEY, Leo
LINDNER, Arthur
LINDREA, Charles Arthur
LINDSAY, Allan
LINDSAY, Charles Henry
LINDSAY, David
LINDSAY, David George
LINDSAY, Dugald Carmichael
LINDSAY, James Archibald
LINDSEY, Robert Joseph
LING, Harold Bliss
LINKLATER, Harry
LINN, John
LINTON, Richard
LINTON, William Aston
LIONE, Ernest Arthur
LISTON, William
LITTLE, Alfred Ernest
LITTLE, Arthur John
LITTLECHILD, Leonard William
LITTLEFIELD, Clarence Landle
LLEWELYN, Leonard Griffith
LLOYD, Job
LLOYD, Reginald Kenneth
LLOYD-JONES, Henry
LLOYD-WORTH, Frederick John
LOADER, George

LOADER, Roland Eugene Clement
LOBB, Percy James
LOCK, Daniel
LOCK, Thomas
LOCKE, James Leonard
LOCKER, Frederick Thomas
LOCKWOOD, Joseph Albert
LODGE, Wilfred Francis Huggett
LODINGTON, Cuthbert
LOFT, John Henry Wilson
LOGAN, Ernest Charles
LOGAN, George Hewish
LOGAN, James
LOGAN, James Glendinning
    Aitken
LOGAN, James John
LOGAN, Thomas James
LOGAN, William Frederick
LOHSE, Alfred George
LOMAX, Harry
LONDON, Alexander
LONERGAN, Patrick Francis
LONG, Alfred Burgess
LONG, Cuthbert Jones
LONG, George
LONG, Harold James
LONG, Robert Arthur
LONGMORE, Herbert George
    Milne
LONGMORE, Thomas
LONGSTAFF, Richard John
LONGSTAFF, William David
LONSDALE, Everard Claude
LOOMES, Aubrey Randolph
LORD, Ashley Codrington
LORD, Reginald William
LORD, Robert Stanley
LOUGHRAN, John
LOUTTIT, Albert Victor
LOVATT, James Muncaster
LOVE, Alfred Herbert
LOVE, Arthur William
LOVELL, Clyde
LOVELL, Ernest Rudolph
LOVELOCK, George
LOVELOCK, George Henry
LOWE, Ernest Gordon
LOWE, James
LOWE, John Edward
LOWE, Leslie
LOWEN, Walter
LOWN, Mervyn Allen
LOWNDES, Edward Whitaker
LOWRIE, Bertie Douglas
LOWTHER, Percival Arnold
LOXTON, Percival
LUCAS, Charles Edward
LUCAS, Edward
LUCAS, James
LUCKETT, Joseph Edward
LUFFMAN, Bertrand Evelyn
LUGG, Joseph James
LUKE, Edward John
LUKIN, Dudley
LUMSDEN, John Hutchinson
LUNDIE, Leslie
LUNN, Richard Denis
LUSH, John Kenneth
LUSH, Philip
LUSIC, Victor Matthew
LUTHER, John Fitzmaurice Guy
LUTTRELL, Frank
LUXTON, Clarence James
LYALL, Brian
LYALL, Donald
LYALL, William
LYNCH, Francis Patrick
LYNCH, Harry

LYNCH, Henry Joseph
LYNCH, Michael John
LYNCH, Patrick
LYNE, Victor Harold Davison
LYNES, Augustus
LYON, Israel Edward
LYONS, Arthur
LYONS, James
LYONS, John Thomas
LYONS, Stanley
LYONS, Thomas Henry
LYONS, William Edward
MAACK, George Frederick
    Charles
MAAS, John Louis
MACALISTER, Ian Gordon
MACAULAY, Alexander Murdo
MACAULAY, Stephen
MACBEAN, Colin Hendrie
MACBETH, Alexander
MACBETH, Arthur Archibald
MACDERMOTT, Charles Leslie
MACDONALD, Arthur Leslie
    Graham
MACDONALD, David Henderson
MACDONALD, Donald
MACDONALD, Duncan
MACDONALD, Frederick
MACDONALD, John Augustine
MACDONALD, John Robert
MACDONALD, Marshal Roy
MACDONALD, Owen
MACDONALD, Robert
MACDONALD, Robert Burnett
MACDONALD, Walter Russell
MACDOUGALL, Donald
MACDOUGALL, Lachlan Stephen
    Wallace
MACE, William Ralph
MACFARLANE, Edward
    Macfarlane
MACFARLANE, John James
MACFARLANE, Norman
MACFARLANE, Samuel James
MACGIBBON, Alexander John
MACGILLIVRAY, Ivor Eric
MACGILP, John
MACGREGOR, Donald Neil
MACGREGOR, James Anderson
MACINNES, Ian Gordon
MACKAY, Alexander Cameron
MACKAY, Archie Graham
MACKAY, Colin Patrick
MACKAY, David Rankin
MACKAY, Duncan McKenzie
MACKAY, Herbert William
    Henderson
MACKAY, Kenneth Scott
MACKENZIE, Charles Oram
MACKENZIE, Donald
MACKENZIE, Donald
MACKENZIE, Hugh MacKay
MACKENZIE, William Cuthbert
MACKIE, Alexander
MACKIE, Alexander
MACKIE, Charlie
MACKIE, James
MACKIE, Joseph
MACKIE, Robert Stirling
MACKINNON, John Younger
MACLAREN, William James
MACLAURIN, Henry Normand
MACLEAN, Allan Cameron
MACLEOD, Kenneth Alexander
MACLURE, Valentine Murray
MACNAMARA, Lionel
MACNISH, Keith Percy
MACNIVEN, Robert

MCKEAN, Rupert
MCKELVIE, Henry
MCKENDRICK, John Thomas
MCKENNA, David Peter
MCKENNA, Edward Albert
MCKENNA, Hugh Patrick
MCKENZIE, Archibald Frank
MCKENZIE, Charles
MCKENZIE, Frederick
MCKENZIE, George
MCKENZIE, Hector
MCKENZIE, James
MCKENZIE, John William
MCKENZIE, Leslie Keir
MCKENZIE, Robert
MCKENZIE, William Davidson
MCKENZIE-MCHARG, William
MCKEON, Joseph
MCKEOWN, Henry
MCKINNIREY, Michael Joseph
  Mansfield
MCKINNON, Athol William
MCKINNON, Duncan
MCKINNON, Ian Godfrey
MCKINNON, James Donald
MCKNIGHT, Ernest Stanley
MCKOY, Stanley James
MCLACHLAN, Adam
MCLACHLAN, John Henry
MCLACHLAN, Roy Stevens
MCLAREN, Hector
MCLAREN, Hugh Wilson Paton
MCLAREN, Thomas McLean
MCLARTY, James
MCLAUGHLIN, John Jubilee
MCLEAN, Alex
MCLEAN, Alexander
MCLEAN, Angus Robert
MCLEAN, Donald
MCLEAN, Donald Shapley
MCLEAN, Edward Finlay
MCLEAN, Henry Abraham
MCLEAN, James
MCLEAN, John Raymund
MCLEAN, Roderick
MCLEAY, Donald Alexander
MCLEAY, Roderick Keith
MCLEISH, David
MCLELLAN, Donald Matheson
MCLELLAN, Reginald John
MCLENAN, Herbert
MCLENNAN, Angus Ewen
MCLENNAN, James
MCLENNAN, Kenneth
MCLENNAN, Roderick George
MCLEOD, Alexander John
MCLEOD, Angus
MCLEOD, Angus
MCLEOD, David Ferguson
MCLEOD, Donald
MCLEOD, Donald George
MCLEOD, James K
MCLEOD, Kenneth Hugh
MCLEOD, Maurice Leslie
MCLEOD, Ronald
MCLEOD, Talisker Donald
MCLEOD, William Harold
MCLINTOCK, John Sloan
MCMAHON, Francis
MCMAHON, Horace Joseph
MCMAHON, Richard John
MCMAHON, Thomas Francis
MCMANAMEY, James Whiteside
  Fraser
MCMASTER, Allan Hugh
MCMASTERS, Robert Thompson
MCMICHAEL, Leslie William
MCMILLAN, Neil

MCMILLAN, Neil Henry
MCMILLAN, Robert
MCMILLAN, Roy Alexander
MCMURRAY, Edward James
MCNAB, Hamish
MCNAB, John
MCNAE, William Charteris
MCNAIR, Samuel Hay
MCNAIR, William
MCNAMARA, James
MCNAMARA, James Steven
MCNAMARA, John
MCNEIL, Angus
MCNEIL, James Donald George
MCNEILL, Henry George
MCNEILL, Thomas
MCNICOL, John
MCNULTY, Robert John
MCPHAIL, Alec
MCPHAIL, John
MCPHEE, Allan Douglas
MCPHERSON, Alexander George
MCPHERSON, Alexander John
MCPHERSON, Athol Cluny
MCPHERSON, Colin
MCPHERSON, Douglas
MCPHERSON, Thomas Roy
MCPHERSON, William
MCPHERSON, William
MCPHIE, Bernard Fritz Tempest
MCQUAID, John
MCQUIE, Alick Charles H
MCRAE, Gordon
MCRAE, Neil
MCROBERTS, Wilfred Orville
MCSHANE, Alfred
MCSHANE, Daniel
MCSHANE, Ernest Alfred
MCSPARRON, William George
MCTAGGART, Herbert
MCTAGUE, Edward
MCTAVISH, John Alexander
MCVAY, David
MCWATT, Malcolm James
MCWHIRTER, Samuel George
MCWILLIAM, Joseph Glaister
MCWILLIAM, Stirling Alexander
MEADE, Arthur Stuart
MEADE, John Henry
MEAGER, Hubert Richard
  William
MEAKINS, Arthur James
MEALAND, Charles Albert Cecil
MEALE, Frederick Roy
MEARNS, Malcolm Livingstone
MEDLEY, John James
MEDLIN, Phillip
MEECH, Richard Alfred
MEEHAN, Michael
MEEK, Cyril Wallace
MEEK, Richard Stanley
MEGAN, John Henry
MEGAW, James
MEGGY, Albert Edward
MEHEGAN, Francis Edward
MEHEW, Reuben
MELEDINE, Louis
MELIA, Edward
MELICAN, Thomas Pembroke
MELLING, Edward James
MELLOR, William
MELROSE, George
MELVILLE, Alexander
MELVILLE, Charles William
MELVILLE, John Rossiter
MELVIN, John
MENADUE, William
MENYWEATHER, Mervyn

MENZIES, David
MERCER, Owen Thomas
MEREDITH, Thomas Herbert
MERIVALE, John Laidley
MERRETT, George Henry
MERRICK, John
MERRY, James Samuel
METCALF, Alfred Sargison
METCALF, John Atkinson
METCALFE, Frank Reginald
METCALFE, Frederick Butler
MEW, Herbert Alexander
MICHAEL, William
MICHELL, Albert Edward
MICHIE, William
MIDDLEBROOK, William
MIDDLETON, George Irvine
MIDDLETON, John West
MIDDLETON, Stanley John
MIDDLETON, Thomas Ernest
MIDGLEY, Thomas
MIELL, Albert
MIHAN, Arthur William
MILBOURNE, Jack Drake
MILES, George
MILES, John William
MILES, Keith Wentworth
MILES, Thomas Richard
MILEY, Clarence Walter
MILFORD, Walter
MILGATE, Frederick John
MILLAR, Percy Edgar Wraight
MILLEN, Charles John
MILLER, Albert
MILLER, Albert Henry
MILLER, Alexander
MILLER, David
MILLER, Ernest Cresswell
MILLER, George
MILLER, James
MILLER, James Edgar
MILLER, James Russell
MILLER, John
MILLER, John Christian
MILLER, John Marshall
MILLER, John Moffat
MILLER, John William
MILLER, Leonard William
MILLER, Leslie Washington
MILLER, Percy
MILLER, Randolph
MILLER, Robert Glencairn
MILLER, Thomas
MILLER, William Ernest
MILLER, William Herbert
MILLHOUSE, Horace Clyde
MILLINGTON, Harry Lees
MILLOY, Edward John
MILLS, Albert James
MILLS, Charles John
MILLS, David George
MILLS, Ernest Murray
MILLS, Frederick John
MILLS, Hessel Sydney
MILLS, John Brier
MILLS, Thomas Hamlyn
MILNE, James
MILNE, James Spence
MILNE, Peter
MILNE, William
MILSON, Stewart
MILTON, William Henry
MINCHAM, Walter Wilton
MINOGUE, William David
MINORS, William
MINTER, Henry
MITCHELL, Angus
MITCHELL, Archibald McFadyen

MITCHELL, Charles Sinclair
MITCHELL, Edward John
MITCHELL, Edwin
MITCHELL, Harold
MITCHELL, Hubert Clarence
MITCHELL, John Harrington
MITCHELL, Keith
MITCHELL, Robert Reid
MITCHELL, William
MITCHELSON, Frederick Daniel
MITCHISON, Matthews
MOAR, William Douglas
MOBBS, William George Delmar
MOBILIA, Lawrence Felix
MOFFAT, Ernest Cameron
MOFFATT, Richard Benjamin
MOFFLIN, Percy Sutherland
MOGG, Leslie Valentine
MOIR, Joseph Russel
MOIR, Robert Webster
MOLONY, Leo Thomas
MONCRIEFF, George
MONEY, William Henry
MONGER, Adrian Calero
MONKS, Leslie Thomas
MONKS, William Gladstone
MONSEY, Harold Charles
MONTAGUE, Alexander
MONTEITH, Frederick Charles
MONTGOMERY, James
  Alexander
MONTGOMERY, Wallace
  Douglas
MOODY, Charles Edward
MOODY, Fred
MOODY, Robert Alexander
MOON, Phillip William George
  Elphick
MOOR, Edward
MOORE, Alexander
MOORE, Arthur
MOORE, Edmon Alfred
MOORE, Ernest
MOORE, Ernest Ephraim
MOORE, George Douglas
MOORE, George Ernest
MOORE, James Anderson
MOORE, John Ramsey
MOORE, Oswald Walter
MOORE, Reginald Johnstone
MOORE, Stanley Gordon
MOORE, Thomas Ernest
  Llewellyn
MOORE, William
MOOREHEAD, Frank McCrae
MOORHOUSE, Ernest William
MORAN, Daniel William
MORAN, Francis
MORE, Arthur
MORELL, Charles
MOREN, William George
MORETON, Archibald Herbert
MORGAN, Daniel
MORGAN, George
MORGAN, Henry Eustace
MORGAN, Hugh Fuller
MORGAN, Patrick
MORGAN, Patrick
MORGAN, Robert William
MORGAN, Walter
MORGAN, Walter John
MORGAN, William John Pike
MORGAN, William Marshall
MORGAN, William Thomas
MORISON, Donald Rutherford
MORLEY, Rupert George
MORLEY, Walter

MORPHETT, Glenton Stuart
  Victor
MORPHETT, Robert Ernest
MORPHETT, William
MORRELL, Harold Joseph
MORREN, Frederick William
MORRICE, William John
MORRIS, Cecil William
MORRIS, Edward Hezekiah
MORRIS, Edward Owen Wynne
MORRIS, Francis Robert
MORRIS, Frank
MORRIS, George
MORRIS, George
MORRIS, George Henry
MORRIS, Herbert Richard
MORRIS, John Cyril Ashton
MORRIS, Morgan
MORRIS, William
MORRIS, William Edwin Cecil
MORRISBY, Percy Frank
MORRISH, Frank Sinclair
MORRISON, George
MORRISON, John Max
MORRISON, Milo James
MORRISON, Robert
MORRISON, Roderick Evan
MORRISON, Roderick Henry
MORRISSEY, Michael
MORRISSEY, Patrick
MORRISSEY, Pierce Patrick
MORROGH, Henry Edward
MORROW, Albert
MORROW, Norman Harold
MORSCHEL, Patrick Francis
MORSHEAD, Herbert Dillon
  Edward
MORTIMORE, Edward John
MORTON, Gavin
MORTON, George Adolphus
  Herbert
MOSELEY, John Percy
MOSEY, George Bertram
MOSS, Arthur
MOSS, Edward Elias
MOSS, Frederick Vincent
MOSS, George William
MOSS, Herbert
MOSS, John
MOSS, Robert Hugh
MOTTARELLI, Ferdinando
MOUAT, Frank Wilson
MOULAND, Edgar
MOULE, Humphry Osborne
MOULTON, Richard Ralph
MOUNSEY, George Reginald
MOUNTAIN, Arthur Henry
  Torres
MOUNTAIN, Laurence Smith
MOUNTJOY, John Adam
MOURITZ, Leofwin Beresford
MOW, William Victor
MOWAT, William Duncan
  Finlayson
MOWBRAY, John
MOY, James
MOY, Patrick Joseph
MOYNIHAN, Patrick James
MOYNIHAN, William Daniel
MOYSEY, James Edgar
MOZAR, Alwyn Willie
MUDDLE, Ernest
MUDIE, John
MUIR, Frederick Warren
MUIR, Hugh
MUIR, William Herbert
MUIRSON, Richard Thomas
MULCAHY, Michael Thomas

MULLAN, John
MULLANE, William Edward
MULLER, Albert Herbert
MULLER, John Clifford
MULLIGAN, Leo
MULLIN, Albert
MULLOY, Edward
MULVEY, Frederic Christie
MUMBY, Thomas
MUMMERY, Albert
MUNCEY, Thomas Francis
MUNCKTON, Robert
MUNN, Allan Shepherd
MUNN, Ronald Thompson
MUNRO, Donald
MUNRO, Frederick
MUNRO, Gordon Albert
MUNRO, Hector Watson
MUNRO, James
MUNRO, Joseph Graham
MUNRO, Norman Alexander
MUNRO, Philip Henry
MUNRO, William Henry
MUNTON, Thomas
MURDEN, James
MURDEN, Robert Raymond
MURDOCH, Reece Morris Lee
MURE, George Ellery
MURPHY, Cecil William
MURPHY, Cornelius Joseph
MURPHY, Francis Joseph Patrick
MURPHY, George Lawrence
MURPHY, Henry Blaney
MURPHY, James
MURPHY, John
MURPHY, John George
MURPHY, Peter John
MURPHY, Richard William
MURPHY, Thomas
MURPHY, Timothy Anthony
MURPHY, William Clifton
MURPHY, William Patrick
MURR, Henry Thomas
MURRAY, Angus
MURRAY, Austin Henry
MURRAY, Charles
MURRAY, David James
MURRAY, Frederick Mozart
MURRAY, James Joseph
MURRAY, James Martin
MURRAY, John Henry
MURRAY, Joseph Gray
MURRAY, Norman Louis
MURRAY, Owen
MURRAY, Thomas Frederick
MURRAY, Thomas Richard
MURRAY, Vernon William
MURRAY, William Herbert
MURTAGH, Henry
MUSGRAVE, Andrew Bremner
MUSGROVE, Reginald
  Hainsworth
MUSTARD, Alexander
MYCHAEL, Archibald John
MYERS, Frank Horace
MYNARD, Charles
NAGHTEN, John
NAISH, Ernest
NAISMITH, William Ivie
NANKIVILL, Lee Bray
NAPIER, Charles Archibald
NAPIER, George Alfred
NAPPER, Leonard Templar
NASH, Allan William
NASH, Brunel John
NASH, Harold Leslie
NAWELL, Charles Henry
NAYLOR, Arthur Albert

NEAL, Frederick McRae
NEAL, George
NEATE, William Harringay Evelyn
NEAVE, George Danford
NEAVES, Alfred Ernest
NEEDHAM, Charles William
  Hector
NEELY, John
NEGRO, Frederick James
NEIL, John
NEILSON, Harry
NEILSON, William
NELMES, Arthur Reginald
NELSON, Albert Ernest
NELSON, Gordon Ernest
NESBITT, Thomas Hudson
NESBITT, Thomas John
NETTLETON, Burdett Philip
NEVETT, William Percy
NEVILLE, William
NEVISON, Donald
NEWALL, George Lawrence
NEWBEGIN, Frank Albert
NEWBOUND, George Albert
NEWBURY, William Herbert
NEWELL, Henry Lewis
NEWHAM, John Drummond
NEWHOUSE, George
NEWMAN, Edward Joseph
NEWMAN, Ernest Walter
NEWTON, John
NEWTON, Owen Eric
NEWTON, Roland
NEWTON, Walter Edward
NICHOLLS, Frank
NICHOLLS, Hilton Stuart
NICHOLLS, Roy Elgin
NICHOLS, Norman Leslie
NICHOLSON, Hugh Milne
NICHOLSON, Robert Hugh
  Bright
NICKLEN, Ernest
NICOLL, George Alfred
NICOLL, John
NICOLL, William Hamilton
NICOLSON, Archibald
NICOLSON, John
NISSEN, Charles Bertholdt
NIVEN, William David
NIXON, Edward
NOAD, Harry Bowlin
NOAKE, Ralph Israel Marshall
NOAKES, Thomas George
NOBLE, Allan
NOLAN, Edmund James
NOLAN, Gerald
NOLLER, William Arthur
NOONAN, Thomas
NORBURY, Ernest Edward
NORDBERG, George Francis
NORMAN, Alfred
NORMAN, Charles Henry
NORMAN, Edward
NORRIS, Edwin Charles
NORRIS, Thomas Milton
NORRIS, Walter Herbert
NORTH, William Edward
NORTHEY, William Reginald
  Eustace
NORTON, Alfred Joseph
NORTON, Clarence Edwin
NORTON, Roland
NORTON, William
NORTON, William Thomas
NORWOOD, Sydney Oxborough
NOTT, Leslie Norman
NOWLAN, James Michael
NUGENT, Arthur George

NUGENT, Eugene
NUNN, Ernest Verril
NYE, Lawrence
O'BREE, William Henry
O'BRIEN, Branden Charles Joseph
O'BRIEN, Frederick Leslie
O'BRIEN, John
O'BRIEN, Michael Thomas
O'BRIEN, Percy John
O'BRIEN, Philip
O'BRIEN, Terence Leslie
O'BRIEN, Thomas Vincent
O'BRIEN, William
O'BRIEN, William Arthur
O'BRIEN, William Harold
O'BRIEN, William Patrick
O'BRYAN, John Thomas
O'BYRNE, Thomas
O'BYRNE, Thomas Patrick
O'CALLAGHAN, Michael
O'CONNOR, Daniel
O'CONNOR, Edward
O'CONNOR, James
O'CONNOR, John James
O'CONNOR, John Joseph
O'CONNOR, Michael
O'CONNOR, William Henry
O'CONNOR, William Miles
O'DELL, Martin
O'DONAHOO, Arthur Herbert
  Graham
O'DONNELL, Ewart Sylvester
O'DONNELL, Hugh Brian
O'DONNELL, James Charles
O'DONOGHUE, James Maurice
O'DONOHUE, Maurice
O'DONOVAN, Daniel
O'DWYER, Michael John
O'FARRELL, James Patrick
O'GRADY, Bernard Edward
O'GRADY, John
O'GRADY, Standish Lockhardt
  Matheison
O'HALLORAN, Arthur Hector
O'HARE, Michael
O'HEA, Michael David
O'KEEFE, Patrick Joseph
O'LEARY, Daniel James
O'LEARY, David Patrick
O'LEARY, Henry Augustus
O'LEARY, John
O'LEARY, John
O'LEARY, Thomas
O'LEARY, William John
O'LOGHLEN, Francis Anthony
  Butler
O'LOUGHLIN, George
O'LOUGHLIN, Michael
O'LOUGHLIN, Patrick John
O'MALLEY, Jeremiah Thomas
O'MEARA, John
O'MULLANE, Bernard Lindsay
O'NEIL, Albert
O'NEILL, Jeremiah
O'NEILL, Lyle Hugh Florian
O'NEILL, Sydney John
O'NEILL, William
O'NEILL, William Henry
O'REILLY, Edward James
O'ROURKE, James Lawrence
O'ROURKE, Samuel
O'SHANNASSY, Richard Ernest
O'SHEA, Vincent Churchwood
O'SULLIVAN, John
O'SULLIVAN, Otho Joseph
OAKES, Alexander Montague
OAKES, Arthur Wellesley
OAKES, Harry

OAKLEY, William Henry
OATS, Herbert George
ODGERS, Archie
ODY, John Andrew Wilberforce
OGILVY, James
OGLE, William
OLDHAM, Edward Castle
OLDHAM, Reginald Le Poer
OLDS, Cyril
OLIVE, Walter George
OLIVER, Cecil Claude
OLIVER, Robert Jonah
OLLEY, Allan Robert
OLSEN, Charles
OLSEN, Charles Thorwald Sererin
OMAN, John
ONLEY, William Henry
OPIE, Victor Alan
ORCHARD, Gilbert Andinwood
ORMEROD, George Booth
ORMSBY, Robert Henry
ORR, Joseph
ORTT, George Ernest
OSBORN, Oliver James
OSBORN, Stephen
OSBORNE, Alexander Henry
OSBORNE, George Ernest
OSBORNE, Ray Foster
OSBORNE, William Henry John
OSWIN, Albert Edward
OTIS, Ernest George
OWEN, John Henry
OWEN, John Richard
OWEN, John Stanley
OWEN, Percy Thomas
OWEN-SMYTH, Trevor
OWENS, John
OWENS, Leslie John
OXER, Arthur Lucas
OXFORD, Bernard Fred
OXLADE, Edward
OZANNE, Eugene Charles Arthur
PACEY, Montague John Durnford
PACEY, William Lenard
PADDON, Frederick George
PAGE, Charles
PAGE, Cleveland Edmund
PAGE, Stanley
PAGE, Thomas Alwyn McDonald
PAICE, Charles Edward
PAINE, Henry Arthur
PALFREYMAN, John Wilson
PALIN, Archibald Edward
PALLOT, Ernest Ralph
PALMER, Charles Frederick
PALMER, David William
PALMER, Edwin Samuel
PALMER, Maurice Weston
PALMER, Roger Ebden Harcourt
PALMER, Rupert Alexander
PALMER, Thomas George William
PANTLIN, James Randall
PAPLEY, Leonard Aloysius
PARIS, George Charles
PARISH, Leslie
PARISH, Montague
PARK, Albert
PARK, Archibald Royston
PARK, Clyde Hamilton
PARK, James
PARK, John William
PARK, Wallace
PARK, William Wallace
PARKER, Arthur
PARKER, Erroll Alexander
PARKER, Harry Frederick
PARKER, Henry William
PARKER, John Wallace

PARKER, Joseph
PARKER, Louis Victor
PARKER, William Charles
PARKER, William Clarence
PARKES, David
PARKES, Sidney Ernest
PARKHOUSE, Harry Hubert
PARKINSON, Gordon Wynne
PARKINSON, Harry Stroud
PARKINSON, Vere
PARMENTER, Albert Osborne
PARMITER, Charles
PARNABY, George
PARRINGTON, William Eric
PARROTT, Lionel Eric
PARRY, Athol Wynne
PARRY, Harry Leslie
PARRY, Herbert Henry
PARSONS, Alfred James
PARSONS, George Ernest
PARSONS, Percy James
PARSONS, Thomas
PARSONS, William
PARSONSON, Cecil Claude
PARTRIDGE, Edgar Charles
PARTRIDGE, Ernest
PARTRIDGE, Thomas Douglas
PASCALL, Arthur Edwin
PASCOE, Joseph Henry
PASCOE, Victor Harold
PASSMORE, Phillip Marich
PATCHETT, John
PATERSON, Daniel Wallace
PATERSON, David
PATERSON, Francis Milton
PATERSON, Harold James
PATERSON, John
PATERSON, Stanley Duncan
PATON, James Hart
PATON, William Hannah
PATRICK, Walter John Wardrop
PATTERSON, Penistan James
PATTERSON, Raymond Walter
PATTERSON, Robert Gerald
PATTON, Eric Wyatt
PATTRICK, Erroll McLeod Nunn
PAUL, Andrew Cameron
PAUL, Claude Stanley
PAUL, Ernest Clifton
PAUL, Frank Henderson
PAUL, John Charles
PAUL, Lawrence James
PAULET, Arthur Forbes
PAULEY, William Thomas
PAULIG, Albert James
PAULIG, Henry Julius
PAULL, Leslie Ewart
PAVEY, Harold Gilbert
PAVEY, James Edward
PAVITT, George
PAVLICH, Henry John
PAWLEY, Arthur James
PAYNE, Elford Athol
PAYNE, Frederick
PAYNE, Leonard Parker
PAYNE, Wilfred Henry
PAYNE, William Thomas
PEACOCKE, Gerald Fitzroy
PEAD, Seymour William
PEAKE, Edwin Ashley
PEARCE, Abraham
PEARCE, Ambrose Stanley
PEARCE, Arthur Mueller
PEARCE, Charles
PEARCE, Edward Charles Henry
PEARCE, Frank Eugene
PEARCE, Henry Hathaway
PEARCE, Richard Henry

PEARCE, Samuel Albert
PEARCE, Wilfred Ernest
PEARCE, Wilfred Morris
PEARSE, Bertram Wellesley
PEARSON, Arthur Albert
PEARSON, Frederick Francis
PEARSON, James Burrows
PEARSON, John Bell
PEARSON, Russell
PEARSON, Stanley Crawle
PEARSON, William James
PEASLEY, Leonard Francis
PEAT, Charles Riach
PEAT, Leonard Hugh
PECK, Frederick John
PEDEN, Harry
PEDLEY, Ernest Victor Starkey
PEGLER, Henry
PELL, Frederick Edgar
PENE, Norman
PENHALIGON, Sydney John
PENINGTON, William Ronald
PENN, Mayson
PENNELLS, Charles Percy
PENNINGTON, Rowland John
   Robert
PENNY, Ernest William
PENROSE, Reginald Arthur
PENTECOST, Thomas
PENTLAND, Sydney
PENTON, William
PERKINS, Clarence Norbert Clyde
PERKINS, Robert Raymond
PERKINS, William John
PERKINS, William Taylor
PERMEZEL, Cedric Holroyd
PERNONIE, Clarence Sydney
PERRAU, Robert James Joseph
PERRETT, Francis Evan
PERROTT, Cecil Hubert
PERROTT, Harry James
PERROTTET, Bernard James
PERRY, Frank Davey
PERRY, Leslie
PERRY, Malcolm George
PESCOD, Ernest Owen
PESCOD, Lewis George
PETER, Robert
PETERS, David
PETERS, Herbert John
PETERS, William George
PETERSEN, George
PETERSEN, William Jens Peter
PETERSON, Edward
PETERSON, Grahame King Page
PETERSON, John George
PETERSON, Leonard
PETERSON, Lionel Joseph
PETERSON, William
PETTERSON, Sydney Leonard
PETTET, Stanley Robert
PETTIGREW, Angus George
PETTIGREW, Trafford Cyril
PETTINGER, George Lawrence
PETTIS, Alfred James
PHEASE, Reginald Arthur
PHELPS, Harry
PHILIP, George
PHILIPPSON, William Felix
PHILLIPS, Aaron Frederick
   William
PHILLIPS, Albert
PHILLIPS, Charles Raymond
PHILLIPS, Clifford Oswald
PHILLIPS, Frederick Roquette
PHILLIPS, James Hamilton
PHILLIPS, John Eddy
PHILLIPS, Leslie Robert

PHILLIPS, Martin Oliver
PHILLIPS, Thomas Harold
PHILLIPS, Waterford
PHILLIS, Horace Vincent
PHILLPOTTS, Hugh Arthur
PHILP, David
PICAUD, Michell
PICKARD, Percy
PICKERING, Sydney Albert
PICKETT, James Burnett
PICKETT, John Victor
PICKUP, William John
PIDGEON, Thomas Sidney
PIERCE, Iveson John
PIERCE, Jack
PIESSE, Vernon Frederick
PIGGOTT, Charles Henry
PIGGOTT, Ellis James
PIGGOTT, Frederick Edward
PIGGOTT, John
PIKE, Hillary Austin
PIKE, Leonard Charles
PILE, Norman Wallace
PILKINGTON, Ashley Ford
PILKINGTON, Thomas
PIMM, Frederick
PIMM, William Henry
PINDER, Thomas Wesley
PINK, Thomas George
PINKERTON, William
PINKERTON, William Harold
PINKNEY, Frederick James
PINKSTONE, Victor John
PINTO, Thomas Joseph
PIPER, Jack Dolph
PIPER, Keith Stuart Mackenzie
PITHER, Frederic Henry
PITTENDRIGH, Edmund
PITTENDRIGH, Norman Thomas
PITTENDRIGH, Robert Reginald
   H
PITTS, Arthur Thomas
PLACE, Ernest William
PLANE, Alfred
PLANT, Percy George
PLATER, Charles William
PLATT, Francis Joseph
PLATT, George
PLATT, James William
PLAYER, Reginald
PLAYNE, John Morton
PLIMMER, Harold
PLUMB, Philip
PLUMLEY, Charles Edward
PLUMMER, Charles Edward
PLUMMER, Edward
PLUMMER, James Willis
PLUMMER, John Thomas
PLUNKETT, George
POHATU, Karanema
POLDEN, William
POLKINGHORNE, Clifford
POLLARD, Fred
POLLEY, Harry
POLLOCK, James Sterling
POLLOCK, Walter Stevenson
POLLOCK, William Alexander
POLSSON, Axel Oscar
POOL, Charles Thomas
POOLE, Gordon Alfred
POOLE, Leslie Joseph
POOLE, Robert William
POOLE, Samuel
POPE, Frederick
POPE, Herbert
POPE, John Gladstone
POPLE, William
POPPLEWELL, Cecil

POPPLEWELL, John
PORTEOUS, Robert
PORTER, Norman James
PORTER, Sydney Nathaniel
PORTER, William James
POSSINGHAM, Alfred Harold
POSTLETHWAITE, John Joyce
POTTER, Arthur Clarence
POTTER, Arthur Valentine
POTTER, Thomas Henry
POTTS, William John
POUGET, William
POUNTNEY, Claude Hastings
POWELL, Baynard
POWER, James
POWER, James Alfred Michael
POWER, William Jeffrey
POWIS, Michael
POWLEY, Charles
POYNER, William
POYNER, William Lees
POYNTZ, Rowland Ridgway
POZZI, Leonard Lambert
PRAIN, William Charles
PRATER, Bertie Lawrence
PRATT, Charles Frederick
PRATT, Frederic Charles
PRATT, George James
PRATT, Leopold Clarence
PREDDY, Frederick Robert
PREECE, Allan
PREECE, Henry Edward Ernest
PRENTICE, Victor
PRESTON, Geoffrey Allison
   Congdon
PRESTON, George
PRESTON, George William
PRESTON, Richard
PRESTON, William
PRETTY, Frank
PRETTY, Fred Victor
PRICE, Andrew
PRICE, Arthur
PRICE, Charles Edward
PRICE, Harry Edward
PRICE, Hilton Clifford
PRICE, James Owen
PRICE, John Leslie
PRICE, Leslie Cecil
PRICE, Percy
PRICE, Walter
PRICE, William George
PRIDEAUX, George Richard
PRIESTLEY, Henry James Vivian
PRIMROSE, Frederick Devine
PRING, Harold James
PRINGLE, George
PRINGLE, Thornburn
PRIOR, Harry
PRISK, Herbert George
PRITCHARD, Allen Johnson
PRITCHARD, Jesse
PRITCHARD, William
PROBETS, Arthur
PROCKTER, Charlton Hogarth
PROCTER, Walter William Gourd
PROCTOR, Charles Howard
PROTHEROE, Thomas Alexander
PROUSE, James Charles
PRUTTON, Frank
PRYCE, Alan
PRYOR, Charles Joseph
PRYOR, James Joshua
PSHEVOLODSKEY, Marian
PUCKLE, Charles Edward Murray
PUDDEPHATT, Frederick Charles
PUGSLEY, Arthur Horace
PUGSLEY, William Roy

PULLEINE, James Bryant
PULLING, Charles Willoughby
   Lee
PURCELL, James Osmond
PURCELL, Owen
PURVES, Godfrey Liddell
PURVES, William Richard Walter
PUTLAND, George Arthur Temple
PUTLAND, Wesley James Ethersey
PUTT, Arthur Sydney
PYE, Harold Hume
PYE, Reginald Leslie
PYKE, John Frederick
PYLE, George Henry
PYNE, Patrick Thomas
QUAMBY, John Thomas
QUARRELL, George Joseph Basil
QUARRIE, Walter Hugh
QUARTERMAN, Guy William
QUEGAN, John
QUIGLEY, James William
QUINN, Charles
QUINN, Hugh
QUINN, John William
QUIRKE, William Michael
RACKSTRAW, Alexander Russell
RADCLIFFE, Alan Arthur
RADCLIFFE, Frederick
RADFORD, Arthur
RADFORD, Walter Francis
RADOS, Peter
RADOSEVICH, George
RAE, Alexander
RAE, Alexander Ramsey
RAE, John William
RAEBURN, Thomas Walter
   Henery
RAFTON, Harry
RAGGATT, Frederick Joseph
RAINBOW, Oscar Allan
RAISTRICK, Harry
RALPH, James Andrew
RAMAGE, Ernest
RAMAGE, Thomas Stanley
RAMSBOTTOM, John Alan
RANDALL, Francis Hugh
RANDALL, William Charles
RANKIN, David
RANKIN, John Edward Alexander
RANKIN, Reginald Henry Bede
RAPKINS, Frank
RAPSEY, Jesse
RASDELL, Harold William
RATCLIFF-GAYLARD, Cecil
   Charles Alexander
RATCLIFFE, James
RATCLIFFE, John Percy
RATHIE, Archibald Anderson
RATTRAY, Benjamin
RAWLINGS, Frank Albert
RAWLINS, Arthur
RAWLINSON, Arthur James
RAY, Alexander Leslie
RAY, Walter
RAYFIELD, Edward Woodman
RAYMOND, Victor Nassau
RAYNER, Alfred Stanley
RAYNER, William Thomas
REA, Walter Everard
REABURN, William
READ, Alexander James
READ, Cyril George Moore
READ, Richard James Reginald
READE, Colin Morgan
READING, Leslie James
REAY, William
REDCLIFFE, Gordon
REDFERN, Joseph Thomas

REDFORD, John Alan
REDFORD, Thomas Harold
REDMAYNE, James
REDMOND, Herbert
REDPATH, Robert John Irvine
REECE, Edward
REECE, Joseph Thomas
REED, Clair William
REED, Leonard Harold
REED, Mark
REEN, Cecil Felix
REES, George Alfred
REES, William Goldney
REEVE, Harold Thomas Fredric
REEVE, Harry Morrell
REEVE, Leslie Harold
REEVES, Frederick
REEVES, Thomas Henry
REEVES, Walter
REGESTER, William Edward
REID, Cyril Lindsay
REID, Ernest Gray
REID, Frederick Charles
REID, Harry Lansbury Urquhart
REID, James Moffat
REID, John
REID, John Dill
REID, Mordant Leslie
REID, Reginald Malcolm
REID, Thomas
REIDY, Henry Joseph
REIS, Robert Vincent
RENEHAN, Anthony Thomas
RENFREW, Robert Houston
RENN, Ernest George
RENNER, Louis Frederick
RENNIE, Fred
RENSHAW, Albert Edward
RENSHAW, Frederick William
REUBENICHT, Robert
REX, Percy Hugh
REYNELL, Carew
REYNOLDS, Albert Lawrence
REYNOLDS, Edward Thomas
REYNOLDS, Fred
REYNOLDS, Frederick
REYNOLDS, Harry Bertram
REYNOLDS, Hugh
REYNOLDS, James William
REYNOLDS, Walter
REYNOLDS, William George
RHODES, John Henry Wilcock
RICE, Frank Sutherland
RICE, Henry Phillip
RICE, Sylvester Albert
RICH, Stanley Clement
RICH, Thomas
RICHARDS, Edward Sydney
RICHARDS, Ernest
RICHARDS, Frederick Jas
   Archibald
RICHARDS, Frederick William
RICHARDS, George Victor
RICHARDS, Harry
RICHARDS, Leslie Lancelott
RICHARDS, Lionel
RICHARDS, Samuel Jabez
RICHARDSON, Alfred
RICHARDSON, Arthur
RICHARDSON, Cuthbert Noel
RICHARDSON, Francis Gordon
RICHARDSON, Frederick
RICHARDSON, George Henry
RICHARDSON, George Laurence
RICHARDSON, George Thomas
RICHARDSON, Reginald Wallace
RICHARDSON, Roy Everard
RICHARDSON, Rupert Noel

RICHARDSON, William Henry
RICHMOND, Alexander
RICHMOND, Alexander Hood
RICKARD, Harry Cecil
RIDDELL, John Brownen
RIDDLE, George
RIDGE, Albert Victor
RIDGE, William
RIDGWAY, Isaac Althorp
RIDLEY, James
RIDLEY, Wallace Purcell
RIEKIE, Henry John
RIGBY, William John
RIGBY, William Thomas
RIGBYE, Percy
RILEY, Albert
RILEY, William Edward
RILEY, William Thomas
RILOT, Joseph Charles
RING, William John
RIORDAN, John Hastings
RISMONDI, Francis Leslie
RITCHIE, Frank Lane
RITCHIE, Thomas
RIVETT, David Edgar
RIXON, George Vincent
RIXON, William Keith
ROACH, Wallie Passmore
ROADS, Richard Leslie
ROBARDS, Edgar Reuben
ROBB, John George
ROBBINS, Frederick Daniel
ROBBINS, Thomas
ROBERTS, Abraham Reginald
ROBERTS, Alexander Francis
    Dawe
ROBERTS, Charles Aubrey
ROBERTS, Darcy James
ROBERTS, David
ROBERTS, Ernest Ambrose
ROBERTS, Geoffrey William
ROBERTS, George MacFarlane
ROBERTS, Harry
ROBERTS, Henry George
ROBERTS, John Elias
ROBERTS, John George
ROBERTS, John Meyrick
ROBERTS, John Powe
ROBERTS, Norman
ROBERTS, Percy McDonald
ROBERTS, Samuel Arthur
ROBERTS, Trevor Evans
ROBERTS, Walter Frank
ROBERTS, William Donald
ROBERTS, William Lennard
ROBERTSHAW, Bartimas
ROBERTSHAW, Herbert Maurice
ROBERTSON, Alexander John
ROBERTSON, Colin Ernest
ROBERTSON, David
ROBERTSON, David
ROBERTSON, Donald Athol
ROBERTSON, Frank Leslie
ROBERTSON, George
ROBERTSON, Gordon Holmes
ROBERTSON, John
ROBERTSON, John Thomas
ROBERTSON, Kenneth
ROBERTSON, Leslie Ernest
ROBERTSON, Ralph
ROBERTSON, Robert
ROBERTSON, Roy Henderson
ROBERTSON, Sydney Beresford
ROBERTSON, Thomas
ROBERTSON, William
ROBERTSON, William David
ROBERTSON, William George
    Weston

ROBERTSON, William Henry
ROBERTSON, William Ormiston
ROBERTSON, William Thomas
ROBIN, Philip de Quetteville
ROBINS, Alfred Arthur
ROBINS, Angus Bruce
ROBINSON, Arthur John
ROBINSON, Bertie
ROBINSON, Cecil James
ROBINSON, Charles Archibald
ROBINSON, Harold Frederick
ROBINSON, Hugh
ROBINSON, Jack
ROBINSON, James Murray
    Hannah
ROBINSON, John Henry
ROBINSON, John William
ROBINSON, Joseph William
ROBINSON, Oliver Francis
ROBINSON, Robert
ROBINSON, Robert Melville
ROBINSON, Samuel Moreland
ROBSON, Frederick
ROBSON, Henry
ROBSON, Percy
ROBSON, Thomas Keith Macleod
ROCHE, David
ROCHESTER, Alfred Windsor
ROCKE, Cecil Harry
RODDIS, George Frederick
RODEN, George
RODERICK, Frederick
RODGERS, Thomas
ROE, Arthur Charles
ROE, Edward
ROE, Henry Graem
ROE, Sydney Clarence
ROEBUCK, Francis Henry
ROFFEY, Frank Alan
ROGASCH, Edward Albert
    George
ROGERS, Albert Thomas
ROGERS, Arthur Ernest
ROGERS, David
ROGERS, George Rowland
ROGERS, George Sandilands
ROGERS, John
ROGERS, John
ROGERS, John Alexander
ROLFE, Henry
ROLLASON, John Thomas
ROLLESTON, William
ROLLS, Oscar Silvester
RONALD, Kenneth McGeorge
RONALD, William Alfred
RONCHETTI, Charles Thomas
    Gould
ROOKE, Charles Keith Jago
ROOKE, Francis Pyburn
ROONEY, John J
ROONEY, Norman Prior
ROOTES, William Henry
ROSA, Oscar Eurtol
ROSE, Andrew
ROSE, George Thomas
ROSE, George William
ROSE, Harold Herbert
ROSE, John
ROSE, Oswald
ROSE, William Clifton
ROSENBROCK, Reginald
ROSKAMS, Leopold James Cecil
ROSS, Charles Hulm
ROSS, Frederick
ROSS, Hugh Chisholm
ROSS, James
ROSS, James Forbes
ROSS, John

ROSS, John
ROSS, Peter John
ROSS, Philip Andrew Rowan
ROSS, Thomas Spurgeon
ROSS, Walter Charles
ROSS, William
ROSS, William
ROSS, William Allardyce
ROSS, William Andrew
ROSSER, Hubert
ROSSITER, Reginald James
ROTHERY, Henry Norman
ROTTON, Henry George Eardley
ROUT, Charles Francis
ROUTLEDGE, John
ROW, Richard
ROWAN, Andrew Percival
ROWAN, David
ROWAN, John Scott
ROWDER, Guy Walter
ROWE, Alfred Edward James
ROWE, Louis Bernard
ROWE, Oswald Robert
ROWE, Reginald Lewis
ROWE, Rowland
ROWE, Thomas James
ROWE, William
ROWELL, Frank Milton
ROWLAND, Arthur John
ROWLAND, Henry Herbert
ROWLAND, Herbert James
ROWLANDS, Robert Whitfield
ROWLES, Victor
ROWLEY, Ernest Fitzroy
ROWLEY, George Albert
ROWLEY, William Ronald Leslie
ROY, Eric Gentle
ROY, William
RUBIE, George Robert
RUDD, Thomas Adamthwaite
RUDD, William
RULE, James Campbell
RUMBOL, George Frederick
RUMNEY, Harold
RUNDLE, John
RUSH, George Alfred
RUSH, Harold
RUSHFORTH, Norman Mervyn
RUSHTON, Charles William
RUSHTON, George William
RUSHTON, John Baker
RUSK, Richard John
RUSK, Walter Jordan
RUSSELL, Charles Alexander
    George
RUSSELL, Percy Benedict
RUSSELL, Phillip Henry
RUSSELL, Robert
RUSSELL, Russell Gordon
RUSSELL, Timothy
RUSSELL, William George
RUTHVEN, Sutherland Charles
RUTLAND, John Bishop
RUTTER, Frederick William
    Gabert
RUWOLDT, Heinrich Carl Ludwig
RYAN, Daniel James
RYAN, Edward
RYAN, James
RYAN, James
RYAN, James
RYAN, James Harold
RYAN, James Richard
RYAN, John Barry
RYAN, Michael Frances
RYAN, Michael Joseph
RYAN, Patrick Francis
RYAN, Robert Matthew

RYAN, William Stanislaus
SABBERTON, Ernest Edward
SABINE, Ralph Thomas
SACLIER, Felix David
SADLER, Henry
SADLER, William Edward
SAGE, Thomas Radford
SAKER, Richard
SALMON, Albert Ernest
SALMON, Nathan George
SALMONI, Frederick Stanley
SALOWAY, Charles Henry
SALTAU, Victor Leslie
SALTER, Alfred William
SALTER, John
SAMES, Arthur Albert
SAMPSON, Charles Ernest George
SAMPSON, William
SAMPSON, William Aaron
SAMS, Jack Clyde
SAMWAYS, William Scott
SANDBERG, Frederick
SANDER, Arnold
SANDERCOCK, William Edward
SANDERS, Alexander Macleay
SANDERS, Frederick
SANDERS, Thomas
SANDERS, Victor Joseph
SANDILANDS, Claude Fairfax
SANDSTROM, Swen Addvin
SANDY, George Frederick Henry
SANDY, Henry John
SARGENT, Frederick
SAUNDERS, Colin
SAUNDERS, Reginald Jacob
SAUNDERS, Thomas Henry
SAUNDERS, William George
SAWFORD, Percy Charles
SAWLEY, Harry
SAWTELL, Sydney Clyde
SAXTON, Reuben Oliver
SAYER, George Gordon
SAYERS, Ralph
SAYERS, William John
SAYWELL, Charles William
SCANLAN, Cornelius John
SCARBOROUGH, Herbert
SCHADEL, Ernest John
SCHAEFFER, William Bismark
SCHARNESS, Charles
SCHEIDEL, Norman Phillip
SCHMEDJE, Simon Flood
SCHMIDT, Alexander
SCHMIDT, Henry John
SCHMITT, Joseph
SCHOCROFT, Spencer Lane
SCHOFIELD, Frank
SCHOFIELD, Herbert Victor
SCHOFIELD, Norman Charles
SCHOFIELD, Reginald George
    Hornby
SCHRADER, Carl Lauenstein
SCHUMACHER, Fred
SCHWEITZER, Stanley Grenfell
SCOBIE, Robert
SCOLLIN, William Edward
SCOONES, George Henry
SCOTCHFORD, William George
SCOTT, Albert Stanley
SCOTT, Basil Archdeacon
SCOTT, Clarence
SCOTT, David
SCOTT, David Brand
SCOTT, Douglas Elliott
SCOTT, Edward
SCOTT, Ernest Charles Gordon
SCOTT, Frederick Stanley
SCOTT, George Phillip

SCOTT, Harold
SCOTT, Henry Thomas
SCOTT, James Henry
SCOTT, John Andrew
SCOTT, John Burns
SCOTT, John Kirkpatrick
SCOTT, John Sydney
SCOTT, Kenneth Lindsay
SCOTT, Neil
SCOTT, Robert Thomas
SCOTT, Walter Henry
SCOTT, William
SCOTT, William Alexander
SCOTT, William Pollok
SCOULLER, John Gordon
SCRIVENER, Robert
SEABORN, Harold
SEABROOK, George Henry
SEAGER, George Rothwell
SEAGER, Leonard
SEAMAN, Percy Fredrick William
SEAMAN, Roy
SEAMAN, Walter Batley
SEANEY, Henry James
SEAR, Sackville Joseph
SEARLE, Frank Vivian
SEARLE, John Alexander
SEARLES, Cecil George
SECCOMBE, Frank William
SECCOMBE, Walter Thomas
SEDERY, Charles
SEEGER, John Alfred
SEELEY, Francis James Laurence
SEELEY, Harold George
SEINOR, Reason Hugh
SELDON, Richard Thomas Francis
SELLERS, Frederick
SELLS, Samuel George
SELLS, William John
SELMON, Leonard
SELVAGE, Frederick Charles
SENIOR, Sacheveral George
SERGEANT, John Edwin
SERJEANT, Robert Malachy
SETON, Thomas
SETTERICH, Charles Conrad
SEWELL, Augustus William
SEWELL, Edward
SEWELL, John Thomas
SEYD, Harry George
SEYMOUR, Arthur Thomas Hayes
SEYMOUR, Ernest John Pierpoint
SEYMOUR, Eustace Evelyn Guy
SEYMOUR, Hobart Alfred
SEYMOUR, James
SEYMOUR, William John
SHALLBERG, John Reginald
SHANAHAN, James
SHANNON, John James
SHAPLEY, Edmund Anthony
SHARMAN, Henry James
SHARMAN, Norton John
    Randolph
SHARP, Clarence Roy
SHARP, David John
SHARP, Frederick
SHARP, James Howe
SHARP, John
SHARP, William Ernest
SHARPE, Cecil Herbert
SHARPE, Guy Allen
SHAW, Alfred Thomas
SHAW, Charles
SHAW, Hurtle Charles
SHAW, James
SHAW, James
SHAW, Jesse
SHAW, John George

SHAW, Robert Davidson
SHAW, Sidney Wigmore
SHAW, Thomas
SHAW, William James
SHEARER, Royard Gough
SHEARING, Herbert Harold
SHEARSMITH, Ernest Lloyd
SHEARSTON, Arthur William Reginald
SHEED, William
SHEEDY, James John
SHEEHAN, Albert Edward
SHELDON, Cecil Job
SHELDON, Frederick Laurence
SHELDON, Herbert Stephen
SHELFORD, William
SHELTON, William Haswell
SHENFIELD, Ernest Arthur
SHEPARD, Alec John
SHEPHERD, Benjamin James
SHEPHERD, Clarence
SHEPHERD, John Livingstone
SHEPHERD, Norman Thomas
SHEPHERD, Philip Edwin Bartlett
SHEPHERD, Thomas James
SHEPLEY, Thomas Alan
SHEPPARD, George Henry
SHEPPARD, Sherbourne Haliburton
SHEPPEE, Frederick John
SHERBURNE, Lafayette Alonzo
SHERIDAN, Charles Henry
SHERIDAN, James
SHERIDAN, Stanley Henderson
SHERIDAN, Walter
SHERIDAN, William Owen
SHERLOCK, Alex John
SHERMAN, Godfrey John
SHERMAN, Percy Frederick
SHERRING, Aubrey John Bickley
SHERWIN, Harold Phillip
SHERWOOD, Frederick Herbert
SHERWOOD, Harold Samuel
SHIELLS, David
SHILLINGLAW, John Rowe
SHILLITO, Donald Robert
SHIPHAM, William Casper
SHIPP, Alfred Nathan
SHIPP, Frederick Herbert
SHIPP, Peter Wilfred
SHIRLEY, Raymond Ferres
SHOEBRIDGE, Arthur William
SHOOTER, Harry
SHORE, Phillip Patrick
SHORNEY, Arthur Burton
SHORT, Arthur Gawler
SHORT, Edwin Douglas
SHORT, James Henry
SHORTLAND, Herbert Leslie
SHOUT, Alfred John
SHOWERS, Archibald Robert
SHRUBB, John Howard
SIDDALL, Norman
SIDNEY, Ernest Cecil
SILVA, Vincent Albert
SIMCOCK, David John
SIMM, Frank
SIMMONDS, George Frederick
SIMMONS, Edgar
SIMMONS, Herbert
SIMON, Faulkner Charles Roy
SIMONS, Leslie John
SIMONS, Richard Clyde
SIMONS, Stafford
SIMPSON, Archibald
SIMPSON, Charles Sydney
SIMPSON, George Barre Goldie
SIMPSON, George Cant

SIMPSON, James
SIMPSON, Thomas Gordon
SIMPSON, William Henry
SIMS, James William
SINCLAIR, Augustus William
SINCLAIR, Donald John
SINCLAIR, Herbert Thomas Joseph
SINCLAIR, James
SINCLAIR, Robert Francis Darcy
SINCLAIR, Robert Hector
SINCLAIR, Thomas
SINCLAIR, William
SINCLAIR, William George
SKELLERN, James William
SKENE, Joseph Leo
SKEVINGTON, Frederick
SKIDMORE, Edward William
SKIDMORE, Hector Allan
SKILTON, William Richard Norton
SKIMMING, John Campbell
SKINNER, Charles
SKINNER, Henry William
SKINNER, Herbert
SKINNER, John Robert
SLADE, Frank Thomas
SLADE, Henry Arthur
SLATER, Frank Miller
SLATER, Thomas Henry
SLATTERY, John
SLATTERY, John
SLEDGE, Alfred
SLEE, William
SLEIGHTHOLM, Edmund
SLOAN, James Bowman
SLOAN, Thomas Bowman
SLOANE, William Henry
SLOCOMBE, Robert James
SLOCOMBE, Walter Henry
SLOGGATT, Guy Rosevear
SLOPER, George Edward
SMALE, Alfred John
SMALE, Walter Edward
SMALLEY, Edward Joseph
SMALLS, Michael
SMART, George
SMART, George William
SMART, Henry
SMART, Ira Alfred
SMEDLEY, Arthur Carrington
SMEE, William Henry
SMEETH, Leslie Robert
SMILLIE, James Steel
SMITH, Albert Henry
SMITH, Alexander
SMITH, Alexander John Ross
SMITH, Alexander Sydney
SMITH, Alfred
SMITH, Alfred
SMITH, Alfred Henry
SMITH, Arnold Ashton
SMITH, Arthur
SMITH, Arthur Cecil
SMITH, Arthur James
SMITH, Arthur John
SMITH, Arthur William
SMITH, Bert
SMITH, Charles
SMITH, Charles Leslie
SMITH, Cyril Charles
SMITH, Dale
SMITH, David Augustus
SMITH, David Clement
SMITH, David Thom
SMITH, Edward Thomas
SMITH, Ellis Henry
SMITH, Eoin Lindsay

SMITH, Eric Lyndon
SMITH, Eric Ray
SMITH, Eric Stanley
SMITH, Ernest Albert
SMITH, Ferner
SMITH, Frederick Joseph
SMITH, George
SMITH, George Catt
SMITH, George Frederick Herbert
SMITH, George Holt Henderson
SMITH, George Horace
SMITH, George Robinson
SMITH, George Stoddart
SMITH, George William
SMITH, Gilbert John
SMITH, Harold Bathurst
SMITH, Harold Consort
SMITH, Harold Edward
SMITH, Harold George
SMITH, Harold George
SMITH, Harry Edward
SMITH, Harry Joseph Sinclair
SMITH, Henry Gordon
SMITH, Henry Lewis
SMITH, Herbert
SMITH, Herbert Cleveland
SMITH, Hugh Harold
SMITH, James
SMITH, James
SMITH, James
SMITH, John
SMITH, John Carlisle Alvin
SMITH, John Edward
SMITH, John Inglis
SMITH, John McLennon
SMITH, John Olley
SMITH, John William
SMITH, Joseph
SMITH, Joseph Raymond
SMITH, Leslie Jack
SMITH, Malcolm Teesdale
SMITH, Mark Alexander
SMITH, Maxwell George
SMITH, Muir Paul
SMITH, Norman
SMITH, Percival Leonard
SMITH, Percival Thorne
SMITH, Peter
SMITH, Peter Alix
SMITH, Peter Vincent
SMITH, Quintin Robert
SMITH, Reginald Aubrey John
SMITH, Reuben
SMITH, Richard
SMITH, Richard
SMITH, Richard Joseph
SMITH, Robert Edwin John
SMITH, Samuel
SMITH, Samuel Stanley
SMITH, Samuel William
SMITH, Septimus Sydney
SMITH, Stanley Herbert
SMITH, Sydney
SMITH, Sydney Thomas
SMITH, Thomas
SMITH, Thomas
SMITH, Thomas Hearn
SMITH, Thomas Oscar
SMITH, William Frederick
SMITH, William James
SMITH, William Jeffries
SMITH, William John
SMITH, William John
SMITH, William Patrick
SMYLIE, William Millar
SMYTH, Cyril Bishop
SNELHAM, Arthur
SNELL, Alexander George Henry

SNELL, Francis William
SNODGRASS, Robert
SNOW, Charles Hastings
SNOW, William Arthur
SNUDDEN, Albert
SNUDDEN, William John
SOANES, Henry Donald
SOHIER, Norman Henry
SOLLING, Eric Martin
SOLOMON, Roy Henry
SOMERS, Noel Travers Edgeworth
SOMERVILLE, Edward Reuben
SOMERVILLE, George Davidson
SOONING, James Albert
SOPER, Edgar Alen
SOUTH, Arthur Roy Desborough
SOUTH, Sydney Anthony
SOUTHERN, Arthur Richard
SOUTHERN, Harold Alfred
SOUTHEY, Herbert Edmond
SOWERBY, Robert Coulson
SPAIN, James Michael
SPARGO, Edwin Bennett
SPARKS, Mervyn Hamilton
SPARKS, Roy
SPARROW, Frederick William
SPARROW, Rupert James
SPARSHOTT, Frank
SPELLACY, Frank
SPELLS, Francis
SPENCE, Alfred
SPENCE, Charles
SPENCE, George
SPENCER, Alfred
SPENCER, Christopher Harold
SPENCER, Claude
SPENCER, Edward Howard
SPENCER, Harold John
SPENCER, Henry
SPENCER, John Norman
SPENCER, Robert Ernest
SPENCER, Stephen
SPERBER, William
SPERLING, John Joseph
SPETTS, Charles Wilfred
SPILLANE, Daniel John
SPILSBURY, Edgar Norman Fulton
SPINKS, Laurens Charles
SPOONER, Herbert Frank
SPRAGUE, Francis David Vivian
SPRATT, James Charles
SPRINGALL, John Fred
SPRITCH, Thomas Arthur
SPROSTON, Leonard George
SPRY, Mordaunt
SPURR, Arthur William
SQUIRE, Gordon Clarence
SQUIRES, Frank
STABELL, Charles
STABLES, Edward Pennell
STACE, Thomas
STACH, Vincent Alexander
STACKPOOL, Mathew Aloysins
STAFFORD, Stanley Owen
STAFFORD-MILLS, Ernest Digby
STAGG, John Leslie
STAGGS, Andrew Edward
STAGOLL, John Wesley
STANBRIDGE, Charles Roy
STANBROUGH, Joseph Thomas
STANDFORD, Bert
STANDING, John Albert Theodore
STANFORD, Abraham Joseph
STANISTREET, Andrew
STANLEY, Herbert Edward
STANMORE, Francis
STANNESS, George

STAPLETON, Albert George
STARICK, John Edward
STARKEY, Bernard Samuel Robinson
STARR, Hubert Leigh
STATHAM, Edward Harvey
STATHAM, Sydney Joseph
STEAD, Charles
STEAD, William Henry
STEELE, George William
STEENSON, James Carfrae
STEETH, Walter Joseph
STEIN, Alfred James
STELLING, Gustav
STENT, George
STENZEL, George
STEPHEN, Edwin
STEPHENS, Alan
STEPHENS, Charles
STEPHENS, Robert
STEPHENS, Stanley John
STEPHENS, Thomas
STEPHENSON, John William
STEPHENSON, Noble
STEPHENSON, Roy Kennings
STEPTO, Arthur Phillip Sidney
STEVENS, Eddy Blackwood
STEVENS, Frederick
STEVENS, Harold
STEVENS, Henry Joseph
STEVENS, Richard Harry
STEVENS, Victor Henry
STEVENS, William Henry
STEVENSON, Adam
STEVENSON, Arthur Edward
STEVENSON, George
STEVENSON, James Archibald Brakspear
STEWART, Bruce
STEWART, Charles
STEWART, David
STEWART, Dougald
STEWART, Frank Alfred
STEWART, Hugh Campbell
STEWART, Jack
STEWART, James
STEWART, James
STEWART, James Alexander
STEWART, John
STEWART, John
STEWART, John Donald
STEWART, John William
STEWART, Leslie Stanley
STEWART, Robert
STEWART, Robert Arthur
STEWART, Robert Joseph
STEWART, Russell William
STEWART, Selby Albert Shepherd
STEWART, Thomas
STEWART, William
STEWART, William
STEWART, William
STEWART, William John
STIEBEL, Leonard
STILL, Vivian Roy
STILWELL, Bartholomew George
STINSON, Alexander William
STOBAUS, Ralph Gustav
STOCKDALE, William Hallett
STOKAN, Thomas Clouston
STOKES, Archibald
STOKES, Francis Herbert
STOKES, Henry
STOKES, John George Albert
STOKES, Thomas William
STOKES, Walter John
STOLZ, George Alexander
STONE, Allan Cameron

STONE, George Arthur
STONE, Harry Thomas
STONE, Roy Frank
STONEHAM, Phillip Raphael
STONELL, Alfred Victor
STONELY, Samuel Herbert
STOREY, Frank
STOREY, Frederick
STORRER, Charles Murray
STOTT, Thomas Sydney
STOUT, Henry
STRACHAN, Frederick
STRACHAN, William Leighton
STRACHEY, Claude Otto
STRAHAN, William Henry
STRAKER, George
STRANG, William Andrew
STRATFORD, Herbert Charles
STRATFORD, Joseph
STREET, Joseph Dandy
STREET, Laurence Whistler
STREET, Robert John
STREETER, Roy Charles
STRENGE, Elmore
STRINGER, Jack Edmund
STRUTT, Charles Nettleton
STUART, Gordon Duke
STUART, William Alexander
    Baring Bingham
STUBBS, Hugh Rufus
STUBBS, Vincent Mortimer
STUMBLES, Horace George
STUPART, George Campbell
STURDY, Ernest Walter
STURROCK, David Chalmers
STYLES, Walter John
SUDLOW, Francis Paget
SULLIVAN, Arthur Gilbert
SULLIVAN, Edward Austin
SULLIVAN, James Peter
SULLIVAN, John Phillip
SULLIVAN, Joseph
SULLIVAN, Michael John
SULLIVAN, Raymond
SULLIVAN, Robert Ignatius
SULLIVAN, Thomas
SULLIVAN, William Francis
SULLIVAN, William James
SULLIVAN, William John
SULLIVAN, William Martin
SUMMERS, Ralph
SUMMERS, William Wigan
SUMMERSBEE, Austin Philip
SUMMERSCALES, Percy
SUMMERSFORD, Henry Roy
SUMNER, John William
SURGEY, Thomas Edwin
SUSSEX, Charles Joshua
SUSSEX, Joshua
SUTCLIFFE, Robert
SUTCLIFFE, Victor Briggs
SUTHERLAND, Charles Tytler
SUTHERLAND, John
SUTHERLAND, William
SUTHERLAND, William John
SUTTIE, Robert
SUTTON, Clarence Edward
SUTTON, David George
SUTTON, James Read
SUTTON, John Briggs
SWAFFER, Herbert Harry
SWAIN, Frederick Cecil
SWAIN, Frederick Job
SWALE, Alexander George
SWALLOW, Herbert
SWAN, James Lawrence
SWANEPOEL, Henry David
SWANN, Frank Murray

SWANNELL, Blair Inskip
SWANTON, John
SWARBRICK, William
SWEENEY, James
SWEENEY, Patrick Joseph
SWEENEY, Thomas Thurle
SWEETLAND, Stephen James
SWIFT, Alexander Thomas
SWIFT, Stanley Roy
SWIFT, Thomas William West
SWINBOURNE, Harry Foster
SWINSCOE, Arthur Ralph
SWINTON, Thomas Trowbridge
SYKES, Alfred Tasman
SYKES, Henry Heath
SYME, John William
SYMES, Arthur Edward
SYMMONS, Henry
SYVERSEN, Charles
TABBUT, Fremont Leon
TABREHAM, Arthur Ernest
TACKABERRY, Nicholas
TAINSH, William
TAIT, Allan Roy
TAIT, Lawrence
TALBETT, Norman Thomas
TALLENTIRE, Albert William
    John
TAMBLYN, Frederick
TAMSETT, James Alwyn
TANKARD, Oswald James
TANNER, Richard
TANSLEY, Arthur Wilfred
TANSLEY, Eric
TAPLIN, Charles John
TARRANT, Alfred Ernest
TASSELL, Frederick Ernest
TATE, Ernest James
TATHAM, John
TAUSE, Hector Algie
TAVERNER, Fred Arthur
TAWELL, Leslie Richard
TAXT, John
TAYLOR, Arthur John
TAYLOR, Barrett Leach
TAYLOR, Charles
TAYLOR, Charles
TAYLOR, Charles Frederick
TAYLOR, Charles Thomas
TAYLOR, Denis Charles
TAYLOR, Edward George
TAYLOR, Edwin Hutchinson
TAYLOR, Eric James
TAYLOR, Ernest
TAYLOR, Ernest Arthur
TAYLOR, Ernest George
TAYLOR, Frank Samuel Augustus
TAYLOR, Frederick George
TAYLOR, Gilbert
TAYLOR, Guy Holbrook
TAYLOR, Henry Joseph Thomas
TAYLOR, Herbert George Lindorff
TAYLOR, Herbert Morton
TAYLOR, Herbert Stewart
TAYLOR, James
TAYLOR, James
TAYLOR, James Ashton
TAYLOR, Jesse Herbert
TAYLOR, John
TAYLOR, John Low
TAYLOR, Joseph Richardson
TAYLOR, Leslie Edward
TAYLOR, Oliver Frank Leopold
TAYLOR, Richard Batchelor
TAYLOR, Robert Stanley
TAYLOR, Stanley Howard
TAYLOR, Thomas
TAYLOR, Wilfred Arthur

TAYLOR, William
TAYLOR, William
TAYLOR, William Frederick
    Maxwell
TAYLOR, William Thomas
TAYSOM, James Forbes
TEALE, John
TELFER, George Robert
TELFORD, James Campbell
TELFORD, William Alfred
TEMPLE, Clarence William
TEMPLE, Stanley
TEMPLER, Francis Darvall
TEMPLETON, Sidney Charles
TERNAN, Bernard Francis George
TERRY, Charles Henry
TERRY, Smedley Joseph John
TETLEY, Arthur Norman
TEVENDALE, Charles
THAYNE, Alfred Gregory
THEOBALD, William George
    Morley
THEW, George Joseph
THEWLIS, Charlie
THICKINS, William
THOM, Charles Henry Wallace
THOMAS, Albert Edward
THOMAS, Alfred Duncan
THOMAS, Arthur Evan Ridout
THOMAS, Bert Joseph
THOMAS, Charles Joseph
THOMAS, Colin
THOMAS, Ernest
THOMAS, Frederick William
THOMAS, George Frederick
THOMAS, James
THOMAS, John Robert
THOMAS, Samuel
THOMAS, Stanley George
THOMAS, Thomas Hurtle
THOMPSON, Albert James
THOMPSON, Astley John Onslow
THOMPSON, Bert Arthur
THOMPSON, Charles
THOMPSON, Cyril Weller
THOMPSON, Douglas William
THOMPSON, Frank Woodville
    Dixon
THOMPSON, Frederick
THOMPSON, Frederick Herbert
THOMPSON, Frederick John
THOMPSON, Gilbert Leslie
THOMPSON, Horace William
    Blair Leo
THOMPSON, James Gordon Ford
THOMPSON, John
THOMPSON, John
THOMPSON, John Alfred
THOMPSON, John Charles
THOMPSON, Reginald Charles
THOMPSON, Richard
THOMPSON, Richard Hugh
THOMPSON, Robert Alfred
THOMPSON, Roy
THOMPSON, Sidney
THOMPSON, Stanley Charles
THOMPSON, Thomas
THOMPSON, Victor Frederick
THOMPSON, William
THOMPSON, William
THOMPSON, William Henry
THOMSON, Alexander Cameron
THOMSON, Charles Aitken
THOMSON, Harry James
THOMSON, James
THOMSON, John Cecil
THOMSON, John William
THOMSON, Louis Neil Francis

THOMSON, Percy William
THOMSON, William
THORLEY, Leslie
THORNE, Alan
THORNE, Alfred John
THORNE, Austin John
THORNETT, John James
THORNHILL, George
THORNTON, Arthur Gibbsland
THORNTON, Frank
THORNTON, Joseph Henry
THORNTON, Milton Frank
THORNTON, Raymond Mark
THORNTON, Raymond Slade
THORNTON, Russell Stewart
THORPE, Benjamin Thomas
THORPE, John
THORPE, Robert
THRELFALL, Reginald Hope
THROWER, William
THRUM, Edward James
THUMWOOD, Arthur Henry
THUNDER, Albert William
THURSTON, Harry Ernest
THYER, Walter Hervey
TIBBS, Walter
TICKNER, Charles Lewis
TIDD, William
TIERNEY, Andrew James
TIGHE, Alfred
TIGHE, Edward Victor
TILBEE, Walter Joseph
TILBURY, Clive William
TILEY, Mark Daniel George
TILL, Alan Gordon
TILL, James Victor
TILLIDGE, Henry William
TILLS, George Earnest Willan
TILLY, Rupert James
TIMBERLEY, Charles
TIMBRELL, Gordon
TIMMINS, Herbert Thomas
TIMMS, Owen Stanley
TINSON, Garnet Edmund Iles
TIPPET, George Thomas
TIPPET, Harold Freeman
TIPPET, Percy Albert
TIPPETT, Albert Ernest Arthur
TODD, James Watson
TODD, Robert James
TOLEMAN, William
TOLL, Frederick Vivian
TOLLEY, Charles Samuel
TOLMIE, Roy Colin
TOMLEY, John William
TOMLINSON, David
TOMLINSON, George
TOMLINSON, William
TONG, Frank
TONKIN, Frederick John
TONKIN, Richard Caleb
TONKIN, Walter John
TOOGOOD, Edward
TOOMEY, Alfred
TOOP, Robert Daniel
TOPLIFFE, Charles John
TORPY, John Bermingham
TOSDEVIN, Robert
TOSH, William
TOVELL, John Francis Huon
TOWERS, Walter
TOWNER, Frederick Arthur
    Albert
TOWNSEND, Albert Edward
TOWNSEND, Cecil
TOWNSEND, Fred James
TOWNSHEND, Ernest Richard
TOWNSHEND, Samuel Edward

TRACEY, Claude
TRACY, William Henry
TRAISE, Jack Herbert
TRANTER, Albert Ernest
TRAVERS, Bertram
TREADGOLD, Charles Ashbourne
TREFFONE, Harold Miller
TREHARNE, Evan
TRELEASE, William Inson
TRESILIAN, Frederick Robertson
TREVAN, Jack
TREVASKIS, Thomas Henry
TREVETT, Arthur Cecil
TREVILLIAN, George Leslie
TREWIN, Angus Duncan
TRICKETT, Russell
TRICKEY, Frank
TRINEMAN, Charles
TRINGHAM, Arthur Robert
TROON, Henry
TROYAHN, William John
TRUE, George Haviland
TRUMAN, Leslie Huon
TRUSCOTT, Herbert
TUCK, Albert Victor
TUCK, Percy Clarence
TUCKER, John Stuart
TUCKER, William
TUDENHAM, George Frederick
TUESKI, Henry Edward Cyril
TULLOCH, William
TUNKS, John
TURBET, Claude Douglas
TURNBULL, Alexander Phipps
TURNBULL, George
TURNBULL, John Sanderson
TURNBULL, Oliver Edwin
TURNBULL, Thomas
TURNBULL, Walter
TURNER, Alfred James
TURNER, Austin
TURNER, Charles
TURNER, Frank Joseph
TURNER, George Michael
TURNER, Henry Francis Charles
TURNER, Henry Joseph
TURNER, John
TURNER, John
TURNER, John Henry
TURNER, John James
TURNER, Leonard Woodward
TURNER, Leslie Patrick
TURNER, Miles Nuel
TURNER, William
TURNER, William Monarch
TURNER, William Philip
TURNOCK, James Goodison
TURNOCK, Joseph Arnold
TURTON, William
TURVEY, Charles Henry
TURVEY, George Nicholas
TUTT, Henry Dawson
TWIGHT, George Leo
TWINING, James John
TWOSE, Edwin
TWYFORD, Harrie Raymond
TYLER, George Thomas
TYLER, John
TYNAN, Joseph
TYRRELL, Fred
TYRRELL, Harry James
TYSON, Charles Malcolm Edward
TYTHERLEIGH, John Athelstan
    Corteen
UDEN, Percy
ULRICH, Frank
UNDERHILL, Richard Mallett
UNWIN, Norman Charles

UPJOHN, Edward Henry
UPTON, Clive
URQUHART, Hector
USHER, Francis Lewis
USHER, Jack Wilfrid
USHER, Robert Donald
USSHER, Athelstan Neville
UTHER, Gordon Arthvael
VAGG, Stewart Parnell
VAGUE, Felix
VALLANCE, George
VAN MENXAL, Alexander
VAN SPRINKHUYSEN, Anton
  Bertus Alexander
VANCE, Eric Allan
VANZA, Frederick Camillus
  Diogenes
VARCOE, Albert Edward
VARLEY, Thomas
VARTY, John
VASSY, Peter Constantine
VAUGHAN, Stanley Paul
VEAGE, Charles Lewis
VEAL, Norman Joseph
VEIT, Gordon Henry
VEITCH, Arthur Wilson
VEITCH, Donald
VENNING, Percy William
VERGETTE, John James
VERNON, Cecil Charles
VERSWYVELT, Joseph Williams
VERTIGAN, John William
VIANT, William Evans
VICARY, Henry Walter
VICK, William Henry
VICKERY, Clive
VIDGEN, Jack Grahame
VILE, Alfred Ernest
VILE, Percy Edgar
VILES, William James
VILLIS, Frank Laird
VILLIS, Leyshon
VILLIS, Stanley
VINCENT, Albert
VINCENT, John Henry Walden
VINCENT, Robert
VINE-HALL, Noel Francis
VINNICOMBE, Walter Lewis
VISTARINI, Hector
VIZE, Harry Blanchard
VOGNSEN, Kristian
VOLKOFF, John
VOLLER, Albert James
VON-STEIGLITZ, Tasman Blacker
VROLAND, James Emil Huntly
VYNER, Charles John
WADDELL, James Robert
WADDELL, Peter
WADE, John Stanley
WAGNER, Roy James
WAGSTAFF, Arthur
WAINE, Frederick Charles
WAINEY, John
WAIT, Edward Walter
WALDEN, Herbert Noel
WALDEN, Joseph Benjamin
  Harold
WALDOCK, Alfred Henry
WALDRON, Leonard James
WALE, Philip George
WALFORD, Norman Alexander
WALKER, Andrew
WALKER, Arthur Edward
WALKER, Charles Alexander
  Theodore
WALKER, Eric
WALKER, Eric De Witte Talmage
WALKER, Ernest Percy

WALKER, George
WALKER, Henry Ernest
WALKER, Horace
WALKER, James
WALKER, John Bryden
WALKER, Kenneth Leigh
WALKER, Reginald John
WALKER, Thomas
WALKER, Thomas Allan
WALKER, William Frederick
WALLACE, Charles
WALLACE, Donald Wally
WALLACE, Norman
WALLACE, Thomas Alexander
WALLACK, Gordon Townshend
WALLER, Charles Stephen
WALLER, George Henry
WALLER, John Henry
WALLIS, Aver William Mitchell
WALLIS, Lindsay Gordon
WALLIS, Lycester Gordon
  Armstrong
WALLIS, Thomas Louis
WALLS, Stuart
WALSH, Andrew William
WALSH, Claude Hallastone
WALSH, Edward
WALSH, James Lawrence
WALSH, John Francis
WALSH, John Thomas
WALSH, Thomas
WALSH, Timothy
WALSH, William John
WALTER, Clement Wallace
WALTERS, Albert Phillip
WALTON, Arthur
WALTON, Ernest Joseph
WALTON, Victor Kenneth
WANSBROUGH, Cyril
WARD, Charles Alfred
WARD, Edward
WARD, Harold John
WARD, Henry Holdford
WARD, John
WARD, Joseph Clarence
WARD, Joseph Henry
WARD, Robert David
WARD, Roland Grant
WARD, William Richard
WARDROP, William Bertie
WAREHAM, Edward Graham
WARNECKE, Albert Hugh
WARNES, Albert Percy
WARNES, William Edward
WARR, Arthur Bolton
WARREN, Francis Edgar
WARREN, George William
WARREN, Gordon Stanley
WARREN, James Percy Soltau
WARREN, Robert
WARREN, William
WARRENER, Alan Smithies
WASHINGTON, James Roy
WASLEY, Matthew Randall
WASLIN, William Pickard
WASSELL, Frank
WASSON, Reginald John
WATERS, Harry Percy
WATERS, James Harold
WATERS, Leo Stanislaus
WATERS, Leslie John
WATERS, Reginald Rutherford
WATERS, Richard Stephen
WATERS, Stanley
WATHERSTON, Frank Patten
WATKINS, Harold Thomas
WATKINS, Owen Meredith
WATKINS, William Henry

WATKINSON, Arthur Henry
WATLING, Alfred
WATLING, Arthur
WATMAN, Percy Hewitt
WATSON, Alfred Godfrey
WATSON, Douglas Linly Roy
WATSON, Edward
WATSON, Eric Stanley
WATSON, Frank Edward
WATSON, Frank Wentworth
WATSON, Frederick William
WATSON, George
WATSON, James
WATSON, James Thomas
WATSON, John Moore
WATSON, John Roberton
WATSON, Keith
WATSON, Percy
WATSON, Reginald Thornton
WATSON, Thomas William
WATSON, Wallace Frederick
WATSON, Walter McFarlane
WATT, Archibald James
WATT, George Redpath
WATT, Joseph William
WATT, Keith Everard
WATT, Oscar Harold McLure
WATT, Ronald Alan Mills
WATT, Sidney Alexander
WATT, Walter Thomas
WATTERS, Frederick Theodore
WATTERSTON, Birkett William
WATTIE, George Elmslie
WATTS, George
WATTS, George Ernest
WATTS, Harold
WATTS, Harold William
WATTS, Leonard Charles
WATTS, Raymond Thomas
WAUGH, William Edward
WAYGOOD, Henry William
WAYLAND, Claude Frederick
WAYTE, John Joseph
WEATHERBURN, John Stapleton
WEATHERHEAD, John Fortescue
  Law
WEATHERS, Thomas Francis
WEAVER, Frederick Henry
WEAVER, Horace Kurnell
WEAVER, Leslie Pooler
WEAVERS, Joseph Clyde
WEBB, Albert
WEBB, Arthur Claude
WEBB, Charles Henry
WEBB, Edwin
WEBB, Francis Russell
WEBB, Harry
WEBB, Joseph John
WEBB, Norman Reginald
WEBB, Rhys
WEBB, Thomas
WEBB, William Arthur
WEBBER, George Patrick
WEBSTER, Arthur Edwin
WEBSTER, Arthur William
WEBSTER, Eric Osmond
WEBSTER, Frank Green
WEBSTER, Isaac Oswald
WEBSTER, Joseph
WEBSTER, Richard Wynne
WEBSTER, Tasman Laurence
WEBSTER, Thomas
WEBSTER, Walter James
WEDERELL, James Percy
WEDMORE, George
WEEKES, William
WEEKS, Samuel James
WEEKS, Stanley Ernest

WEILER, Albert
WEINGOTT, Samuel
WEINRICH, Joseph Herman
WEIR, Duncan Archibald
WEIR, Frank Percy
WEIR, George Thomas
WEIR, James E
WEIR, Joseph
WELCH, George
WELCH, Mervyn Bede
WELCH, William Bradley
WELLISCH, Frederick
WELLS, Cecil Fredk John
WELLS, Charles
WELLS, Clifford Edwin Arthur
WELLS, Daniel
WELLS, Francis Leslie
WELLS, Richard William
WELMAN, Roy Cameron Patrick
WELSH, Frank August
WELSH, William
WELSMAN, Ernest Walter
WEMYSS, Oswald Stewart
WENTWORTH, Charles Benjamin
WERE, Clive Wellington
WERNER, William Edward
WEST, Edwin Spragg
WEST, Frederick Michael
WEST, Thomas
WEST, Walter Charles
WESTCOTT, Wilfred George
WESTON, Frederick Harold
WESTON, George Edward
WESTON, John Charles
WESTON, Leonard Herbert
WESTON, Victor Edmund
WESTRUPP, Walter
WESTWOOD, Lewis Herman
WETHERALL, Walter Bert
WETHERBY, Lucien Porter
WETZLER, Philip Joseph
WHALAN, Glyndwr Montague
WHALEY, Arthur
WHALEY, Peter
WHARTON, George Willie
WHARTON, Harry Hopetoun
WHATTON, Ernest Bartholomew
WHEATLEY, Anthony
WHEATLEY, Noel Charles
WHEATLEY, Percy Alfred
WHEATLEY, Thomas Charles
WHEELAGHAN, James Brydon
WHEELER, Harold E
WHEELER, Herbert John
WHEELER, William Henry
WHELAN, Patrick
WHIDBORNE, Charles Hobson
WHIFFEN, Charles
WHIPPS, Frederick
WHITAKER, Charles Leonard
WHITBOURN, George Daniel
WHITE, Alexander Henry
WHITE, Alfred Ernest
WHITE, Charles Harold Ophir
WHITE, Charles William
WHITE, Clarence Maldon
WHITE, Dudley Clifford
WHITE, Edward Geoffrey
WHITE, Edwin James
WHITE, Eric
WHITE, Frederick James
WHITE, George
WHITE, George Oliver
WHITE, George William
WHITE, Henry Edward
WHITE, Henry Francis
WHITE, James Edward
WHITE, James Leslie

WHITE, John Harvey
WHITE, John Wesley
WHITE, Walter Henry
WHITE, Wilfred Allan
WHITE, William Forsyth
WHITE, William Henry
WHITE, William John
WHITECROSS, A Duncan
WHITECROSS, William
WHITEFORD, Jack Patrick
WHITEHEAD, Eric
WHITEHEAD, Frederick
WHITEHEAD, Robert
WHITEHEAD, William Bickerton
WHITELAW, Loftus
WHITELEY, Jack Smithurst
WHITEMAN, Reuben George
WHITFIELD, Edward Percy
WHITFORD, Alexander
WHITING, David
WHITING, Eric Anderson
WHITLEY, Langlo Arthur
WHITTAKER, George
WHITTALL, Percy George
WHITTERON, Edmund Reginald
WHITTLE, Arthur Gilbert
WHITTLE, William Arthur
WHYMAN, Bertram Robert
WHYTE, Robert
WHYTE, Thomas Anderson
WHYTT, Richmond
WICKING, Herbert Charles
WICKINS, Vernon John
WICKS, George Sidney Thomas
WIDDICOMBE, Robert Herbert
WIDDON, Albert Edward
WIGG, Herbert James
WIGGER, Charles Hugh Llewellyn
WIGGER, Reginald Charles
WIGGINS, Albert George
WIGGINS, Ernest Alfred
WIGHT, Arthur Henry
WIGHT, Powell John
WIGNALL, Robert
WILCOX, Herbert Wattam
WILCOX, Leslie Joseph Victor
WILCOX, William John
WILDE, James
WILDEN, Arthur
WILKERSON, James Thomas
WILKINS, Alfred
WILKINS, James
WILKINSON, Albert
WILKINSON, Cecil
WILKINSON, Charles
WILKINSON, Charles Pyrmont
WILKINSON, Clarence William
  Anstruther
WILKINSON, Frederick Charles
  Erasmus
WILKINSON, James Harvey
WILKINSON, Leslie Arthur
WILKINSON, William
WILLAN, Roy
WILLCOX, George
WILLIAMS, Alan Charles
WILLIAMS, Albert Henry
WILLIAMS, Alfred Spedding
WILLIAMS, Anthony George
  Herbert
WILLIAMS, Arthur James
WILLIAMS, Charles Henry Ernest
WILLIAMS, Charles Llewellyn
WILLIAMS, Charles Louis
WILLIAMS, David John
WILLIAMS, David Lionel
WILLIAMS, David Victor John
WILLIAMS, Edmund Thomas

WILLIAMS, Edward Homer
WILLIAMS, Frank
WILLIAMS, Frederick Arthur
WILLIAMS, George Charles
WILLIAMS, Henry Wallis
WILLIAMS, Herbert
WILLIAMS, Herbert Charles
WILLIAMS, Herbert Edwin
WILLIAMS, Humphrey
WILLIAMS, Hurtle Gordon
WILLIAMS, John
WILLIAMS, John Anthony
WILLIAMS, John Edward
WILLIAMS, John Joseph Hamford
WILLIAMS, Leonard
WILLIAMS, Leslie Lloyd
WILLIAMS, Llewellyn
WILLIAMS, Percival
WILLIAMS, Percy
WILLIAMS, Percy James
WILLIAMS, Reginald
WILLIAMS, Samuel Clay
WILLIAMS, Sydney Leonard
WILLIAMS, Thomas
WILLIAMS, Thomas Alfred
WILLIAMS, Victor Clarence
WILLIAMS, Walter
WILLIAMS, William David
WILLIAMS, William Edwin
WILLIAMS, William Henry
WILLIAMSON, Albert James
  Ramsey
WILLIAMSON, Alfred James
WILLIAMSON, Basil Bruce
WILLIAMSON, David Murray
WILLIAMSON, Harold
WILLIAMSON, Harold
WILLIAMSON, Henry
WILLIAMSON, Leslie
WILLIAMSON, Peter Arthur
WILLIAMSON, Richard
WILLICK, Bertie Clyde
WILLIS, Archibald Henry
WILLIS, Arthur Joseph
WILLIS, William Organ
WILLISON, Robert Edgar
WILLMOT, Arthur Henry
WILLMOTT, Albert Edward
WILLMOTT, Charles Jonathan
WILLMOTT, George

WILLOUGHBY, Francis
WILLOUGHBY, Thomas
WILLS, John
WILLS, Vivian Malcolm
WILLS, William Henry
WILLSON, George
WILLUMSEN, Sydney
WILSON, Alexander Kyle
WILSON, Alfred
WILSON, Allan Elwood
WILSON, Andrew
WILSON, Augustus George
  Maryon
WILSON, Cecil Sturt
WILSON, Clarence Edward
WILSON, Edgar James
WILSON, Edgar Ralph
WILSON, Edward Thomas
WILSON, Eliot Gratton
WILSON, Elvas Roy
WILSON, Frank Ness
WILSON, Frederick Gladstone
WILSON, Frederick Jerry
WILSON, Graeme Lang
WILSON, Harry
WILSON, Herbert Swarbrick
WILSON, James Joseph
WILSON, John
WILSON, John
WILSON, John Robert
WILSON, Joseph Benjamin
WILSON, Leslie Samuel
WILSON, Luke John
WILSON, Raymond Oscar
WILSON, Richard Noble
WILSON, Robert
WILSON, Robert
WILSON, Robert McLauchlan
WILSON, Stuart McIllwraith
WILSON, Thomas Clark
WILSON, Thomas Henry
WILSON, William
WILSON, William Clark
WILSON, William George
WILSON, William James
WILSON, William John
WILSON, Willie
WILSON, Wright
WINAL, James
WINCH, Cecil Henry

WINCH, Cecil Robert
WINCH, Harold Forbes Clark
WINDLE, Thomas
WINDROSS, Theodore Northcote
WINDSOR, John
WING, Ralph
WINGATE, James Peter George
WINGROVE, Charles Melbourne
WINNETT, John Wylie
WINNING, James
WINSLET, Bertram
WINSLETT, Harry
WINTER, Richard
WINZER, Luther Alfred
WIRE, Bertram John
WISE, Arthur Edward
WISE, Henry
WISE, Robert
WISEMAN, James Arthur
WISEWOULD, James
WISHART, John Charles
WITCOMB, Sydney Trafford
WITHAM, Robert Percival
WITHERS, Henry Albert
WITHERS, William Edward
WITT, Arthur
WITTER, James
WODETZKI, Victor Emanuel
WOLF, Albert Victor
WOLFENDEN, Clarence William
WOLSELEY, Paul Stewart
WOLSLEY, Arthur Garnet
WOMACK, George Edward
WOOD, Alexander Thomas
WOOD, Alfred Edward
WOOD, George William
WOOD, Leofric
WOOD, Thomas
WOOD, William Ferguson
WOODBERRY, Max Llewellyn
WOODBRIDGE, John Michael
  Paul
WOODBURY, William John
WOODCOCK, George
WOODHOUSE, Joseph
WOODHOUSE, Thomas John
WOODHOUSE, William Augustus
WOODIN, Ernest Frank
WOODLEY, Thomas
WOODLOCK, Charles Henry

WOODROFF, Henry
WOODS, Arthur
WOODS, Cecil Talbot
WOODS, Charles Gordon
WOODS, Horace Charles
WOODS, John Albert
WOODS, John William
WOODS, Reginald Norman
  Frederick
WOODS, Robert
WOODS, William Harry Rankin
WOODSBEY, Joseph
WOODWARD, James
WOODWARD, Walter
WOODWARD, William George
WOOLCOCK, Roy Clifford
WOOLLEY, George Joseph Arthur
WOOLLEY, James Nathaniel
WOOTTON, Charles Edmund
WOOTTON, Frank William
WORDSWORTH, John
WORKMAN, Laurence Charles
WORNES, Robert
WORSLEY, Tasman
WORTABET, John Cecil
WORTHINGTON, Victor Robert
WRAGGE, Clement Lionel
  Egerton
WREN, David
WRIGGLESWORTH, Thomas
WRIGHT, Alfred
WRIGHT, Charles
WRIGHT, Charles D'Arcey
WRIGHT, Frank Thomas
WRIGHT, Frederick
WRIGHT, George Clifton
WRIGHT, Harry Taylor
WRIGHT, Herbert Henry
WRIGHT, Herbert Patrick
WRIGHT, John
WRIGHT, John
WRIGHT, Samuel
WRIGHT, Samuel James
WRIGHT, Sydney
WRIGHT, Thomas
WRIGHT, Thomas Alfred
  Reginald
WRIGLEY, Arthur
WUNSCH, Claude Maxwell
WYATT, John Wynn

WYLD, Roy
WYLDE, Herbert William
WYLIE, Allan James Noel
WYLIE, Edward
WYLIE, Roy
WYMAN, Charles William
WYMAN, Leo John
WYMAN, Thomas Wilmore
WYNNE, Edward
WYNNE, Sidney James
WYTHES, James Edward John
YATES, Alexander
YATES, Thomas Richard
YEATES, Andrew Powell
YEATMAN, Allen Patrick
YEOMANS, Bertram William
YOUDEN, Frederick Charles
YOUDS, Howard Leland
YOUNG, Charles Harry
YOUNG, Charles Lyle
YOUNG, David
YOUNG, Edward
YOUNG, Frederick
YOUNG, Frederick Richard
  Charles
YOUNG, Horace
YOUNG, Ivar
YOUNG, James
YOUNG, James
YOUNG, John Douglas
YOUNG, John Henry
YOUNG, Percival John
YOUNG, Phillip Alexander
YOUNG, Robert Edwin
YOUNG, Roland Macdonald
YOUNG, Sidney Douglas
YOUNG, Walter Alexander
YOUNG, William
YOUNG, William
YOUNG-GRANT, Charles
YOUNGER, Thomas
YUILL, George Robert
ZAHNLEITER, Philip
ZARNKE, Albert
ZEISSER, Peter

Index